S0-AAB-163

MARYLAND

Also in This Series

Arizona, Malcolm L. Comeaux

Colorado, Mel Griffiths and Lynnell Rubright

Hawaii, Joseph R. Morgan

Missouri, Milton D. Rafferty

New Jersey, Charles A. Stansfield, Jr.

Texas, Terry G. Jordan, with John L. Bean, Jr., and William M. Holmes

Wyoming, Robert Harold Brown

Forthcoming Through 1984

Alaska, Roger W. Pearson and Donald F. Lynch

Michigan, Lawrence M. Sommers

Mississippi, Jesse O. McKee

North Carolina, Ole Gade and H. Daniel Stillwell

South Carolina, Charles F. Kovacik and John J. Winberry

Utah, Clifford B. Craig

All books in this series are available in paperback and hardcover.

GEOGRAPHIES OF THE UNITED STATES

Ingolf Vogeler, General Editor

Maryland: A Geography

James E. DiLisio

Although one of the smallest of the fifty states, in many ways Maryland is the United States in miniature, bringing together and exemplifying the diverse elements of the country. In it the North and the South meet, and Maryland is one of the original gateways to the West.

Maryland is a study in contrasts, combining the poverty of the Appalachian hill people, the sharecroppers of the South, and the inner-city dwellers of Baltimore with the affluence of country manor estates and fashionable suburbs. Some of America's most rural scenes are interspersed there with some of its largest metropolitan centers. Added to this is a great physical diversity—the Coastal Plain, the Piedmont, the Delmarva Peninsula, the Chesapeake Bay, and the Appalachian Highlands.

This book provides an analytical survey of the physical, social, cultural, and economic geography of Maryland. Though the emphasis is on human geography, significant attention is given to the physical base on which the cultural landscape has developed. Environmental issues, such as Chesapeake Bay pollution, coal mining in Western Maryland, and the urbanization of the beaches, are addressed to show how development has often led to conflicts between people and their environments.

Dr. James E. DiLisio is associate professor and chairman in the Department of Geography and Environmental Planning, Towson State University, Maryland, where he teaches the geography of Maryland. He has been an instructor of economic geography at the University of Oklahoma and a consultant to the U.S. Army Corps of Engineers.

MARYLAND

A GEOGRAPHY

James E. DiLisio

Westview Press / Boulder, Colorado

Geographies of the United States

Unless otherwise attributed, all photographs were taken by the author.

Published in 1983 in the United States of America by
Westview Press, Inc.
5500 Central Avenue
Boulder, Colorado 80301
Frederick A. Praeger, President and Publisher

Library of Congress Cataloging in Publication Data
DiLisio, James E.
Maryland, a geography.
(Geographies of the United States)
Bibliography: p.
Includes index.
1. Maryland—Description and travel. I. Title. II. Series.
F181.D5 1983 975.2′043 83-6637
ISBN 0-86531-092-0
ISBN 0-86531-474-8 (pbk.)

Printed and bound in the United States of America

For
Kay, Kasha, and Jay

CONTENTS

FIGURES

TABLES

PREFACE

The initiation by Westview Press of a geographies of the United States series is an important undertaking. Not since the 1930s has such a series been attempted. I am indeed pleased to have contributed this volume on Maryland.

Although one of the smallest of the fifty states, Maryland stands as an important cog in the nation's social, economic, and political mechanism. In many ways Maryland brings together and exemplifies the diverse elements of the United States. In it North and South meet, and Maryland has historically been a gateway to the West.

My goal in this book is to describe and analyze Maryland's physical and human dimensions and to enable the reader to develop a sense of place about this state. Although the physical geography of Maryland certainly has not been neglected in this volume, the emphasis is on the cultural, social, and economic characteristics of the people. Extensive figures and data are presented to aid the reader in interpreting the Maryland landscape.

I am greatly indebted to a number of colleagues, friends, and family members for their assistance and encouragement during the preparation of this book. Norman Diffenderfer, Kenneth Haddock, Hlib Hayuk, and Curtis Martin, all of Towson State University, gave helpful reviews of chapters. For the cartography, thanks to William Richardson for his dedication and loyalty. I am grateful to Towson State University for support of this project in the form of research grants. I am also grateful to all who kindly permitted me to reproduce portions of their work herein. Many others helped me with suggestions and materials and to each of them my thanks. I would like to give credit also to the many students in my classes who greatly helped me sharpen my perception of the Maryland landscape. And I want to express my appreciation to the series editor, Ingolf Vogeler, who was helpful and supportive of my efforts.

Finally, I offer thanks to my wife, Kay, for her indispensable suggestions, editorial efforts, hours of typing, and inspirational support during the writing. To Kasha and Jay, thanks for enduring many months when Daddy didn't always have the time to give you the amount of attention you deserved.

James E. DiLisio

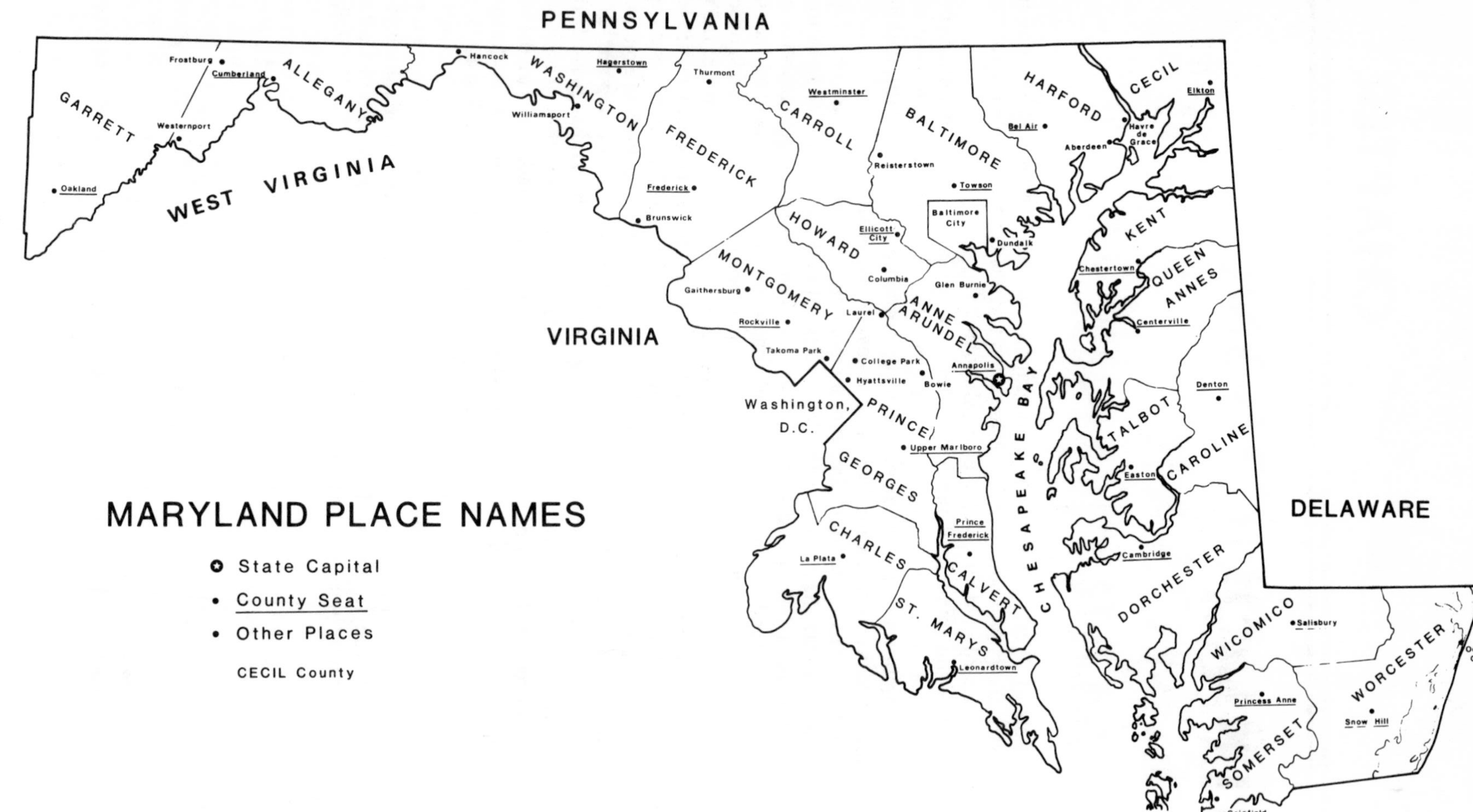
PENNSYLVANIA
MARYLAND PLACE NAMES
State Capital
County Seat
Other Places
CECIL County
GARRETT
Oakland
Frostburg
Cumberland
Westernport
ALLEGANY
WEST VIRGINIA
Hancock
WASHINGTON
Williamsport
Hagerstown
FREDERICK
Thurmont
Frederick
Brunswick
CARROLL
Westminster
BALTIMORE
Reisterstown
Towson
Baltimore City
Dundalk
HARFORD
Bel Air
Aberdeen
Havre de Grace
CECIL
Elkton
HOWARD
Ellicott City
Columbia
MONTGOMERY
Gaithersburg
Rockville
Takoma Park
Laurel
VIRGINIA
Washington, D.C.
ANNE ARUNDEL
Glen Burnie
Annapolis
College Park
Hyattsville
Bowie
PRINCE GEORGES
Upper Marlboro
CHARLES
La Plata
CALVERT
Prince Frederick
ST. MARYS
Leonardtown
CHESAPEAKE BAY
KENT
Chestertown
QUEEN ANNES
Centerville
TALBOT
Easton
CAROLINE
Denton
DORCHESTER
Cambridge
DELAWARE
WICOMICO
Salisbury
WORCESTER
Ocean City
Snow Hill
SOMERSET
Princess Anne
Crisfield
W. RICHARDSON

FIGURE 1.1.

CHAPTER 1

INTRODUCTION: THE MOSAIC OF MARYLAND

This book is about the state of Maryland—its land, people, personality, past landscapes, and future (see Figure 1.1). The geographical portrait of Maryland presented in these pages is one of a diverse region with a people who have a strong sense of place. A region is much more than a physical land base displaying various patterns of climate, vegetation, transportation, settlement, and agriculture; it is also people, life-styles, paces of life, sounds, smells, and symbols. The personality of a region is composed of both tangible and intangible elements. Geographer Jean Gottman described the intangible facets of regional personality when he wrote,

> To be distinct from its surroundings, a region needs much more than a mountain or a valley, a given language or certain skills; it needs essentially a strong belief based on some religious creed, some social viewpoint, or some pattern of political memories, and often a combination of all three. Thus regionalism has what might be called iconography as its foundation: each community has found for itself or was given an icon, a symbol slightly different from those cherished by its neighbors.[1]

The various chapters of this book are designed to reveal the tangible and intangible characteristics of the Maryland landscape and thus allow the reader to develop a true sense of place.

Although Maryland is the forty-second state in size, its landscape displays great physical and cultural variety. In the white sandy beaches, marshes, and swamps around Chesapeake Bay, the fine agricultural lands of the Eastern Shore, the rolling hills of middle Maryland, and the rugged mountains of the Appalachians is represented the full range of physiographic provinces found in the eastern United States (see Chapters 2, 3, and 4).

The fascinating story of the historical development of the cultural landscape of Maryland is reviewed in Chapter 5. Carl Sauer, a geographer at the University of California at Berkeley for many years, wrote in 1927 that cultural landscape constitutes "the forms superimposed on the physical landscape by the activites of man." Another geographer, Derwent Whittlesey, introduced the concept *sequent occupance,* which describes the successive contributions to the evolution of a region's cultural landscape. The sequence of occupance for Maryland has been first, the coming of hunters, trappers, and traders; next, the advance of settlement accompanied by subsistence agriculture; then a transition from subsistence farming to commercial agriculture and the rise of market-oriented production; and finally the growth of nonfarm employment and industrialization.

The great diversity of people, cultures, occupations, and spatial organization of the present Maryland landscape are the topics for the remaining chapters. Maryland's urban system embraces the spectrum of city life, from a metropolis like Baltimore—a world port and fourteenth-largest metropolitan area in the United States—and the suburban counties of metropolitan Washington, D.C.—the nation's seventh-largest metropolitan area—to numerous small rural settlements. Settlements also vary in age from plantations established in colonial times to the new, planned city of Columbia, created within the last fifteen years. Maryland's population includes some of the country's poorest and most disadvantaged people—the hill people of western Maryland, sharecroppers of southern Maryland, and inner-city dwellers of Baltimore—and some of the nation's wealthiest people—the residents of Maryland's country estates and affluent suburbs. (Montgomery County, for example, has the highest average family income of any county in the United States.) A wide range, too, of occupations is found, including farming, fishing, mining, steelworking, and many service-related industries. Of the 451 different kinds of manufacturing classifications used by the U.S. Bureau of the Census in the Standard Industrial Classification, 363, or over 80 percent, are represented in Maryland.

This book, then, is the story of the many interacting systems that give Maryland its geographical character. All of these physical and human pieces of the Maryland puzzle interlock to form the mosaic that is the state. As the roadside sign says, "Maryland Welcomes You" (Figure 1.2).

The spatial interactions and linkages that Maryland has with places outside its borders are also numerous and significant. So before proceeding to material specific to the state, it is necessary to locate Maryland and to describe its setting within the United States. Many of the physical and cultural characteristics of the state can be fully understood only when viewed in the regional and national context.

Figure 1.2. Entering Maryland along Interstate 83 in northern Baltimore County.

THE REGIONAL SETTING

Upon first seeing the countryside around Chesapeake Bay in 1608, John Smith was recorded to have exclaimed, "Heaven and earth seemed never to have agreed better to frame a place for man's habitation."[2] Captain Smith's travels did not take him to the land that lay to the west, to the area that was to become Maryland, but had he traveled there, he would have found a region just as suitable for European habitation. The geographical location of Maryland's future site can be stated in several ways.

In terms of absolute location, that is, position on the earth's latitude/longitude grid, Maryland lies between parallels 37°43′26″ and 39°53′ north latitude and between meridians 75°4′ and 79°29′15″ west longitude. But this information alone is not really very helpful. In recent years, geographers have become much more interested in relative location—the location of a place and its spatial relationship to other places. Promotion map Figure 1.3

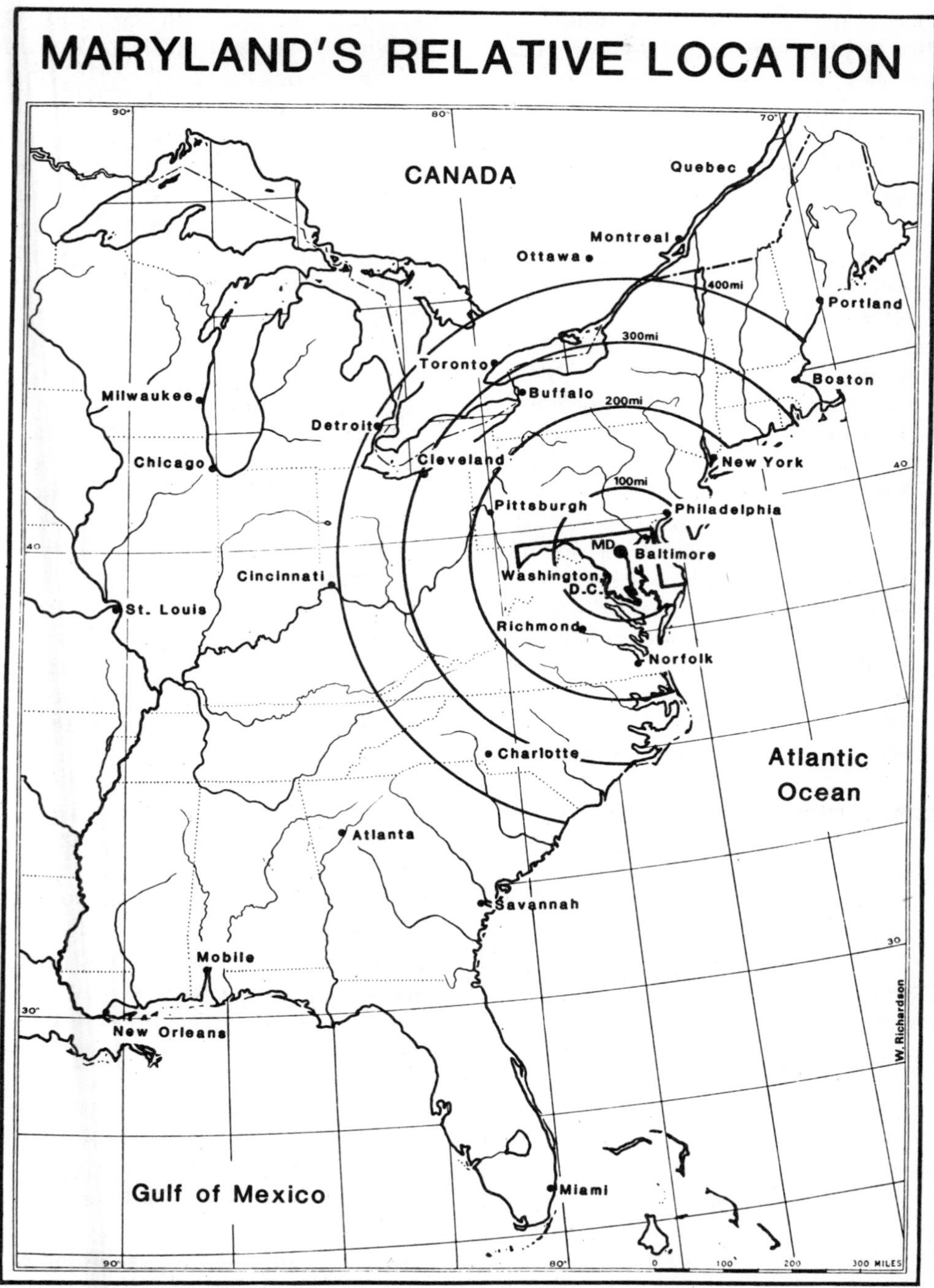

Figure 1.3. Source: Maryland Department of Economic and Community Development.

shows Maryland's relative location within the eastern U.S. market.

The geographical diversity of Maryland is reflected by the numerous regions in which it has been included by geographers attempting to describe its relative location: megalopolis, American Manufacturing Belt, Appalachia, Middle Atlantic region, and South Atlantic region. Regions are areas on the surface of the earth defined in terms of specified characteristics and extending as far as these characteristics are distinctive. Maryland's inclusion in a number of regions reflects the various ways that geographers have regionalized this part of the country, and the relative location of Maryland can be assessed through the characteristics of these various regions.

Megalopolis

A noticeable feature of the United States is the dense urban population in the 500-mile (800-kilometer) arc running northeast-southwest along the East Coast from southern New Hampshire to northern Virginia. This urban corridor was given the name *megalopolis* by Jean Gottmann in his classic 1961 study, an outgrowth of twenty years of research on the area (Figure 1.4). Gottmann included in his study all of Maryland and metropolitan Washington, D.C., extending into northern Virginia. The original region defined by Gottmann has continued to grow and now extends farther north and south to include Richmond, Norfolk, and Newport-News. The national dominance of this region was recognized by Gottmann: "Megalopolis provides the whole of America with so many essential services of the sort that a community used to obtain in its downtown section that it may well deserve the nickname of 'Main Street' of the nation."[3]

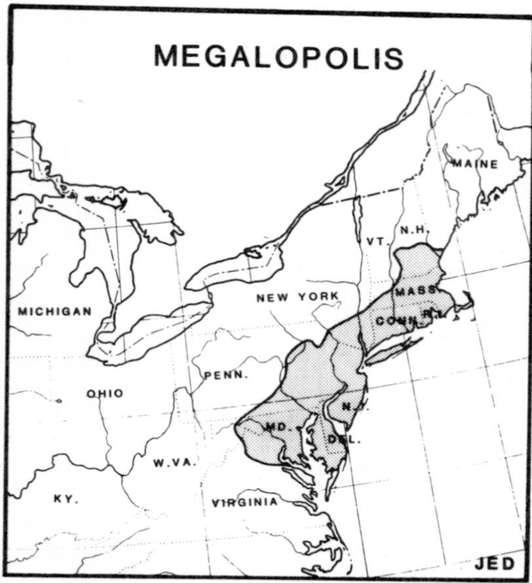

Figure 1.4.

The dominant feature of megalopolis, its urbanness, is reflected in its intense spatial organization. (However, the region is not just a massive collection of urban forms; much green space still exists. Approximately 20 percent of the land area of megalopolis is in urban land use; the rest is woodland and farmland.) Five of the nation's metropolitan areas exceeding 1 million population are found in megalopolis, including the metropolitan areas of Baltimore and Washington, D.C., in Maryland. In 1980, the latest year for which figures are available, megalopolis had 42,099,749 people; this was 20.7 percent of the total U.S. population. This is an impressive figure when coupled with the fact that megalopolis occupies only 1.5 percent of the land area of the United States. Figure 1.5 is a symvu—a demographic model of the distribution of the nation's population. It clearly shows the large population concentration in megalopolis relative to the rest of the country.

Megalopolis is a region of superlatives. It has the country's greatest accumulation of wealth, greatest concentration of poverty, greatest variety of urban amenities, most varied population mix, leading business and governmental centers, and is one of the world's most highly urbanized areas.

The numerous internal and external linkages of megalopolis are complex. This

Figure 1.5. Source: U.S. Census of Population, 1980.

region has a high degree of interchange with other areas. Megalopolis is the western terminus of the world's busiest ocean route across the North Atlantic from western Europe. The convoluted coast of megalopolis contains many fine natural harbors, including that at Baltimore. In addition, many of the large cities of megalopolis have good access to the interior. This accessibility has been very important to the development of Baltimore and Maryland. Goods, people, and ideas have entered megalopolis from overseas and have been absorbed, changed, and sent into the interior. These elements also flow from the interior into megalopolis and thence overseas. For this reason, Gottmann referred to megalopolis as the "hinge" of the continent.

Baltimore is an important segment of this continental hinge. The city is located at the head of navigation on the Patapsco River, about 12 mi (19.2 km) from Chesapeake Bay and 200 mi (320 km) from the mouth of the Bay. Baltimore is the best example in megalopolis of a major city that has penetrated as far inland as possible while still retaining its seaport functions. The city is the center of the rich agricultural district surrounding the bay and has thus been a major food processing center for many years. Processing of imported raw materials, the basis of various industries including copper smelting, sugar refining, manufacture of commercial fertilizer, and steel making, has long been an important activity in Baltimore. For instance, the Bethlehem Steel Sparrows Point tidewater plant, built in 1887, utilizes iron ore that arrives by ship from Bethlehem's Venezuelan and Chilean mines. And finally because it is closer to the Midwest than Philadelphia or New York, freight rates through Baltimore are consistently lower than through these other megalopolitan ports.

The American Manufacturing Belt

The core region of U.S. manufacturing lies in the northeastern quarter of the country. The manufacturing belt was defined over seventy years ago as a quadrangle with corners at Portland, Maine, in the northeast; Milwaukee, Wisconsin, in the northwest; St. Louis, Missouri, in the southwest; and Baltimore, Maryland, in the southeast. Since then the definition has undergone many refinements, but all are centered on the quadrangle. Although many important changes have occurred in the distribution of U.S. industry, the concentration of industry in the Northeast has not been affected.

The United States has 451 different categories of manufacturing that together employ over 19 million people. The geographic distribution of these workers is illustrated in Figure 1.6. On this map, the circles represent manufacturing employment in the combined counties of metropolitan areas and show that the United States can be split into eastern and western manufacturing regions by a line drawn from the southern tip of Texas to the Minnesota–South Dakota border. Manufacturing in the western half is widely spaced, while the eastern region supports nearly 90 percent of the country's manufacturing employment. Over 50 percent of the jobs are

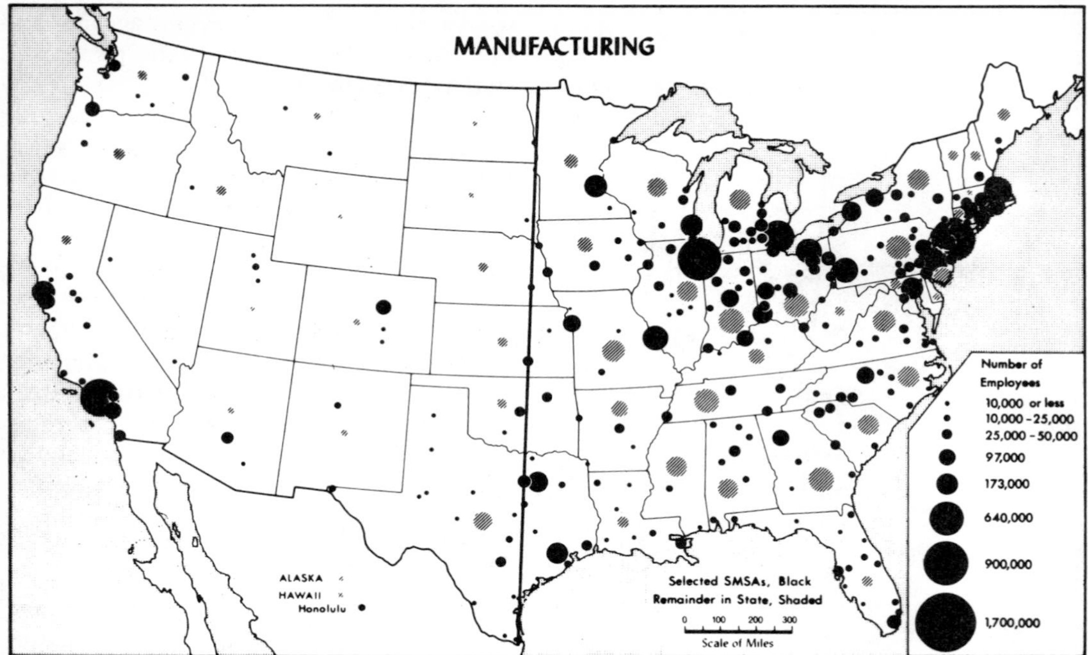

Figure 1.6. Source: John Alexander and Lay Gibson, *Economic Geography,* 2nd ed., © 1979, p. 304. Reprinted by permission of Prentice-Hall, Inc., Englewood Cliffs, New Jersey.

in the Northeast (east of the Mississippi River and north of the Ohio River); this area roughly coincides with the quadrangle.

Within the northeastern manufacturing region, there are several subregions: the New York metropolitan area, New England, the Middle Atlantic states, the Great Lakes, and the Ohio Valley (Figure 1.7). Each subregion possesses a unique personality, reflecting different source areas for raw materials; different historical development patterns; different labor, market energy, and transport factors; and different relative locations.

Maryland is often included in the Middle Atlantic subregion along with eastern Pennsylvania, southern New Jersey, and Delaware. And diversity is the hallmark of manufacturing in Maryland as it is within the rest of the region—nearly every industry is present in at least small amounts. A variety of manufacturing takes place in the state, ranging from heavy industries such as steel mills, shipyards, and petroleum refineries to lighter industries such as electronics and food processing. Figure 1.8 indicates Maryland's status for just two of the many industries.

The relative location of Maryland gives it a number of critical advantages in manufacturing. The heavily populated megalopolitan region is a ready market for its goods, and the Atlantic coastal frontage and fine harbors provide easy access to foreign importing and exporting. The manufacturing centers of Maryland are well connected by transportation lines to the interior, as well as to the rest of the East Coast. These accessibility factors enable Maryland to interact with other places with comparative ease and low cost.

Manufacturing, unlike agriculture, is not continuously developed over an extensive region; it is localized at favorable sites. In addition to industry, the American Manufacturing Belt has a considerable amount of agricultural and forest land in the interstices between centers of manufacturing.

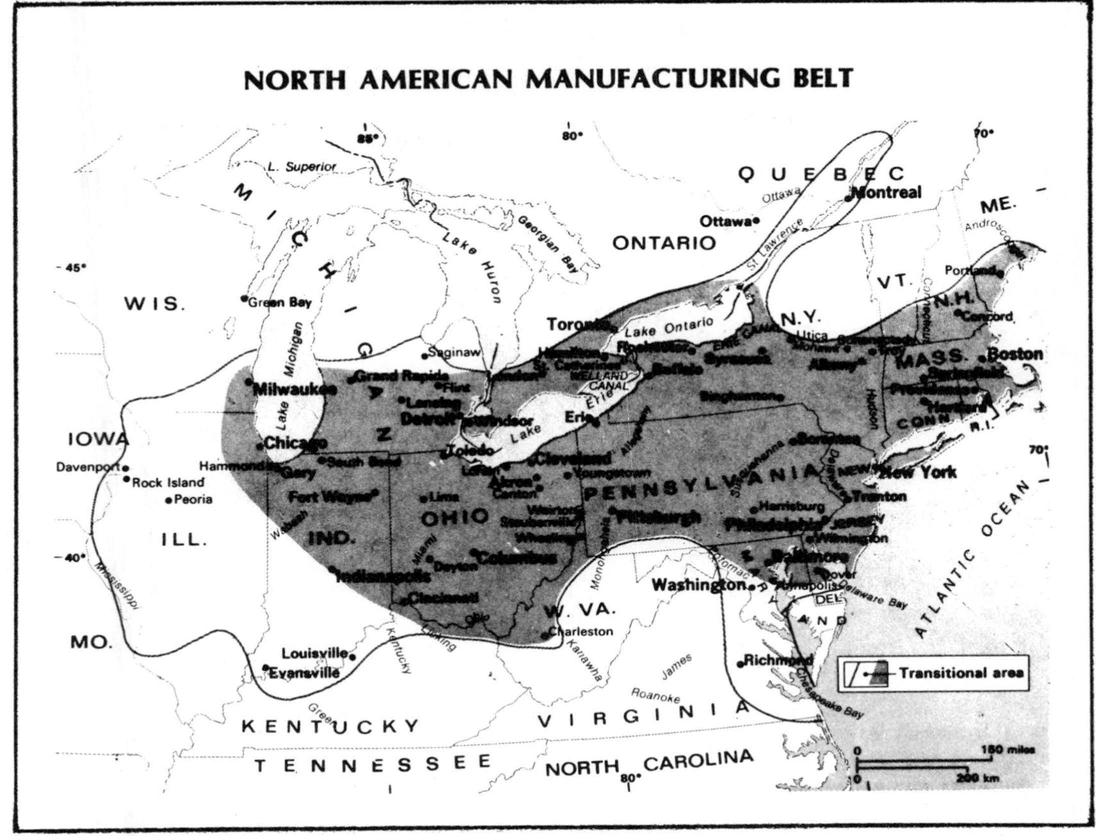

Figure 1.7. Source: Stephen Birdsall and John Florin, *Regional Landscapes of the United States and Canada,* © 1978, p. 77. Reprinted by permission of John Wiley & Sons, Inc., New York.

In Maryland, prime agricultural land accounts for almost one-third of the state's total land area; forests cover almost half of Maryland's land surface, whereas the national average is one-third.

As Maryland lies within both the American Manufacturing Belt and megalopolis, an appropriate question is: what are the connections between growth patterns of industrialization and urbanization? Very often these two processes are strongly interdependent (there are exceptions as in the case of Washington, D.C., which has very little industry for a metropolitan area of its size).

A number of advantages found in urban areas help to explain the interlocking growth patterns of cities and industries. One such characteristic is economies of scale, the economic advantages of large-scale production that allow the manufacturer to spread the fixed costs (building, machinery, land, and so forth) over more units of production. The result is lower prices or higher profits for the large-scale producer. Another characteristic of urban areas is agglomeration economies, i.e., a clustering of related industries in which component parts produced by various firms are brought together for assembly by one firm. Related industries thus clustered also can share the skilled-labor market. Large urban areas provide more accessible markets than do rural areas. Finally, in addition to laborers and consumers, the urban areas provide transportation and communication networks,

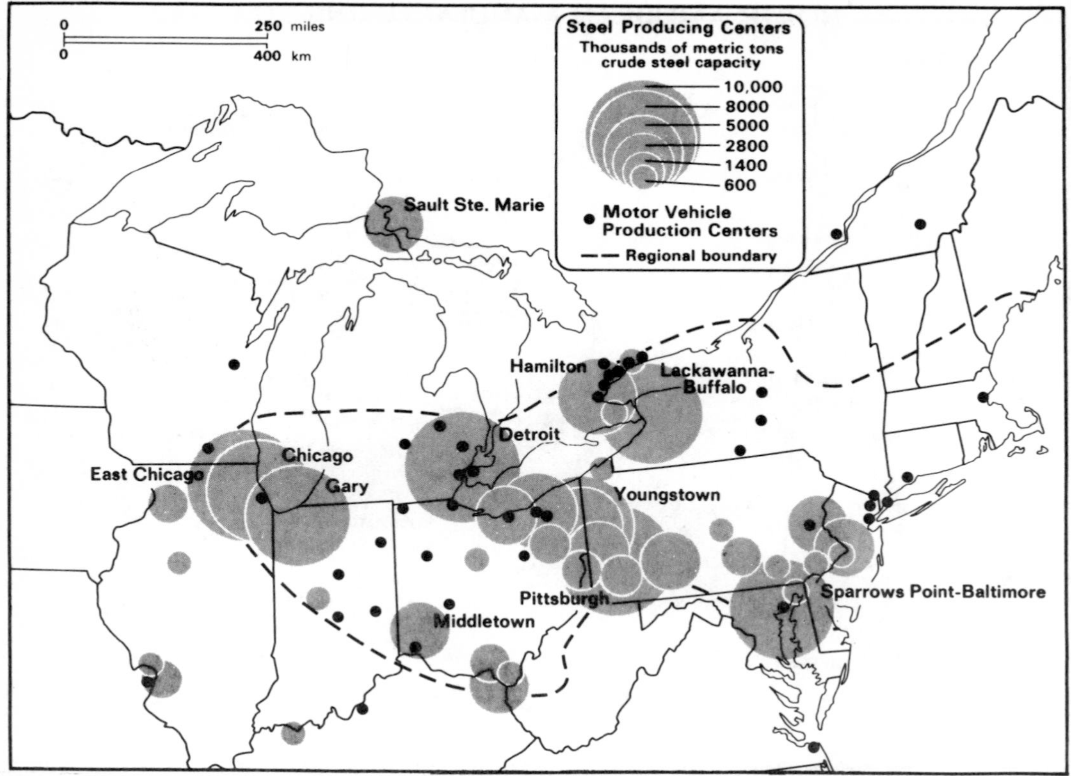

Figure 1.8. Source: Stephen Birdsall and John Florin, *Regional Landscapes of the United States and Canada,* © 1978, p. 98. Reprinted by permission of John Wiley & Sons, Inc., New York.

utilities, public services such as fire and police protection, schools and recreation for workers and their families, and a host of other amenities. All of this complex interplay can be directly witnessed in the urban-industrial areas of Maryland.

Appalachia

Another facet of the Maryland kaleidoscope is revealed by the inclusion of Garrett, Allegany, and Washington counties in the Appalachia region (Figure 1.9). This western part of Maryland has a physical and cultural character quite distinct from that of the rest of the state. Most advanced countries have one or more backward regions that linger near the threshold of the development road. These regions, for a number of reasons, fail to keep pace with the rising standards of living and structural economic changes that occur in the growth areas of the country. In the United States, Appalachia is one such region: an extensive area of rural poverty that stretches southwest along the highland region from New York State.

The definition of Appalachia as a region is complex. First and foremost, it is a physical region possessing the unity of a single geologic system. The definitions of "mountain" and "hill" are far from exact, but much of this region can be considered mountains. These are by no means the high mountains of the United States; the Sierra Nevada and the Rocky Mountains have peaks that rise over a mile higher than the highest Appalachian peaks. The geologic system of Appalachia is composed

APPALACHIA–OZARKS

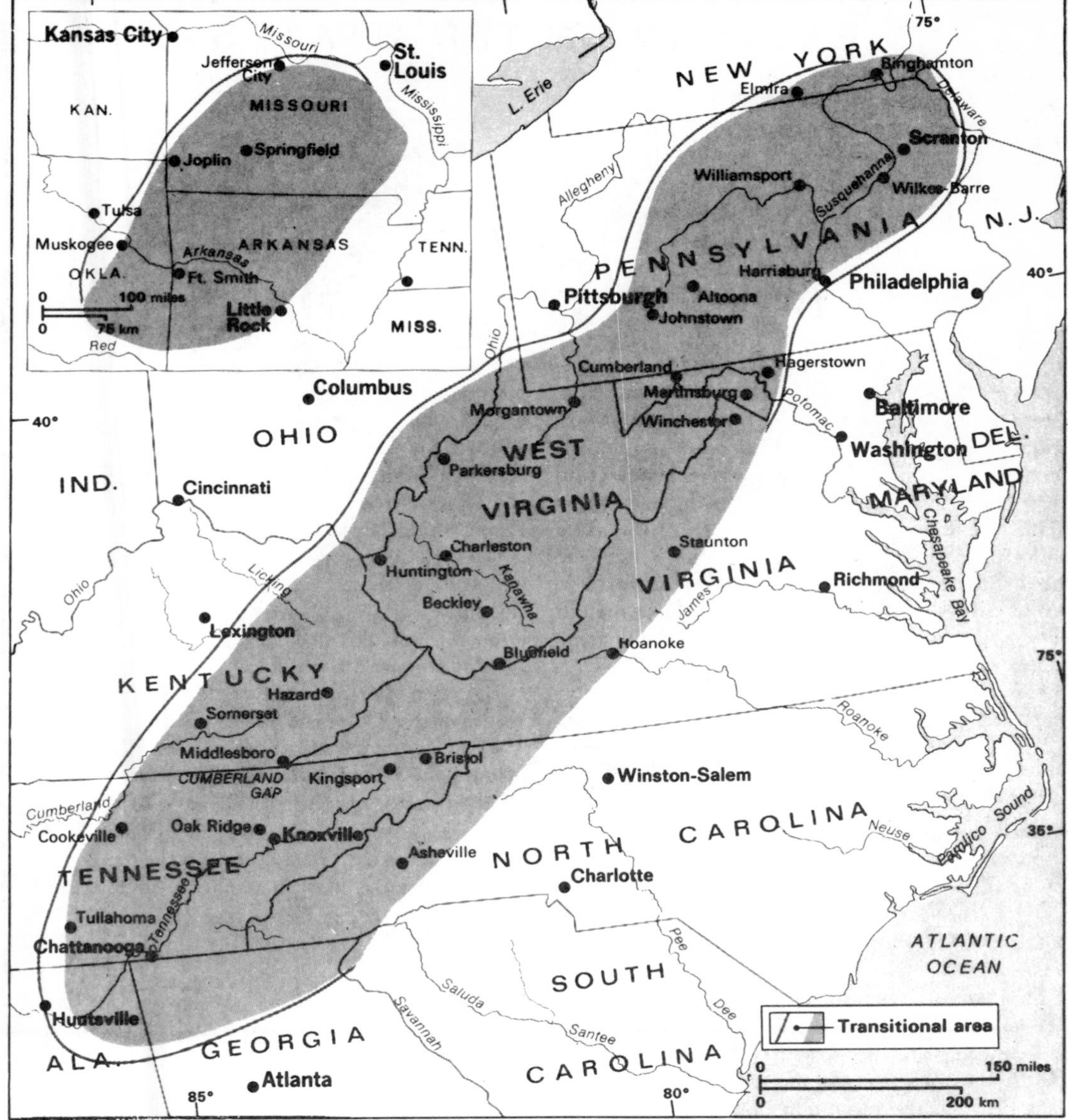

Figure 1.9. Source: Stephen Birdsall and John Florin, *Regional Landscapes of the United States and Canada,* © 1978, p. 140. Reprinted by permission of John Wiley & Sons, Inc., New York.

of three distinct physiographic regions that run parallel to each other as they stretch north-south. Traveling west the Blue Ridge is the first province of the Appalachians encountered, next comes the Ridge and Valley section, and then the plateau area. All of these provinces are represented within the borders of Maryland (Figure 1.10; see also Figure 2.20 in Chapter 2).

The physical characteristics alone do not

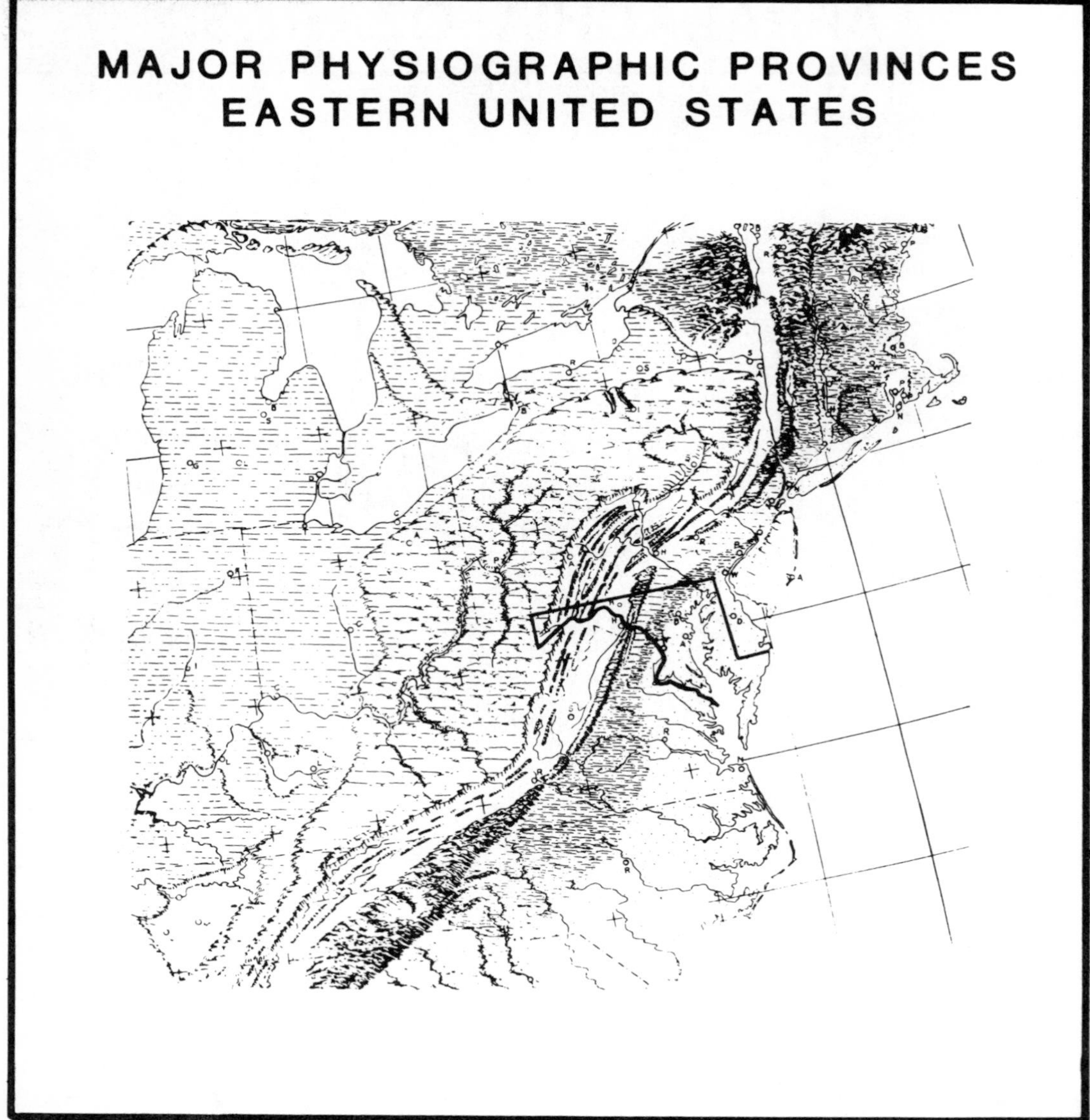

Figure 1.10. Source: Adapted from A. K. Lobeck, *Physiographic Diagram of the United States,* © 1957. Reprinted by permission of The Geographical Press, Maplewood, New Jersey.

explain adequately the way in which the name "Appalachia" is used, because it carries a political and a cultural meaning. Historically, the Appalachian system has been a barrier to the east-west movement of migration-settlement patterns, and settlers did not cross the Blue Ridge into the highlands until late in the colonial period. In 1732 Cecilius Calvert, second Lord of Baltimore, officially proclaimed western Maryland open for settlement, but it wasn't until the late 1700s and early 1800s that the area was settled. (Additional economic and political factors in the opening of the Maryland frontier will be discussed in Chapter 5.) As time passed, this region became isolated and separated from other areas. Transportation was difficult: even

Figure 1.11. A scene of rural poverty in Appalachian Maryland. Courtesy, U.S. Department of Housing and Urban Development.

the famous Wilderness Road that cut through the Cumberland Gap and on to the Bluegrass Basin of Kentucky was a difficult passage. The region developed outside the national pattern.

Culturally, Appalachia does not fit the description of a unified region with common characteristics throughout. Although it is vaguely defined as a region on the basis of a common syndrome of poverty, limited human opportunity, and stagnated economic development, the cultural variations within Appalachia are great. Appalachians in Maryland may resemble Appalachians in Mississippi in education, life-style, and income, but they are not linked by any significant trade or migration flows. Economist Edgar Hoover states that "Appalachia should be regarded as a succession of hinterlands to various centers located mainly outside the region as officially defined; a row of back yards as it were."[4]

Appalachia has often been described in a negative manner with an emphasis on its problems: farm lands have declined; coal production and employment declined for many years; schooling has been backward (Figure 1.11). The better educated and energetic people often left the area, creating a "brain drain" that was serious for a region with a scarcity of these human resources. Businesses such as coal mining and lumbering often are controlled by corporations from outside the region; this means that much of their profits also leave Appalachia.

As a result of regional immobility and isolation, a cultural distinctness has persisted in Appalachia. In his penetrating analysis of the region, *Night Comes to the Cumberlands,* Henry Caudill stated,

> In spite of the desirability of migration from certain depressed areas, studies have shown a pronounced reluctance on the part of the people to move. The social attachments to the area in terms of association with churches and clubs, the strong family ties, the distinctive local ways of life, and the difficulties of adjustment to a metropolitan environment all tend to reduce potential outmigration.[5]

These Appalachian people, often called "hillbillies," are mostly white, Anglo-Saxon, and Protestant. They represent the largest group of low-income people in the United States who are predominantly white (over one-third of the families live below the federally defined poverty level). The people also can be described as conservative and provincial.

Appalachia is a region that specializes in the kinds of employment for which demand has either grown slowly or declined, e.g., coal mining and general farming. As a result, the labor force lacks experience in more dynamic occupations and thus is at a disadvantage when seeking work elsewhere. Although the national image of Appalachia is one of a rural area, the high rural densities are not supported by a commercial agricultural system. Small general farms and coal mines are where most of the labor is employed.

In Appalachia, when the time came in the sequence of occupance for the transition from the stage of subsistence agriculture to the stage of commercial, market-oriented agriculture, the farmers were largely unsuccessful. The average Appalachian farm is small and remote. The rugged topography, poor soil, and short growing season all work against commercial farming; the efficient use of machinery is not possible here because of the lack of large, level farms. The general farming carried on here is a mixture of many products with no one dominating the region as corn does in parts of the Midwest. In western Maryland the mixture of crops and activities includes maple trees for syrup production, fruit orchards, pastureland, dairying, hay, wheat, and poultry.

One feature that unites this region is coal mining. The coal of Appalachia became important after the Civil War with the development of railroads and the steel industry, and the region provided the coal for the U.S. industrial revolution. Mining, which adversely affected the land and the quality of life of the people, provided employment for many. Then during the depression and after World War II, the coal industry declined and economic distress hit Appalachia hard. Unemployment in coal counties soared as mechanization caused the number of jobs to decline. Some counties lost over a quarter of their population due to the resultant outmigration from 1950 to 1960. By 1980, however, the coal industry was experiencing increased production rates that set new records.

John F. Kennedy became aware of the situation in Appalachia while campaigning there for the presidency in 1960. His promise to remedy these great regional disparities was addressed after his death when in 1965 the Appalachian Redevelopment Act was passed as an extension of the Area Redevelopment Act of 1961. The definition of Appalachia adopted by the act was broad and based on vague criteria: high unemployment; low income; low levels of housing, health, and educational facilites; dominance of the regional economy by one or two industries in a long-term decline; substantial outmigration of labor and/or capital; and low growth rate of aggregate output. In the final analysis it was left largely to the states to decide what was and what was not Appalachia. The political-administrative development region that has emerged stretches from New York State to Mississippi and includes 373 counties in eleven states.

In the act, $1.1 billion was made available to the Appalachian Regional Commission to be spent on projects agreed upon

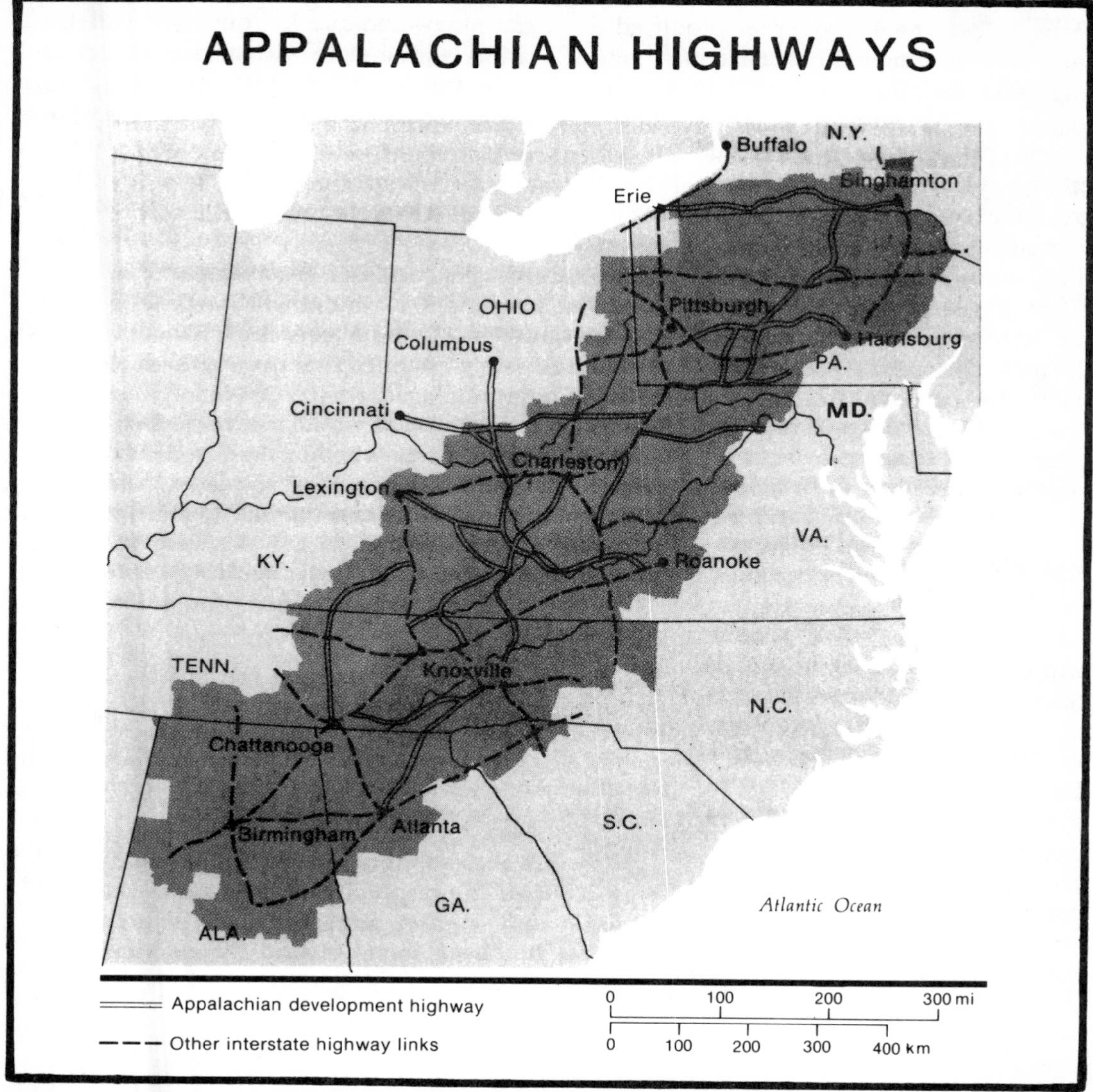

Figure 1.12. Courtesy, Appalachian Regional Commission.

between federal and state officials. Since 1965, the original allocation has been added to and the commission has spent several billion dollars for health centers, vocational training, erosion control, schools, libraries, sewerage facilities, recreational facilities, and roads. By far the largest share of the funds (80 percent of the original allocation) has been used to build roads, in hopes that they would decrease isolation and encourage industries to come into the region (Figure 1.12). Criticism has been leveled at the commission for committing so much money for roads, as the goal of the planners that development corridors would result from the roads has not been fully realized. In many instances the improved roads have allowed motorists to travel through the area faster and have facilitated outmigration.

As stated earlier, there has been a reversal of trends in Appalachia since the early 1970s. The energy crisis produced a surge in the demand for coal, and out-migration has been replaced by net in-migration. The number of families below the poverty level has decreased. The improved highway network has provided greater accesibility. In all, it is now becoming evident that long-term efforts in the areas of health and education are paying off as the human resources of the region are becoming more fully integrated into the national economy. Appalachia will most likely not become part of the U.S. manufacturing core nor will poverty disappear there, but at least there is hope for future steady improvement in the quality of life.

AMERICA IN MINIATURE: AN OVERVIEW

The themes presented in this chapter will be more fully developed and analyzed throughout the book. The regional setting of Maryland explains the full meaning of its description as "America in Miniature." Despite its small size, Maryland contains a rich variety of physical and cultural landscapes: wealth and poverty, urban centers and rural areas, plains and mountains, centrality and isolation, manufacturing and farming—and the list does not end here. Maryland, a state with a long history and rich traditions, is pulsating with change from the Eastern Shore ruled by its squirearchy, across the fox-and-hounds country, to the coal mines of Garrett County. H. L. Mencken once wrote an essay describing Maryland as the most "average" of states. In doing so, this distinguished Baltimore writer was recognizing the presence in Maryland of the elemental character of the nation.

NOTES

1. Jean Gottmann, *A Geography of Europe,* 4th ed. (New York: Holt, Rinehart, and Winston, 1969), p. 76.
2. Harold Vokes, *Geography and Geology of Maryland,* Geological Survey Bulletin 19, revised by Jonathan Edwards (Baltimore: Maryland Geological Survey, 1968), p. 1.
3. Jean Gottmann, *Megalopolis: The Urbanized Northeastern Seaboard of the U.S.* (New York: 20th Century Fund, 1961), p. 8.
4. Edgar Hoover, *An Introduction to Regional Economics* (New York: Alfred Knopf Pub., 1975), p. 289.
5. Henry M. Caudill, *Night Comes to the Cumberlands* (Boston: Little, Brown and Co., 1962), p. 179.

CHAPTER 2

THE LAND

A prerequisite for consideration of the geography of Maryland is to understand the land itself, for it is upon this physical base that the people left their mark over the centuries. This imprint made by people upon the land, called the cultural landscape, includes elements such as settlements, transportation routes, and agricultural, manufacturing, and recreational facilities. People interact with the natural environment to create their own cultural landscapes. At one time, the major theme in geography was environmental determinism, i.e., a belief that human behavior is to a large degree controlled or determined by the natural environment. Today, geographers have adopted a more realistic belief—the belief that people are active agents in their environment and make decisions based on their cultural and environmental perceptions. Nevertheless, the possible constraints of the environmental resistances that people must overcome cannot be ignored.

Maryland has a physical environment that is delightfully varied. The low-lying areas of eastern Maryland, which border the Atlantic Ocean along the 32-mile (51.2-kilometer) coastline of Worcester County and surround Chesapeake Bay, have a climate with a maritime influence. West of the bay, beyond the fall-line zone, are found the low, rolling-and-pitching hills of the Piedmont. These hills give way to the ridges, valleys, and upland plateau of the Appalachians in western Maryland.

While the diversity of the physical environment is the central topic of this chapter, consideration also will be given to Maryland's boundaries and location in relation to the state's climate, soil, vegetation, water resources, and landforms. Each of these elements of the total physical system of the state extends beyond the political boundaries of Maryland and into adjacent states. All of the elements interact with each other as parts of an environmental system: it is not possible to understand Maryland's climate, for example, without considering the landforms and distribution of water bodies throughout the state.

THE TERRITORIAL EXTENT OF MARYLAND

Maryland is one of the smaller states of the nation, ranking forty-second in area. The state covers 12,303 sq mi (31,865 sq km), which can be separated into 9,874 sq mi (25,574 sq km) land, 1,726 (4,470) Chesapeake Bay, 106 (275) Chincoteague Bay, and 597 (1,546) inland and tidal waters. The east-west distance across Maryland is less than 250 mi (402 km). North-south the extent varies greatly, from 125 mi (201 km) in the east to a mere 1.9 mi (3.1 km) at the wasplike waist near Hancock in Washington County. For purposes of comparison, Maryland is six times larger than Delaware, a little less than one-third the size of Pennsylvania.

The present shape of Maryland has

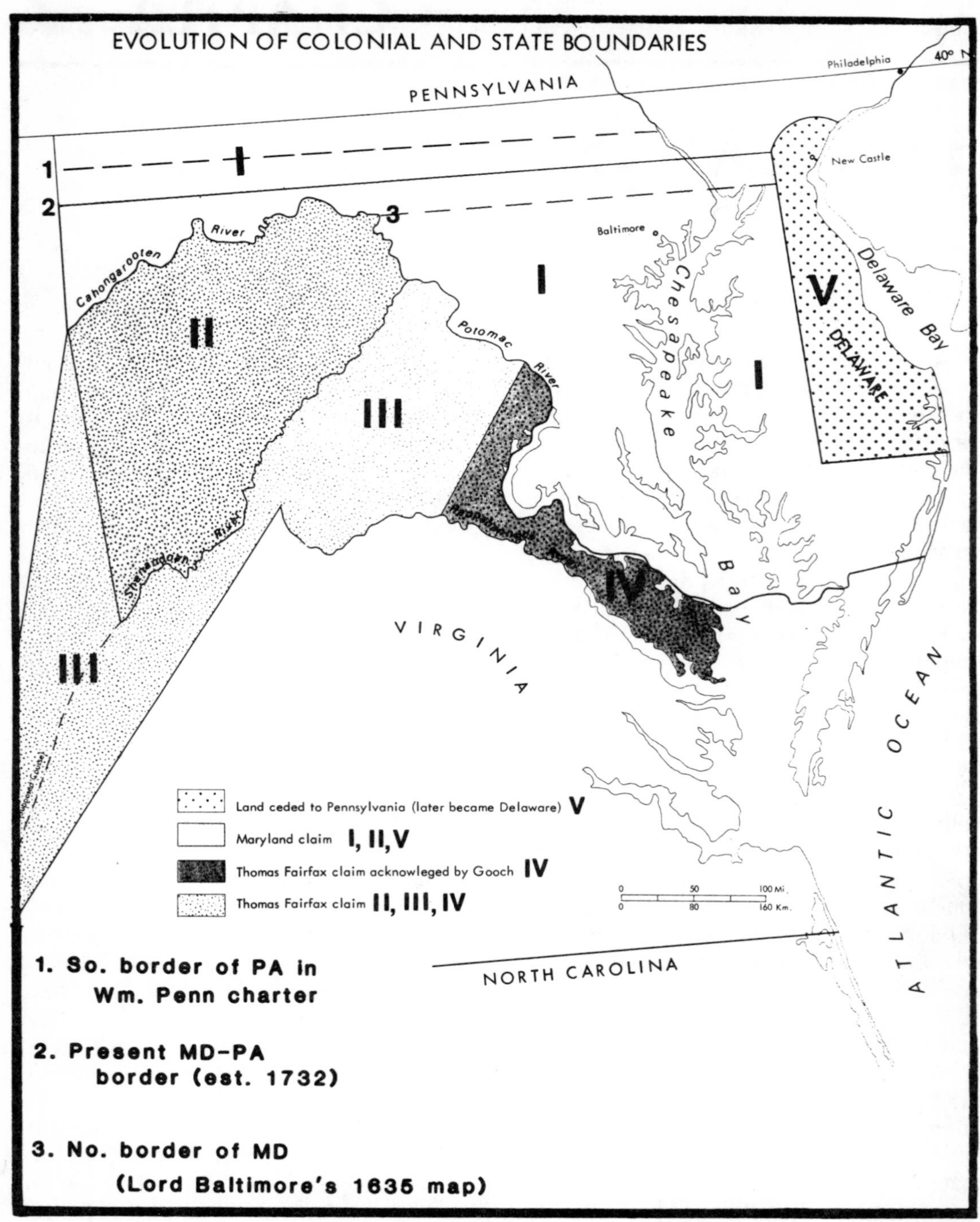

FIGURE 2.1. Source: Derek Thompson, ed., *Atlas of Maryland,* © 1977 (College Park: Department of Geography, University of Maryland). Reprinted with permission.

evolved since the original grant to Lord Baltimore in 1632. The northern, western, and most of the eastern boundaries are straight lines. The irregular southern boundary follows the southern shore of the Potomac River; the Potomac is entirely in Maryland.

The charter of Maryland issued on June 20, 1632, by King Charles I of England described the boundaries of the colony as extending from the Potomac River north to the 40th parallel (this includes the present site of Philadelphia) and westward from the Atlantic Ocean to the first "fountain" of the Potomac. Unfortunately, the officials in London had no accurate geographic information about the interior of the region. In 1680, a part of the same territory was granted to William Penn. And another part of the Maryland grant, which had been settled by Swedes (what is now Delaware), was granted to the Duke of York who, after becoming James II, ceded the area to Penn in 1682.

Endless boundary disputes plagued Maryland until the close of the nineteenth century (Figure 2.1). Pennsylvania and Virginia were reluctant to recognize the legality of Lord Baltimore's grant. Their arguments centered on the unclear terminology of the Charter of 1632, such as the grant of "land hitherto unsettled" from the Potomac to a line "which lieth under the fortieth degree north latitude from the quinoctal," and extended westward to a line due north from the "first fountain of the Potomac." In 1760 an English court set the Maryland-Delaware-Pennsylvania corner, as shown in Figure 2.2. In 1763 two English surveyors, Charles Mason and Jeremiah Dixon, were contracted to demarcate these boundaries. It took them until December 1767 to run the northern boundary, along which each mile was marked by a stone from a quarry on the Isle of Portland, England. The northern side of the marker displayed a *P* and the southern side an *M*. This boundary, known as the Mason-Dixon line, actually emerges as a visual feature when viewed from the air. Figure 2.3 shows it

MD.-DEL.-PA. CORNER

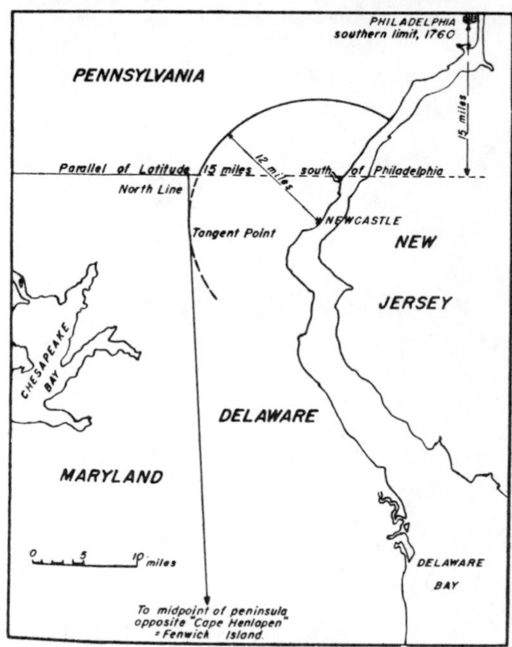

FIGURE 2.2. Source: Harold Vokes, *Geography and Geology of Maryland,* revised by Jonathan Edwards, Maryland Geological Survey Bulletin 19, 1968, p. 3.

in an area northwest of Towson in Baltimore County, looking west with Pennsylvania on the right and Maryland on the left.

The western border of Maryland was disputed with Virginia, and after the Civil War differences arose with West Virginia. It was not until the United States Supreme Court decision on May 7, 1912, that the western boundary of the state was firmly established. The southern boundary was disputed as late as 1930 with Virginia. At that time a commission established by the governors of the two states agreed to the low-water mark on the Virginia side of the Potomac River as the boundary.

Maryland lost all of its major boundary disputes with neighboring colonies and later with states. Other colonies closed in on Maryland and settled the periphery; territorial retreat followed each court defeat.

FIGURE 2.3. The Mason-Dixon line along the Maryland-Pennsylvania border is clearly visible today. Offset property boundaries and different field patterns make this cultural imprint visible. Courtesy, N. R. Diffenderfer.

The Calvert family did not aggressively pursue its land grant. Much of their failure to protect the integrity of Maryland's boundaries was due to a lack of geographical information, but it also can be understood in another context. The Calverts were a prominent and wealthy Roman Catholic family. As the early seventeenth century was not a pleasant time for Catholics in England, the Calverts did not desire to stir up any controversies with the largely Protestant colonies surrounding Maryland. The Papists in Maryland were barely tolerated in these early years.

THE PHYSICAL FRAME

Climate

Maryland has a moderate mid-latitude climate that can be described as mesothermal. Climates to the north and west are more rigorous; those to the south are milder.

Climatic characteristics sometimes vary significantly at different geographical scales. At the continental scale, the general climate within this small state does not display any significant variations. When viewed at a more local scale, distinct climatic variations over the Maryland landscape are unmasked. Slight variations in temperature and precipitation throughout the state are significant to the people living on this land. These variations affect farming, forestry, and recreation, among other activities. For instance, there is enough climatic variation in Maryland to allow skiing in Garrett County and cypress swamps in Calvert County. To understand the climatic differences in Maryland, consideration must be given to elevation, the extent of land and water surfaces, continentality, and human settlements, as well as to latitudinal location. The Appalachian Highlands in western Maryland have a climate significantly different from the Coastal Plain area to the east that lies adjacent to two major bodies of water, Chesapeake Bay and the Atlantic Ocean. There are also significant differences in the Baltimore and Washington, D.C., metropolitan area heat islands.

Climate is the long-term pattern of weather conditions typical of a place. The two obvious elements are temperature and moisture, which have direct influences on agriculture, water supply, human comfort, industry, and recreation. Climate, therefore, is an important natural resource. The following description of Maryland's climate considers spatial variations (place to place) and temporal variations (season to season).

Temperature. Mean annual temperatures in Maryland range from 48°F (8.9°C) at

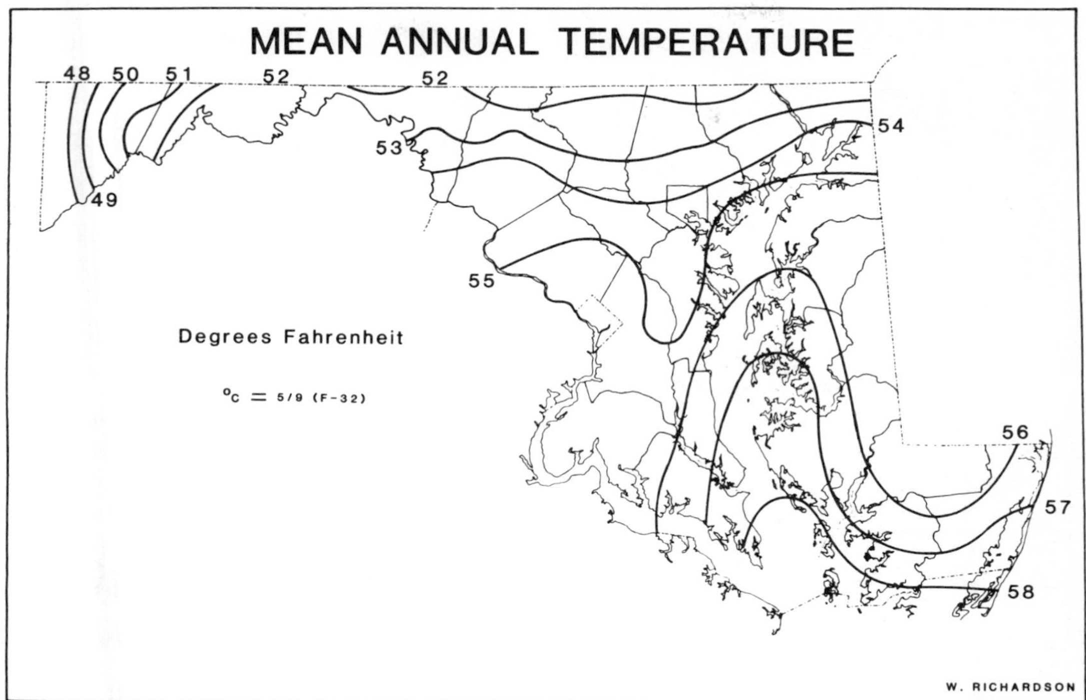

FIGURE 2.4. Source: National Oceanographic and Atmospheric Administration, *Climatic Data, Maryland and Delaware* (Washington, D.C.: U.S. Department of Commerce, annual volumes 1951 through 1975).

high elevations of Garrett County to 58°F (14.4°C) on the Coastal Plain of southern Maryland (Figure 2.4). Seasonal temperatures vary around the annual mean by about twenty degrees Fahrenheit (11 degrees Celsius) i.e., mean winter temperatures are about twenty degrees lower and mean summer temperatures about twenty degrees higher (Figures 2.5, 2.6).

Urban areas have a microclimate associated with them that is warmer than the surrounding hinterland. Called an urban heat island, it results from the intense discharge of heat and pollutants from various urban activities. The heat islands of Baltimore and Washington, D.C., show up clearly on Figures 2.5 and 2.6. Heat islands are especially noticeable during the summer when winds are weaker and heat-pollution domes build up over the two cities. The heat island effect is not as pronounced in the winter. At that time the Baltimore heat island is more intense than that of Washington, D.C., a difference explained by the industrial activities in each city. Baltimore has a strong mixture of heavy and light industries that release much heat into the atmosphere. Washington, D.C., on the other hand, is a more service-oriented city and has very little industry to produce waste heat.

Climatic data for the seven locations in Maryland listed in Table 2.1 are displayed in Table 2.2. Baltimore City has a mean annual temperature of 57.5°F (14.2°C), while Baltimore-Washington International (BWI) Airport located south of the city, just outside the heat island, has a mean annual temperature of 55°F (12.8°C). The difference between the mean annual temperatures of Snow Hill and Baltimore, both at the same elevation, results from the fact

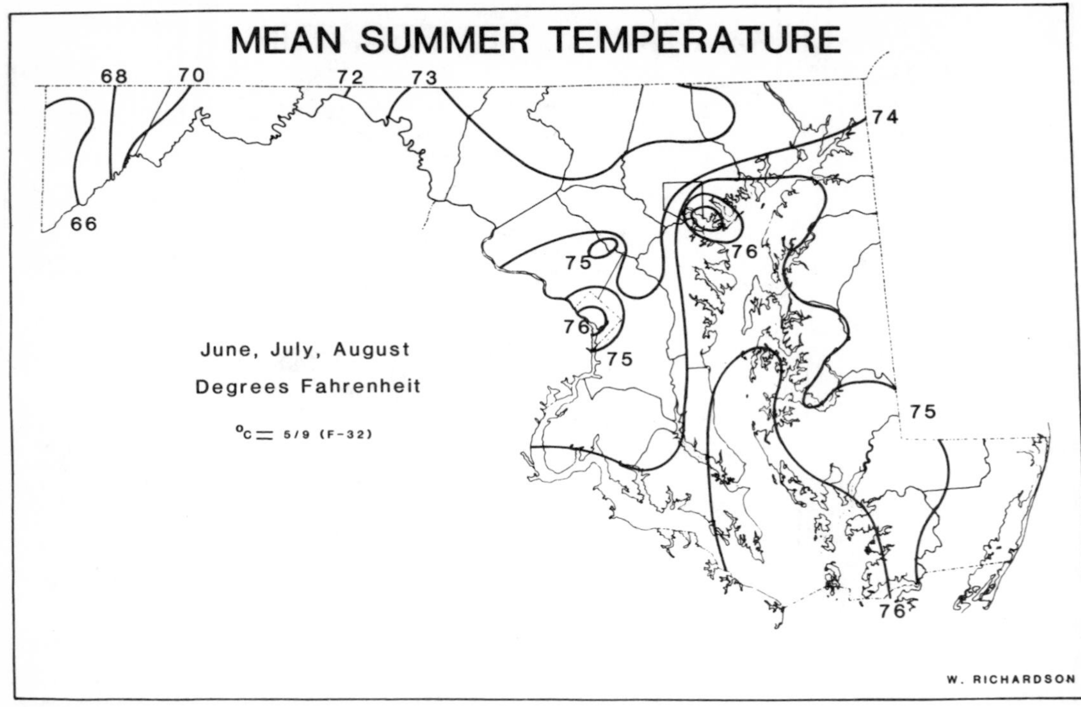

FIGURE 2.5 (*above*). FIGURE 2.6 (*below*). Source for both figures: National Oceanographic and Atmospheric Administration, *Climatic Data, Maryland and Delaware* (Washington, D.C.: U.S. Department of Commerce, annual volumes 1951 through 1975).

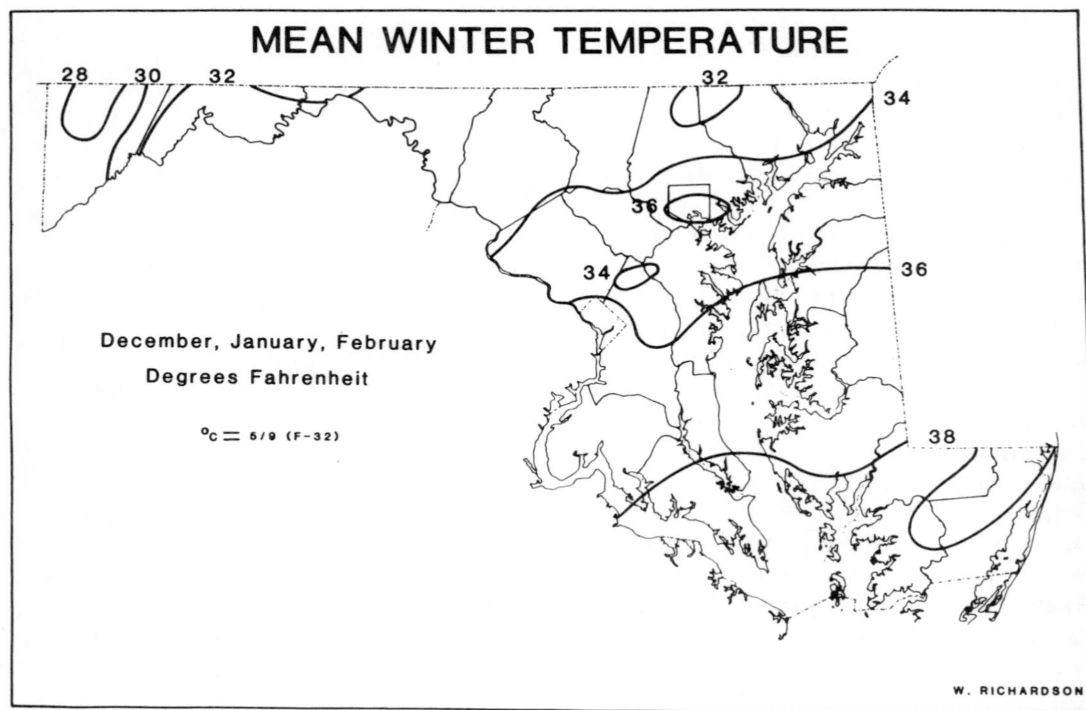

TABLE 2.1
SELECTED WEATHER STATIONS

Station	Latitude North	Longitude West	Elevation (Feet)
Baltimore (City)	39° 17'	76° 37'	14
Baltimore-Washington International Airport	39° 11'	76° 40'	148
Cumberland	39° 39'	78° 45'	945
Oakland	39° 24'	79° 24'	2,420
Snow Hill	38° 11'	75° 24'	14
Westminster	39° 35'	77° 00'	770

Source: Maryland Statistical Abstract 1979, p. 67, Table 38.

that Snow Hill is not a major city with a heat island. On the other hand, the difference in elevation of Westminster, Carroll County, at 770 ft (234.7 m) and Oakland at 2420 ft (737.6 m) in the extreme western part of Maryland, explains the 5.2°F difference in the mean annual temperatures of the two towns.

These variations in temperature from place to place reflect four major factors: latitude, elevation, urbanization, and proximity to large bodies of water. In Figure 2.4, the isotherms (lines connecting points of equal temperature) trend north-south over the mountains of western Maryland and over the Chesapeake Bay area. In central Maryland, where the influence of the mountains and the bay is not pronounced, the isotherms trend more east-west along the lines of latitude. The mean winter temperatures shown in Figure 2.6 reflect the effects of latitude and elevation. Southern Maryland is nearly 5°F warmer in winter than the northeast corner of the state; yet both areas are near sea level.

The highest temperature recorded in Maryland is 109°F (42.7°C); this was at Keedysville, Washington County, on August 6, 1918, and at Cumberland, Allegany County, and Frederick, Frederick County, on July 10, 1936. The coldest temperature in the state is −40°F (−40°C), recorded at Oakland, Garrett County, on January 13, 1912. All of these locations are in western Maryland, away from the moderating influence on temperature of Chesapeake Bay and the Atlantic Ocean. These large bodies of water, which store heat during the summer, release it during the winter to moderate nighttime cooling. The occurrence of days with a minimum temperature below 32°F (0°C) is less for places close to these bodies of water (Figure 2.7). In the summer, the water absorbs heat, and the result is fewer days with a maximum temperature exceeding 90°F (32.2°C) over the adjacent landmass (Figure 2.8). Thus the Eastern Shore and the Chesapeake lands experience milder winters and slightly cooler summers with higher humidity. Farther inland the marine influence gives way to a continental influence, producing more extremes of seasonal temperatures.

Of great importance to agriculture in Maryland is the length of the growing season, the period of time between the last frost in the spring and the first frost in the fall. It is difficult to define "killing frost" because plants vary in their minimum temperature tolerance, but 32°F (0°C)

TABLE 2.2

MEAN ANNUAL TEMPERATURE AND PRECIPITATION AT SELECTED WEATHER STATIONS, 1941-1970

Station	Jan	Feb	Mar	Apr	May	Jun	Jul	Aug	Sep	Oct	Nov	Dec	Annual
Baltimore (City)													
Mo. Temp. (°F)	36.5	37.2	43.7	55.7	66.9	73.8	79.2	77.6	70.9	60.2	48.9	38.8	57.5
Ppt. (In)	3.00	2.92	3.80	3.23	3.63	3.84	4.12	4.01	3.25	2.86	3.21	3.44	41.31
BWI Airport													
Mo. Temp. (°F)	33.4	34.8	42.8	53.8	63.7	72.4	76.6	74.9	68.5	57.4	46.1	35.3	55.0
Ppt. (In)	2.91	2.81	3.69	3.07	3.61	3.77	4.07	4.21	3.12	2.81	3.13	3.26	40.46
Cumberland													
Mo. Temp. (°F)	31.8	33.7	41.4	53.1	62.4	70.2	73.6	72.7	66.1	55.8	43.6	33.9	53.2
Ppt. (In)	2.42	2.51	3.59	3.47	3.56	3.97	3.12	3.19	2.97	2.54	2.61	2.61	36.56
Oakland													
Mo. Temp. (°F)	27.5	28.8	35.9	47.7	56.6	64.4	67.4	66.5	60.3	50.4	36.9	29.2	47.9
Ppt. (In)	3.84	3.33	4.68	4.28	4.48	4.28	4.78	4.36	3.09	2.91	3.27	3.81	47.11
Snow Hill													
Mo. Temp. (°F)	36.3	37.9	44.6	54.5	63.9	72.0	75.8	73.4	68.0	58.8	47.4	38.2	55.9
Ppt. (In)	3.60	3.62	4.69	3.35	3.43	3.85	4.37	5.01	3.82	3.65	3.56	3.69	46.64
Westminster													
Mo. Temp. (°F)	31.4	33.0	41.1	52.5	62.0	70.4	74.5	72.7	66.2	55.7	41.5	33.4	53.1
Ppt. (In)	2.97	2.79	3.88	3.43	3.69	3.85	4.52	4.10	3.04	2.94	3.35	3.47	41.84

Source: Maryland Statistical Abstract, 1979.

°C = 5/9 (F-32)

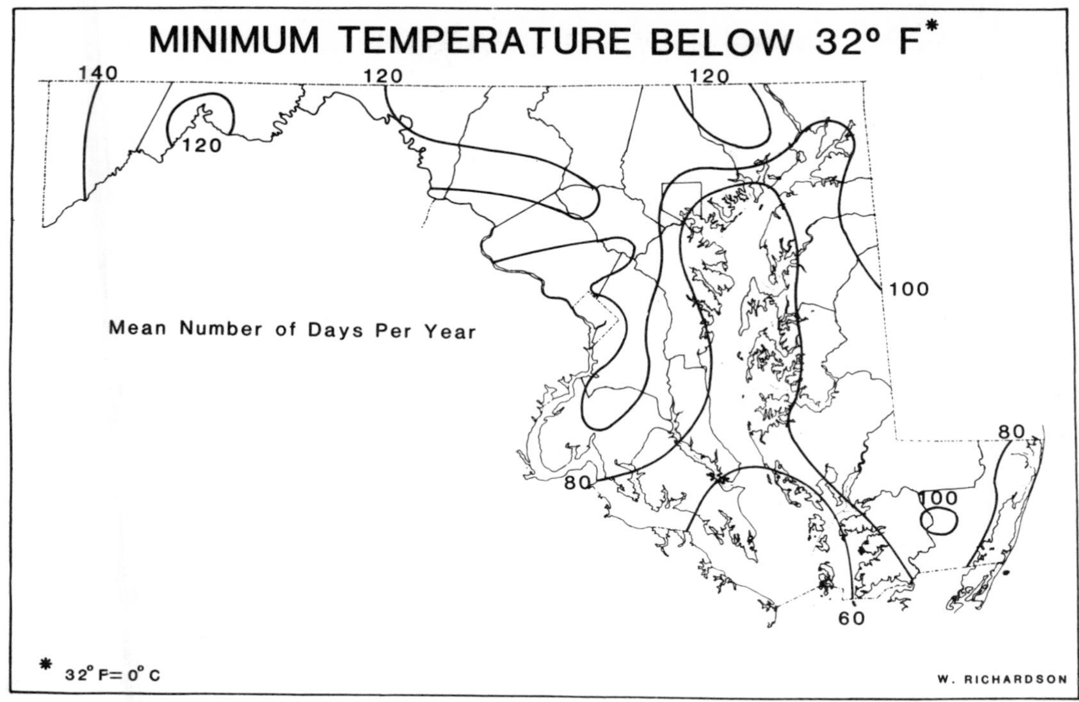

FIGURE 2.7 (*above*). FIGURE 2.8 (*below*). Source for both figures: National Oceanographic and Atmospheric Administration, *Climatic Data, Maryland and Delaware* (Washington, D.C.: U.S. Department of Commerce, annual volumes 1951 through 1975).

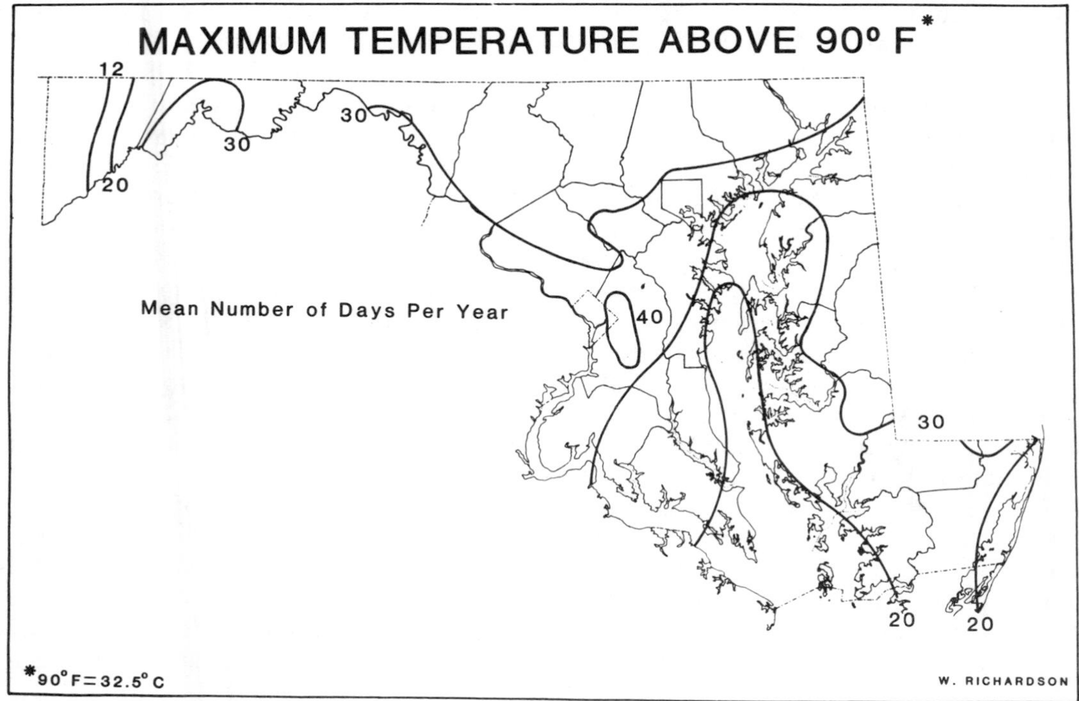

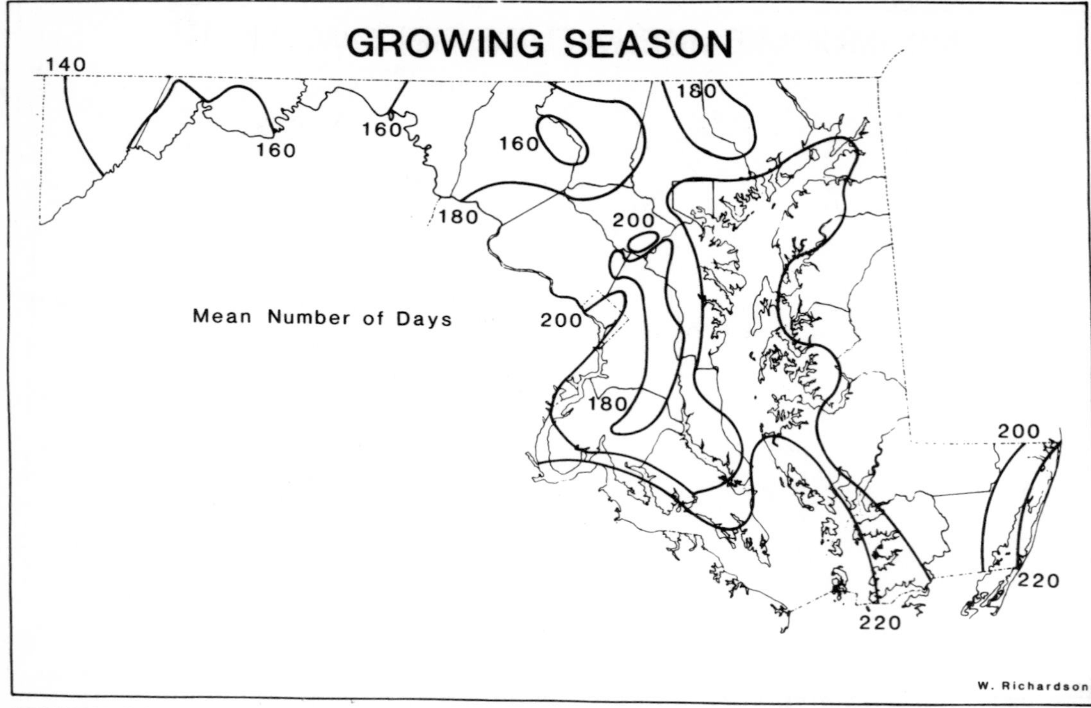

FIGURE 2.9. Source: National Oceanographic and Atmospheric Administration, *Climatic Data, Maryland and Delaware* (Washington, D.C.: U.S. Department of Commerce, annual volumes 1951 through 1975).

is often used as an indicator of frost occurrence. The number of days in the growing season (Figure 2.9) is based on the period of time between the mean spring and fall frost dates (shown on Figures 2.10 and 2.11). The longest growing seasons in Maryland are found near Chesapeake Bay and along the ocean, because of the ameliorating influence of the water, and in the Baltimore and Washington, D.C., areas as a result of the urban heat islands.

The frost dates shown represent means; frosts may occur earlier or later in any given year. Frosts have occurred as late as May 12 and early as October 1 in Baltimore and as late as June 24 and early as August 21 in Oakland. Ninety percent of the time the first frost in fall occurs within three weeks of the mean date. Frost variability in the spring is less in the coastal areas than in the upland area of western Maryland. Local topography can also affect the occurrence of frost, so that low-lying valleys and hollows may experience a frost later in spring and earlier in fall than hilltops.

Moisture. Precipitation amounts do not vary widely throughout Maryland, but a general pattern is noticeable. However, temperature is much more predictable in Maryland than is precipitation.

Annual precipitation totals vary from less than 38 in (96.5 cm) to over 48 in (122 cm); the mean for the state is 42 in (107 cm) (Figure 2.12). The noticeably lower averages in the area around and east of Cumberland indicate the Ridge and Valley section of the Appalachians, which lies at a lower elevation than the Allegheny Plateau immediately west of Cumberland. Since the winds are generally from the west and northwest, Cumberland and the area to the east experience a noticeable rain shadow effect. It can be seen in Table 2.2 that Oakland, Garrett County (which lies

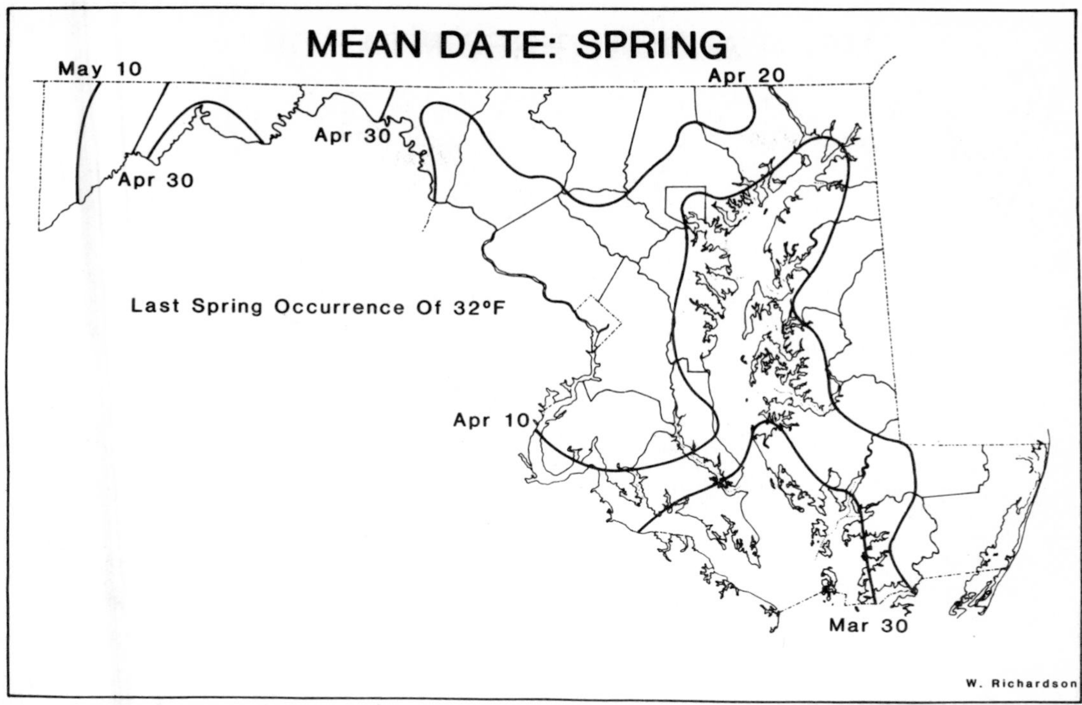

FIGURE 2.10 (*above*). FIGURE 2.11 (*below*). Source for both figures: National Oceanographic and Atmospheric Administration, *Climatic Data, Maryland and Delaware* (Washington, D.C.: U.S. Department of Commerce, annual volumes 1951 through 1975).

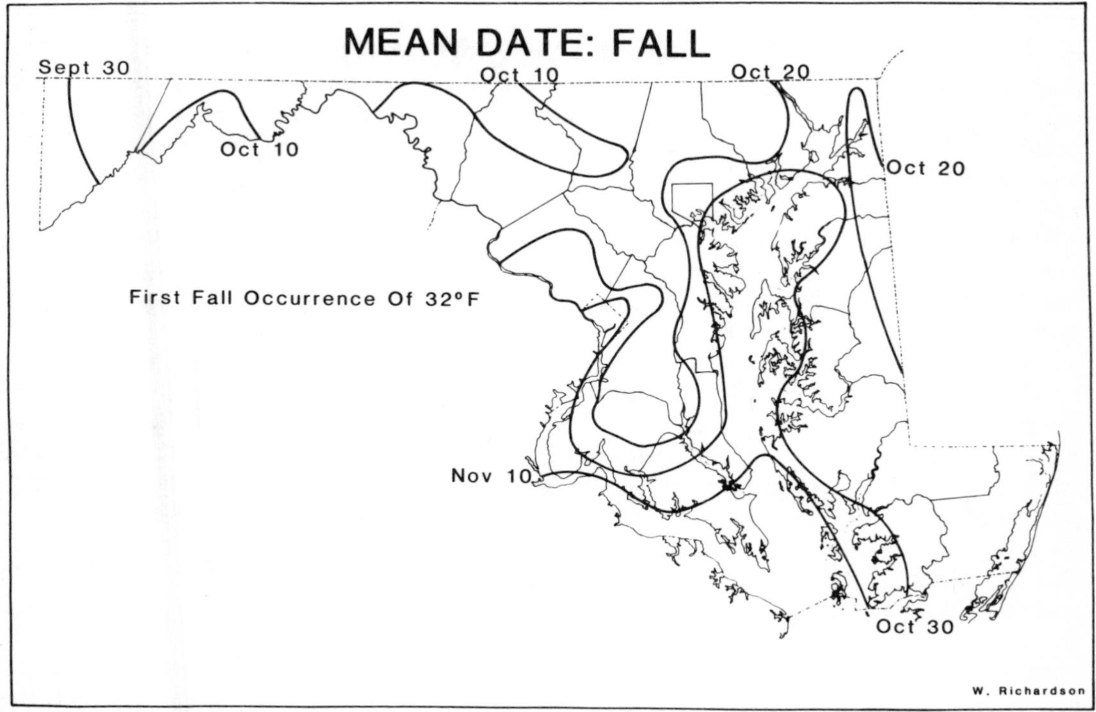

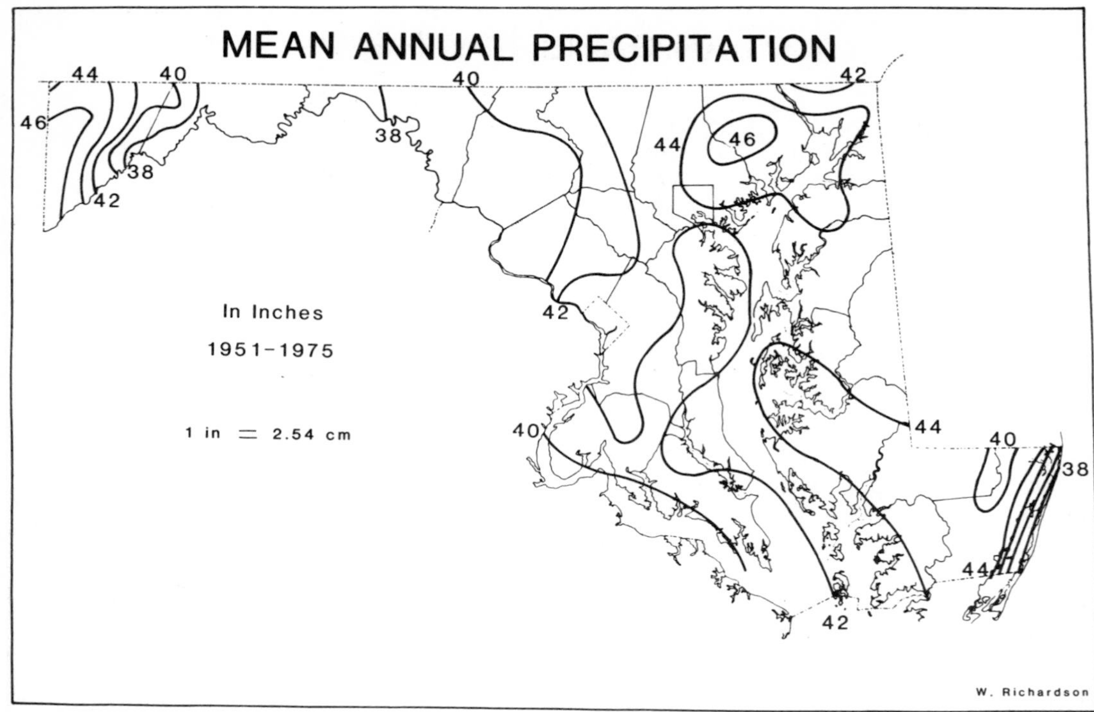

FIGURE 2.12 (*above*). FIGURE 2.13 (*below*). Source for both figures: National Oceanographic and Atmospheric Administration, *Climatic Data, Maryland and Delaware* (Washington, D.C.: U.S. Department of Commerce, annual volumes 1951 through 1975).

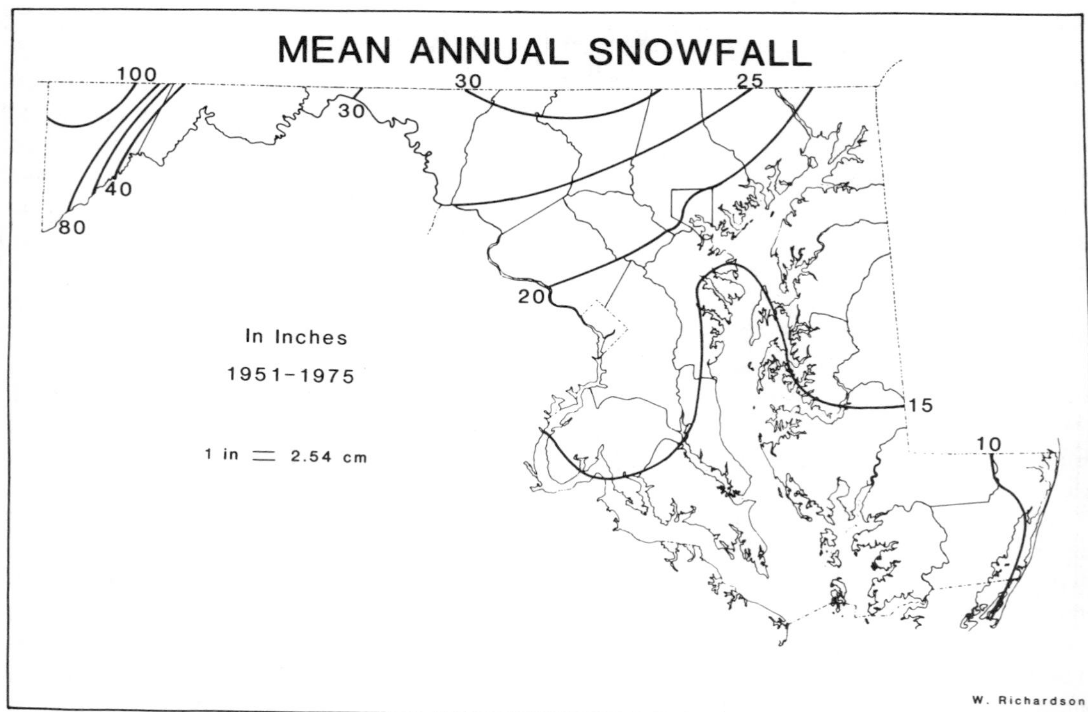

at 2,420 ft [737.6 m] elevation on the Allegheny Plateau just 40 mi [64.4 km] west of Cumberland), receives on the average 10.55 in (26.8 cm) more precipitation per year than Cumberland. Allegany County receives less precipitation than any other county in the state.

Mean annual snowfall varies greatly, from over 100 in (254 cm) on the Allegheny Plateau in Garrett County to less than 10 in (25.4 cm) in the extreme eastern part of the state (Figure 2.13). Snow usually remains on the ground for only a short period of time in most of Maryland.

Overall, Maryland has a moist climate with no dry months. In this water-surplus climate, annual precipitation normally is greater than evapotranspiration (evaporation of surface water or soil moisture plus plant transpiration), and extended droughts are infrequent. Short drought periods occur more often; these may be serious if they occur during the growing season.

The climograph shown in Figure 2.14 for Westminster, Carroll County, depicts seasonal variations in temperature and precipitation. Precipitation is greatest in early summer, exceeding 4.5 in (11.4 cm) in July; this coincides with the maximum mean monthly temperatures of 75.5°F (24.4°C). Most of this summer precipitation is from convectional thunderstorms. Evapotranspiration, near zero all winter, increases with warming temperatures, and during June, July, and August evapotranspiration usually exceeds precipitation in all of Maryland except Garrett County, where precipitation exceeds evapotranspiration all year. From April through September, much of Maryland's rain is from showery and thunderstorm conditions; from October through March, much of the precipitation comes from frontal storms.

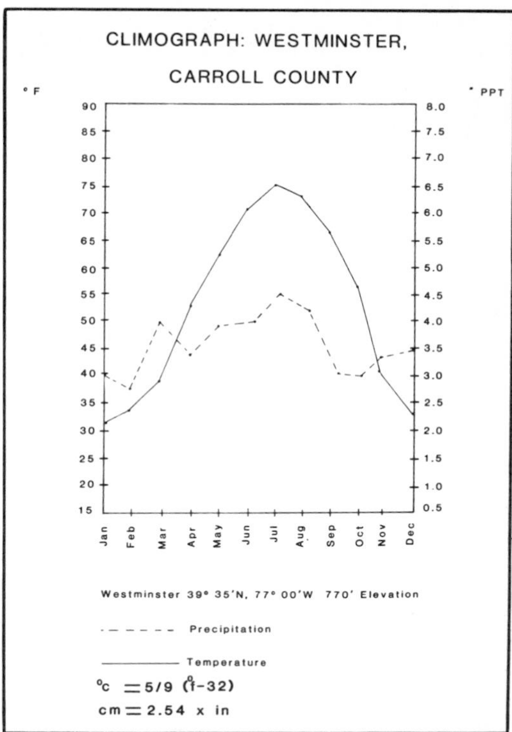

FIGURE 2.14. Source: Maryland Geological Survey.

Winds and Storms. The latitude of Maryland places it in the prevailing westerly wind belt. The winds do vary somewhat by the season, as the global wind patterns change: from October to April the prevailing wind direction is from the northwest, from May to September from the south and southwest. In the mountains of western Maryland the west-northwest winds are common all year. The mean wind velocity is greatest in March and lowest in August. Although they do occur, high destructive winds from tornadoes and tropical hurricanes are infrequent in Maryland.

Weather patterns usually approach Maryland from the west. Cold air masses that bring cold winter days and cool summer days originate over central Canada and travel over the Midwest to Maryland. Warm, dry air masses originating over the southwestern United States occasionally, but very seldom, reach Maryland. Warm, humid air masses travel to Maryland from the Gulf of Mexico and Atlantic Ocean.

Daily temperatures in Maryland are affected by the degree of cloudiness. The greatest daily ranges occur on cloudless days in the spring and fall. The absence of clouds during the day allows a great

TABLE 2.3
CLOUD COVER CONDITIONS IN MARYLAND

	Annual No. of Days of Cloud Cover [a]		
	CR [b]	PC [c]	CDY [d]
Baltimore area	109	108	148
Washington, D.C., area	104	103	158
Lower Eastern Shore	110	104	151
Upper Eastern Shore	96	105	164
Western Maryland	49	110	206

Source: See Table 41 Maryland Statistical Abstract, 1979.

[a] Based on records for 1941-1970.

[b] CR = 0-.3 Cloud cover

[c] PC = .4-.7 Cloud cover

[d] CDY = .8-.10 Cloud cover

amount of solar insolation to reach the surface and warm the atmosphere. During the night, conversely, the absence of clouds allows the heat to rapidly escape the atmosphere. Cloudiness has the opposite effect and reduces the daily temperature range, with snowy and rainy days often having only a slight temperature variation. Thus the degree of cloudiness in an area is important for agriculture. The number of days per year with varying cloud conditions is shown in Table 2.3. The lower Eastern Shore has the greatest number of clear days in the state, followed by the Baltimore and Washington, D.C., areas. The low number of clear days (49) and high number of cloudy days (206) in western Maryland stands out.

Much of the human activity in the eastern part of Maryland centers around Chesapeake Bay, which is generally more free from dangerous high winds than any other large body of water in the United States. The inlet is at a right angle to the main trend of the bay so that the Eastern Shore acts as a windbreak from the main force of Atlantic Ocean storms despite the low profile of the area. The bay's dimensions, averaging 15 mi (24 km) east-west and 180 mi (290 km) north-south, are not great enough to favor the frequent development of high, dangerous winds, because the prevailing westerly winds sweep the bay over its narrow dimensions. In the summer, Chesapeake Bay is conducive to good air circulation over eastern Maryland, and southeast land breezes often refresh the western shore, including Baltimore, on summer afternoons.

Climatic Zones. The result of the climatic factors described in this section is a pattern of five general climatic zones (Figure 2.15). The characteristics of each zone are summarized in Table 2.4. Al-

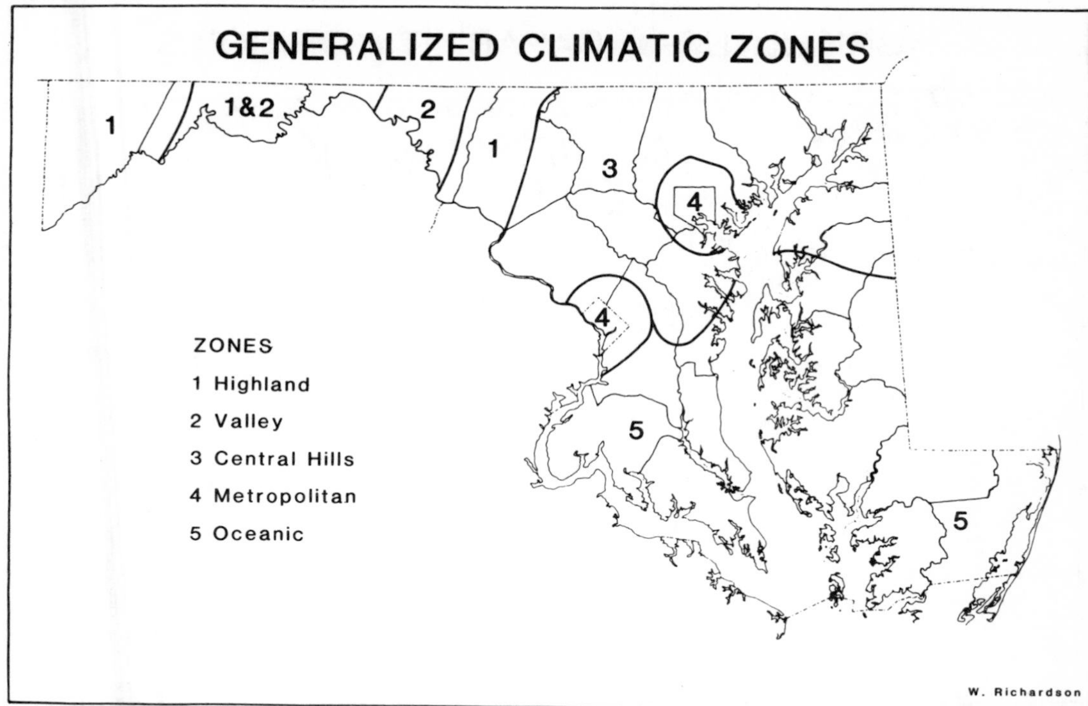

FIGURE 2.15.

TABLE 2.4
Climatic Zones

Zone	Moisture	Temperatures
Highland	Very Wet	Cool Summer, Cold Winter
Valley	Dry to Moderate	Warm Summer, Cold Winter
Central Hills	Moist	Warm Summer, Cool Winter
Metropolitan	Moist	Hot Summer, Mild Winter
Oceanic	Moist (Dry on Seashore)	Cool Summer, Mild Winter

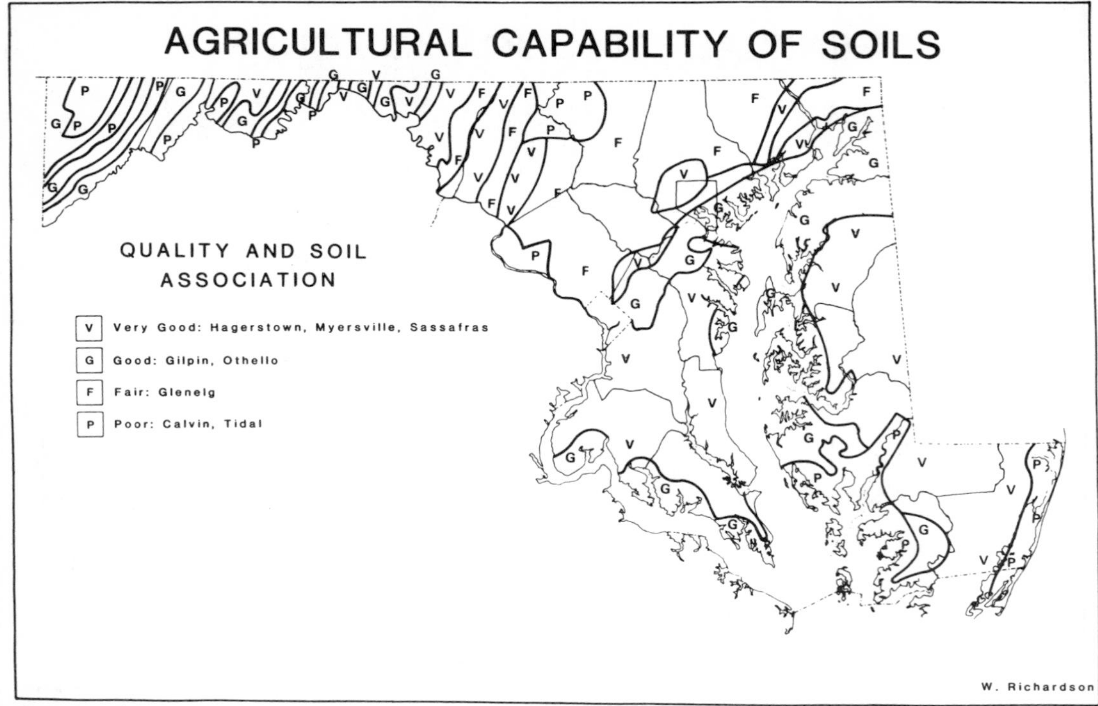

FIGURE 2.16. Source: Maryland Agricultural Experiment Station, College Park, Maryland.

though the climatic differences throughout Maryland are not dramatic when viewed at a macroscale, a microanalysis does reveal some differences. The importance of these climatic differences will become more evident in the discussion of agriculture in Chapter 3.

Soils

Land-use variations in Maryland are largely a product of land surface conditions such as climate, slope, soil, vegetation, and drainage. Climate was discussed in the previous section; the emphasis in this and the following sections will be on the other factors.

Except on the Eastern Shore, local slope varies greatly around the state, with slopes up to 20 percent. Slopes of 3 to 10 percent need special treatment to prevent erosion when used for urban development or cropland; slopes greater than 10 percent should not be used for these purposes. Only activities such as forestry and recreation are appropriate for slopes over 20 percent where the soils are extremely thin.

The largest area of such steep slopes and thin soils in Maryland occurs west of Frederick in the Blue Ridge and the Ridge and Valley sections of the Appalachian highlands (these provinces will be described later in this chapter). There are also some scattered steep slopes on the Piedmont of central Maryland and the Coastal Plain of eastern Maryland. Large areas of gentle slopes and thicker soils are found on the Eastern Shore, the western periphery of the Coastal Plain, and in the valleys around Frederick and Hagerstown.

The soils in these areas vary greatly by type.[1] In terms of land use, the agricultural capability of soils (Figure 2.16) is more important than the classification by soil types. The soil information in Figure 2.16 is highly generalized, as there are 225 soil-series types in Maryland, each with distinct

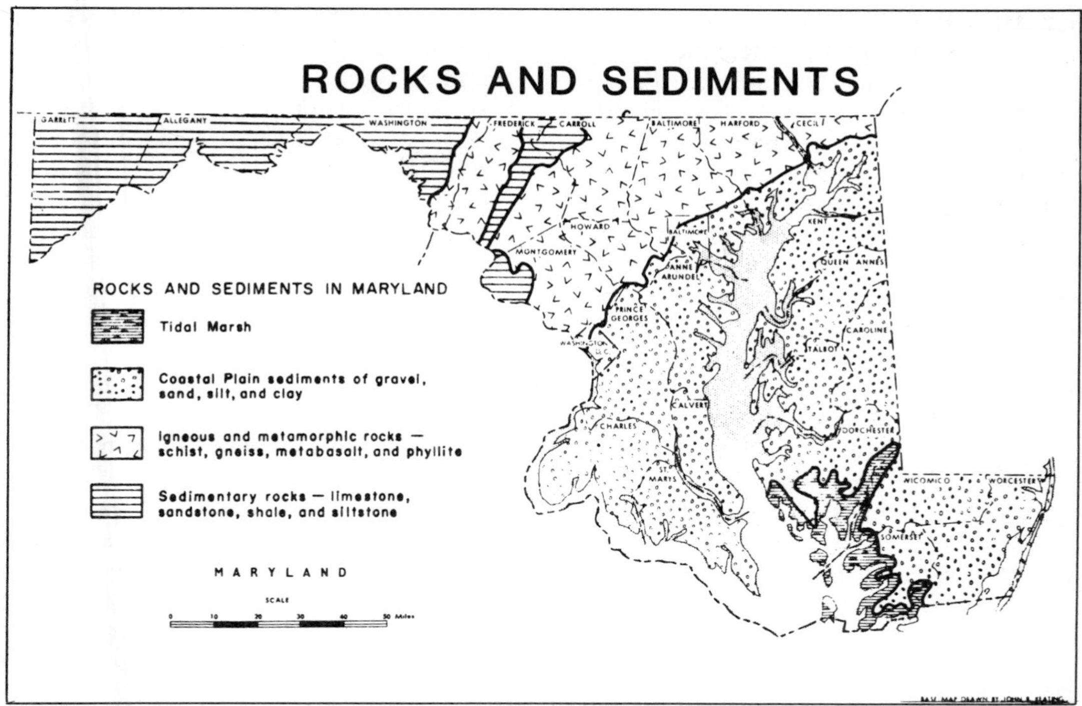

FIGURE 2.17. Source: Fred P. Miller, *Maryland Soils,* Cooperative Extension Service Bulletin 212 (College Park: University of Maryland, 1967).

characteristics. Soils best suited for agriculture are deep, fertile, well drained, and have a high moisture-holding capability. Soils least suited for cropland are thin, shallow, stony, and poorly or excessively drained. Prime agricultural land accounts for less than one-third of the total land area of Maryland; only half of this is currently used as cropland.

Figure 2.17 shows the underlying rock types and sediments in Maryland. A comparison of Figures 2.16 and 2.17 reveals that there are productive and unproductive soils in each of the major physiographic regions of the state. The sedimentary rock area of western Maryland has areas of excellent soil developed on limestone: a deep, well-drained, fertile, and loamy soil known as the Hagerstown soil association. The "good" soil area in western Maryland, shown on Figure 2.16, is called the Gilpin association. This soil, formed on shale and sandstone, is deep and well drained, whereas the Calvin association is thin, stony, found on steeper slopes, and formed mainly of sandstone.

On the Piedmont of central Maryland, the best soils are the Myersville association and the "fair" soils are the Glenelg association. To be useful for agriculture, both types require heavy applications of lime and fertilizer.

The sediment soils of the Coastal Plain vary from excellent to very poor. The Sassafras association soils are excellent and are well drained. The Othello soils are "good," while the Tidal soils are unproductive and sandy. Soil category, quality, and suitability for agriculture are all vital to the success of farming.

Vegetation

Patterns of natural vegetation vary in Maryland with latitude, elevation, slope, climate, and soils. Before Maryland was colonized by Europeans, the natural vegetation pattern was quite different than it is today. The Eastern Shore was an area of oak, pine, cypress, and gum forests. On the western shore there was an oak, hickory, and pine forest. The Piedmont area was forested by chestnut, walnut, hickory, oak, and pine. In western Maryland, the pattern was pine and chestnut on the hilltops with oak, poplar, maple, and walnut in the valleys. Today, only a fraction of this original pattern remains because people have cut, cleared, plowed, urbanized, and changed the landscape in many ways.

Forests have great economic value in Maryland in terms of jobs, lumber products, and increased land values. Maryland's commercial forests cover 2,523,000 acres (1,034,430 ha), nearly 40 percent of the state's land area (Table 2.5). This varies from a low of 30 percent in Carroll and Talbot counties, where much farming is done, to 70 percent in Allegany and Garrett counties (Figure 2.18). Baltimore County and the heavily populated counties surrounding Washington, D.C.—Montgomery and Prince Georges—still have 35 to 45 percent of their land area in commercial forest land. The major uses of the nonforested 58.1 percent of Maryland's land area are pasture, cropland, marshland, sand dunes, rock outcrops, and urban areas.

Commercial forest land in Maryland is largely in private hands (94 percent). Farmers and farm operators own 25 percent (767,000 acres or 310,635 ha), and forest industries own 3.5 percent (101,000 acres or 40,905 ha). Many other types of private owners, such as businessmen, wage earners, and professional people, own nearly two-thirds of the commercial forest land; most of their holdings are tracts of fewer than 100 acres (40.5 ha).

Public agencies own 6 percent of the commercial forest (189,000 acres or 76,545 ha). Of this the state owns 144,000 acres (58,320 ha), municipalities 31,000 acres

TABLE 2.5
FOREST LAND AREA IN MARYLAND AND NEIGHBORING STATES AND THE CONTINENTAL UNITED STATES: January 1, 1977

	Acreage (1,000)					
TYPE	UNITED STATES	MARYLAND	PENNSYLVANIA	DELAWARE	VIRGINIA	WEST VIRGINIA
Total Land Area	2,263,548	6,330	28,778	1,268	25,459	15,405
Forest Land Area	740,147	2,653	17,832	392	16,417	11,669
% of Total Land	32.7	41.9	62.0	30.9	64.5	75.7
Commercial Forest Land	487,726	2,523	17,478	384	15,939	11,484
% of all Forest Land	65.9	95.1	98.0	98.0	97.1	98.4
Noncommercial Forest Land	252,421	130	354	7	479	185
% of all Forest Land	34.1	4.9	2.0	1.8	2.9	1.6

Source: U. S. Department of Agriculture, Forest Service, *Forest Statistics of the U. S., 1977*, Review Draft--All Data Subject to Revision, issued 1978, Table 1.

Hectares = .41 x acres

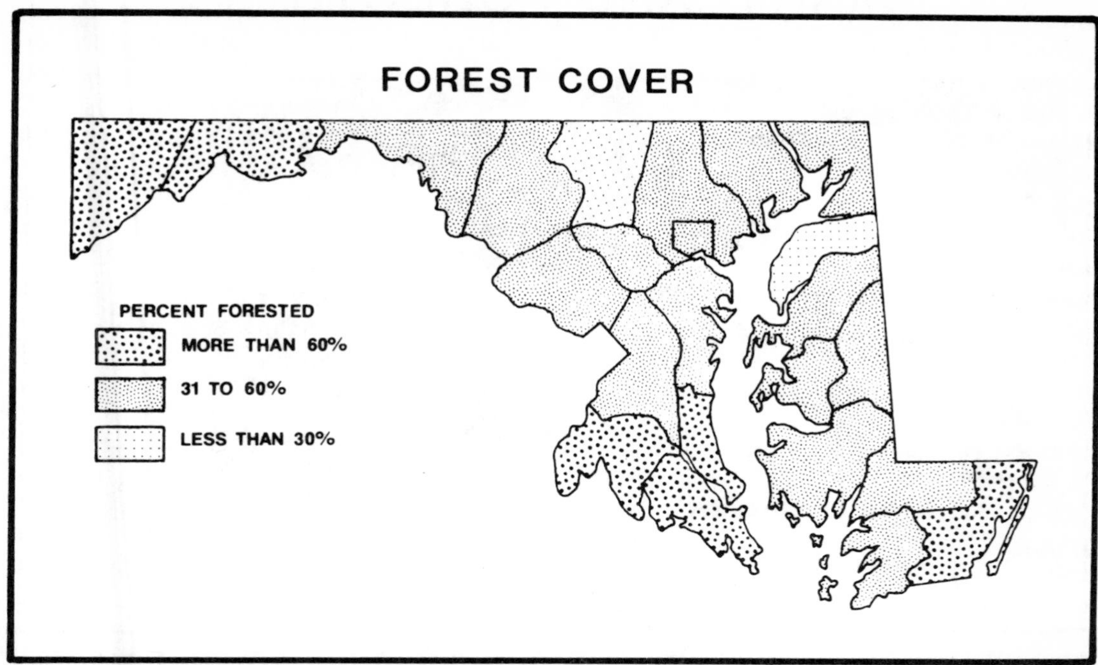

FIGURE 2.18. Source: *Forest Vegetation in Maryland* (Baltimore: Maryland Department of State Planning, 1974).

(12,555 ha), and federal agencies 14,000 acres (5,670 ha). Federally owned forest land has decreased since 1950, while state forest land has increased with the acquisition of Wicomico State Forest and wildlife management areas such as Dans Mountain and Warrior Mountain in Allegany County.

Maryland's forests can be grouped into five categories (Figure 2.19). The southern pine forest type occupies 557,130 acres (228,423 ha) or 21 percent of Maryland's forest land. Virginia and loblolly pines are the chief species in these areas, but pond, pitch, and shortleaf pines are also found. Loblolly pine is especially common in the southern Eastern Shore, extending northwest beyond the Bay Bridge, and some loblolly is found in southern Maryland. Virginia pine is often found in nearly pure stands on drier sites of the Eastern Shore.

The oak-hickory forest type covers 49 percent, the largest acreage of any forest type in Maryland: 1,299,970 acres (532,988 ha). Yellow poplar is the principal species (324,993 acres or 133,247 ha). This forest type is important in western Maryland, where it accounts for 75 percent of the total forest area. In north-central Maryland the oak-hickory type covers 58 percent of the forest land; in southern Maryland, only 23 percent.

Oak-gum forests are the third-largest type (12 percent) in Maryland, covering 318,360 acres (130,528 ha). Most of these areas are in sweetgum, blackgum, river birch, green ash, and swamp oak. Oak-pine forests cover 10 percent or 265,300 acres (108,773 ha), chiefly in the western shore and the Ridge and Valley areas. The remaining forest areas, a mixture of many types, cover 8 percent or 212,240 acres (87,018 ha).

Maryland's forests are predominantly hardwoods, which account for 79 percent of the state's growing-stock volume. Oaks are the principal species and are found all over the state; they account for 46 percent of the hardwood volume (Table 2.6). Soft-

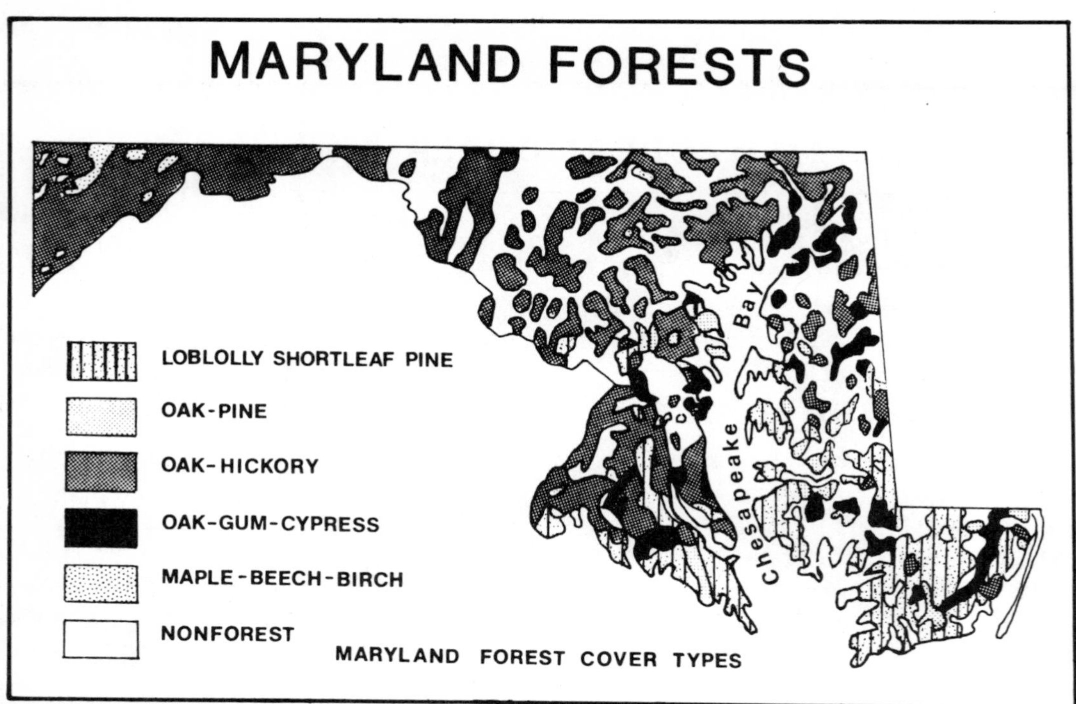

FIGURE 2.19. Source: *Forest Vegetation in Maryland* (Baltimore: Maryland Department of State Planning, 1974).

TABLE 2.6
NET VOLUME OF SAWTIMBER AND GROWING STOCK ON COMMERCIAL TIMBERLAND IN MARYLAND AS OF JANUARY 1, 1977

Species	Sawtimber (Million Bd. Ft.)	Growing Stock (Million Cu. Ft.)
Total Softwoods	1,726	793
Shortleaf & Loblolly Pines	1,239	483
Other Yellow Pines	420	251
Eastern Red & White Pines	29	42
Other Eastern Softwoods	38	17
Total Hardwoods	6,440	2,699
Select White Oaks	1,005	400
Select Red Oaks	481	186
Other White Oaks	382	180
Other Red Oaks	1,216	468
Hickory	253	115
Hard Maple	50	33
Soft Maple	515	281
Beech	288	95
Sweetgum	455	221
Tupelo and Blackgum	213	99
Ash	134	71
Yellow Poplar	1,070	350
Black Walnut	35	18
Other Eastern Hardwoods	300	154
Black Cherry	43	28

Source: U. S. Department of Agriculture, Forest Service, Forest Statistics of the U. S., 1977, Review Draft--All data subject to revision, issued 1978, Tables 25, 26, 27, and 28.
Cubic meter = .28 x cubic feet

woods compose the remaining 21 percent of the growing-stock volume. The pattern varies more in eastern Maryland than in the west.

PHYSIOGRAPHIC REGIONS

As it stretches from east to west Maryland's landscape displays a cross section of three major physiographic provinces and a number of subdivisions by cutting across their northeast-southwest grain. From east to west the provinces are the Coastal Plain, Piedmont (eastern upland and western lowland divisions), and Appalachian Highlands (Blue Ridge, Ridge and Valley, and Allegheny Plateau divisions). Figure 2.20 shows the boundaries of the physiographic provinces and their divisions. Figure 2.21 is a more detailed physiographic diagram of Maryland that includes cross sections. The different geologic structures and the sequential physical surface processes have produced a physiographic landscape that displays much diversity.

The Coastal Plain

This province covers approximately 5,000 sq mi (12,950 sq km), half the area of Maryland. The Coastal Plain is an extensive, partially submerged, undulating to flat surface consisting mainly of recent marine sediment deposits; it is characterized by a number of seaward-dipping beds of unconsolidated clay, sand, and gravel. These materials have washed from the Appalachian highlands over millions of years of erosion.

The Coastal Plain extends from below sea level on the continental shelf westward to the fall-line zone, a general boundary separating the more highly elevated crystalline rocks of the Piedmont from the unconsolidated sediments of the Coastal Plain. Streams frequently have falls or rapids where they flow from the older, more

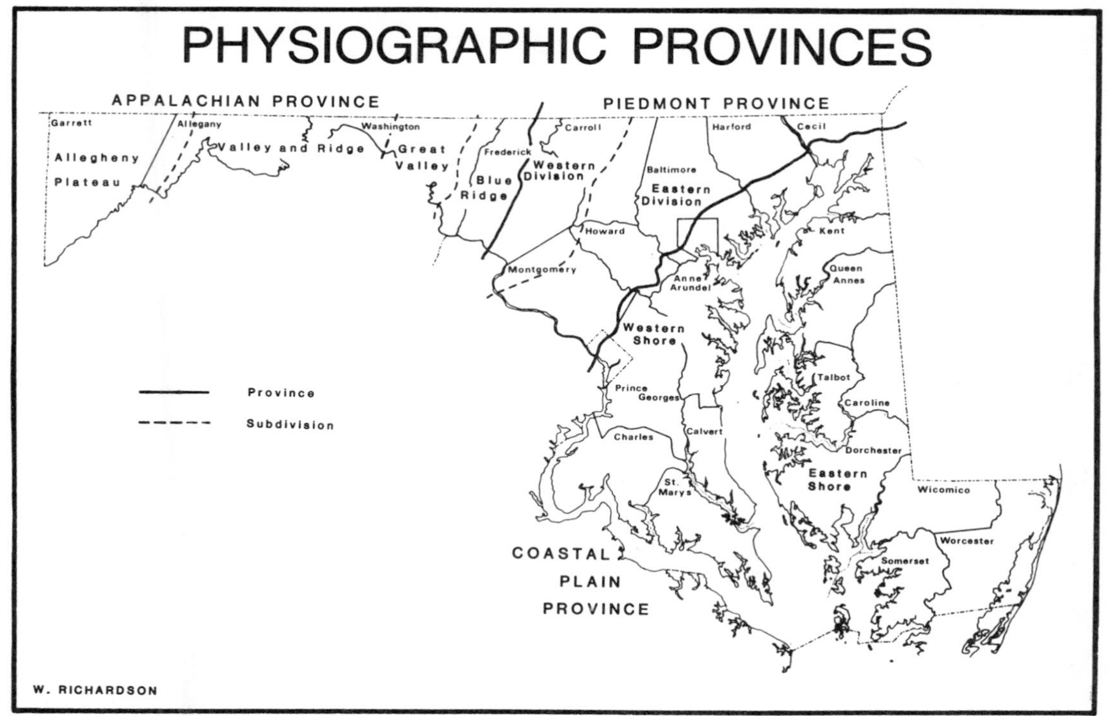

FIGURE 2.20. Source: Fred P. Miller, *Maryland Soils,* Cooperative Extension Service Bulletin 212 (College Park: University of Maryland, 1967).

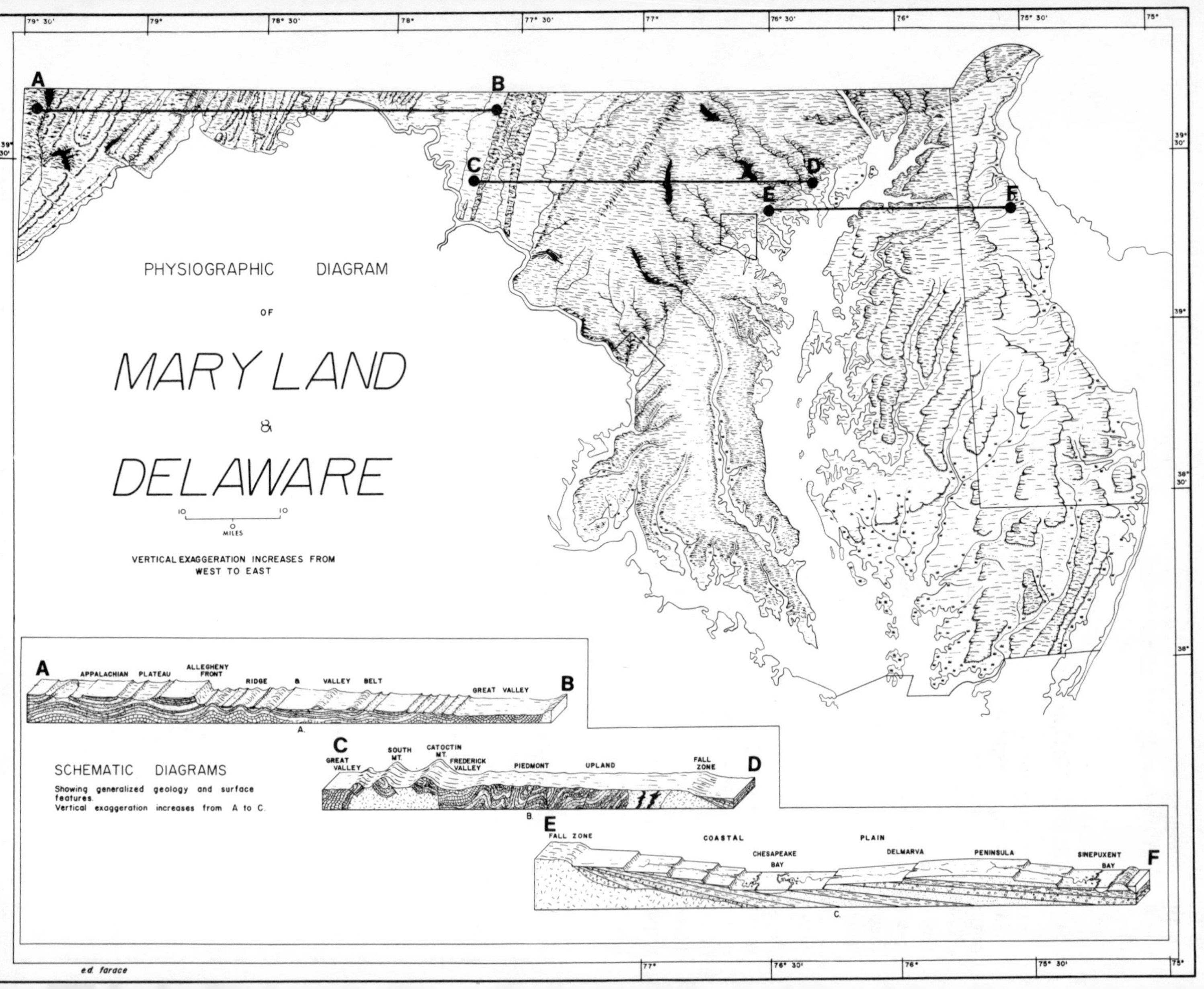
PHYSIOGRAPHIC DIAGRAM
OF
MARYLAND
&
DELAWARE
10 0 10
MILES
VERTICAL EXAGGERATION INCREASES FROM WEST TO EAST
A
B
C
D
E
F
APPALACHIAN PLATEAU
ALLEGHENY FRONT
RIDGE & VALLEY BELT
GREAT VALLEY
SCHEMATIC DIAGRAMS
Showing generalized geology and surface features.
Vertical exaggeration increases from A to C.
GREAT VALLEY
SOUTH MT.
CATOCTIN MT.
FREDERICK VALLEY
PIEDMONT
UPLAND
FALL ZONE
FALL ZONE
COASTAL
PLAIN
CHESAPEAKE BAY
DELMARVA
PENINSULA
SINEPUXENT BAY
ed. farace

FIGURE 2.22. Great Falls of the Potomac in Montgomery County where the Potomac River begins to leave the Piedmont and descend onto the Coastal Plain. Courtesy, Maryland Department of Economic and Community Development.

resistant metamorphic uplands of the Piedmont onto the Coastal Plain (Figure 2.22), and a line on a map connecting these falls would mark the fall-line zone. It is most likely that the fall line was first mapped by boat, because the rivers are generally wider and deeper on the seaward side of the fall line and the falls and rapids mark the upper limit of navigation from the sea. During the early settlement period of Maryland, these cargo break-of-bulk places became the sites of a number of settlements, including Baltimore. Other settlement location factors along the fall line included a ready source of water power for milling and manufacturing and the port site.

Overall, the Coastal Plain nearly lacks relief; it is a complex network of stream drainage and deeply indented, branching bays and estuaries at low elevation. Chesapeake Bay divides the Coastal Plain into the Eastern and western shores. "Eastern Shore" was the name used by Captain John Smith in 1608 to describe all of what is now the Delmarva Peninsula; the Eastern Shore of Maryland is found east of the bay and south of Elk River. Elevation on the Eastern Shore ranges from sea level along the coast and riverine locations to approximately 60 ft (18.3 m) in the north, and as a result, the streams of this area have a gentle gradient with wide and shallow valleys. Low-lying wetlands account for 20 percent of the land area of the Eastern Shore. This embayed coastal plain does become somewhat rolling in the north

FIGURE 2.21. Courtesy, E. D. Farace, Salisbury State College, Salisbury, Maryland.

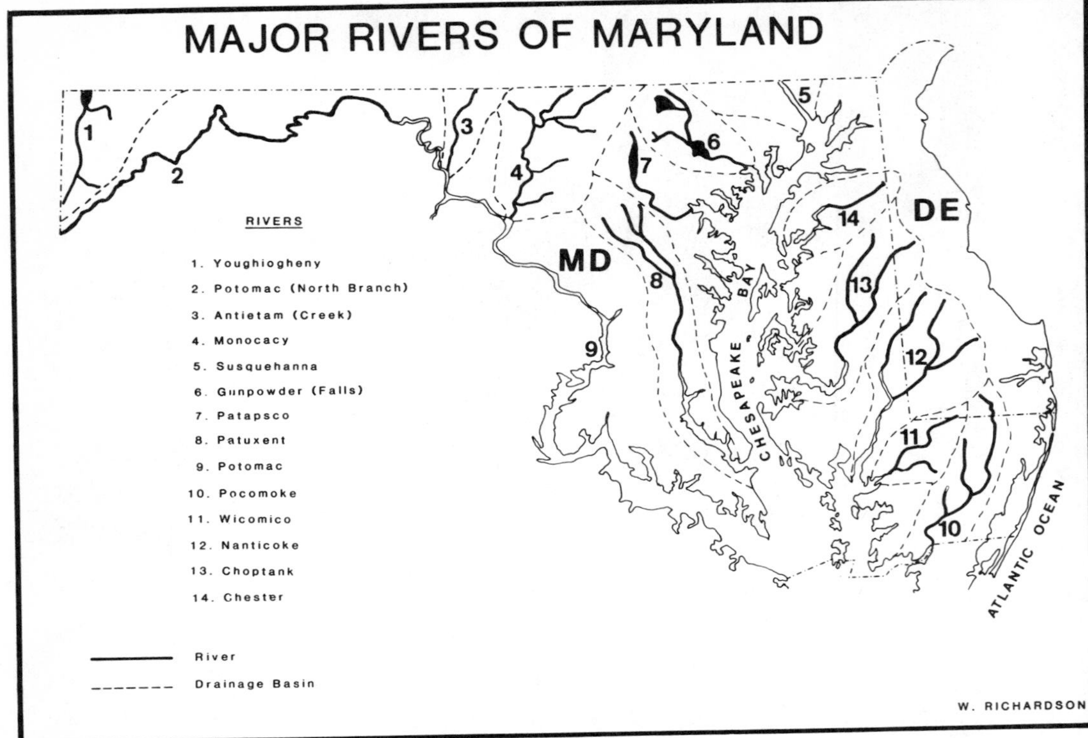

FIGURE 2.23.

as it approaches the Piedmont and takes on some of the characteristics of that province.

West of Chesapeake Bay is the western shore, rising to 270 ft (82.3 m) elevation. Some major rivers coming off the Piedmont have dissected this area, for example, the Patuxent, Patapsco, and Gunpowder Falls rivers in the vicinity of Baltimore (see Figure 2.23). The rivers flowing across the western shore are much greater in volume than the smaller, low-velocity rivers of the Eastern Shore. The western shore area is characterized by many low knobs and ridges. That part of the area called southern Maryland is an upland dissected by the Potomac and Patuxent rivers, with elevations ranging from 0 to 270 ft. In Calvert County, dissection has produced flat-topped ridges and a steep cliff along Chesapeake Bay (Figure 2.24).

When the great Pleistocene glaciers melted, the level of the sea rose and drowned the stream valleys of the western shore to the fall line. On the Eastern Shore, the rivers were drowned 10 to 40 mi (16.1 to 64.4 km) from the present shoreline. The highly irregular coastline of Chesapeake Bay is an indication of the submerged nature of this embayed area of tidal estuaries.

On the Atlantic coast a series of beaches extends south from Cape Henlopen, Delaware, along Maryland to Virginia. In Delaware, the barrier beaches are attached to the mainland, but in Maryland they are barrier islands separated from the mainland by tidal lagoons, locally called "bays." The beaches are composed of material eroded at Cape Henlopen and carried south by strong longshore currents that cause littoral drift. The great long islands of Fenwick and Assateague are along the Maryland coast. Fenwick Island is separated from

FIGURE 2.24. Calvert Cliffs on the western shore in southern Maryland. Courtesy, Maryland Department of Economic and Community Development.

the mainland by Assawoman Bay; Assateague Island by Sinepuxent Bay in the north and Chincoteague Bay in the south. Until 1933, Fenwick and Assateague islands were one. In that year a hurricane breached the island, producing what is today called the Ocean City Inlet. The inlet has now been regularized and the sides stabilized with rocks to prevent it from closing. (The problems associated with development and urbanization along these fragile beaches in the Ocean City area will be discussed later.) In Maryland and Virginia, the 37-mile (59.5-kilometer) stretch of Assateague Island has been designated the Assateague Island National Seashore.

The Piedmont

Between the Coastal Plain and the Blue Ridge lies the Piedmont ("foot of the mountain"). The eastern boundary of the Piedmont is the fall-line zone; the western boundary is Catoctin Mountain. The Piedmont is a province of varied topography, with low, wooded hills separated by well drained, fertile valleys.

The entire Piedmont covers approximately 2,500 sq mi (6,475 sq km), one-fourth of Maryland's area. It has two geologically and topographically distinct subdivisions: the eastern division, called the Piedmont upland, and the western division, the Piedmont lowland. The Piedmont upland is underlain by metaphoric rock, its diversified, broadly undulating topography is low to moderate in relief. Parrs Ridge, 880 ft (268.2 m), and Dugs Hill Ridge, 1,200 ft (366 m), are the highest areas of the Piedmont upland. They form a drainage divide that separates the flow

FIGURE 2.25. The Conowingo hydroelectric dam on the Susquehanna River between Harford and Cecil counties. Courtesy, Philadelphia Electric Company.

east to Chesapeake Bay from that west to the Potomac River. Major streams have deeply dissected the Piedmont upland, and a number of dams have been built across narrow stream valleys (Figure 2.25) to meet the need for water, electricity, and recreation of the large, nearby population concentrations along the Baltimore–Washington, D.C. urban corridor. Reservoirs have been created along several rivers: Triadelphia and Rocky Gorge reservoirs on the Patuxent River, Liberty Reservoir on Patapsco River, and Prettyboy and Loch Raven reservoirs on Gunpowder Falls River.

The Piedmont lowland centers on the Frederick Valley, extending north from the Potomac River to the vicinity of New Midway, Frederick County. Because it is underlain by limestone, the area was worn down faster than the more-resistant metamorphic rock to the east. The Monocacy River drains the fertile Frederick Valley, a prosperous dairying area with a low relief averaging 300 ft (91.4 m). To the north, west, and south is that part of the Piedmont called the Triassic lowland, an area of sedimentary rock of Triassic age with a relief averaging 500 ft (152.4 m). A prominent feature along the boundary of the Piedmont upland and lowland in southeastern Frederick County is the erosional remnant called Sugarloaf Mountain, elevation 1,280 ft (390 m).

The Appalachian Highlands

The Blue Ridge. West of the lower Piedmont is the edge of the Appalachian Highlands. The blue haze that often hangs over the mountains gives them the collective name, the Blue Ridge. Actually this mountain belt consists of three separate ridges:

FIGURE 2.26. Overlooking the Middletown Valley in Washington County. Courtesy, Maryland Department of Economic and Community Development.

Catoctin Mountain, South Mountain, and Elk Ridge.

Catoctin Mountain lies a bit east of the Blue Ridge proper and is considered a prong, or outlier. It is separated from the Blue Ridge by the Middletown Valley (Figure 2.26). Located in the Catoctins is the 10,120 acre (4,099 ha) Catoctin Recreational Demonstration Area that includes the historical presidential retreat named Shangri La by President Franklin Roosevelt and later renamed Camp David by President Dwight Eisenhower, after his grandson. The retreat lies west of Thurmont, Frederick County; it is 60 mi (96.5 km) from Washington, D.C. The National Park Service has jurisdiction over this area.

West of Catoctin Mountain across the Middletown Valley is South Mountain, the actual beginning of the Blue Ridge. To the west of South Mountain lies Pleasant Valley, then Elk Ridge. The crests of all these ridges were long ago removed by weathering and erosion; what remain are erosional remnants. The Potomac River has cut a spectacular water gap in the ridges of the Blue Ridge, which lies perpendicular to the river's course. Steep, sharp slopes characterize the Potomac's valley as it cuts through the metamorphic quartzite of the area, and the channel of the Potomac is strewn with rock outcrops forming rapids from Harpers Ferry, West Virginia, to Point of Rocks, south of Frederick in Maryland.

The Ridge and Valley Division. Extending approximately 65 mi (105 km) west from South Mountain and Elk Ridge to Dans Mountain (the local name for the Allegheny Front) is the Valley and Ridge division. The two distinct subdivisions of this region are the Valley-Ridge section and the Great Appalachian Valley, called the Hagerstown Valley in Maryland, Shenandoah Valley in Virginia and West Virginia,

FIGURE 2.27. The city of Cumberland in Allegany County lies in the foreground. In the background the Cumberland Gap can be seen cutting through the mountains. Courtesy, Richard C. Springer, General Graphics Inc., Cumberland, Maryland.

and Cumberland Valley in Pennsylvania. The Hagerstown Valley lies between South Mountain and Elk Ridge on the east and Powell and Fairview mountains on the west. This broad, rich valley contains many farms; fruit orchards are especially frequent. The lowland has an average elevation of 500 to 600 ft (152 to 183 m), increasing from 400 ft (122 m) at the Potomac River to 800 ft (244 m) at the Maryland-Pennsylvania border. The two main rivers draining the Hagerstown Valley are Antietam Creek in the east and Conococheague Creek in the west; both have their source in Pennsylvania and flow south into the Potomac River. Conococheague Creek is the most prominent feature in the valley, as it is incised approximately 100 ft (30.5 m) into the surface of a belt of soft shale that is 22 mi (35.4 km) long and 3.5 mi (5.6 km) wide, and it has many pronounced meanders along its course.

From Powell and Fairview mountains west to Dans Mountain is a series of northeast-southwest trending ridges separated by narrow valleys, resulting from a series of alternately weak and resistant sedimentary rock. These ridges run parallel to each other and are nearly even in elevation. One such valley, the famous Cumberland Gap, is shown in Figure 2.27.

Allegheny Plateau. Dans Mountain, immediately west of Cumberland, Allegany County, marks the eastern edge of the Allegheny Plateau. This physiographic division includes western Allegany County and all of Garrett County. Although it is called a plateau and the Allegheny Front along Dans Mountain gives the appearance of being the edge of a plateau, the area is far from being an elevated table land. To the west are found a series of gentle, open folds of compressed sedimentary rock, which have been eroded to produce a coarse, grained surface with ridges standing 500 to 800 ft (152 to 244 m) above the land surface.

From east to west the Allegheny Plateau can be subdivided into Georges Creek Valley (dissected along its axis by Georges

FIGURE 2.28. Muddy Creek Falls in Swallow Falls State Park, Garrett County. Courtesy, Maryland Department of Economic and Community Development.

Creek), Deer Park Valley (dominated by the Savage River system), Casselman Basin, Accident Dome, and the Youghiogheny River Basin. Along the Maryland-Pennsylvania border, drainage is to the north by the Casselman River system. The southern area is drained by tributaries of the Youghiogheny. Sandwiched between the Casselman and Youghiogheny basins is Accident Dome. Big Savage Mountain is in the eastern part; its southern extension, Backbone Mountain, is the highest point in Maryland, 3,360 ft (1,024 m), north of Kempton.

A remarkable feature of this area is the Youghiogheny River Valley, which is deep and steep walled and has several falls. The falls shown in Figure 2.28 are along Muddy Creek, a tributary of the Youghiogheny. The narrow water gap of the Youghiogheny is ideal for the development of reservoirs for water, electricity, and recreation. At the narrow gap of Savage and Backbone mountains, the Savage River has been impounded by a dam. A small dam near the confluence of Deep Creek and the Youghiogheny River has produced Deep Creek Lake, the largest lake in Maryland, covering 4,000 acres (1,620 ha). (All of Maryland's lakes are man-made.)

SELECTED ENVIRONMENTAL ISSUES

This section is concerned with some of the interactions that occur along the human–natural environment interface. Scientists often use the word entropy as a measure of relative disorder: a disorderly system has high entropy, an orderly system low entropy. Ecologist G. Tyler Miller has described an "entropy trap" that exists along the human–natural environment interface: "Man's ability to create disorder in the environment while trying to order part of the world is greater than that of any other organism."[2] The production of food and the manufacture of chemicals, clothes, shelter, and other supplies all increase disorder in the environment; examples of this in Maryland are described here.

Chesapeake Bay: The Degradation of an Estuary

When Spanish explorers first saw Chesapeake Bay, they described it as the best and largest port in the world and named it Bay of the Mother of God. "The Bay," as it is usually called in Maryland today, is the largest estuary in the United States and one of the largest estuarial systems in the world. The origin of the name Chesapeake is not clear. It has been stated that a group of English explorers visiting the area named it "Chesepiuc" after a local tribe of Indians. In 1608, Captain John Smith explored and mapped the bay; his map used the spelling "Chesapeack," reported to be an Indian word meaning great shellfish bay. Elsewhere it has been reported that the name was "Chesapiooc" from "Kchesepiock," an Indian word for a country on a great river.[3] There seems to be little doubt that the name is of Indian origin and refers to the body of water or adjacent land in some manner.

Origins, Dimensions, and Characteristics of the Bay. Chesapeake Bay almost cuts Maryland into two parts and covers nearly one-sixth of the state. But it was not always this way—many years ago this area was covered by a coastal plain. The ancient Susquehanna River cut a gorge through the coastal plain in an area that today is in the central part of the Bay and joined the sea some 657 ft (200 m) below present sea level. The worldwide rise in sea level associated with the melting of the Pleistocene glaciers approximately 10,000 years ago had a great effect on this low-lying area. As the sea level rose, the land slowly subsided and the ocean invaded, or drowned, the lower stream valleys to the fall-line zone. An obvious indicator of the submerged nature of this area is the highly irregular coastline of the bay; in fact, Chesapeake Bay is a classic example of a coastline of submergence.

The lower portions of the river systems flowing into the bay are not true rivers, but rather are tidal estuaries. The bay itself is an estuary, a semienclosed body of water that has a free connection with the open sea and within which sea water is measurably diluted by fresh water from land drainage.

Chesapeake Bay is approximately 185 mi (298 km) long and varies in width from 3 mi (4.8 km) to 22 mi (35.4 km). The narrowest part of the Bay is near Annapolis, where the 4.4-mile (7.1-kilometer), twin-span Chesapeake Bay Bridge crosses over to Kent Island (Figure 2.29). The deepest part of the bay, 174 ft (53 m), is in the ancient Susquehanna River Valley off Bloody Point on the southern end of Kent Island; the mean depth is 21 ft (6.4 m). The entire bay covers an area of 3,237 sq mi (8,384 sq km), of which 1,726 sq mi (4,470 sq km) are in Maryland. The extensive, irregular coastline extends nearly 8,000 mi (12,872 km); 4,100 miles (6,597 km) are in Maryland.

The estuarial system focuses on Chesapeake Bay, but extends far beyond the local bay region. Over 64,000 sq mi (165,760 sq km) of land are included in the drainage basin of the bay. This includes areas in Pennsylvania, Virginia, West Virginia, Delaware, Maryland, and as far away as western New York, the headwaters of the Susquehanna. Over fifty major rivers flow into the bay. The major ones in Maryland are the Susquehanna, Northeast, Elk, Bohemia, Sassafras, Bush, Gunpowder Falls, Middle, Back, Patapsco, Choptank, Patuxent, Honga, Nanticoke, Wicomico, Pocomoke, and Potomac rivers. The many rivers flowing into Chesapeake Bay vary in chemical

FIGURE 2.29. The twin-span Bay Bridge connects the eastern and western shores. Courtesy, Maryland Department of Economic and Community Development.

composition according to the types of areas drained and the materials carried.

One of the most important characteristics of the bay is salinity, which ranges from 0 parts per thousand (ppt) in the north to 35 ppt at the mouth of the bay (fresh water ranges from 0 to 3.5 ppt, while saline water has over 3.5 ppt). The general circulation pattern in the bay is that of warmer, less-saline water at the surface flowing south and colder, more-saline water deeper down flowing north. A constant flushing and cleansing action occurs between the estuary and the ocean.

In addition to differences in salinity by depth, there are differences from north to south and east to west: salinity is less in the north and west. Above the Potomac river the Susquehanna River provides 80 percent of the freshwater flow into the bay (overall it provides 50 percent), so it forms a freshwater pool in the upper bay. During the spring high-flow period, a large freshwater pool occurs in a zone from Spesutie Island to Turkey Point (Figure 2.30). The west side of Chesapeake Bay is less saline than the east. A number of major rivers enter on the west and dilute the water, whereas the rivers coming off the Eastern Shore are smaller in volume, and thus diluting the eastern side of the bay less. Another factor is Coriolis force, which deflects currents to the right in the Northern Hemisphere; it drives the more dense saline waters to the eastern side of the bay.

During the winter and early spring the salinity of the bay decreases, and it is richer in dissolved oxygen. During the summer and early fall, salinity increases as the water flow into the bay decreases. Chesapeake Bay is biologically a special place where both freshwater and saltwater organisms can live. The ecological balance can be upset if salinity changes. The very dry weather in 1914 caused salinity in the bay to increase; saline water nearly reached the freshwater intake on the Susquehanna at Havre de Grace, while at Turkey Point the

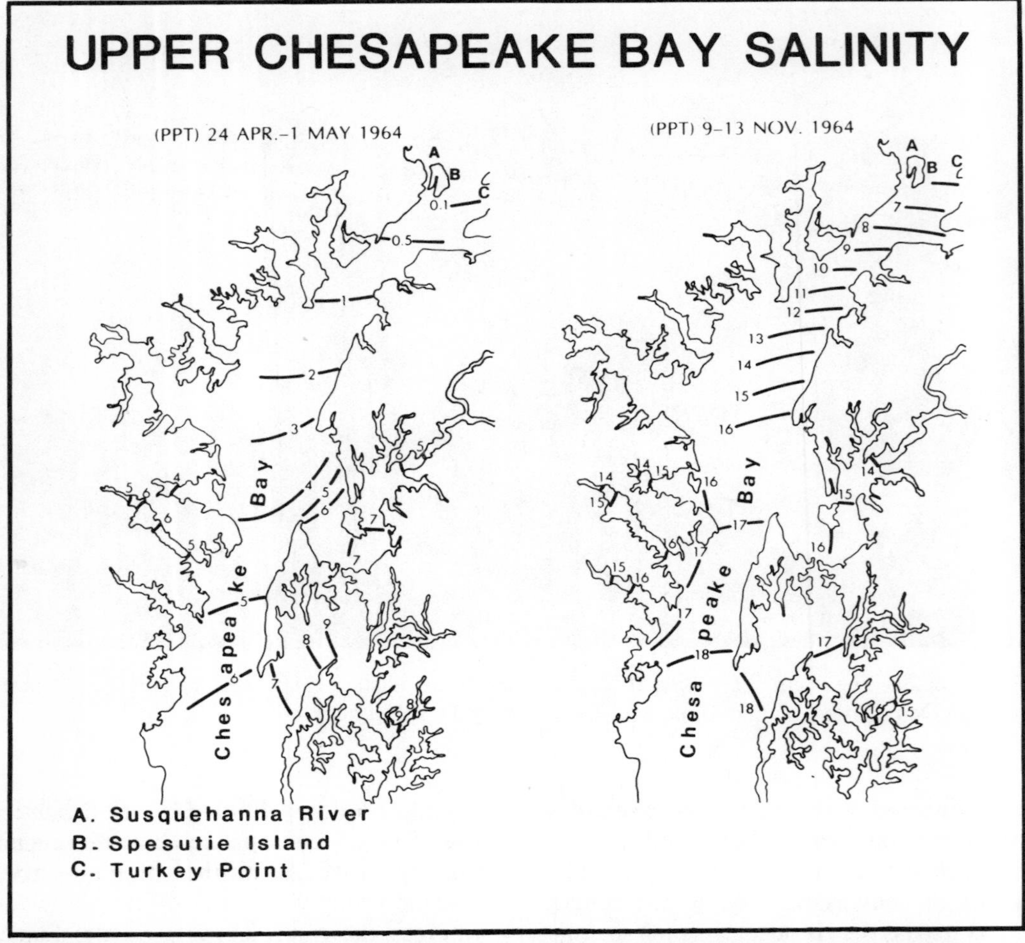

FIGURE 2.30. Source: Maryland Department of State Planning, *Integrity of the Chesapeake Bay,* 1972.

salinity increased from .1 ppt to 6 ppt. This greatly hurt the shad and rockfish spawning, which usually occurs in nearly fresh water. In 1972, rains from the severe storm Agnes increased the flow of fresh water into the bay 15.5 times normal. The decrease in salinity killed 2 million bu (242,259,000 l) of oysters, which need saline conditions.

Another factor leading to increased salinity in the upper bay was the construction of the 13-mile (20.8-kilometer) Chesapeake and Delaware Canal connecting Chesapeake Bay to the Delaware River and the Atlantic Ocean. The canal was first opened in 1829 and enlarged in 1938. Fresh water flows out of the bay in the upper waters of the canal, as brackish waters enter the bay at lower depths (Figure 2.31).

Chesapeake Bay is a rich body of water; many plants thrive there because the bay is shallow and sunlight can penetrate the water. These plant "food factories" are eaten by tiny animals that in turn are eaten by larger species, thus forming a food chain. Maryland has 35,000 acres (14,175 ha) of rich tidal-marsh areas, called wetlands, where much of the plant food grows.

Nearly 1 million ducks and geese winter along the wetlands of Chesapeake Bay, one of the most important areas of the Atlantic Flyway. The bay shoreline is 88 percent

FIGURE 2.31. The Chesapeake and Delaware Canal is seen here from the air. Chesapeake City, Maryland, is on the left bank; Chesapeake Bay is in the upper direction and the Delaware River in the lower direction on the photograph. Courtesy, Maryland Department of Economic and Community Development.

privately owned, with most of the wetlands managed by local governments that are in need of increasing the tax base. The destruction of wetlands by diking and filling for new industries or housing is common. The public has recognized the problem; the Maryland wetland laws enacted in 1970 are intended to prevent dredging and filling of wetlands without a permit.

The configuration of some parts of Chesapeake Bay is constantly changing as current and tides eat away and rebuild. Smith Island, offshore from Crisfield, is one the last of the bay's inhabited islands. The U.S. Army Corps of Engineers is studying erosion there, to determine how to stabilize the shore, but the outlook is not good. This stronghold of Chesapeake watermen and the old way of life, where a dialect echoing earlier times is spoken, loses up to 50 ft (15.2 m) to erosion in some years. There may be little left of Smith Island thirty years from now. Like the fictional Devon Island and Rosalind's Revenge of James Michener's *Chesapeake,* Smith Island and other bay islands will erode and vanish, while new ones appear. The specific configuration of the coastline is indeed ephemeral.

The shoreline is constantly under attack by wind, water-driven tides, and currents. Between 1845 and 1942 about 6,000 acres (2,430 ha) of land were lost to erosion along the Maryland shoreline of the bay; the average loss during this 97-year span was 26 acres (10.6 ha) per mile of shoreline. Shoreline losses can be great in some areas, negligible in others: the rate of erosion at a specific place depends on the shoreline configuration, direction and velocity of the prevailing winds, reach of open water over which winds blow, and composition of the materials that make up the shoreline.

Pollution from the Land. The magnificent Chesapeake Bay is not without ecological problems. In the past it was generally believed that the bay had an infinite capacity to break down and scatter wastes. This "dilution is the solution to pollution" mentality has led to some severe problems.[4]

There is great concern among scientists, government officials, and environmental groups about how to assure the maintenance of the bay's natural integrity in order to maintain its valuable yields and its tremendous ability to produce fish, shellfish, and waterfowl and to break down human sewage waste. A water body has a limited capability to assimilate nutrients. Algae blooms have already been observed in the upper bay, indicating areas where algae are thriving on increased nutrients in the water. Decaying algae consume oxygen in the water, producing a eutrophic environment that has disastrous effects on other forms of life. Both shellfish and finfish alike can die due to starvation or suffocation in a water environment that is murky and low in oxygen content. Species such as the rockfish spawn near the freshwater-saline interface in the upper bay. Menhaden, sea trout, spot, croaker (hardhead), harvest fish, winter flounder, and drum spawn near the mouth of the bay; as the deep water drifts up the bay, it carries their eggs and larvae to the richer, upper-bay feeding areas.

It is estimated that the current human population of almost 3.6 million in the bay region will climb to 9 million in the Maryland bay region by the year 2020. The bay area's population is supported by rich farmland, vast woodlands, and intensely developed industrial areas. An increase in population means that more water is drawn off before the fresh water enters Chesapeake Bay, and the bay's salinity increases. The additional water is used for irrigation and industrial processes, as well as for generation of electricity. During the period from 1955 to 1980, nearly 1.4 million new residents moved into Maryland, while the state lost 1.6 million acres (.65 million ha) of open space; this is conversion at the incredible rate of 1 acre (.41 ha) lost per person! As the population grows, so will the needs for recreational, residential, and commercial space.

The overall problem is how to reconcile the need for disposal of solid and liquid waste with requirements for other bay uses. There are a number of major waste disposal problems. Domestic wastes in the form of treated municipal sewage enter Chesapeake Bay at a rate of 270 million gal (1.021 billion l) per day from Maryland counties and 300 million gal (1.135 billion l) more per day from the Washington, D.C., Blue Plains Treatment Plant on the Potomac River.

Industrial wastes vary from nontoxic rinse water or cooling water to very harmful chemicals, heavy metals, oil, and grease; wastes from agriculture include animal excrement, pesticides, herbicides, and fertilizers. Surface runoff and percolating groundwater carry all these pollutants into the bay. Animal wastes and fertilizer rob large quantities of oxygen from the water, carry disease-causing organisms, and accelerate the growth of aquatic plants. Pesticides and herbicides also are a critical threat to the health of the bay's ecosystem. Estimates are that quantities of agricultural wastes are at least equal to municipal sewage, but treatment of waters from farmlands at selected points is not feasible due to their dispersed distribution. One insecticide, Kepone, has levied a heavy toll on Chesapeake Bay. In 1975 it was found that workers were being poisoned at a plant producing Kepone in Hopewell, Virginia, on the James River. Kepone from the river has entered the bay, and its affinity for bottom sediment causes it to be retained in the bay ecosystem rather than being flushed out by water circulation.

Chesapeake Bay accommodates vessels ranging from large ships to small pleasure craft, which creates several problems. The amount of raw sewage discharged into the bay by vessels in transit is equivalent to that from a community of 20,000 people. Problems occur in marina and anchorage areas that lie near bathing beaches or shellfish harvest areas. Because of its potential magnitude, an even more serious problem is that of oil spills. As the region's population grows, so will its need for oil. The growth of the port of Baltimore requires that the channel into the harbor be deepened from the present 42 ft (12.8 km) to 50 ft (15.2 km). The question is, where will the 120 million cu yd (91.8 million cu m) of dredged and largely toxic bottom sediment be put? Officials plan to use much of the dredge waste to fill in behind a dike, thus enlarging Hart and Miller islands located north of the harbor. This has become a controversial issue in the state.

Solid waste disposal is a growing problem. Because the greatest need for sanitary landfills exists in the populated areas, where the land is very valuable, wetlands are often looked at for new sites. By the year 2000, over 500 acres (202.5 ha) per year will be needed for solid waste disposal sites in the Maryland bay region. Chesapeake Bay will become increasingly attractive for solid waste disposal.

It is predicted that over 80 percent of the state's population will continue to be concentrated around the bay. This means that, with increased needs for electricity, most of the thermal-waste discharge from additional power plants will impinge upon the bay and its tributaries. The discharge of heated water causes thermal pollution that can harm fish and aquatic life.

The rivers flowing into the bay, especially those on the western shore, carry an enormous amount of sediment. Between 1845 and 1924, over 15 ft (4.6 m) of sediment accumulated in the Patapsco River near Baltimore. Frequent dredging in many areas is necessary. The sediment covers the bottom of the bay and often smothers bottom-dwelling marine life. From 80 to 90 percent of the annual sediment load is carried into the bay during February and March when spring precipitation and melt-water flow is high. At that time soils are thawing, rocks and soil have been loosened by frost, and there is little vegetation to hold the soil in place.

Environmental disturbances can destroy fish and shellfish habitats and disrupt life cycles. Natural hazards include storms, floods, extreme variations in salinity, limited nutrient supply, sedimentation, predators, and parasites. Human impacts include destruction of habitats by diking and filling wetlands, dredging and dumping spoil, diversion of freshwater flow, accelerated sedimentation from agricultural and urban development, and domestic and industrial pollution.

What Happens Next? The problems so far described are part of a land-water dilemma. Chesapeake Bay is a coupled system, i.e., it is linked to the uplands of its entire drainage basin. Symptoms of problems can be seen in the bay, but environmental scientists are claiming that we must look to the land for solutions. The surrounding land is a free-market commodity whose use is determined by short-term economics. It is recognized in the federal Clean Air and Clean Water acts that these two elements are in the public domain, but the land by tradition and law is largely private. Around Chesapeake Bay, farmland vanishes at a rate of 122 sq mi (316 sq km) per year as it is rezoned for housing; local control of zoning means that 10 percent of the bay region's population decides how 93 percent of the land is to be used. Deforestation in Maryland is the most severe in the northeastern United States: between 1964 and 1976 deforestation claimed 13 percent of all Maryland forests, an area the size of Baltimore County. A balance between growth in the region and the integrity of Chesapeake Bay is needed. Thus far there has been a strong bias for managing the bay by engineering techniques and by the use of economic growth models, not ecological models.

If current trends continue, portions of Chesapeake Bay and its tributaries will become eutrophic, with little or no oxygen, especially in the summer. Some species of fish and shellfish—the shad, striped bass (rockfish), and maybe even the oyster—may be completely gone by the year 2000. Much of the shoreline will be denuded of life-giving grasses. Oil spills will occur; sediment from development will cloud the water and fill the channels; the flow of fresh water into the bay will decrease.

Crabs, when available, will cost a fortune. This bleak picture could become a reality if current patterns of use and abuse continue.[5]

Tom Wisner of Solomons, Maryland, a former biologist turned balladeer, sings a song in his new album *Chesapeake Born* called "Clean Water Remembered":

> Well, can Congress with its mighty notions
> rebuild the waters from the mountains to
> the oceans?
> Will the people of the Piedmont plain
> see clear water once again?[6]

Kudzu Menace

Kudzu is a lush, fast-growing vine that has been engulfing much of the southern United States for several decades. A hairy vine with broad, three-pointed leaves, kudzu came to the United States in 1876 from Japan, when the Japanese used the plant as an ornament in their exhibit at the U.S. Centennial celebration in Philadelphia. One hundred years later, the vine covered over 1 million acres (405,000 ha) in the southern United States. The vines, now found in Maryland, have been creeping northward. Once planted to provide ground cover and nourish the soil, kudzu vines now spread rapaciously into field and forest. Some vines grow up to 1 ft (.3048 m) a day, and it is not unusual for them to grow 100 ft (30.48 m) longer in one summer.

To the tourist, kudzu looks like a verdant and beautiful cover plant. Environmentalists and farmers are quick to point out that where kudzu grows, nothing else does: the vines swallow up everything in their path.

At first kudzu was welcomed as a ground cover. Chickens, cows, and goats like to eat the plant, and county agricultural agents soon began to promote kudzu as a supplemental forage crop, since it has a nutritive value comparable to alfalfa. Its 7-foot (2.1-meter) roots aerate the soil and reach deep for water during dry periods. Kudzu is a member of the legume family, thus it restores nitrogen to the soil. The plant's promoters felt that the plant would grow on the hard, red-clay soil, stop erosion, and provide good grazing and an attractive ground cover.

During the New Deal period in the 1930s, kudzu was strongly promoted. The Agricultural Stabilization and Conservation Service, which was created to reclaim land, began a massive kudzu promotion campaign, and the Soil Conservation Service grew millions of kudzu plants in its nurseries from Maryland to Texas. The Civilian Conservation Corps planted them along highways in eroded gullies.

Kudzu grown in the United States is a poor seed producer, but it can produce a new plant from each joint, about every 12 in (30.48 cm). Seeds were also imported from Japan prior to World War II. By the end of the war, kudzu clubs had sprung up and Auburn, Alabama, had elected a kudzu queen.

By the mid 1950s a number of problems with kudzu became apparent. Kudzu could not stand up to intensive grazing; the tangled vines could not be harvested as easily as hay; the vines freely jumped fences and ran wild. Among the critics of kudzu have been the U.S. Forest Service and the lumber industry, as the vine kills timber by cutting off sunlight and smothering the trees. Farmers now see kudzu as a scourge that damages field crops and fruit and nut trees. Telephone companies have reported that kudzu pulls down telephone poles, and power companies must spray herbicides yearly to keep the vine off high voltage towers (occasionally the vines cause an electrical arc producing extensive damage).

Kudzu is not going away. Chemical controls are not being applied over widespread areas because of adverse environmental effects. As kudzu spreads unchecked, the acreage in Maryland covered by the vine will certainly increase and the state will be faced with a major biological problem.

Urbanization on the Ocean City Shoreline

Magnetism of the Coast. Increasingly the U.S. coastline is becoming a victim of its own magnetism, attracting development that fouls its beauty and undermines its ecological balances. Environmentalist Anne Simon stated in her book *The Thin Edge,*

> In the last ten years, the coast's magnetic pull has become stronger than ever—more industry, more oil, more people, hotels, motels, boatels, more sewage, more waste. The coast is informing us that there is a saturation point beyond which its natural functions no longer flourish, often diminish, or simply cease.[7]

Many environmentalists feel that much of the Atlantic shore seems destined to become a stretch of boardwalk and pizza-parlor tackiness.[8] The voices of concern about the coast penetrated the White House; President Jimmy Carter declared 1980 the Year of the Coast.

When powerful economic arguments for "needed growth" to bring new jobs, profits, and tax revenues to coastal communities are combined with the fact that people have acquired the resources to afford second homes and have more leisure time, the result is the kind of rapid development that has occurred on Fenwick Island, Maryland, since the early 1960s. The difficulty in planning and directing coastal development is compounded by property ownership patterns. Over 90 percent of the U.S. coastline is privately owned; 5 percent is controlled by the armed forces; less than 5 percent is open to the public! Yet over 50 percent of the U.S. population lives in coastal counties.[9]

Hazards associated with natural processes are found in conjunction with urban development all along the Atlantic and Gulf coasts. Fenwick Island, where the resort center of Ocean City is located, is a prime example of these people-environment conflicts. Decisions about development of the Ocean City shoreline should be made on the basis of information concerning rates of natural processes; planners could use such information to guide future development to those areas of least hazard. Unfortunately, this has not been the case at Ocean City. The narrow but important coastal margin is used for recreation, industrial and commercial activities, waste disposal, and food production. Those who choose to live close to the coast experience risks associated with hurricanes and other storms. The tremendous increases in development and population at Ocean City intensify these risks.

The Nature of Barrier Islands. Barrier islands are the most unstable coastal lands utilized by people. Beaches and dunes are only temporary in form; they are continually shifting and moving in response to natural forces.[10] Barrier islands are found along the coast of the United States from Maine to Texas and form the primary terrestrial-marine interface. When left alone, this ecological system naturally adjusts by building new beach, destroying old beach, and shifting position. When people enter the picture, they try to halt these natural processes with various kinds of engineering constructions. Development of this rapidly changing landscape is based on the belief that the landscape is stable or can be engineered to be stable.[11]

Barrier islands, however, are unstable because of the constant movement of sand by wind and currents, the occurrence of catastrophic storms, and the general trend of a rising sea level causing coastal recession. Sandy barrier-island beaches are stable only if sand arrives at the same rate that it is carried off. A surplus of sand causes beach building to seaward, and a deficiency of sand results in coastline retreat. Recently, the amount of sand leaving the mid-Atlantic coast has generally exceeded that being carried in. The net result of these forces is the movement of barrier islands closer to the mainland. It is the natural coastal retreat process occurring along the beaches at Ocean City that has caused much concern to property owners, planners, scientists, and community leaders.

The two principal causes of major change on Fenwick Island (a typical barrier island) have been hurricanes and extratropical storms (northeasters). Records going back to the seventeenth century show that although numerous storms have passed nearby, between 1672 and 1970 only three hurricanes with winds in excess of 75 mph (121 km/hr) have struck Fenwick Island. The August 23, 1933, hurricane had wind velocities averaging 60 mph (96.5 km/hr) with 10-foot (3-meter) waves, and the tide reached a record level of 7.5 ft (2.3 m) above mean low water. Total damage from the storm amounted to $500,000. The hurricane opened the Ocean City Inlet, a breach 10 ft (3 m) deep and 250 ft (76.2 m) wide, which would have closed naturally had it not been for maintenance by the U.S. Army Corp of Engineers.[12]

However, each year between thirty and forty northeasters cause surge waves of at least 5 ft (1.5 m) above normal along the Ocean City shoreline. The most damaging northeaster was the March 1962 Ash Wednesday storm.[13] This northeaster had winds averaging 50 mph (80.5 km/hr) over several days. Waves ranged from 10 to 15 ft (3 to 4.6 m), and the tides were 9 ft (2.7 m) above mean low water. Much of Fenwick Island was covered for two days at depths up to 8 ft (2.4 m). Damage from the storm totaled $7 million. Although this storm ravaged Ocean City, it set the stage for vast reconstruction and development that began immediately.

Coastal scientists use statistics from studies of storm and wave conditions to construct storm-return-interval graphs. A storm producing a maximum deep water wave height of 25 ft (7.6 m) offshore from Ocean City can be expected to occur every twenty-five years.[14] Many ocean-side resorts such as Ocean City, with large numbers of new high-rise apartments and condominiums, have yet to be tested by major storms, because the hurricane cycle was in an unusual lull during the 1970s when much of the new construction took place (Figure 2.32).

Varying gravitational attractions associated with the moon, earth, and sun can affect the level of the sea along the coast. The highest spring tides at Ocean City occur twice each month when the moon, earth, and sun are aligned; this increases the tidal range by 20 percent. Tides have their greatest adverse effect if coastal flooding occurs, but not all high tides or coastal storms cause flooding. Under certain circumstances, uncommonly high tides (perigean spring tides) coincide with strong onshore winds and flood the island; this is what happened on Ash Wednesday in March 1962.

The Growth of Ocean City. Ocean City has become a model of beach overdevelopment, but this problematic situation developed only recently. During the colonial period, the island was used as pastureland. In the 1830s the market for oysters, clams, diamondback terrapin, and waterfowl encouraged more settlement. In 1872 several Worcester County people joined with some Baltimore businessmen to form the Sinepuxent Beach Corporation to promote a resort (the original name for Ocean City was Sinepuxent Beach). The Atlantic Hotel opened its doors in 1875 and welcomed visitors who had come to the shore directly across from Ocean City on the railroad extension built in 1872 from Berlin, Maryland. In 1878 the railroad was extended across Sinepuxent Bay to Ocean City.[15]

Ocean City remained a small resort community until after World War II. Starting from the small town center on the southern end of what is now Fenwick Island, Ocean City began to spread north to the Delaware border. The series of maps in Figure 2.33 depicts the urbanization process from 1901 to 1972. The present growth spurt started in the early 1950s and intensified in the 1960s and 1970s.

From 1950 to 1972 the urban area on Fenwick Island more than doubled, mostly at the expense of wetlands. An important factor was the opening of the Chesapeake Bay Bridge connecting Sandy Point on the western shore to Kent Island on the Eastern Shore. Before the bridge was opened in 1952, the trip to Ocean City from Baltimore or Washington, D.C., took three to four hours via ferry. After the bridge opened, the time was reduced to two and a half

FIGURE 2.32. Most of these new condominiums in Ocean City were built in the 1970s. Courtesy, U.S. Geological Survey.

hours. The reduced travel time, coupled with more leisure time and affluence, led to an explosion in development and property values in the 1960s and 1970s. The 1970s became the decade of the condominiums. Some of this development, including mobile homes and filled wetlands, can be seen in Figures 2.34 and 2.35.

Since 1970 many apartments and condominiums, as shown in Figure 2.32, have been built very close to the beach. Some of these buildings in "high-rise row" are over twenty-two stories high. Although development stretches along 10 mi (16.1 km) of Ocean City shoreline, only two blocks are open for public recreation. Of the 26,663 housing units in Ocean City in 1974, nearly 75 percent were in hotel, motel, apartment, and condominium units. Although Ocean City's permanent population has always been small (in 1960 there were fewer than 983 people and only 4,000 by 1975), the peak weekend summer visitor population exceeds 200,000!

Beach Stabilization Measures. All along the Maryland coast from Delaware to Virginia, beach sand is being lost, carried southward by littoral drift. In addition, sand is being lost by winds blowing westward (deflation) and by seaward losses during violent storms. Erosion has caused the beach along the shoreline at Ocean City to recede over the past fifty years at a mean annual rate of 2.4 ft (.73 m). Between 1850 and 1965, the mean high-water contour shifted landward 270 ft (82.3 m). Of this movement, 86 ft (26.2 m) has occurred since 1930, coinciding with the period of greatest growth at Ocean City.

Shoreline protection measures have been of three general types: (1) seawalls, (2) groins and jetties, and (3) artificial nourishment of beaches. Seawalls are meant to absorb and reflect wave energy; they protect

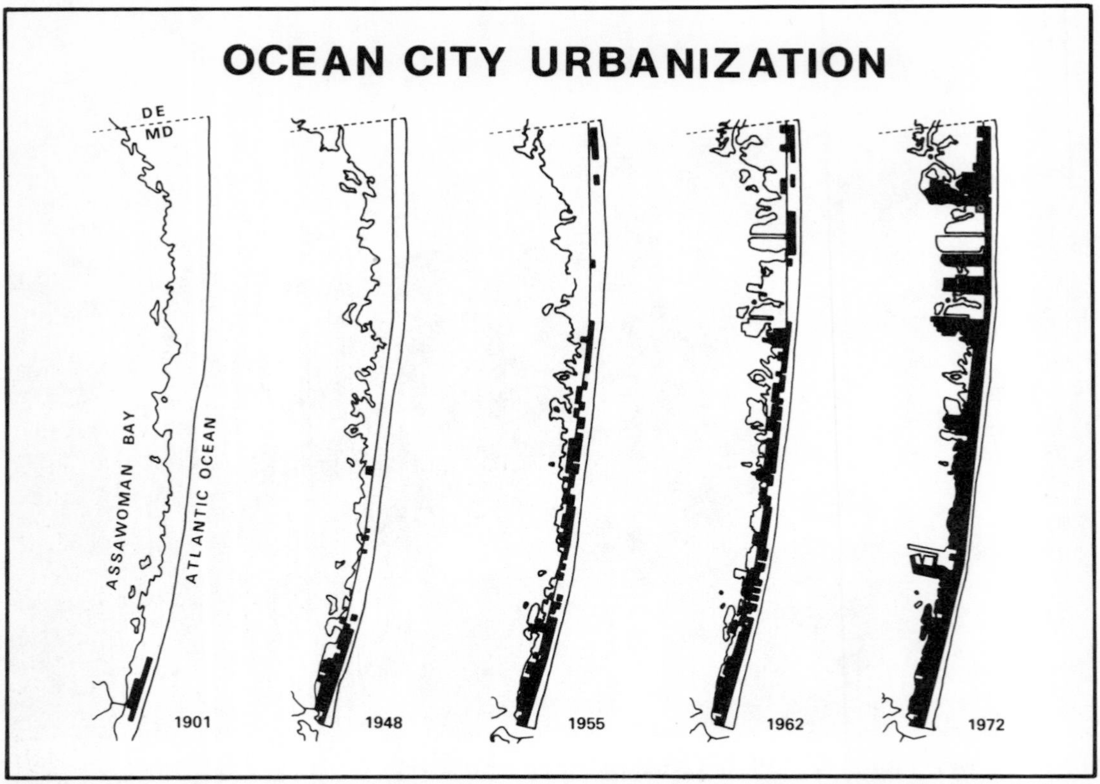

FIGURE 2.33. Source: Robert Dolan, Harry Lins, and John Stewart, *Geographical Analysis of Fenwick Island, Maryland, a Middle Atlantic Coast Barrier Island,* U.S. Geological Survey, 1980.

FIGURE 2.34. Development on the wetlands of Fenwick Island includes these mobile homes in the foreground. Courtesy, U.S. Geological Survey.

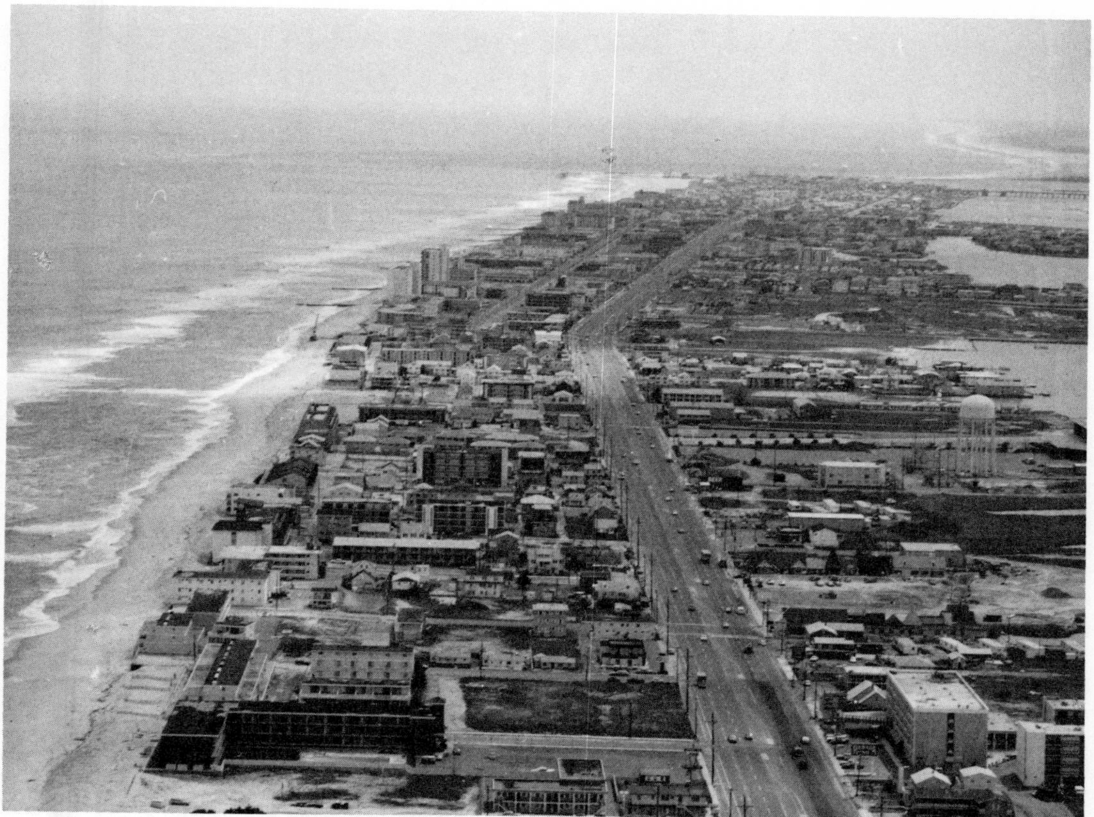

FIGURE 2.35. The 1962 storm flood surge covered most of the area shown in this photograph of Ocean City. Courtesy, U.S. Geological Survey.

the elevated land behind them. Because the beach in front of a seawall often loses sand at an accelerated rate, seawalls have not been used at Ocean City. A groin is a structure built perpendicular to the shoreline to impede littoral drift of sand. At Ocean City sand is entrapped on the north side of the groins, while a shortage of sand is experienced downbeach. To use groins efficiently, littoral drift must be significant in volume and the land downbeach must be expendable. Groins and jetties (a type of groin used also as a retaining wall) have long been used at Ocean City to trap sand and protect the beaches. However, in a study of the Ocean City situation, the U.S. Geological Survey (U.S.G.S.) has concluded that by and large, groins and jetties have not been successful—indeed, they have aggravated the problem.[16]

Today there are forty-two groins, constructed between 1922 and 1978, on Ocean City beaches. Groins and jetties must be located as a system to be successful; those at Ocean City were not. Instead, sites were subjectively selected by the mayor of Ocean City along the 9 mi (14.5 km) of coastline considered to be problem areas.[17]

The north jetty, built in 1934 and located on the northern side of the Ocean City Inlet, has created a massive impoundment of sand that blankets the most southerly mile of Ocean City's shore up to about Ninth Street. This impoundment has benefited the beaches to the north, as well as keeping some of the sand out of the Ocean City Inlet. The inlet must still be dredged from time to time. In 1935 the south jetty was built on the southern side of the inlet. Before then, the southward-moving sand

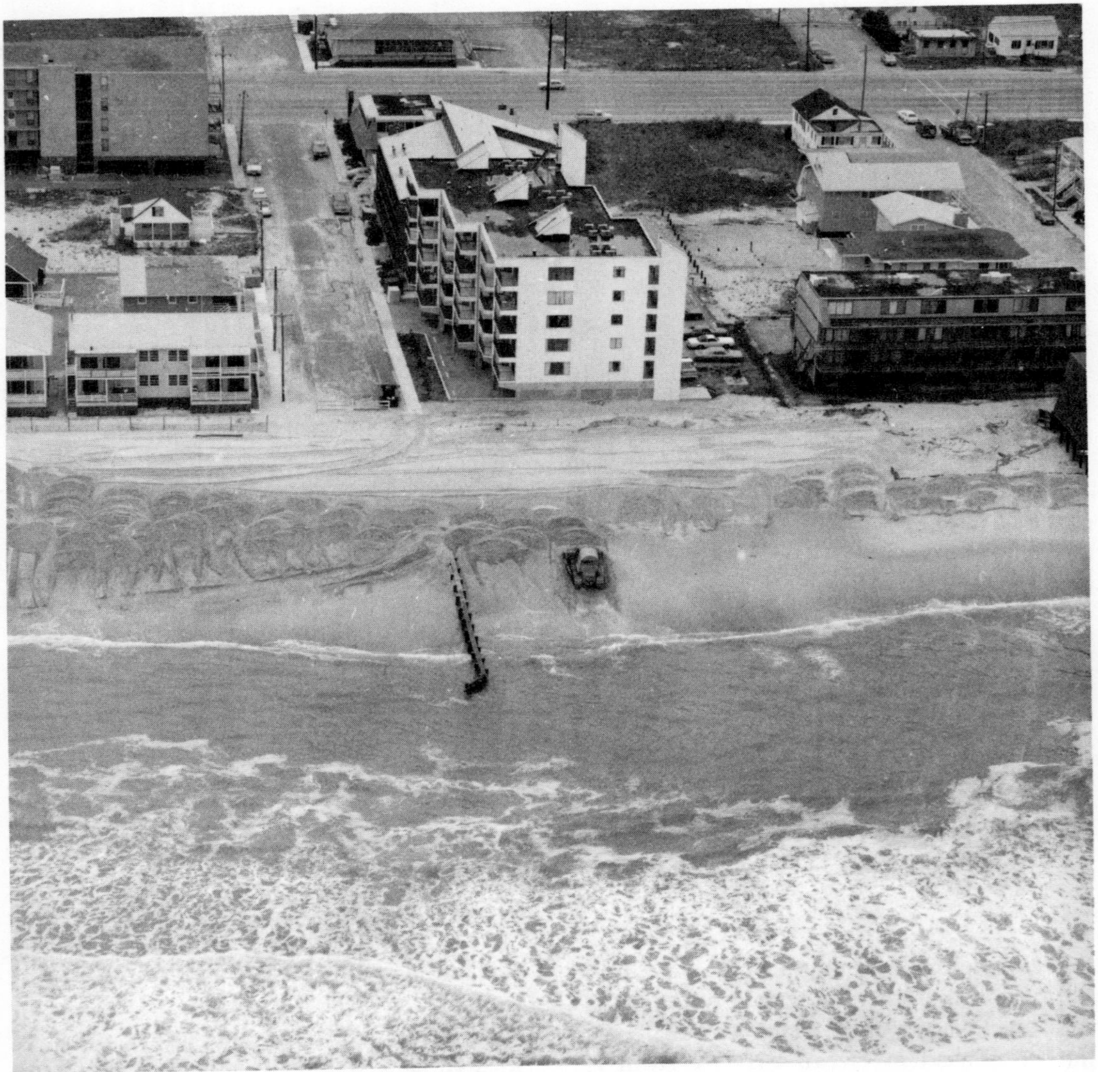

FIGURE 2.36. Bulldozing the Ocean City beaches is a controversial measure, as is the location of groins such as the one in this photograph. Courtesy, U.S. Geological Survey.

moved onto what is now Assateague Island; since the breach in 1933 and the construction of the jetties, very little sand has reached Assateague from the north. This has resulted in the massive erosion of the shore face of the northern 3 to 4 mi (4.8 to 6.4 km) of Assateague. From 1943 to 1963 the beach retreated 800 ft (244 m)![18] The March 1962 storm ripped a space through the decimated northern end of Assateague Island, later repaired by the U.S. Army Corps of Engineers.

The U.S.G.S. and the Corps of Engineers favor a beach nourishment program, in which sand would be moved onto the beaches from offshore borrow areas, as the most desirable method of protection.

Another approach is to bulldoze sand from the surf area and stockpile it on the upper beach. The bulldozing concept was organized in 1973 by Mayor Harry Kelley of Ocean City. In the winter of 1976–77, approximately 8 mi (12.9 km) of beach were reconditioned (Figure 2.36). The effectiveness of bulldozing has not been fully analyzed, but the results seem to indicate that the sand mounds might offer a fair degree of protection during the first two hours of attack by 5.5 ft (1.7 m) waves.[19] The U.S.G.S. report warns against possible adverse effects of bulldozing, as it causes a change in the beach profile that may trigger other changes.[20]

In June 1976 the secretary of the Maryland Department of Natural Resources created the Coastal Resources Advisory Committee (CRAC) with ninety-eight members representing local, state, and federal governmental agencies, citizens' interest groups, the academic community, and the public. A private engineering firm was hired to assess the problem at Ocean City and to recommend action. The firm's report strongly supported the short, stone groin as the best measure.[21] CRAC soon after adopted this recommendation, but the Maryland Department of Natural Resources has admitted that an extension of the groin system will exacerbate the erosion problem on Assateague.[22]

A study by the Maryland Department of Community and Economic Development justifies the extension of the groin system on economic grounds.[23] This study concludes that public funds should be used to protect the beaches with a system of groins from Ocean City north to the Delaware border. The rationale is presented in terms of employment, income, tax revenue, and pleasure provided by the beach attraction (Tables 2.7 and 2.8). Over 95 percent of the travelers to Ocean City are tourists who stay only a couple of days. Between July 1978 and June 1979, they spent approximately $170 million (Table 2.8). The report concluded that "the use of public funds to stabilize and protect the Ocean City beaches and the tourism industry founded on them appears to be quantitatively justified.[24]

Efforts to stabilize the barrier island landscape have had serious ecological effects. Inhibiting overwash and concentrating windblown sands in the form of manmade dunes alters overwash channels, changes vegetative communities, and interferes with the natural landward migration of the island, while inhibiting longshore currents with groins causes shore accretion on the upcurrent side and erosion on the downcurrent side. The construction of roads, parking lots, and campgrounds alters sediment processes, and freshwater runoff is changed.[25] There is a clear conflict be-

TABLE 2.7
Estimated Impacts Of Tourist Expenditures In Ocean City, 1978-1979

Type of Impact	Value or Numbers
Local Employment	9,390 persons
Local Income	$ 54.7 million
Local Sales	$248.8 million
Local Tax Revenue	$ 13.7 million
Local and State Tax Revenue	$ 15.0 million

Source: Penny Davis and Vernon Fahle, Economic Rationale for Preservation of Ocean City Beaches (Annapolis: Maryland Department of Economic & Community Development, January 4, 1980), p. 5.

TABLE 2.8
ESTIMATED TOURIST EXPENDITURES IN OCEAN CITY, 1978-1979

Expenditure Category	Value ($ Million)	Percent
Lodgings	51.0	30.0
Restaurants and Liquor Stores	42.2	25.0
Food Stores	18.3	11.0
Gas Stations and Repair Services	11.9	7.0
Miscellaneous Retail Stores	12.3	7.0
Personal and Business Services	7.1	4.0
Amusements and Recreation	27.2	16.0
TOTAL	170.0	100.0

Source: Penny Davis and Vernon Fahle, Economic Rationale for Preservation of Ocean City Beaches (Annapolis: Maryland Department of Economic & Community Development, January 4, 1980), p. 3.

tween environmental concerns and the economic concerns supported by the tremendous amount of growth on Fenwick Island. The approach adopted by Maryland emphasizes halting the natural barrier-island beach processes because it is "economically feasible and quantitatively justified."

Where Do We Go from Here? To face the problems of development, erosion, and storm surge, projections on island conditions in the future are needed. Data must be continually updated; a systematic monitoring program, including remote sensing and fieldwork, is needed. Economic and environmental concerns are not necessarily mutually exclusive, but development should be preceded by identification of the hazards, assessment of the risks, and estimation of the costs and effectiveness of mitigation measures.

Funds for beach restoration and flood insurance should not be spent so as to encourage development in hazardous areas. The National Flood Insurance Program administered by the Federal Insurance Agency (FIA) provides assistance in reducing the potential property losses on barrier islands; the program helps to rebuild what will almost surely be destroyed again some day. (After hurricane Allen ravaged the Texas coast in August 1980, developers immediately began to build fifteen new condominiums on the southern end of Padre Island.) The FIA requirements are more design oriented than location oriented and are mainly structural; they induce developers to construct buildings so as to reduce susceptibility to flood damage. Buildings that meet structural requirements still can be located in hazardous areas; this ignores basic geographic facts.

The expansion of the groin system, the National Flood Insurance Program, and other measures such as the Hurricane Protection and Beach Restoration Plan of the Corps of Engineers (essentially a plan to artifically nourish the beaches) should be more carefully analyzed. There seems to be a lack of coordination of efforts by local, state, and federal agencies concerning this problem.

Barrier islands are attractive places to live on or visit, but they have the potential of being hazardous. Gilbert White, an environmental geographer at the University of Colorado, has stated that "the most rapidly growing site for catastrophic events in the United States is the Gulf and Atlantic coast of the country."[26]

NOTES

1. For a detailed description of the many soil types of Maryland, see Fred P. Miller, *Maryland Soils,* University of Maryland, Cooperative Extension Service Bulletin no. 212 (College Park, 1967).

2. G. Tyler Miller, Jr., *Energy and Environment: The Four Crises* (Belmont, Calif.: Wadsworth Pub. Co., 1980), p. 14.

3. Pearl Blood, *The Geography of Maryland* (Boston: Allyn and Bacon, 1961), coverpage; also see Allan C. Fisher, Jr., "My Chesapeake Queen of Bays," *National Geographic* 158 (1980):428.

4. Some of these problems are studied in the Chesapeake Bay model operated by the U.S. Army Corps of Engineers at Matapeake on Kent Island. The model is used by technicians, scientists, and engineers to stimulate changes in the tides, flow of tributaries, floods, and salinity of the Bay. All of the changes are effected through computer-controlled valves and sluiceways. The model covers 8 acres (3.2 ha) inside a 14 acre (5.7 ha) building, and the walking tour is near 1 mi (1.6 km).

5. "What Will the Bay Be Like in Twenty Years?" *Chesapeake Citizen Report,* no. 14 (July–August 1980), p. 7.

6. Tom Wisner from *Chesapeake Born* booklet, used by permission Folkways Records.

7. Anne W. Simon, *The Thin Edge: The Coast and Man in Crisis* (New York: Harper & Row Publishers, 1978), p. 21.

8. John S. McDermott, "America's Abused Coastline," *Time* (September 15, 1980), p. 28.

9. Ibid.

10. Robert Dolan, Harry Lins, and John Stewart, *Geographical Analysis of Fenwick Island, Maryland, A Middle Atlantic Coast Barrier Island* (Washington, D.C.: Government Printing Office, for the U.S. Geological Survey, 1980), p. 1.

11. Ibid., p. 2.

12. *Environmental Effects Report for Interim Beach Maintenance at Ocean City, Maryland* (Annapolis: Maryland Department of Natural Resources, Tidewater Administration, 1980), p. 1.

13. Dolan, Lins, and Stewart, *Geographical Analysis of Fenwick Island, Maryland,* p. 5.

14. E. F. Thompson, *Wave Climate at Selected Locations Along U.S. Coasts* (Fort Belvoir, Va.: U.S. Army Corps of Engineers, 1977), p. 32.

15. D. V. Truitt and Les Calette, *Worcester County: Maryland's Arcadia* (Ocean City, Md.: Worcester County Historical Society, 1964), p. 8.

16. Dolan, Lins, and Stewart, *Geographical Analysis of Fenwick Island, Maryland,* p. 17.

17. *Environmental Effects Report for Interim Beach Maintenance at Ocean City, Maryland,* p. 3.

18. Ibid., p. 56.

19. Ibid., p. 4.

20. Dolan, Lins, and Stewart, *Geographical Analysis of Fenwick Island, Maryland,* p. 18.

21. *Preliminary Report: Interim Beach Maintenance at Ocean City* (Annapolis, Md.: Trident Engineering Associates, Inc., 1979).

22. *Environmental Effects Report for Interim Beach Maintenance at Ocean City, Maryland,* p. 66.

23. Penny Davis and Vernon Fahle, *Economic Rationale for the Preservation of the Ocean City Beaches* (Annapolis: Maryland Department of Economic and Community Development, 1980).

24. Ibid., p. 10.

25. Dolan, Lins, and Stewart, *Geographical Analysis of Fenwick Island, Maryland,* p. 14.

26. Gilbert White, ed., *Natural Hazards* (New York: Oxford University Press, 1975), p. 57.

CHAPTER 3

HOW THE LAND IS USED: PRIMARY ACTIVITIES

GENERAL ECONOMIC PROFILE OF MARYLAND

If people and their economic activities were distributed evenly over the earth, there probably would be little interest in economic geography. However, any economic atlas will attest to the uneven distribution of people and their activities,[1] and Maryland is no exception. People in Maryland earn their livelihood from a variety of occupations—from farming and fishing to research and development—representing all sectors of the economy, but specific occupations tend to be concentrated in specific areas or locations.

All six major activity sectors of the economy are strongly represented in Maryland: (1) procurement in the primary sector, (2) production in the secondary sector, (3) marketing in the tertiary sector, (4) servicing in the quaternary sector, (5) consumption, and (6) transportation, the connecting link among them all.[2] The relationships among the sectors are shown in Figure 3.1.

Activity Sectors

People employed in primary activities procure commodities in natural form from the earth's seas, mines, forests, and farms. In Maryland, as in the United States as a whole, only a small percentage of the labor force is employed in the primary sector. As regions become more economically advanced, employment declines in the primary occupations, but this does not mean that primary activities are less important. The primary occupations in Maryland are not less important, indeed they are now appreciated more than ever due to the recognition of the finite nature of food, energy, and industrial resources.

In the secondary sector, form utility is added to primary commodities as the manufacturing process turns the commodities into products. The manufacturing industries of Maryland range from electronics firms to shipyards and steel mills.

The tertiary (marketing) sector includes wholesale and retail activities that display products for purchase by customers. The quaternary or service sector provides all types of services to the other sectors. Some services are producer oriented (Type I on Figure 3.1); they are concerned with extracting, moving, manufacturing, and selling items. Other services, called consumer or personal services (Type II on Figure 3.1), are provided directly to the consumer. Tertiary and quaternary services occupy only a small part of the land area of Maryland, but account for a large and growing segment of the work force (Figure

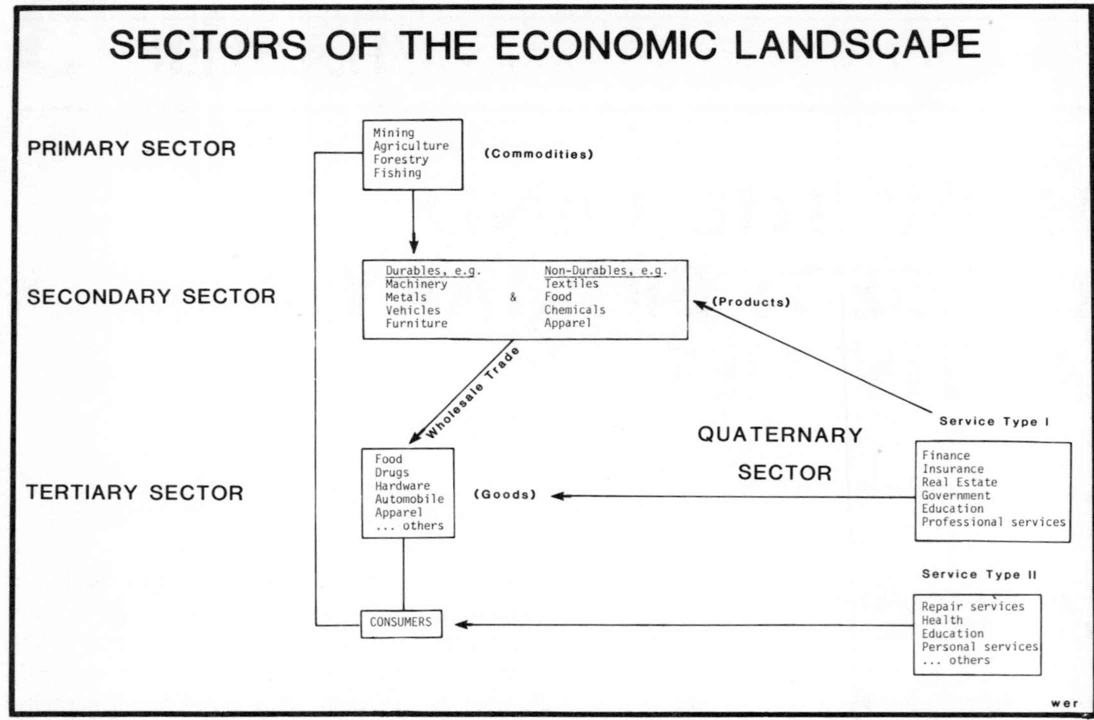

FIGURE 3.1.

3.2).[3] These market-oriented activities are found in urban centers.

The consumer sector initiates demand. Goods and services are supplied to this sector, which includes the total population. All sectors of the economy are tied together by various modes of transportation and communications.

Farmers, miners, and fishermen (called watermen locally) are found in the rural areas of Maryland. Urbanites work in heavy industries such as steel plants, shipyards, and port activities. Figure 3.2 shows that the biggest employer in the state is government, which at all levels employes 23.3 percent of the state's work force. The leading economic activities in Maryland are not agriculture, fishing, mining, and manufacturing, but are urban-centered activities.

Manufacturing and agriculture were still major employers in 1900, but by 1920 the commodity-producing sectors accounted for only about 50 percent of the Maryland work force. The most recent growth area is the service sector, which now accounts for 18.4 percent of the work force. Included in this sector are new activities such as research and development, information handling, electronic communications, and services to businesses, government, and individuals; these activities are coming to dominate the Maryland economy.

The decline in primary- and secondary-sector employment and the expansion of employment in the tertiary and quaternary sectors is shown in Figure 3.3. The trends for Maryland and the United States as a whole from 1940 to 1970 were similar.

By 1979, over 1.9 million Maryland residents were employed; nonagricultural employment in Maryland has grown in recent years in all categories except the federal government, which has declined slightly. Nevertheless, the role of federal government employment in Maryland

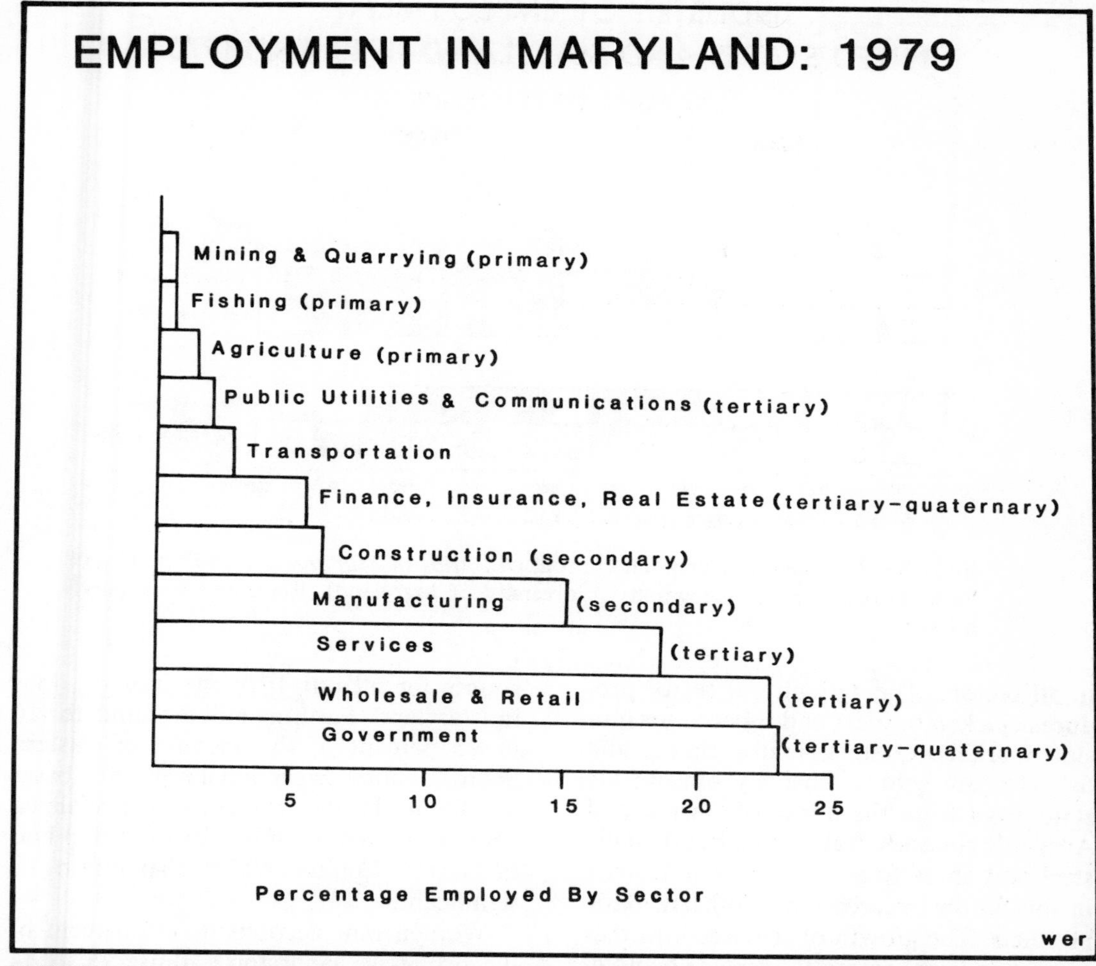

FIGURE 3.2. Source: *Maryland Statistical Abstract, 1979* (Annapolis: Maryland Department of Economic and Community Development, 1980).

should not be overlooked. Over 130,300 civilians were employed in various federal agencies in Maryland in 1979, and an additional 45,200 civilian and military employees (2 percent of Maryland's labor force) work for the Department of Defense.[4]

Basic and Nonbasic Occupations

According to economic base theory, employment in Maryland can be grouped into two types of occupations: basic and nonbasic. Nonbasic occupations are service or residentiary jobs that take care of the needs of the population of the region. Basic occupations serve the area, but what is more important, they also serve outside areas with goods and services. By their nature, basic activities are not as ubiquitous as nonbasic; that is, basic activities are located more sporadically. Basic activities draw income into Maryland from outside the state. In addition, they attract similar and related businesses, resulting in agglomeration economies and growth; this regional economic phenomenon is called the regional multiplier effect, or sometimes cumulative causation.

Basic activities in Maryland are found

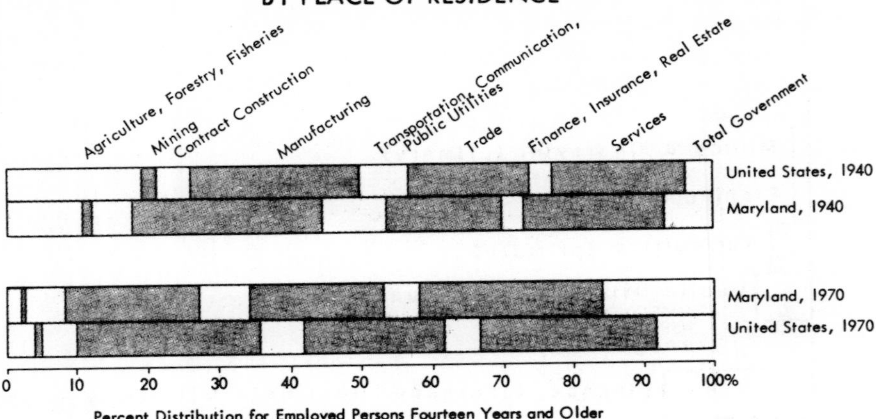

FIGURE 3.3. Source: Derek Thompson, ed., *Atlas of Maryland,* © 1977 (College Park: Department of Geography, University of Maryland). Reprinted with permission.

in all sectors. The agricultural sector produces chicken broilers and tobacco for outside markets. Oysters, crabs, clams, and fish also are sold extensively outside the state. Coal from the mines of Garrett and Allegany counties leaves Maryland daily; steel and ships from the heavy industries in the Baltimore area are significant basic products. The growth of services for other areas has been dramatic; especially noteworthy have been the commercial and financial activities of the port of Baltimore, higher education, medical research, general research and development, wholesaling, tourist services, and the activities of federal installations.

Still, the majority of the people in Maryland earn a living from jobs that are nonbasic, e.g., retail trade, transportation, local government, teaching, residential construction, social work, and police and fire protection. These kinds of jobs will continue to be important in the future.

Special Characteristics

Industrial counties vary significantly in their economic base. The urban corridor from Baltimore to Washington, D.C., accounts for all but 10 percent of the jobs in Maryland. Farming still accounts for 10 to 75 percent of the income of Eastern Shore counties. Exceptional economic bases are found in the government-specialized counties (Anne Arundel, for example) and in Garrett County, where coal mining is significant.

Women now account for 50 percent of the prime-age labor force, those 25 to 54 years old.[5] Maryland is consistently below the national unemployment rate; even the cities of Baltimore and Washington, D.C., are below national rates. Some counties in Maryland have marked seasonal variations in unemployment, e.g., Somerset, Worcester, and Garrett; Allegany County has a high level of unemployment. Much of this rural unemployment is tied to a decline in agriculture and fishing.

In the remainder of this chapter, attention is focused on the primary activities in Maryland.

AGRICULTURAL ACTIVITIES

The theme of diversity within a relatively small area clearly carries over into

Maryland agriculture. The agricultural diversity is related to a number of physical, cultural, and economic factors: soil types, elevation and topography, growing season, proximity to markets, transportation, and labor. The varied physical environment described in Chapter 2 affords the possibility of carrying on a wide range of agricultural activities within the state. In addition, Maryland has a well-connected transportation network; coupled with the state's location within the huge market of Megalopolis, this means that Maryland broilers, fruits, vegetables, dairy products, and other agricultural commodities are in demand.

Eastern Shore farms are noted for their broilers, vegetables, grains, and cattle. Croplands and forests are mixed in the four southernmost counties of the Eastern Shore; here the light, sandy-loam soils are excellent for raising vegetables. On the northern part of the Eastern Shore, the proportion of land used for agriculture reaches the highest percentage in the state: 75 percent in Kent County, as compared to 42 percent of the land in the entire state (Figure 3.4). The heavier soils of the northern Eastern Shore support such crops as wheat, corn, and hay. The area of the four counties of the lower Eastern Shore accounts for 34 percent of the total state agricultural receipts primarily because it is one of the nation's leading producers of broiler chickens. Grains are also important on the Eastern Shore, mainly as feed for the poultry.

Southern Maryland is tobacco country. Although tobacco acreage has been decreasing over the past few decades, it still remains an important crop and accounted for 4.6 percent of the state's total agricultural receipts in 1977 (Table 3.1). In addition to tobacco, the light loam soils in this part of Maryland are used to grow some wheat, alfalfa, and an increasing amount of soybeans.

North-central Maryland is an area of general farming, livestock production, and dairy farming. The mixed-farming area of dairy products and crops in Frederick, Washington, and Carroll counties alone accounts for 20 percent of Maryland's total gross receipts from farming.

Farming in western Maryland is more restricted because of the higher elevation, thinner soils (except in valleys), and shorter growing season. Here is found a concentration of fruit orchards, along with some production of potatoes, livestock, and maple syrup.

Greenhouse and nursery farming is increasing around the population centers of Maryland. In 1977, these activities accounted for 3.8 percent of the total gross receipts from agriculture (Table 3.2).

These general agricultural patterns in the state are summarized in Figure 3.5, which shows the level of cash receipts from livestock and crops by county in 1973, as well as the percentage of receipts from various types of agriculture for each county. The outstanding counties in total receipts are Wicomico, Worcester, and Somerset counties on the Eastern Shore; and Frederick, Carroll, and Washington counties on

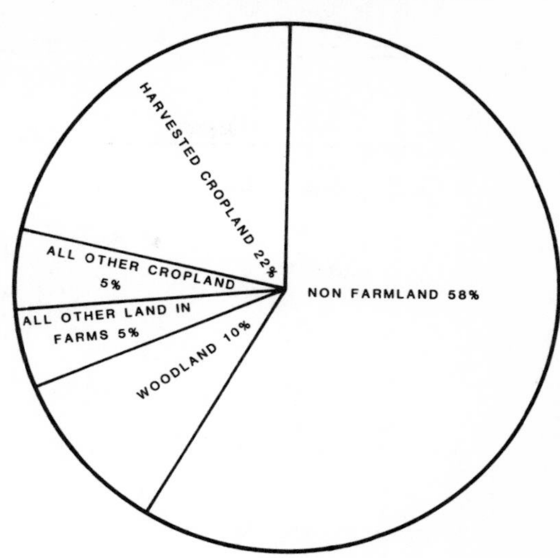

FIGURE 3.4. Source: Maryland Department of Agriculture, *Maryland Agricultural Statistics Summary for 1978.*

TABLE 3.1
CASH RECEIPTS FROM MARYLAND FARMING 1977

1977		Cash Receipts	% Of Total Receipts From:	
Livestock & Products		$ 428,282,000		64.8
Broilers	185,566,000		28.1	
Dairy Products	162,168,000		24.6	
Cattle & Calves	37,243,000		5.6	
Hogs	17,677,000		2.7	
Other: eggs farm chickens turkeys sheep & lambs honey wool	25,628,000		3.8	
All Crops		229,185,000		34.7
Corn	68,856,000		10.4	
Soybeans	41,089,000		6.2	
Tobacco	30,200,000		4.6	
Vegetable	25,766,000		3.9	
Fruit	10,721,000		1.6	
Greenhouse & Nursery	25,000,000		3.8	
Other	27,553,000		4.2	
Government Payments		3,398,000		.5
Total Receipts		$ 660,865,000		100.0 %

Source: Based on information from Statistical Abstract of Maryland 1979, Table No. 193, pages 260-261.

the Piedmont. The largest component of production in the Eastern Shore counties is poultry, while that of the Piedmont counties is dairying and other livestock. The importance of tobacco in the southern counties of Prince Georges, Calvert, Charles, and St. Marys is indicated by the data on the map, as is the relative importance of fruit in Allegany and Washington counties.

Like most other states, especially those in Megalopolis, Maryland has been undergoing a shift in employment from rural, agricultural jobs to those in urban manufacturing and service industries. As a result, the total land in agriculture, the number of farms, and the number of farm workers has been declining (Tables 3.2, 3.3). Long-term trends in the decline of Maryland farm acreage are shown in Figures 3.6 and 3.7. Although the acreage farmed and the number of farms has been decreasing, the mean size of farms in Maryland has increased from 108.3 acres (43.9 ha) per farm in 1950 to 175.3 acres (71 ha) in 1979. These trends are similar to those throughout the United States.

The farm employment numbers given in Table 3.2 represent a mean of employment figures for the months of April, July, October and January. These employment figures, especially those for hired labor, vary significantly by season. Of special interest are migrant workers who come to Maryland, in particular its Eastern Shore, from as far south as Florida. Most of these migrant workers, the majority of whom

TABLE 3.2
WORKERS ON FARMS IN MARYLAND

Type	Annual Average[a] 1978	1977	1976	1974
Family workers	17,000	20,000	21,000	24,000
Hired workers	12,000	12,000	13,000	10,000
Total	29,000	32,000	34,000	34,000

Source: Maryland Department of Agriculture, Maryland Agricultural Statistics, Publication No. 85 (June 1979), and Publication No. 69 (June 1978).

[a]Annual average of persons employed based on the last full calendar week ending at least one day before the end of the months of April, July, October, and January.

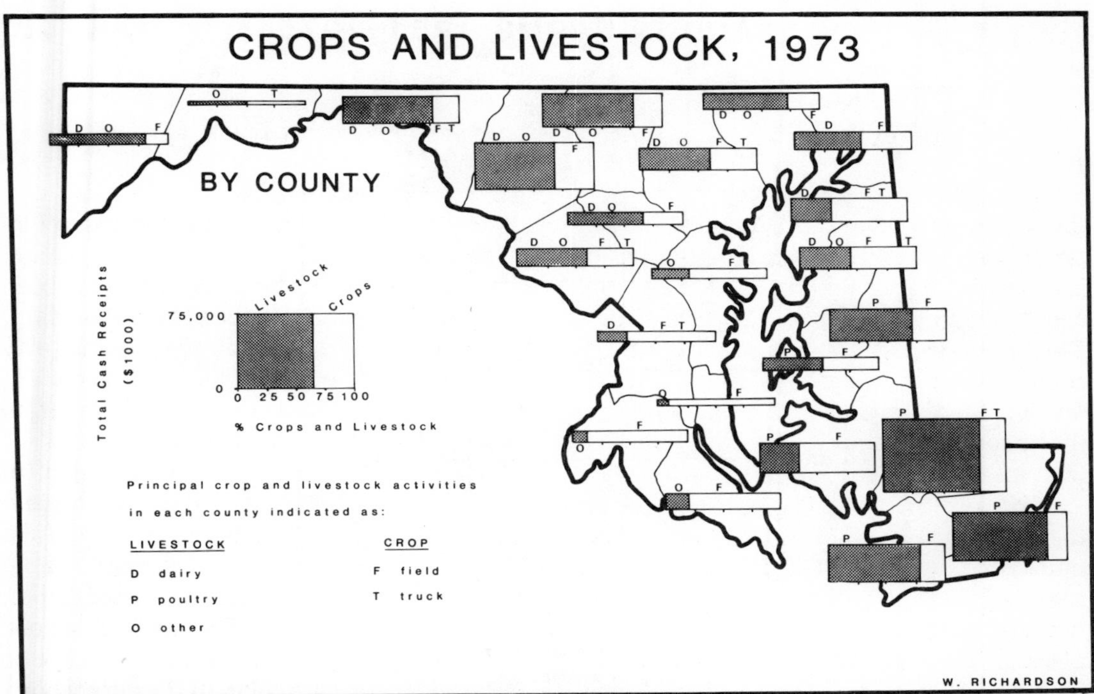

FIGURE 3.5. Source: Derek Thompson, ed., *Atlas of Maryland,* © 1977 (College Park: Department of Geography, University of Maryland). Reprinted with permission.

TABLE 3.3
NUMBER OF FARMS AND LAND IN FARMS, MARYLAND

Year [a]	Number of Farms [b]	Land in Farms [b] (1,000 Acres) [c]
1979	16,000	2,805
1978	16,100	2,815
1977	16,100	2,820
1976	16,300	2,840
1975	16,400	2,855
1974	17,800	2,955
1973	18,000	2,970
1972	18,200	3,010
1971	18,500	3,050
1970	18,500	3,080

Source: Maryland Department of Agriculture, Division of Marketing, Maryland Agricultural Statistics, Publication No. 85 (June 1979).

[a] Beginning in 1975, places with annual sales of agricultural products of $1,000 or more.

[b] Official estimate of Maryland-Delaware Crop Reporting Service.

[c] Formula to convert acres to hectares is: Acres = Hectares / .41

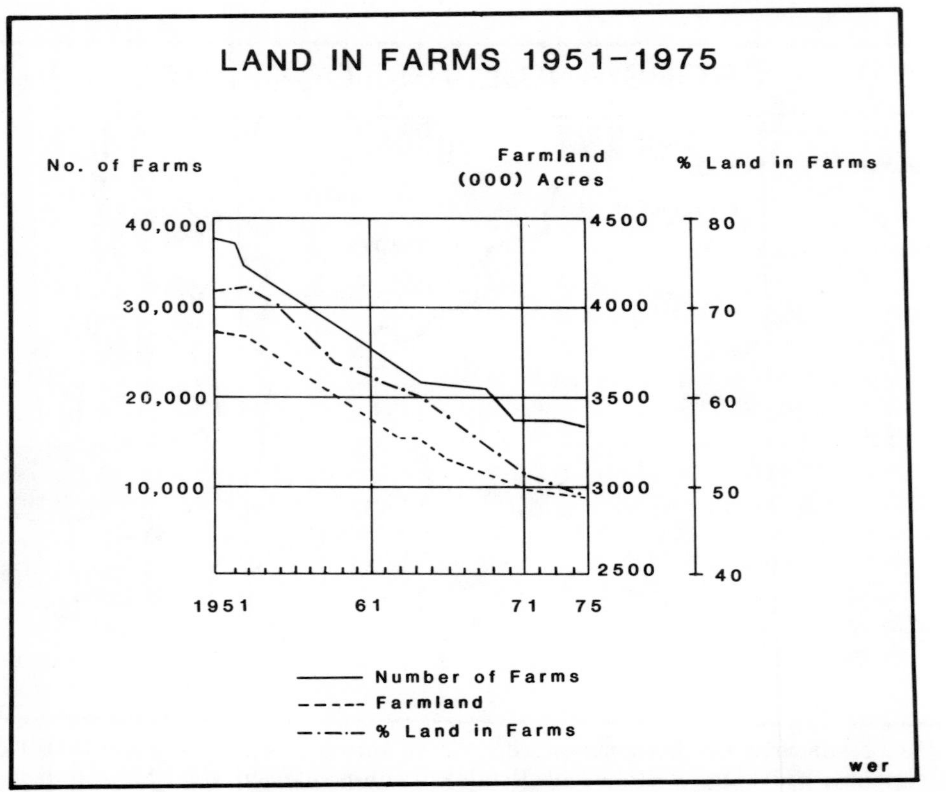

FIGURE 3.6. Source: Maryland Department of Agriculture.

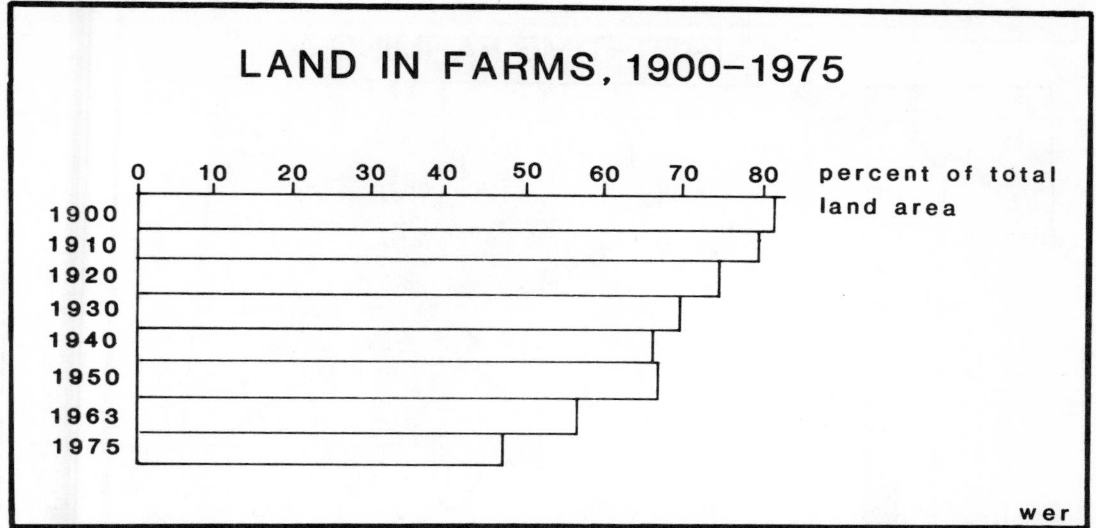

FIGURE 3.7. Source: Maryland Department of Agriculture.

are blacks and Hispanics, come north by bus and stay about five months, picking vegetables. They live in labor camps owned by contractors who supply workers to local farmers. The camps are usually fenced in and made up of cabins that are hot and provide poor living conditions. Money to pay for the cabins, utilities, and gasoline for travel to and from the fields is deducted from the workers' salaries by the contractor. The state of Maryland provides some medical care clinics that visit the camps, but this effort is limited by underfunding. These laborers remain outside the local society, almost as aliens, yet many of them return year after year all their lives.[6]

In addition to the regular farm activities, there are a number of part-time farmers in Maryland (Figure 3.8). Part-time farming supplements an income from another job, is an avocation, or is carried on by retired individuals. Coal miners in Allegany County own and operate part-time farms, as do watermen in Wicomico County.

Crops

Truck Farming. Truck farming—raising small fruits and vegetables in large quantities to be sent either to nearby large urban markets to be sold fresh or to canneries for processing—is an important component of Maryland agriculture. The Eastern Shore is Maryland's leading truck-farming area (Table 3.4), and indeed is one of the outstanding truck-farming areas in the nation. In 1978 the Eastern Shore produced 78 percent of Maryland's commercial vegetables and melons for the fresh market and processing; the four counties of the lower Eastern Shore accounted for 29 percent of that production, while the central and upper Eastern Shore counties grew 49 percent of the crops.[7] In addition to having the necessary long growing season and good soils, the Eastern Shore is readily accessible to the large markets of Washington, D.C., Baltimore, Philadelphia, Wilmington, and the rest of megalopolis. West of Chesapeake Bay, Baltimore County is the leading truck-farm area, with much of its produce going to the metropolitan Baltimore market.

Most truck farms are small to medium in size, as these activities are labor intensive. Some crops still must be picked mainly by hand, e.g., melons, strawberries, and beans. It is to these areas that the seasonal laborers come for the harvest.

Although the Eastern Shore is one of

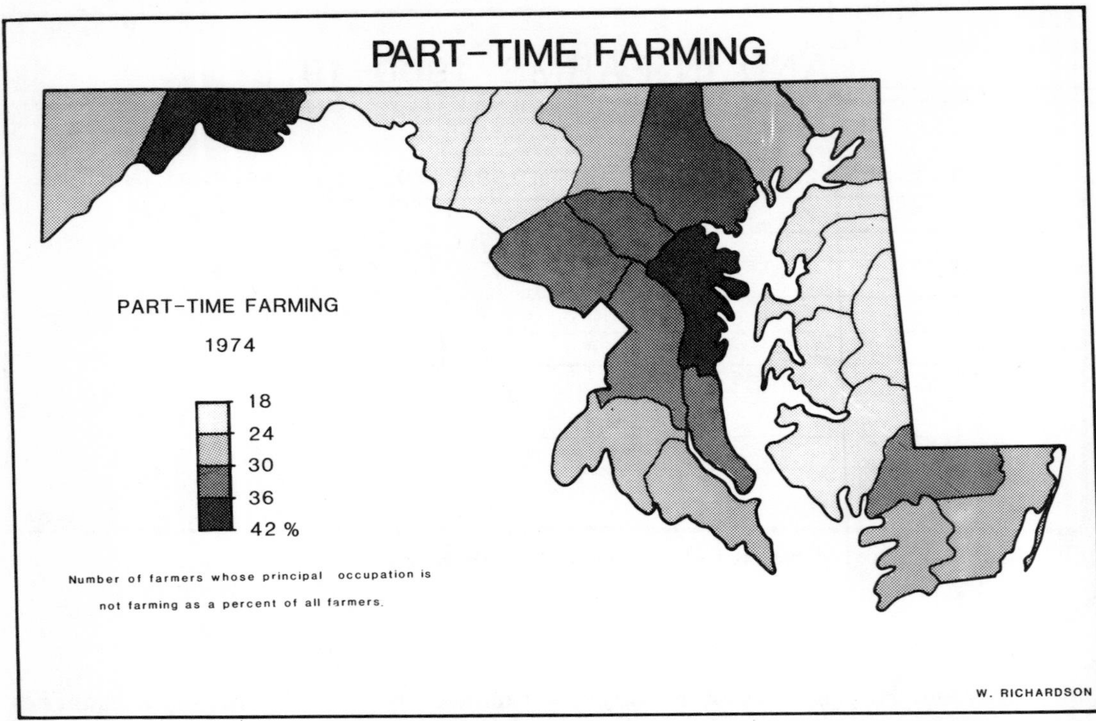

FIGURE 3.8. Source: Maryland Department of Agriculture.

the nation's leading tomato-producing areas, there has been a declining trend in recent years as farmers have turned to more profitable crops requiring less labor.[8] Early in this century, Maryland was the nation's leading producer of tomatoes; today it accounts for only a small share of the market. In the 1930s Maryland farmers planted an annual average of 51,200 acres (20,736 ha) of tomatoes for processing, while California farmers planted 53,400 acres (21,627 ha). During the 1940s and 1950s, Maryland's acreage declined, while California's increased. From 1945 to 1955, Maryland farmers planted an annual average of 33,900 acres (13,730 ha) in tomatoes compared to 111,300 (45,077 ha) for California. These figures diverged even more from 1959 to 1963, to 9,100 acres (3,686 ha) in Maryland and 142,500 (57,713 ha) in California. By 1979, Maryland farmers were planting only 3,900 acres (1,580 ha) of tomatoes for processing and 2,400 acres (972 ha) for the fresh market.

Since 1940, the number of tomato canneries in Maryland has dropped from 450 to 40. The cannery industry started on the East Coast in the 1930s. Most of the Maryland canneries were small, family-owned businesses. As the industry moved west, the size of the canneries became larger, and it became increasingly difficult for Maryland canneries to compete with the monstrous California operations. West Coast canneries have other advantages in addition to the economies of scale associated with larger operations: longer growing season, larger yield per acre, and more mechanization. However, some Maryland farmers feel that high energy costs could cause a resurgence of tomato growing and canning in the state, because its location in the major U.S. market could make the savings on transportation costs significant.

Maryland is an important producer of early potatoes, which go to market in late June. Early potatoes are produced chiefly on the Eastern Shore, where light soils and

TABLE 3.4
COMMERCIAL VEGETABLES AND MELONS HARVESTED, 1978

Crops	Total Acres Harvested For Processing & Fresh Market			
	Lower Eastern Shore	Central & Upper Eastern Shore	West of the Chesapeake Bay	State
Snapbeans Fresh Mkt. only	810	180	1,100	2,090
Cabbage	10	180	460	650
Sweet Corn Processing only	1,970	7,350	2,180	11,500
Cucumbers Fresh Mkt. only	1,075	335	90	1,500
Green Peas Processing only	*	4,030	*	6,000
Tomatoes	3,410	1,940	950	6,300
Watermelons	2,340	250	110	2,700
Asparagus, cucumbers for pickles, spinach, lima beans, snap beans for processing	3,860	8,210	5,270	15,370
TOTAL	7,650	20,770	7,270	35,690

Source: Maryland Agricultural Statistics (June 1979), p. 24.
Note: Formula for conversion of acres to hectares is: Acres = Hectares / .41
*Combined to avoid disclosing operations of individuals.

an early spring make it possible to plant in March. On the Piedmont, some early potatoes are grown, but most of the crop is for late harvest. Sweet potatoes are also grown on the sandy soils of the Eastern Shore; many are stored and cured for later use or are canned.

Field Crops. Field crops are by far the leading types of crops grown in Maryland (Table 3.1). The major ones are listed in Table 3.5. Corn for grain is the leader, with significant production both east and west of Chesapeake Bay. Most of the field corn grown on the Eastern Shore is used as feed for chickens and other livestock, while much of that grown west of the bay is used to feed dairy and beef cattle. Other grains are used to mix livestock feed, but corn is the main ingredient. Corn was grown in Maryland by the Indians before the white colonists arrived, and it was a good crop for early settlers, because it could be grown among the rocks and stumps on rough land. Some corn is raised in all

TABLE 3.5
FIELD CROP DATA 1978

Crop	Acreage Harvested	East of Bay	West of Bay	Total Production
Corn for Grain	590,000	32,985,000 bu	24,245,000 bu	57,230,000 bu
Soybeans	345,000	10,047,000 bu	993,000 bu	11,040,000 bu
Wheat	108,000	1,879,000 bu	2,117,000 bu	3,996,000 bu
Barley	85,000	2,098,000 bu	1,727,000 bu	3,825,000 bu
All Hay	249,000	93,700 tn	537,300 tn	631,000 tn
Tobacco	23,000	0	32,200 lb	32,200 lb

Source: Based on various tables from Maryland Department of Agriculture, Maryland Agricultural Statistics 1978, publication No. 95.
Kilograms = .45 x pounds
Tonnes = .9 x short tons
Liters = 35.2 x Bushels

twenty-four counties, but several counties are outstanding producers: Kent, Queen Annes, Carroll, Worcester, Dorchester, Caroline, Talbot, Frederick, and Montgomery (Figure 3.9). The rolling Piedmont is physically well suited for growing corn because of the long, hot, wet summers as well as the clay loam soil.

The second largest field crop in Maryland is soybeans (Table 3.5). This crop has been increasing in importance in Maryland, as it has been in the entire nation. Soybeans are a versatile crop, being used to produce oil, meat substitute, and plastics, as well as being used as a hay, silage, and cover crop. In 1925, only 6,000 acres (2,430 ha) of soybeans were raised in Maryland. By 1951, this figure had increased to 77,000 acres (31,185 ha), and by 1978 there were 345,000 acres (139,725 ha) in soybeans. Figure 3.10 indicates that the leading counties in soybean acreage are clustered on the Eastern Shore: Queen Annes, Caroline, Talbot, and Dorchester. The smaller production west of Chesapeake Bay is found mainly in St. Marys, Charles, Baltimore, and Prince Georges counties. Much of the western shore soybean crop is grown in the tobacco region of southern Maryland.

The bulk of the hay crop is grown west of the bay where the thriving dairy industry of central Maryland requires hay as feed; both cattle and horses eat large amounts of hay. More of this valuable roughage feed is produced in Frederick County than anywhere else in the state. On the Piedmont, alfalfa, timothy, and clover are important elements in the hay crop. On the Eastern Shore and in southern Maryland, more soybeans and cowpeas are used as hay.

Winter wheat was not grown extensively in Maryland before the Revolution. Soon after the war, the three Ellicott brothers from Pennsylvania established a mill on the fall line at what is today Ellicott City.[9] Soon much of the local land that had been exhausted from tobacco production was planted in wheat. With the help of fertilizer, these Piedmont soils began to produce good wheat crops; at one time, wheat was such an important crop that the tax levy was valued in bushels of wheat. Wheat was exported, helping to establish Baltimore as a leading grain-handling port. Winter wheat is sown in the early fall, so that plants are well started before the winter freeze. In

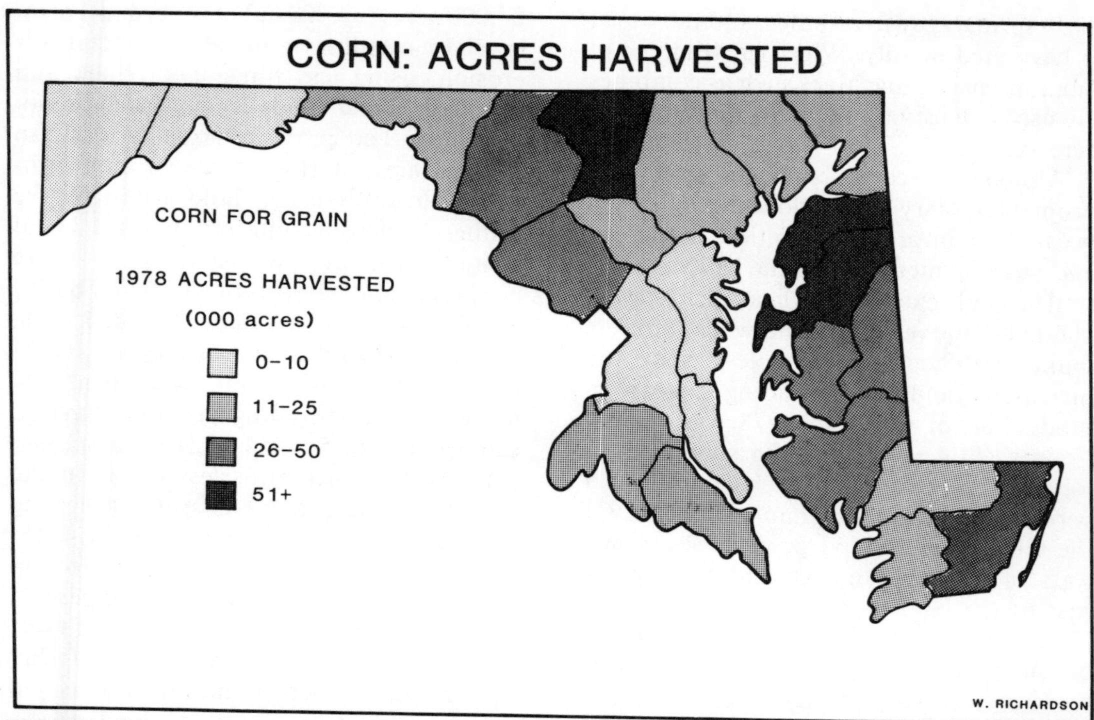

FIGURE 3.9.

SOYBEANS: ACRES HARVESTED

SOYBEANS FOR BEANS

1978 ACRES HARVESTED

(000 acres)

0-1.9

2.0-10

11-30

31-40

41+

W. RICHARDSON

FIGURE 3.10.

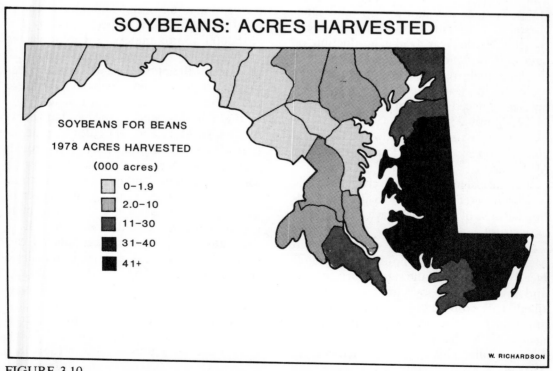

early spring, growth resumes, and the wheat is harvested in July. Wheat growing is not labor intensive; machines such as combines are used extensively on the Piedmont wheat acreage.

Although acreage planted to wheat has dropped in Maryland, yields have increased because of improved varieties, fertilizers, and farming methods. As the Midwest was settled and extensive wheat fields were planted, however, Maryland wheat farmers found it difficult to compete despite the increased yields. The leading county in production of wheat in 1978 was Carroll County (11.4 percent of the state's crop), followed closely by Frederick County (10.5 percent); both are Piedmont counties. Of the total state crop, 53 percent was grown west of Chesapeake Bay and 47 percent east of the bay.

Barley is a popular grain feed that can be substituted in part for corn, and it requires less labor to produce the same amount of feed value. Barley is grown both east and west of the bay. The Eastern Shore leads in state production, with Caroline (15 percent of the state's crop) and Dorchester (14 percent) the leading counties.

After World War II the production of oats in Maryland declined drastically, as the large-scale replacement of horses and mules by machines reduced demand. Barley has replaced much of the oat acreage. In 1978, only 23,000 acres (9,315 ha) were planted in oats. Oats grow better in a climate cooler than that found in most of Maryland.

The last significant field crop, tobacco, will be covered separately in the next section because of its special place in Maryland agriculture.

No-till Cultivation. A new trend in Maryland agriculture is no-till cultivation.[10] Nearly 50 percent of the state's corn acreage and much of the soybean acreage is not tilled at all: crops are planted in the stubble and mulch of the previous crop. In 1970, nearly 50,000 acres (20,250 ha) of corn was not tilled; by 1979 this increased to 350,000 acres (141,750 ha) of corn and 80,000 acres (32,400 ha) of soybeans. Farmers claim no-till saves moisture and controls erosion, using less time, labor, fuel, and fertilizer; higher yields are produced on no-till acres. The practice slows erosion, so streams are not clogged with runoff sediment. No-till is taking hold fastest on the rolling Piedmont country; it could be of greatest value on the Eastern Shore where land is flat and harvests of wheat and barley are followed by, or double cropped with, soybeans. No-till does not require an expensive tractor for sowing, just a relatively inexpensive sod-seeding machine. Savings can amount to 5 gal (18.9 l) of diesel fuel per acre and two-thirds less labor. In the fall, when the ground is wet, harvesting combines ride more easily over no-tilled land; there is a reduction in soil erosion, especially in hilly terrain. Today 60 percent of Piedmont farming is of the no-till type.

Chesapeake Bay watermen claim that the herbicides used by no-till farmers kill aquatic vegetation as well as land weeds, but research has shown that no-till cultivation results in less herbicide runoff than conventional farming. The U.S. Department of Agriculture projects that by the year 2000, approximately 77.5 million acres or 31,387,500 ha (45 percent of total U.S. cropland) will not be tilled. Maryland, Kentucky, Virginia, and Pennsylvania have taken the lead in no-till cultivation.

Western Maryland. In the highland areas of western Maryland, agricultural production drops off dramatically. The rough mountainous terrain and shorter growing season make it difficult to grow many crops; freezes occur later in spring and earlier in the fall; winters are colder and summers cooler. Allegany County ranks lowest in the state in almost every agricultural category. Some livestock and feeds are raised in these areas, and in Garrett and Allegany counties, maple syrup is an important local forest product.

By far the most important crops of western Maryland are fruits. In 1978, Maryland orchardists grew 42,500 tn (38,548 t) of apples and 12,000 tn (10,884 t) of peaches.

Production is centered in Washington County's Hagerstown Valley (part of the Great Appalachian Valley), a rich limestone-soil valley that is one of the finest apple-producing regions of the United States. West of the Hagerstown Valley, extensive orchards are found on the hillsides, especially around Hancock. The reason for planting fruit trees on hillsides is to take advantage of air drainage.[11] During the day, solar insolation heats the earth, which in turn reradiates heat to the atmosphere. At night the thin air containing less moisture, on the hilltops, loses heat faster than air in the valleys, and heavy, cold air flows down the slopes into the valleys, pushing up warmer, light air. The warm rising air spreads out to warm the slopes, thus creating a thermal belt. Farmers take advantage of this warmer thermal belt by planting fruit trees there. Frosts may occur in the valleys but not on the slopes. To assist the circulation of air, some orchards have air circulators that look like large propellers mounted on high towers above the trees.

Tobacco

Tobacco is a field crop that deserves special attention because of its historic and continuing importance to Maryland. Since colonial days, a distinct way of life or culture has developed in Maryland's tobacco region. Tobacco has been grown in the state for over 300 years: it is still grown today in areas that were originally planted in colonial times, and Maryland farmers still utilize much the same growing, curing, and marketing processes as did previous generations. Maryland ranks eighth among the states in total tobacco production. Although Maryland's production is dwarfed by other areas today, it produces a distinct type of tobacco leaf not found in any other state. The unique characteristics of Maryland tobacco make it much sought after by cigarette manufacturers in the United States and Western Europe.

As early as 1637, tobacco was the dominant crop in Maryland. During the colonial period, the British purposely limited the amount of currency in America; tobacco was so important that it became the prime medium of exchange for paying debts, taxes, and salaries. By 1750, tobacco production had reached 13,500 tn (12,245 t) and accounted for 75 percent of the value of all Maryland exports.[12]

No large, important central places developed in the tobacco country of southern Maryland, because ships came up the rivers to the plantations' doorsteps, where hogsheads of tobacco were loaded onto the ships and manufactured goods were unloaded. (Figure 3.11 shows several hogsheads of tobacco as they were still packed in the 1930s.) Because places were better connected by water, overland roads were poor. The lack of large central places is still evident in southern Maryland. Sotterley, an early plantation (Figure 3.12), can be visited today on the south bank of the Patuxent River, which flows through the core of the Tobacco area.

The tobacco region is made up of five contiguous counties in southern Maryland; Prince Georges, Anne Arundel, Calvert, Charles, and St. Marys (Table 3.6). All of Maryland's commercial tobacco is grown in these counties, which have shown a remarkable locational persistence for this crop. Because they are close to large urban centers, Anne Arundel and Prince Georges counties are more urbanized than the others. The Patuxent River basin occupies a central position in southern Maryland between Chesapeake Bay to the east and the Potomac River to the south and west. Along the middle course of the Patuxent, between Benedict and Queen Anne, lies the single greatest concentration of rich tobacco-producing land in southern Maryland.[13] This rural area with few large-order urban places reflects a past when the highly discrete, fragmented, and widely distributed nature of early marketing procedures did not necessitate the formation of large central places.[14]

Tobacco wears out the soil quickly. As earlier farmers abandoned old fields for

FIGURE 3.11 (*above*). Hogsheads of tobacco as they once were shipped from Maryland. FIGURE 3.12 (*below*). Sotterley is a colonial plantation on the banks of the Patuxent River near Hollywood in St. Marys County.

TABLE 3.6
TOBACCO ACREAGE AND PRODUCTION 1978

County	Acres Harvested	Production (1000 pounds)
Anne Arundel	4,400	6,160
Calvert	4,500	6,300
Charles	4,700	6,674
Prince George's	3,900	5,265
St. Mary's	5,500	7,801
TOTAL	23,000	32,200

Source: Maryland Agricultural Statistics (June 1979), p. 17.

Hectares = .41 x Acres

new land, the old land grew over with weeds and trees. Much of this wasted land remains unused today, but some has been reclaimed, especially by the Amish people who have moved into southern Maryland from Pennsylvania.

The climate, topography, and soils of this area are ideal for tobacco. The mild climate averages 56°F (13°C), with precipitation normally around 40 in (102 cm) per year and a growing season of 189 days. Tobacco is grown on sandy-loam soils of the Sassafras series, which have loose surfaces but do not dry out or cake.[15] Tobacco remains the most important cash crop in southern Maryland despite its limited areal extent in comparison to corn, soybeans, winter wheat, and fallow land.

Much of the work on Maryland tobacco fields is done by hand. Machines are used mainly to prepare the fields and set out the plants. In October, seedbeds of fertile soil are prepared; the following March, the seedbeds are sown and packed firmly. Muslin covers are draped over the delicate plants to keep them warm and protect them from insects. In May the plants are transferred to well-drained, light, sandy loam fields. While maturing, sprouts on the sides of the plant, called suckers, are removed to preserve the quality of the large leaves. After sixteen to twenty leaves have grown, the top of the plant is broken off below the seedhead to allow the lower leaves to develop (a process called topping). After topping, the plants grow another two to four weeks before being harvested in August (Figure 3.13). At harvesttime the stalks are cut close to the ground and left in the field to wilt; once they are easy to handle, each stalk is pierced and strung on a tobacco stick, and the plants are then removed to a curing barn (Figures 3.14, 3.15). Tobacco-curing barns are a common sight in southern Maryland. These tall, unpainted barns have hinged side boards to allow for air flow.

Once strung, tobacco cures in the circulating air of the barn until later winter or early spring, without the use of artificial heat. The dry, brittle tobacco softens up with the spring humidity. The leaves are then removed from the barn and graded into bunches of twelve to fifteen leaves, called a hand. Each hand is placed into a large pile called a burden.

Tobacco is a relatively tolerant crop in terms of temperature requirements. Some varieties prefer warm, humid conditions as in the Carolinas, while others thrive in more vigorous climates such as Connecticut. In Maryland, high humidity produces

FIGURE 3.13. This tobacco field in Calvert County near Prince Frederick is nearly ready for harvesting.

FIGURE 3.14. The inside of a tobacco-curing barn showing the racks used to hold the tobacco stalks.

FIGURE 3.15. Maryland tobacco is cured in barns such as this. The boards on the sides of the barn can be opened to allow air to flow in and enhance curing.

FIGURE 3.16. The loose-leaf tobacco auction in Upper Marlboro, Prince Georges County, is frequented by tobacco buyers from many companies.

a mild tobacco with thin leaves, low nicotine content, and a steady-burning quality.[16] There are six classes of tobacco: flue cured, fire cured, air cured, cigar filler, cigar binder, and cigar wrapper. Classes are further broken down into types based on quality and color. Maryland tobacco is Class 3 light air cured, types 31 and 32. Type 31, called burley, is the single type most widely grown in the United States, accounting for 25 percent of production. Very little burley is raised in Maryland; most of the state's crop is type 32, called "Southern Maryland." Type 32 is unlike any other tobacco and is difficult to duplicate because of the particular soil and climatic conditions necessary to grow it. Cured type 32 is reddish brown, thin, and very dry. Unlike other tobacco, type 32 continues to burn evenly after lighting until totally consumed. Because it also has no distinctive odor, cigarette manufacturers prefer type 32.

There are two types of tobacco markets in Maryland. Loose-leaf auctions, the most common, have been operated only since 1939. Auctions are held at Hughesville, La Plata, Waldorf, and Upper Marlboro (Figure 3.16). Bundles of tobacco are placed in baskets on the auction floor, and state inspectors grade each basket. As the auctioneer sells each basket, payment is immediate. The second type of market is the hogshead market. A hogshead is a cask approximately 44 in (112 cm) in diameter and 54 in (137 cm) long (Figure 3.11). Tobacco is packed tightly into the hogshead using a mechanized screw. For 200 years Maryland farmers participated in the hogshead market exclusively. Today, the Cheltenham hogshead market is the only one left in the United States. This market is of minor importance since the opening of the loose-leaf market.[17]

In the early 1930s, the American Tobacco Company and the French government were the largest purchasers of Maryland tobacco. By 1933 the company had dropped its purchases drastically, and the French government, which operated a tobacco monopoly, bought none. The purchasers objected to the method of buying only from hogshead samples. A Maryland visitor to a French cigarette factory was shown a yard littered with rocks, rusty plowshares, and other trash found in Maryland tobacco. Soon after, the tobacco-marketing system was revolutionized when Frank M. Hall and R. L. Hall built a large shed in Upper Marlboro and asked tobacco growers to bring their tobacco to sell loose. Buyers could now see the exact quality of tobacco.[18]

A serious threat to the state's tobacco industry at present is the encroachment of the Baltimore-Washington, D.C., urban corridor. There are increasing demands for more residential land in the tobacco counties. In addition, the attractive job opportunities in the urban areas attract labor from the farm areas. Some tobacco farmers have sold out and left the region. A trend in the early 1980s has been the raising of type 32 tobacco in the flue-curing areas of Virginia and the Carolinas. In 1980, Virginia and the Carolinas harvested nearly as much as did Maryland. Despite these pressures, the number of Maryland tobacco farmers and the acreage planted have not declined significantly. There still remains a strong tobacco tradition in southern Maryland.

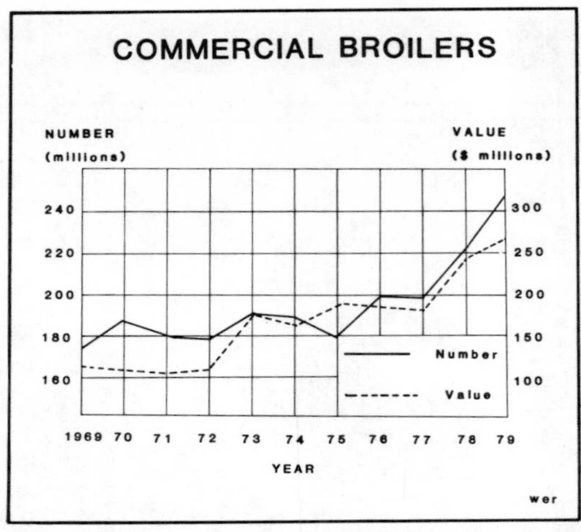

FIGURE 3.17. Source: Adapted from Maryland Department of Agriculture, *Maryland Agriculture Statistics, 1979.*

Livestock

Livestock activities in Maryland accounted for nearly 65 percent of total receipts from agriculture in 1977, as compared to approximately 35 percent for all crops (Table 3.1). The two largest components of livestock production in the state are broilers (28.1 percent of all receipts from agriculture) and dairy products (24.6 percent).

Poultry. The growth of the broiler industry on the Eastern Shore has been impressive. In 1935, Maryland produced 2 million commercial broilers. By 1951, production reached 58,418,000; it climbed to 220,882,000 by 1978 (Figure 3.17). In 1978, Maryland broiler production ranked sixth among the states, totaling 905.6 million lb (407,520,000 kg) of chickens.

The Maryland broiler industry is concentrated on the Eastern Shore in Worcester, Wicomico, and Somerset counties, although some broilers are also raised on the Piedmont. In fact, the Virginia and Delaware parts of the Delmarva Peninsula also produce a significant number of broilers, making it one of the leading chicken-producing areas of the country. The mild climate of the Eastern Shore makes it a good place to raise chickens, which cannot tolerate extreme heat. The location of the Eastern Shore relative to the large markets of Megalopolis is ideal.

Many broiler farmers buy chicks from local hatcheries that get a good portion of their hatching eggs from New England poultry farmers. Up to the early 1950s, most chickens were sold alive in the big cities, but now there are large-scale dressing plants on the Eastern Shore. The broiler business is a big one in Maryland, with a gross income of $235.5 million in 1978 (up 29 percent from 1977).[19] The many elements of the industry include hatcheries, chicken farms, corn feed and other grain production, dressing plants, crate and package production, and refrigerated truck transport. In 1980 there were sixteen poultry-dressing plants in Maryland employing 7,617 people. Of this total, 7,224 were employed in plants on the Eastern Shore (Table 3.7). The plant with the largest number of employees is Bayshore Foods,

TABLE 3.7
EMPLOYMENT IN MARYLAND POULTRY PLANTS 1979

Poultry Dressing Plant	No. Employed	City/Town, County	Region
Allen Family Food Inc.	251	Cordova, Talbot	Eastern Shore
Athens Food Services	5	Baltimore City	Coastal Plain
Bayshore Foods Inc.	1,450	Easton, Talbot	Eastern Shore
Campbell Soup Co.	505	Chestertown, Kent	Eastern Shore
Chesapeake Foods Inc.	450	Parsonsburg, Wicomico	Eastern Shore
Chesapeake Foods Inc.	300	Berlin, Worcester	Eastern Shore
Dover Poultry Prod. Inc.	160	Baltimore City	Coastal Plain
Golden Pride Inc.	700	Berlin, Worcester	Eastern Shore
Golden Pride Inc.	600	Stockton, Worcester	Eastern Shore
Hendler Poultry Co.	8	Baltimore City	Coastal Plain
Holly Farms Poultry Ind.	144	Snow Hill, Worcester	Eastern Shore
Perdue Farms Inc.	1,264	Salisbury, Wicomico	Eastern Shore
Shorgood Poultry	660	Hurlock, Dorchester	Eastern Shore
Showell Farms Inc.	900	Showell, Worcester	Eastern Shore
Sterling Processing Co.	215	Oakland, Garrett	Allegheny Plateau
W & W Poultry Inc.	5	Frederick, Frederick	Piedmont
TOTAL	7,617		

Source: Maryland Department of Economic and Community Development, Directory of Maryland Manufacturers: 1979-1980, p. 279.

Inc., in Easton, followed closely by Perdue Farms, Inc., in Salisbury. On the Eastern Shore over the past fifty years, the trend has been to consolidate poultry firms, the numbers of firms dropping from one hundred to nine. As recently as 1966 there were still twenty firms, but in 1979 Golden Pride, Inc., merged with Perdue Farms, Inc., and Bayshore Foods merged with Country Pride Foods to remain competitive with Perdue.[20] Today, Perdue is the dominant chicken marketer in New York City and is making strong progress in the Boston market.

Dairying. The residents of the large metropolitan areas of Baltimore and Washington, D.C., demand fresh milk daily. Indeed, Maryland's dairy industry had its start with the growth of cities and towns within the state and nearby. Most of the milk from the Eastern Shore goes into local consumption or to the Philadelphia and Baltimore fluid-milk market, while most of the milk from the Piedmont goes to Baltimore or Washington, D.C. The milk produced in Washington County is sold in and around Hagerstown and in nearby parts of Pennsylvania; milk from Allegany and Garrett counties is consumed locally or sold to towns in nearby West Virginia.

The area west of Chesapeake Bay accounts for 83 percent of Maryland's milk production (Figure 3.18). Frederick County is by far the leading milk producer in Maryland, accounting for 27 percent of total state production in 1979 (211,500 tn or 191,831 t). The neighboring counties of Carroll (125,500 tn or 113,829 t) and Washington (104,500 tn or 94,782 t) are also significant producers, followed by Harford

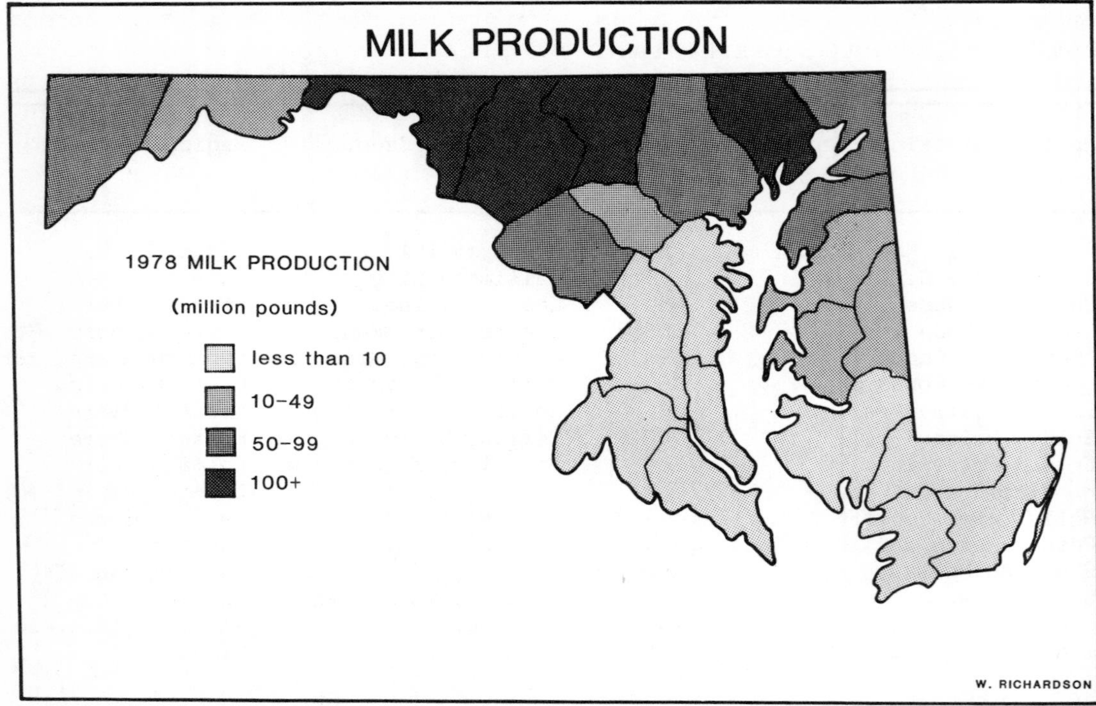

FIGURE 3.18. Source: Maryland Department of Agriculture.

(56,000 tn or 50,792 t).[21] Of a total 370,000 head of cattle and calves in the state in 1978, milk cows accounted for 37 percent.

Dairying is a hard, full-time job with no off-season—cows must be milked morning and evening all year long. One benefit is that income from a dairy farm is steadier than from some other forms of agriculture. The dairy region centered on Frederick County is also Maryland's leading area of hay and field-corn production. These feeds are stored and used during the winter.

Other Livestock. Other livestock raised in Maryland are considerably less important than chickens and dairy cows. Some hogs are raised, but it is difficult to compete with farmers in the Midwest, where corn is plentiful and is converted quickly into pork on a huge scale. The number of hogs dropped in Maryland from 335,000 in 1867 to 270,000 in 1951 and to 215,000 in 1978. In 1978, only 19,000 head of sheep and lambs were recorded in Maryland. Beef cattle made up 16 percent of the state's cattle in 1978.[22]

From 1940 to 1950 the number of horses in Maryland decreased by 50 percent, as farms turned to mechanization. Still, the business of raising horses is important to the fox hunting and racing that are part of the Maryland culture. A number of farms throughout Maryland are devoted to raising thoroughbreds; hunters, saddle horses, and ponies also are raised. Horse racing in Maryland contributes to the well-being of agriculture through the State Farm Board, which receives a share of levies imposed by law on race tracks. In addition, horse-breeding farms are important consumers of farm products such as hay, corn, and oats.

FISHING: THE WATERMEN'S DOMAIN

Although only 1 percent of Maryland's employment is in fishing, it remains an important economic activity, especially on the Eastern Shore and parts of the western shore. Seafood is not only an important resource, it is a component of the culture of Maryland, touching the Atlantic Ocean and Chesapeake Bay as the state does; one can hardly think of Maryland without associating it with oysters and crabs.

In 1978 there were 17,504 licensed watermen in Maryland. Processed seafood products in 1978 were valued at $117.8 million and were produced in 172 plants employing an annual average of 2,795 people.[23] In 1978 Maryland had a dockside commercial catch valued at $32.6 million; this is a substantial under count, as it does not include the catches of a large number of sport fishermen. The major share of the Maryland catch is credited to shellfish, $29.5 million or 90 percent by value. Oysters were the leading catch by value ($14.5 million), followed by clams ($9.6 million) and blue crabs ($5.1 million). Leading finfish catches by value were striped bass (called rockfish in Maryland), bluefin tuna, and flounder (Table 3.8). The rockfish is a local favorite; 90 percent of these delicious East Coast fighters spawn in Chesapeake Bay.

Despite the pollution problems discussed in Chapter 2, the yield from Chesapeake Bay is still high, totaling over 2,500 tn (2,268 t) in 1978. It is estimated, however, that by the year 2000, the maximum sustainable yield (the greatest harvest possible without hurting future yields) will be exceeded for blue crab, spot, rockfish, white perch, flounder, and eel. By 2020, sustainable yields for oysters, soft-shell clams, menhaden, and alewives may be exceeded.[24]

A relatively recent entry into the Maryland seafood industry is the soft-shell clam, *Mya arenaria,* the succulent steamer of New England clambake fame. For years, Chesapeake Bay watermen neglected and despised these clams, locally called "manoes," as being unfit for consumption. In New England, *Mya* lie in the mud at low tide; in Maryland they remain under 10 to 20 ft (3.1 to 6.2 m) of water and must be dredged. In 1950, Fletcher Hanks of Hanks Seafood Company in Easton heard of a serious decline of New England clams; the next year he patented a hydro-escalator clam harvester that was an instant success. In 1952, nearly 95 percent of the U.S. catch of soft-shell clams was taken in New England; by 1960, the Chesapeake Bay mano fleet was supplying over 600,000 bu (211,440,000 l) annually, or 70 percent of U.S. production. Nearly all of the bay clams are sold to New England, but other areas around the country are demanding them also.[25] New England has become second to the bay in total catch of clams (Figure 3.19).

The effect on the shad of pollution, sediment, and overall environmental degradation is representative of the effect on many other species of finfish in the bay. In 1890 the all-time high catch of 3,500 tn (3,175 t) of shad was landed; by 1909, the catch had dropped to 1,500 tn (1,361 t). By the 1920s California, where shad had been transplanted, was shipping 1,000 tn (907 t) annually back east. From 1940 to 1970 the annual commercial catches of shad in Maryland waters ranged from 500 to 1,000 tn (453 to 907 t). Since the early 1970s, the catch has been in a precipitous downward trend (Table 3.9). The state is trying to limit fishing activities, promote hatcheries, and limit obstructions on spawning runs; it is now developing fish-population management models to take the pressure off the fish and allow them to make a comeback.

Menhaden are an important catch in Maryland, accounting for 12.5 percent of the weight, although only .8 percent of the catch value. Menhaden are by and large not sold for human consumption; they are reduced to oil, animal feed, and solubles to manufacture cosmetics, linoleum, and steel. Called the "pogy" in New England, menhaden are called the "moss bunker" in the Middle Atlantic states and the "fatback" in North Carolina. Chesapeake Bay watermen often call them "bunker" or, on the Eastern Shore, "alewife" or "old wife."[26]

Watermen is a curious term. The *Oxford Dictionary* states that the first use of the word was around 1400 in Sir Thomas Malory's *Morte D'Arthur.* From the Eliz-

TABLE 3.8
FISH CATCH IN MARYLAND 1978

Species	Value ($)	% Value	Pounds (1000)	% Pounds
TOTAL	$ 32,622,096		56,437	
Finfish	3,140,401	9.626	13,998	24.802
Bluefish	24,768	.080	289	.512
Butterfish	5,461	.020	22	.038
Carp	2,473	.010	96	.170
Catfish	37,381	.110	350	.620
Croppie	873	.002	4	.007
Croaker	143,365	.439	582	1.031
Drum	863	.002	9	.016
Eels	116,867	.360	206	.365
Flounder	356,259	1.090	677	1.200
Gizzard Shad	60	*	4	.007
Hake	329	*	8	.014
Herring	259	*	7	.012
Hickory Shad	298	*	1	.002
Mackerel	1,941	*	10	.018
Menhaden	288,961	.885	7,333	12.992
Scup	1,317	.004	6	.011
Sea Bass	169,009	.518	427	.757
Sea Trout	89,583	.274	518	.918
Shad	23,844	.073	87	.154
Sharks	10,566	.032	142	.252
Spot	4,890	.014	31	.055
Striped Bass	1,279,826	3.920	1,189	2.107
Sturgeon	1,160	.003	4	.007
Sunfish	681	.002	6	.012
Tuna	367,286	1.126	896	1.588
White Perch	203,962	.625	1,040	1.842
Whiting	962	.003	11	.019
Yellow Perch	5,802	.017	29	.051
Unclassified	919	.003	6	.012
Other	436	.001	7	.012
Shellfish	29,481,695	90.373	42,439	75.197
Blue Crabs	5,132,239	15.732	16,815	29.794
Hard	3,963,281	12.149	15,965	28.288
Soft	1,168,958	3.583	850	1.506
Clam Meats	9,598,711	29.424	11,748	20.816
Horseshoe Crabs	8,450	.026	148	.262
Jonah Crabs	2,070	.006	14	.024
Lobsters	123,311	.378	56	.099
Oyster Meats	14,483,631	44.398	13,470	23.867
Other	133,283	.409	188	.333

Source: *Maryland Statistical Abstract*, 1979, pp. 96-99.
*Less than .000%
Kilograms = .45 x Pounds

FIGURE 3.19. Refrigerated seafood trucks from New England are shown here on Kent Island, as their drivers pick up a shipment of clams.

TABLE 3.9
MARYLAND SHAD CATCH

Year	Pounds
1970	1,037,731
1971	946,426
1972	821,260
1973	597,793
1974	220,482
1975	183,757
1976	109,173
1977	73,015
1978	53,818
1979	20,660

Source: Sunday Sun (August 29, 1981), p. A-1.
Kilograms = .45 x pounds

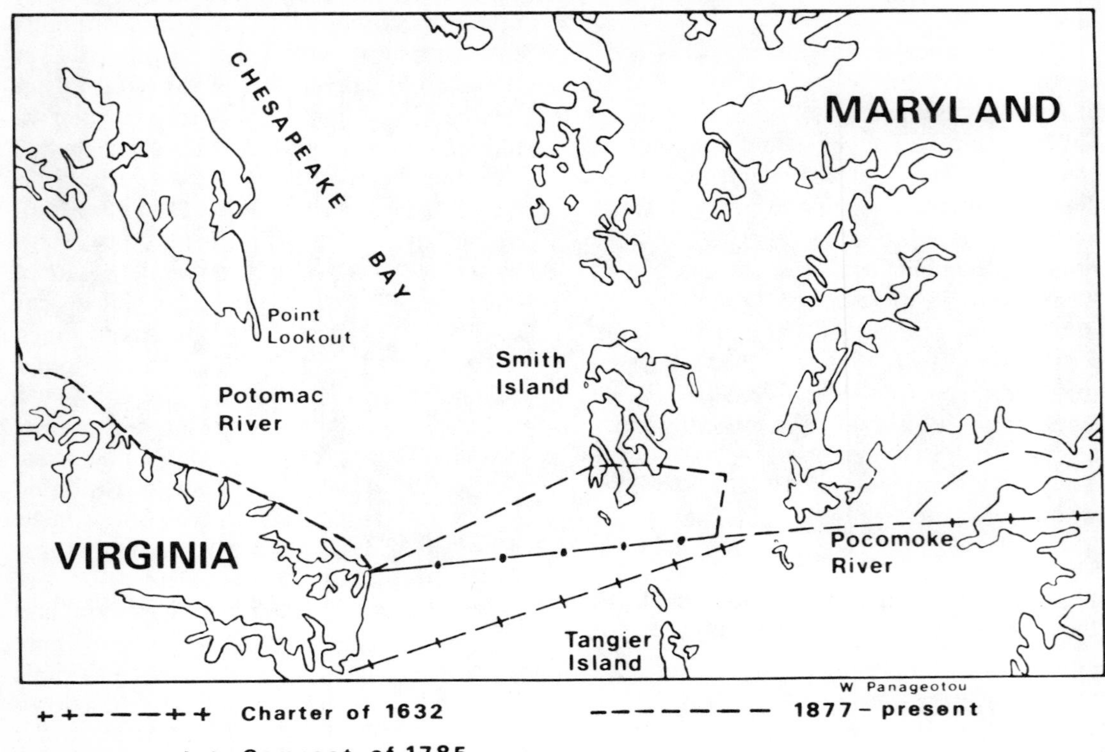

FIGURE 3.20.

abethan period on, frequent references are confined to the Thames River in England to denote waterborne taximen. Today the term has only limited and archaic use in England; it is used mainly in August when the London Fishmonger's Company sponsors the annual Waterman's Race. It is not known exactly why in America the term took root only along the shores of Chesapeake Bay. It may be that early Chesapeake watermen plied for hire on the rivers. The word came to be used to differentiate those who had the resources to acquire land from those who didn't and were forced to follow the water for subsistence.[27]

Since the 18th century Maryland and Virginia have had a number of conflicts over fishing rights along the water boundary between the states (Figure 3.20). In 1785 a new compact was signed that recognized the boundary that had existed in fact since 1668. It allowed residents of both states to fish the Potomac River, although Virginia conceded that the river was entirely within Maryland. As oyster supplies diminished, Maryland passed laws that Virginia refused to honor. In 1957 the Maryland legislature finally abrogated the Compact of 1785, and in 1958 the two states drew up a new compact that recognized the boundary that had existed in fact since 1877. Under the terms of this compact, a joint commission regulates the Potomac fisheries and patrol boats from both states enforce the laws. Until 1958, slot machine casinos were operated on the ends of piers stretching out from Virginia. Although illegal in Virginia, the gambling was occurring in Maryland waters. Finally in 1958, Maryland outlawed these casinos.[28]

On Chesapeake Bay fishing laws vary significantly from Maryland to Virginia; Maryland's laws tend to be more conservation oriented. Fishermen are not allowed to cross the state boundary, but incursions and incidents remain common. Both states actively patrol the border in the bay. One notable incident occurred in July 1949 when the boat of Earl Lee "Pete" Nelson, a Maryland crabber out of Smith Island, was boarded by a Virginia Fisheries Commission inspector. When Nelson refused to go to a Virginia port for impoundment, a shot was fired and Nelson was killed. Today the border is clearly marked with white and orange buoys.

Oystering

From the rocky coast of Maine to the sandy beaches of California, when people talk of Maryland they eventually discuss the Chesapeake Bay and the oyster, "Those succulent, tender, juicy, plump, delicious, magnificent Chesapeake oysters which Marylanders thrive upon, brag about, and even lie about, are certainly the crown jewels of the world of gastronomy."[29] The oyster and the bay are indeed an important component of Maryland's culture. Oystering ("arstering" on the Eastern Shore) is more than a job, it is a way of life. Chesapeake Bay, for all its size and impersonal statistics, is an intimate place where land and water intertwine in infinite varieties of mood and pattern.[30]

By value, the oyster is Chesapeake Bay's leading resource (over $14 million in 1978). In 1885 Maryland watermen harvested 15 million bu (528.6 million l) of oysters, but since then there has been a steady decline. Still, Maryland remains the leading state in harvesting oysters (over 2 million bu or 70,480,000 l in 1978). Maryland controls 703 sq mi (1,821 sq km) of Chesapeake Bay and Virginia 985 sq mi (2,551 sq km); together they produce 25 percent of the total U.S. oyster catch.

The state boundary has proven to be a hindrance. The Virginia area is plagued by predators, disease, and pollution. Although the Maryland waters are largely free of these problems, they lack the vital oyster seedbeds and have an archaic system of tenure and management. Chesapeake Bay and the lower portions of its tributaries have 557,482 acres (225,780 ha) of natural oyster bars, restricted by the 30-foot (9.14-meter) isobath (a line connecting points of equal water depth) (Figure 3.21). The deeper waters have too little oxygen and too much of the unstable silt and clay that can smother oysters.

Salinity is the principal environmental factor affecting oysters. The Chesapeake oyster, *Crassostrea virginica,* is restricted to waters ranging from 5 to 30 ppt salinity. As noted in Chapter 2, bay salinity ranges from nearly 0 ppt at the head to 25 ppt at the mouth and varies by season and with climatic patterns. The Eastern Shore of Chesapeake Bay is saltier due to Coriolis force that deflects fresh water moving down the bay from the north and west to the right, the western shore, and dense, salty water moving up the bay to the right, the Eastern Shore. In the lower bay, the higher salinity allows a number of predators and diseases to flourish.

Severe damage is inflicted on the oysters by oyster drills, *Urosalpinx cinerea* and *Eupleura caudata.* These small snails kill 60 to 70 percent of the seed oysters of the East Coast and are likely responsible for the lack of oyster bars on the Virginia portion of the Eastern Shore (Figure 3.22).[31]

Two pathogens more damaging to oysters than oyster drills are the fungus, *Dermocystidium,* and a parasite, *Minchinia nelsoni* (MSX). *Dermocystidium,* which first appeared in Chesapeake Bay in 1949, infects the oyster via the digestive tract, resulting in death. MSX appeared in the bay in 1959; it invades the connective tissue around the intestines and is also fatal. *Dermocystidium* extends up the bay as far as the 15 ppt fall isohaline, thus inhabiting the extreme southern portion of Maryland

NATURAL OYSTER BARS

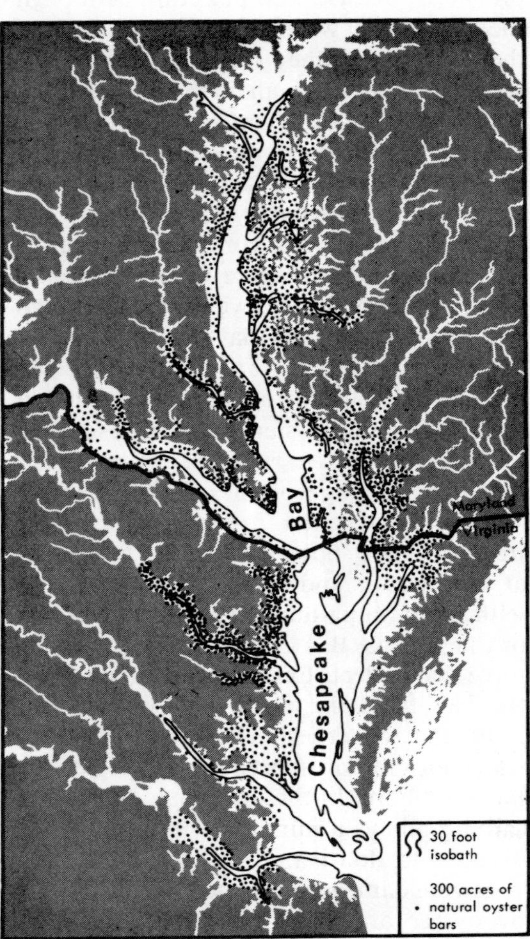

FIGURE 3.21. Source: John Alford, "The Chesapeake Oyster Fishery," *Annals Association American Geographers* (June 1975), p. 230. Reprinted by permission of the Association of American Geographers.

SALINITY AND OYSTER DRILLS

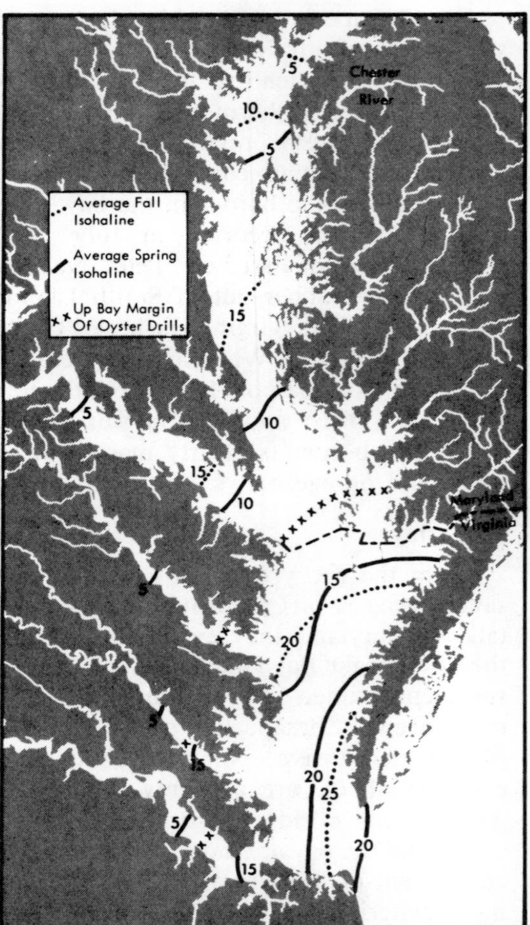

FIGURE 3.22. Source: John Alford, "The Chesapeake Oyster Fishery," *Annals Association American Geographers* (June 1975), p. 231. Reprinted by permission of the Association of American Geographers.

waters. Most of the oysters on the ground for over two years in the southern half of the Bay are infected by *Dermocystidium.*

MSX is a much greater problem. In 1959 Virginia harvested 12,500 tn (11,388 t) of oyster meat. MSX caused this figure to drop to 4,000 tn (3,628 t) by 1968. Almost all of the Maryland waters have been spared from MSX, as it cannot tolerate salinities less than 15 ppt. During dry periods when salinity in the upper bay increases, MSX moves northward. In Virginia, especially at the mouth of the James River and immediately to the north, the oyster fishery fatality level is at 60 percent.

In Chesapeake Bay, the oyster beds with the best production lie between the spring 5 ppt and the summer 15 ppt isohalines

PATHOGENS IN THE BAY

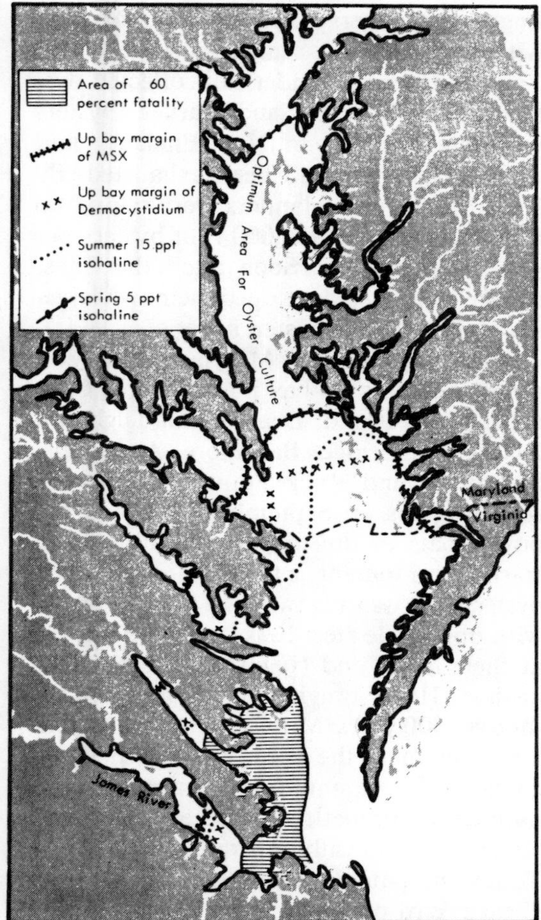

FIGURE 3.23. Source: John Alford, "The Chesapeake Oyster Fishery," *Annals Association American Geographers* (June 1975), p. 232. Reprinted by permission of the Association of American Geographers.

(Figure 3.23); this area, entirely in Maryland, is protected from floods from the north and predators from the south. Some scientists feel that good oyster years are related to dry, climatically stable summers such as that of 1980. It is during this period that spawning and the attachment of spat (young oysters) to objects takes place. Scientists from the University of Maryland regularly sample and count the spat in the bay's oyster bars; Figure 3.24 shows that the pattern is very erratic. The two kinds of oyster bars, growth bars and seed bars, are found in different areas. Growth bars, which sustain rapid development because of availability of food, are in waters that have more circulation. Seed bars are in quiet waters needed to minimize larvae dispersal; they receive heavy sets of oyster larvae and are overcrowded. Most of the seed bars are in Virginia; most of the growth bars, in Maryland. In 1970, over 90 percent of seed-oyster production in the U.S. market came from Virginia, especially from the James River, reputed to be the greatest natural seed-producing area in the world.[32] As Virginia's waters are infested with various predators, disease, and pollution, it would be reasonable to move the seed

MARYLAND OYSTER REPRODUCTION COUNTS

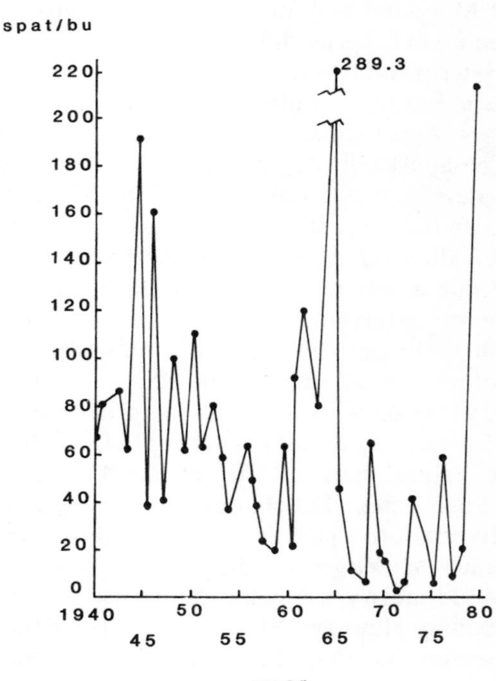

FIGURE 3.24.

oysters to Maryland's growth bars. Oysters will grow 1 in (2.54 cm) per year; it takes three years to reach the legal 3 in (7.6 cm) size, yet most oysters lying on Virginia bottoms for over two years are infected. If moved to cleaner Maryland waters soon enough, the oysters are able to flush out the pollution and are fit for consumption. The Chesapeake Bay oyster fishery would be more productive if Virginia watermen concentrated on seed oysters and Maryland's on growth and fattening. The major problem is the Virginia laws that restrict the movement of large quantities of seed oysters to Maryland.

In Maryland, a per bushel tax on oysters, along with other state appropriations, supports a program to enhance the quality of the oyster bars by means of shell replanting. Millions of oyster shells, once used to build roads in the tidewater counties, are reclaimed from packing houses, barged to the bars, and dumped. This procedure improves the chances for a good spat catch in the summer, as the young oysters often attach themselves to the shells.

Maryland and Virginia laws concerning tenure of fisheries differ. In Maryland, most oyster production is from public oyster bars, but in Virginia, most is from private bars. Approximately 92 percent of private Chesapeake fishery acreage is in Virginia waters, and the major part of the Virginia catch for the past forty years has been from private grounds. The ecologically inferior Virginia waters often outproduce the superior Maryland waters. Virginia has 240,000 acres (97,200 ha) of natural bars; before the infestation of MSX it leased 135,000 acres (54,675 ha) for private use. Maryland has 324,000 acres (131,220 ha) of natural bars in Chesapeake Bay plus 32,000 acres (12,960 ha) in the Potomac River; if Maryland's waters produced as much as Virginia's did before MSX, it would mean a tremendous increase in production. However, Maryland watermen oppose private grounds, because they feel that the greater production would depress prices. Oystering on private grounds is tightly controlled; on public grounds it's a mad scramble.

About the time of the War of 1812, New England schooners invaded Chesapeake Bay with a strange device called a dredge. These Yankee fishermen under sail collected oysters for the New England market. Oysters were big business in New England, and oyster bars there had been exhausted. By 1860, the New Englanders were taking up to 650,000 bu (22,906,000 l) of oysters per year from the bay. Soon after, the Chesapeake watermen developed their own large-scale commercial oyster fishery.

Oystering, and the Maryland fishery in general, centers on bay ports such as Crisfield, Smith Island, Deal Island, Tilghman Island, Cambridge, Baltimore, Annapolis, Solomons, and Rock Point.[33] The oyster season opens on September 15, when the powerboats of the tongers are allowed to start. Hand tonging is the method of taking oysters by scissoring two long wooden shafts with opposable steel baskets, or tongheads, at their lower end (Figure 3.25), while at anchor. Hand tonging has changed little for over 300 years. Most of the hand tongers are older men; the younger watermen are going in for patent tonging, a more economically competitive method that uses larger, hydraulically operated tongheads. Today the patent tongers dominate Chesapeake Bay oystering; their small 40- to 45-foot (12.19- to 13.72-meter) boats with crews of two or three outproduce the other types of oyster craft.

On November 1, the aging but still graceful skipjacks are allowed to commence oyster dredging ("drudgin' " on the Eastern Shore). This dwindling fleet, estimated at twenty-eight boats in 1980, is made up of the last working commercial sailing craft in the United States. Deal Island is home of the fleet. The glamorous skipjack has been placed on the National Register of Historic Places, quite a distinction for a seagoing vessel (Figure 3.26). The skipjacks, with crews of seven, are slowly disappearing as they are expensive to operate and maintain.

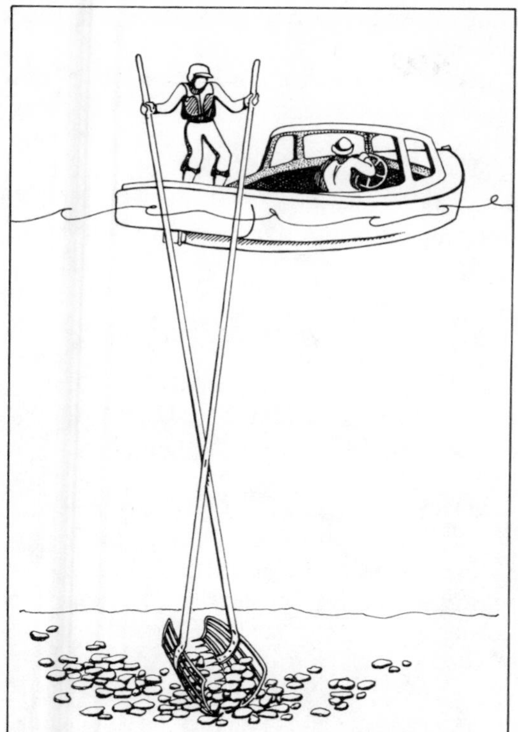

FIGURE 3.25. Hand tonging for oysters with a pair of long-handled tong rakes, hinged like pliers with collecting baskets on the ends. (Drawing by Kay DiLisio.)

A Maryland law of 1865 is still in force requiring that oysters be dredged, i.e., taken in motion, under sail. Powerboats are not allowed to dredge in Maryland waters, with the exception of small push boats carried by skipjacks that are allowed to dredge 150 bu (5,286 l) per day on Monday and Tuesday only. The oyster season runs over the winter months and ends in April.

Once the oysters are landed at the port, they are loaded by conveyor belt onto a truck and taken to a processing plant (Figure 3.27) to be cleaned, shucked, and canned by hand labor. Canning oysters was started in 1820 by Thomas Kensett of Baltimore. A big problem today is the lack of skilled shuckers. Although attempts are being made to develop a mechanical shucker, the operation is still done mainly by hand. An Eastern Shore tongue twister reads, "How many oysters could an oyster shucker shuck if there were enough shuckers to shuck oysters?"[34] The answer to this question, from Eastern Shore processors, is about three times as many. Because there are not enough shuckers, local oysters are shipped to processing plants in Virginia, New Jersey, and North Carolina (Virginia plants alone shuck 60 to 70 percent of the Maryland oyster catch). Somerset County, with the highest rate of unemployment in Maryland, sought to train fifty shuckers, but few people showed an interest. Skilled shuckers average \$150 to \$175 per week, while a waterman earns \$50 to \$75 per day for his share of a good catch. Shucking is seasonal—September to March. Most of the shuckers come from the Eastern Shore's black population; today they want more stable jobs. The trend seems to be fewer Maryland shuckers (only 2,000 in 1980) and more Maryland oysters leaving the state to be processed.

The Japanese oyster fishery possesses techniques that are of interest to Chesapeake Bay resource managers. The Japanese produce 10,000 tn (9,070 t) of oysters annually on an area one-sixth the size of the bay, by use of vertical aquaculture in which shells are threaded on lines and suspended from rafts to collect spat. The advantages of this three-dimensional aquaculture are that: (1) the growth rate is doubled, (2) spat are protected from crawling predators, (3) any type of bottom is suitable, (4) harvesting is easy and certain, and (5) rafts are easily identified private property. Tests done on Cape Cod are encouraging, but the technique is not yet being used in Chesapeake Bay.

Crabbing

Chesapeake Bay has provided more crabs for human consumption than any other body of water in the world. Of greatest commercial value by far is the bay's blue crab. Soon after the oyster season ends in April, many of Maryland's watermen turn to pursuit of the blue crab, which in Mary-

FIGURE 3.26. The skipjack fleet at work dredging oysters.

land is something of a state symbol, as the cod is in Massachusetts. The Atlantic blue crab, *Callinectes sapidus* (*Callinectes* is the Greek word for beautiful swimmer and *sapidus* the Latin for tasty or savory), is sought after, caught, and more eagerly consumed than any other crab.[35] Although it takes the amateur's baited line readily, the blue crab is difficult to catch in commercially valuable quantities, as it moves about and migrates with the seasons.

In late summer and early fall, a layer of freshly oxygenated sea water moves slowly upstream along the bottom of the bay and its tributaries. Above it lies the tired, biologically exhausted water that is oxygen starved after the long, hot summer. In late fall and early winter, the now-cooling surface water sinks as the deeper, oxygenated waters rise. The change in temperature and the churning action is a cue for the blue crabs. The "sooks" (mature females) move down the bay to winter in Virginia waters (most of the blue crabs hatched in Chesapeake Bay are hatched in the more-saline Virginia portion). The big "Jimmies" (mature males) and the younger crabs head for the deep central part of the bay, where they bury themselves in the sediment for the winter.

In the spring the vertical mixing occurs again, though in reverse of the fall pattern. As the waters warm, the sooks head up bay and the Jimmies come out of the deep channel; both head for the warm shoal waters and eelgrass of the lower creeks and tributaries. To make a living by catching the blue crab, the waterman must fully understand its life cycle and be somewhat of a biologist.

FIGURE 3.27. Oysters are landed at dockside and loaded by conveyor belt onto a truck. In this scene at St. Michaels, Talbot County, the hand tongs can be seen on the vessel.

Although the Atlantic blue crab is fished commercially from Delaware to Texas, Chesapeake Bay is the leading area with 50 percent of the national catch; that translates into 150 to 240 million crabs annually. Radical fluctuations in catch have characterized the blue crab industry for over 100 years. The catch in 1966 was an all-time high of 47,500 tn (43,083 t), but 1968 started so poorly that the U.S. House of Representatives' Committee on Merchant Marine and Fisheries held the first hearings ever on the *Blue Crab Shortage and the Chesapeake Bay Crab Industry Problems.* After such rhetoric, the hearings ended in July, just as the catches suddenly increased. "Goes to show you," a dredge captain said, "Ain't no one person knows all about crabs."[36]

Two forms of crab are caught: hard and soft. Most hard crabs are caught in crab pots (Figure 3.28). These steel-mesh, baited traps allow the crab to enter via a funnel-shaped mesh; escape back through the funnel is rare. Hard crabs are also caught on trotlines, the classical method for catching crabs for over 100 years before the introduction of the pot. Trotlines are up to one-third mi (.53 km) long, with bait (preferably eel) attached every 3 ft (.914 m). The line is anchored at the ends and marked with buoys. The crabber visits the trotline daily to pull it in, being careful to scoop the crabs with a deep net before they hit the surface, when they let go of the bait. Running trotlines is hard, messy work. Not much trotlining is done in Virginia; it is done mostly in the eastern part of Chesapeake Bay south of Kent Island, Maryland, and in the marshlands of Dorchester County. Maryland largely restricts the more efficient crab pots to the open bay; the creeks, tributaries, and subestuaries are the domain of the trotliners.

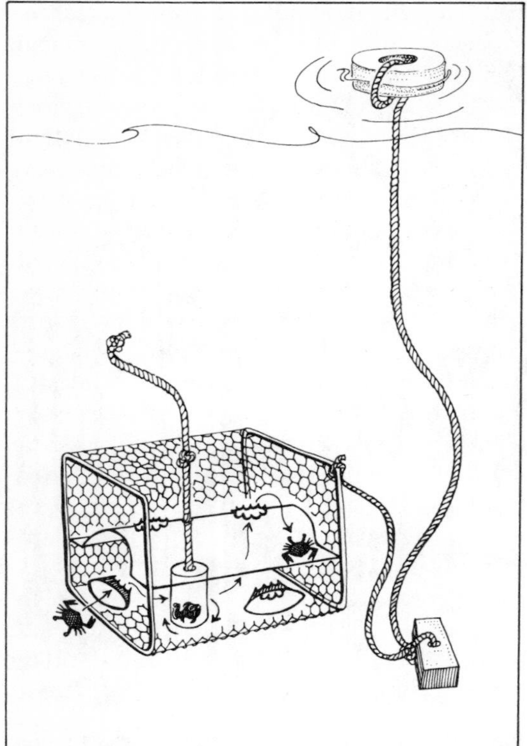

FIGURE 3.28. A crab pot is commonly made of poultry wire. To get at the fresh fish bait, the crab enters the pot through funnels and is unable to find its way out. (Drawing by Kay DiLisio.)

Ninety-five percent of succulent soft crabs are caught in Chesapeake Bay. It is not a matter of habitat, but of the skill, hard work, and infinite patience needed to hold crabs in float pens. Crabs grow by shedding, or moulting, and reforming a new shell soon after. As they do not eat while shedding, soft crabs cannot usually be caught in baited pots or on trotlines. They are mostly caught from late May to September by the use of crab scrapers (a steel-rod and net device) in the shallow grass bottoms; a specially designed shallow draft boat, called a "Jenkins Creeper," is used in scraping. Most crabs are caught while still hard or about to shed; crabbers call them "peelers." The crabs are placed in a shedding float, a rectangular floating enclosure made of strips of lathing about .25 in (.64 cm) apart that allow water to circulate while preventing schools of hungry minnows from devouring the helpless soft crab. The floats are moored with stakes inside protected waters. Acres of floats can be observed on the way into Tylerton on Smith Island; many shedding floats can also be seen at Deal Island, Crisfield, and Dorchester County marsh towns. Pound operators try hard to keep the peelers healthy and happy. Their claws are nicked to discourage damaging combat, and the floats are constantly monitored to remove "stills"; often 50 percent of the peelers die in float pens.

When ready, the soft crabs are packed in trays and covered with seagrass and ice. If their gills are kept wet, the crabs can live for several days. Each tray holds three dozen jumbo or six dozen medium crabs, and three trays make a 60 lb (27.2 kg) box. Specialized seafood-trucking firms pick up the boxes of soft crabs in an area between Cape Charles and St. Michaels and deliver them overnight to markets in Baltimore and Philadelphia and to New York's famous Fulton Fish Market. Air shipments are now made of frozen soft crabs to cities of the interior where the dish is becoming popular, such as Kansas City, Louisville, Chicago, and Detroit. The soft crab is even invading the markets of New England, land of the lobster.

Although soft crabs are gaining new national popularity, the hard crab is still the heart of the industry. Crabs are sold at dockside to a crab house, where they are cooked whole to firm up the flesh. Pickers then split, quarter, and dissect the crabs by hand to obtain every last gram of meat. Pickers, mostly women, are paid by the pound or hourly (minimum wage), whichever is higher. Picking is a difficult skill, but a good picker can pick 40 to 50 lb (18.2 to 22.7 kg) of meat in each seven- or eight-hour work day.

Maryland's leading crabbing area is around Smith Island.[37] The Virginia watermen on nearby Tangier Island catch more crabs than the Smith Islanders only because they are allowed to join the winter crab-dredging fleet in the lower bay. Winter on Smith Island means the oyster, but in the summer, Smith Island is the champion of the bay's soft-crab production.

MINERAL INDUSTRIES

Maryland's Metallic Mineral Heritage

Beginning in the colonial period and continuing into the late 1800s, Maryland was a significant producer of metallic minerals: principally ores of iron, copper, and chrome. As new and more abundant sources of these ores were found in the United States and elsewhere, Maryland's production declined.

Captain John Smith reported the occurrence of iron ore in the clays along the Patapsco River estuary as early as 1608. During Maryland's early days as a colony, England was the source of such iron items as tools, hinges, and nails. Local iron production did not begin until 1681.[38] The early iron was made in small furnaces, called bloomeries, which produced spongy bloom masses of iron that were hammered into shape at a forge.[39] Maryland had the requisites for producing iron: iron ore on the surface (often in bogs), wood for the charcoal to burn in smelting, and easy transportation by water. In 1719 the Maryland Assembly passed an Act for the Encouragement of an Iron Manufacture within this Province,[40] and before long Maryland was producing enough iron for its own needs and for export to England, where wood for charcoal was becoming scarce.

Cecil County was the site of Maryland's first furnace producing good quality, slag-free iron, the Principio Furnace (Figure 3.29). A second furnace was opened in 1723 on Gwynns Falls; today the site is within Baltimore City. Between 1719 and 1885 about fifty-five furnaces using local bog iron ores found in clay were operated in Maryland (Figure 3.30).[41] As the United States industrialized and its railroads expanded, the demand for iron increased, especially from 1830 to 1855. The principal furnaces in Maryland included Curtis Creek Furnace near Glen Burnie in Anne Arundel County (established in 1759); Antietam Furnace near Antietam in Washington County (1765); Catoctin Furnace near Thurmont in Frederick County (1774); Friendsville Furnace near Friendsville in Garrett County (1828); Nassawango Furnace near Snow Hill in Worcester County (1830); Georges Creek Coal and Iron Company Furnace at Lonaconing in Allegany County (1837); Ashland Furnace near Cockeysville in Baltimore County (1837); and Muirkirk Furnace at Muirkirk in Prince Georges County (1847).[42] The Muirkirk Furnace, the last one producing iron from local ores, closed in 1916. The discovery of the vast deposits of rich iron ores in the Mesabi Range on the Superior Upland of Minnesota, along with cheaper and more efficient transportation, was the chief factor in the demise of the Maryland iron industry.

Four different kinds of iron ore minerals found in Maryland were used in these early furnaces. Siderite occurred in the clays of the Arundel formation on the western edge of the Coastal Plain in Anne Arundel, Baltimore, Cecil, Harford, and Prince Georges counties. Limonite was found throughout the state, but most often in swamps or bogs; it came to be called "bog iron." Hematite was mined with copper from a body of igneous rock between Sykesville and Finksburg in Carroll County. Hematite also was present in Allegany County on Wills Mountain, Evitts Mountain, and south of Tussey Mountain; this deposit was part of the famous Clinton iron ore of the Appalachian chain. Magnetite, the fourth type, was found on the east side of Catoctin Mountain near Thurmont, Frederick County, and in the schists of western Harford County and western Carroll and Howard counties.[43]

Maryland was an important copper producer from before the Revolutionary War into the 1840s. Copper had been found in

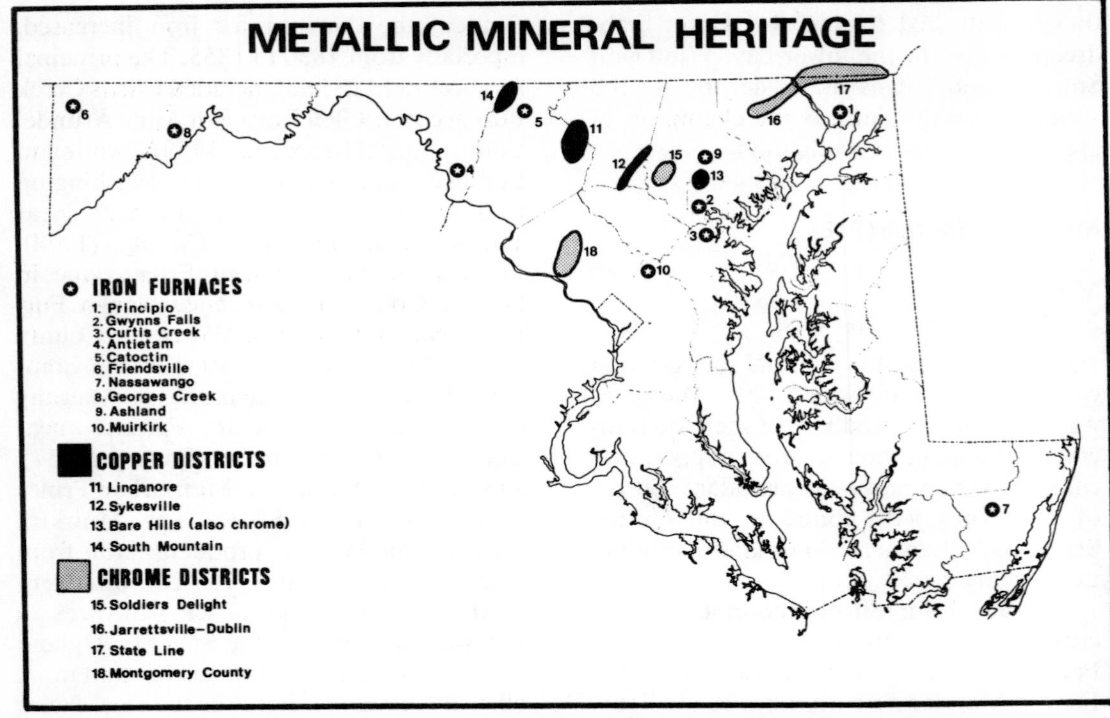

FIGURE 3.29 (*above*). Source: Based on a map from Jonathan Edwards, "Maryland's Metallic Mineral Heritage," *Maryland Conservationist* (August 1967), p. 2. FIGURE 3.30 (*left*). The remnants of the Catoctin Furnace near Thurmont in Frederick County. Courtesy, Maryland Department of Economic and Community Development.

Maryland in 1722, but profitable extraction was not started until 1750; the rich Lake Superior copper ores eventually drove all of the major Maryland copper mines out of business by 1890. Copper was produced in four areas: the Linganore District of eastern Frederick County and western Carroll County, the Sykesville District of southeastern Carroll County, the Bare Hills District of Baltimore County, and South Mountain (Figure 3.29). The Linganore District was the largest copper ore producer and was mined for the longest period of time. The last ores mined in the state came from the New London mine in the Linganore District in 1917.

At one time, all of the world's production of chrome ore came from Maryland and Pennsylvania. Chromite is found in veins in serpentine in the eastern Piedmont from southeastern Pennsylvania to the Potomac River; in Maryland the chrome-bearing districts were Soldiers Delight and Bare Hills in Baltimore County, Jarrettsville-Dublin in Harford County, State Line in Cecil County, and the Montgomery County District (Figure 3.29). Of these, Soldiers Delight was the most productive district. In 1810 chromite was found at Bare Hills on the property of the Tyson family, and mining began in 1822. From 1827 to 1860, chrome mining was the monopoly of Baltimore industrialist Isaac Tyson, Jr., who also controlled the Jarrettsville locality; Reed Mine in that district became the second largest chromite mine in the United States. The Live Pit Mine in the State Line District lay astride the Mason-Dixon line, with the opening in Pennsylvania and the operation underneath Maryland. After the discovery of chromite ores in Turkey in 1848 and in California in 1860, Maryland's production and export declined, until by the 1880s most of the mines had closed. Some minor production did continue until 1920 in the Soldiers Delight area.

Local metallic ores are no longer produced, yet Maryland has a modern metallurgical industrial complex centering on the steel operations at Sparrows Point in Baltimore County.

Contemporary Mining

The commercially important mineral resources extracted in Maryland today are those used for building materials and fuels. Nearly 165-million-dollars worth of minerals was extracted in 1975. The leading commodities were bituminous coal (30 percent of the total value) and stone (26 percent); sand and gravel accounted for another 18 percent (Table 3.10).

Limestone is quarried throughout the Piedmont and Appalachian provinces; the chief uses for it are crushed stone aggregate, cement, and agricultural lime (Figure 3.31). Limestone quarrying is important in Baltimore, Carroll, Frederick, Howard, Harford, Allegany, Washington, Montgomery, and Cecil counties (Table 3.11).

Sand and gravel are dug from the Coastal Plain, mainly for use as construction aggregate. The active sand and gravel pits shown in Figure 3.31 are concentrated on the Eastern Shore (Dorchester, Wicomico, and Worcester counties), and on the western shore, especially in the southern Maryland counties of Anne Arundel, Charles, Prince Georges, and St. Marys. A number of other sand and gravel pits are found across the state from Garrett County to Cecil County (Figure 3.32). There are a number of clay pits across Maryland where clay is extracted for brick making.

During the nineteenth century Maryland was an important supplier of building stone such as granite, marble, and sandstone. However, in the twentieth century, concrete has largely replaced stone as a common building material, and Maryland's production of cut stone has almost ceased.[44]

The most important mineral extracted in Maryland, by total value, is bituminous coal. All of the production occurs in Allegany and Garrett counties. Coal has been mined in western Maryland since the middle of the nineteenth century; present estimates of recoverable reserves (known underground inventory of coal recoverable under present economic and technological conditions) are over 500 million tn (453.5 million t).[45]

Coal

Maryland is not well known nationally for its coal production, especially when compared to the prominence of coal activities in nearby Pennsylvania and West Virginia, and indeed, many people outside of the state are surprised to learn that any coal is mined in Maryland. However, coal mining is an important industry for Allegany and Garrett counties. As oil and gas demand and prices skyrocketed in the 1970s, more attention was focused on coal (currently, coal supplies less than 20 percent

TABLE 3.10
MINERAL PRODUCTION IN MARYLAND 1975

Mineral and Unit of Measure	Quantity	Value ($1,000)
Total Mineral Production [a] (Current Dollars)		$164,919 [p]
Clays [b] (1,000 short tons)	580	1,450
Bituminous Coal (1,000 short tons)	2,606	50,502
Gem Stones	n/a	*
Lime (1,000 short tons)	15	434
Natural Gas (1,000,000 cubic feet)	93	25
Sand and Gravel (1,000 short tons)	11,786	29,477
Peat (1,000 short tons)	2	39
Stone (1,000 short tons)	14,796	43,110
Value of items that cannot be disclosed [c]		$ 39,882

Source: U. S. Department of the Interior, Bureau of Mines, Minerals Yearbook, 1975 Volume II Area Reports: Domestic, issued 1978.
n/a - Not available p - Preliminary
* Withheld to avoid disclosing individual company confidential data.
[a]Production as measured by mine shipments, sales, or marketable production (including consumption by producers).
[b]Excludes ball; included with "value of items that cannot be disclosed."
[c]Cement, ball clay, and talc.
Tonnes = .9 x short tons Cubic meters = .28 x Cubic feet

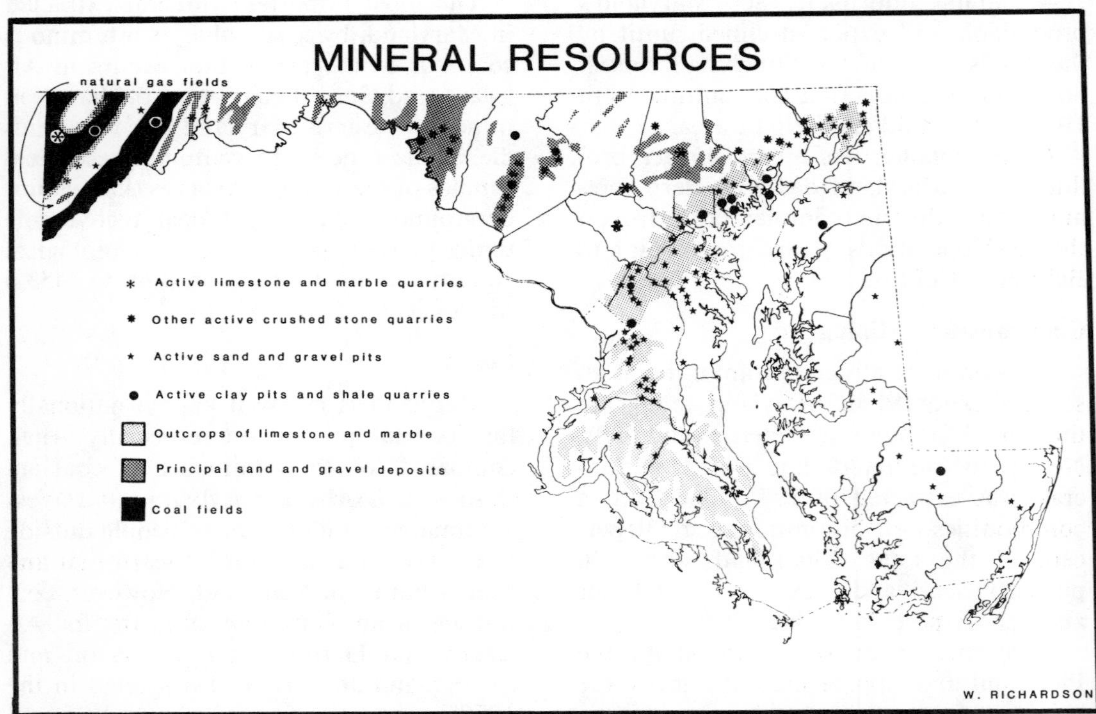

FIGURE 3.31. Source: Maryland Geological Survey, *Geologic Map of Maryland,* 1:250,000 (Baltimore, 1968).

TABLE 3.11
VALUE OF MINERAL PRODUCTION IN MARYLAND, BY POLITICAL SUBDIVISION

Political Subdivision [a]	1975 ($1,000)	1974 ($1,000)	Minerals Produced in 1975 in Order of Value
Maryland	$164,919	$172,880	
Counties			
Allegany	*	*	Coal, stone.
Anne Arundel	3,118	2,819	Sand, gravel.
Baltimore [b]	*	25,125	Stone, sand, gravel, clays.
Carroll	*	*	Cement, stone, clays.
Cecil	8,693	8,406	Stone, sand, gravel.
Charles	*	*	Sand, gravel.
Dorchester	372	368	Sand, gravel.
Frederick	*	19,329	Cement, stone, clays, lime.
Garrett	*	*	Coal, stone, sand, gravel, peat.
Harford	*	*	Sand, gravel, stone.
Howard	*	*	Stone.
Kent	*	51	Clays.
Montgomery	5,765	*	Stone.
Prince Georges	11,464	13,525	Sand, gravel, clays.
St. Mary's	*		Sand, gravel.
Washington	*	*	Cement, stone, clays.
Wicomico	*	*	Sand, gravel.
Worcester	395	396	Sand, gravel.
Undistributed [c]	$135,111	$102,859	

Source: U. S. Department of the Interior, Bureau of Mines, Minerals Yearbook, 1975 Vol. II Area Reports: Domestic, issued 1978.

Note: Data may not add to totals due to rounding.

* Withheld; included in "Undistributed."

[a] Calvert, Caroline, Queen Anne's, Somerset and Talbot counties are not listed because no production was reported. [b] Includes Baltimore City. [c] Includes some natural gas, gem stones, and values indicated by *.

FIGURE 3.32. This sand and gravel pit is in Hollywood, St. Marys County, on the Coastal Plain.

of the energy used in the United States, but comprises 80 percent of our domestic energy reserves[46]), and the coal fields of western Maryland were caught up in the worldwide, renewed interest in alternative energy sources. The port of Baltimore receives much of the Maryland coal by rail; increased demand has overtaxed the coal loading facility at the port, and ships must remain anchored in Chesapeake Bay for days, awaiting their turn to load coal.

Historical Development. There is no certain knowledge of the first discovery of coal in western Maryland. However, George Washington suggested in 1755 that beneath the soil of western Maryland, the fuel of the future might be found.[47] A map published in 1782 showed a coal mine near the mouth of Georges Creek, and by the early nineteenth century, a number of small companies were tunneling into the coal seams. One of these early localities was about a mile north of Frostburg in the valley of Jenning's Run. Between 1828 and 1838 the Maryland Assembly incorporated a dozen coal mining companies.

The chief difficulty was getting the coal to the consumers. At first the coal was floated down the Potomac in flatboats; the first recorded shipment was in 1820. Coal worth six to eight cents a bushel in Cumberland brought fifty to sixty cents at the dock in Georgetown.[48] The situation for Baltimore was not as good. In 1828 the Chesapeake and Ohio Canal was started, but this would not improve the situation of Baltimore, as the canal was being built from Cumberland to Georgetown. In the same year, construction commenced on the Baltimore and Ohio Railroad, and by 1842, the railroad had reached Cumberland, 178 mi (286 km) from Baltimore. The output of Maryland coal increased rapidly from 1,708 tn (1,549 t) in 1842 to a peak production of 5,532,628 tn (5,018,094 t) in 1907 (Figure 3.33). Given good transportation, coal was nothing less than black gold. During the last half of the nineteenth century demand was growing in the industrializing city of Baltimore: coal was needed to keep the growing number of Baltimoreans warm and to produce the

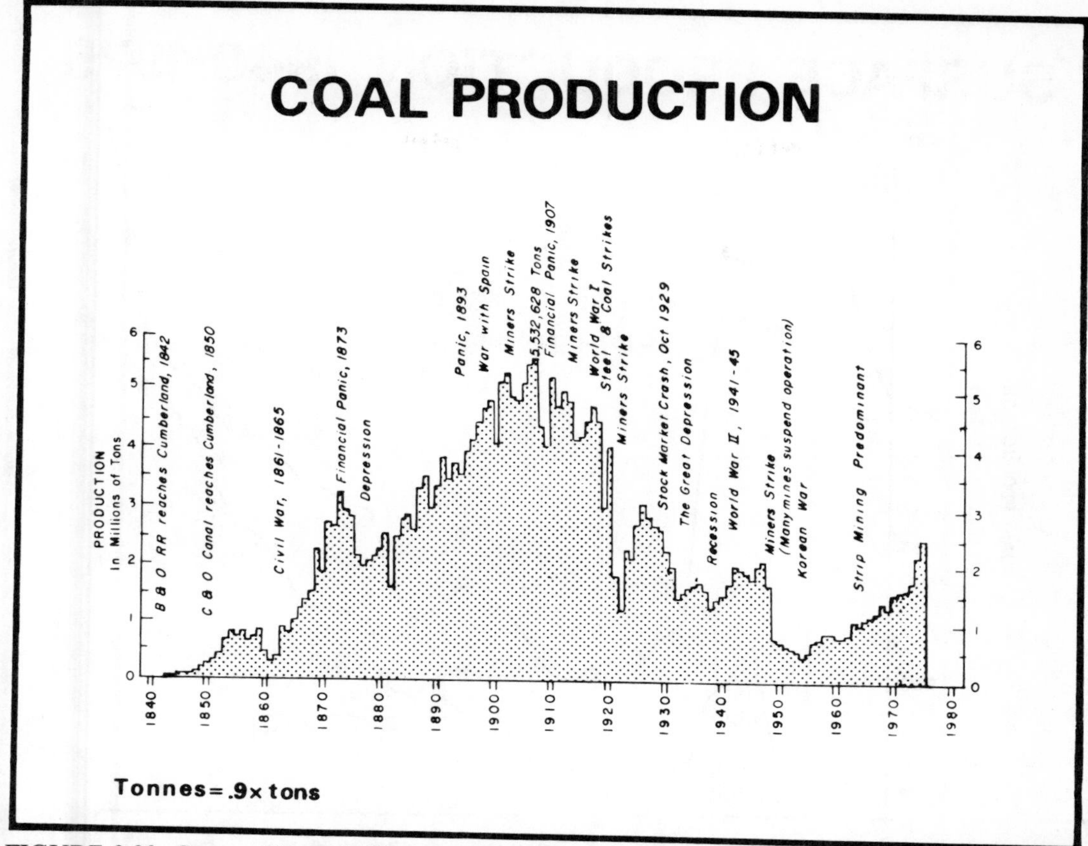

FIGURE 3.33. Source: Kenneth Weaver, James Croffoth, and Jonathan Edwards, *Coal Reserves in Maryland: Potential for Future Development,* Maryland Geological Survey, 1976, p. 2.

steam power their growing factories demanded.

The men who mined the coal had a hard, dirty, and dangerous life. They burrowed into the hillsides, putting up timber braces as they went since the bituminous coal was soft and apt to crumble at any time. Miners were paid by the long ton (2,240 lb). A miner digging 2 tn (1.8 t) a day in 1839 was paid fifty cents per ton.[49] Company towns were established, such as that of the Georges Creek Coal and Iron Company at Lonaconing.[50] At Lonaconing, the company rules specified that every employee would work every day of the year except Sundays and Christmas Day, from sunrise to sunset. Employees were paid once a month, after deductions for debts at the company store, mills, and post office.

After peaking in 1907, coal production averaged 4.5 million tn (4,081,500 t) per year until 1918; after World War I it declined and reached a low of 1,281,413 tn (1,162,242 t) in 1938. A slight revival during World War II was followed by a major labor strike in 1948 that caused many mines to close. By 1954, fewer than 500,000 tn (453,500 t) were mined. Since that year the trend has been upward.[51]

Before World War II almost all coal came from underground mines. As a result of increased demand at a time of manpower shortages during World War II, surface strip mining began. By 1975, 97 percent of the coal mined in Maryland was stripped (Figure 3.34). Employment in Maryland coal

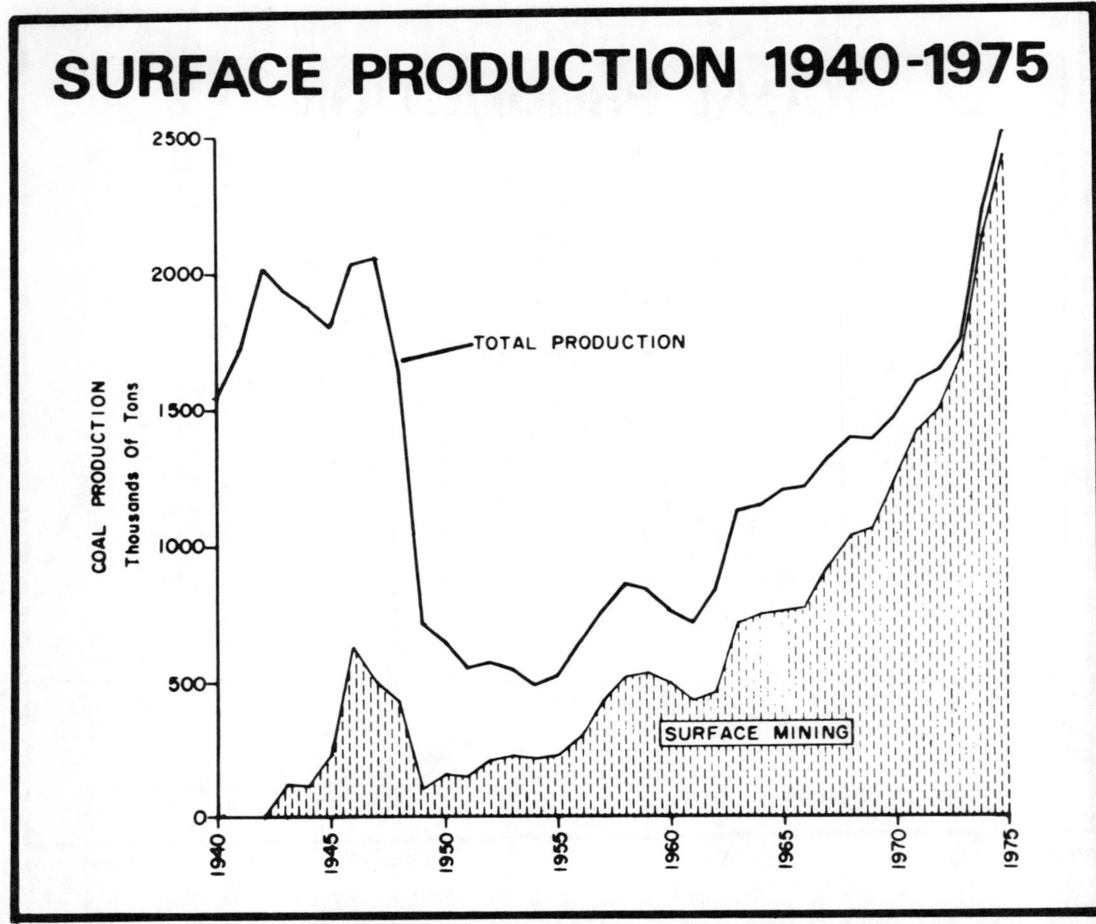

FIGURE 3.34. Source: Kenneth Weaver, James Croffoth, and Jonathan Edwards, *Coal Reserves in Maryland: Potential for Future Development,* Maryland Geological Survey, 1976, p. 3.

mines peaked at 5,000 men in 1907; today there are just over 1,000 employed.

Coal Basins. Located on the eastern fringe of the great Appalachian coal field that extends from Alabama to Pennsylvania, the coal reserves of Allegany and Garrett counties are found in five synclinal basins: the Georges Creek, Upper Potomac, Casselman, and Upper and Lower Youghiogheny (Figure 3.35). The layers of rock in these basins have been downfolded into elongated troughs so that the beds on each limb dip toward the centerline of the basin (Figure 3.36). The basins, composed of Pennsylvanian and Permian age sediments, traverse the two counties in a northeast-southwest direction (Figure 3.35). Most of the rock strata in the coal basins are of shale, siltstone, sandstone, and limestone; the coal seams themselves comprise only a small part of the total rock volume.

The coal of western Maryland is typical of the low volatile coals of the Appalachian Basin, which have a high Btu and sulfur content. Within the coal basins of western Maryland, there are eleven commercially exploitable coal seams (Figure 3.37). Total production from these coal seams in 1978 was 1,082,370 tn (981,710 t) in Allegany County and 1,768,951 tn (1,604,439 t) in

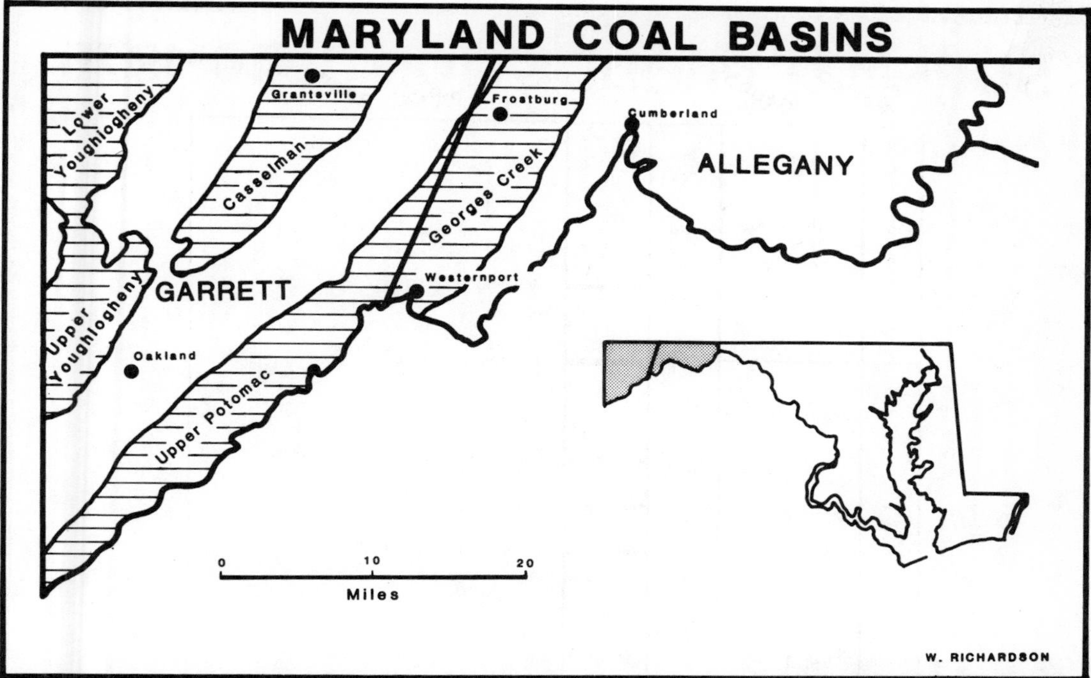

FIGURE 3.35 (*above*). FIGURE 3.36 (*below*). Source for both figures: Kenneth Weaver, James Croffoth, and Jonathan Edwards, *Coal Reserves in Maryland: Potential for Future Development,* Maryland Geological Survey, 1976, p. 4.

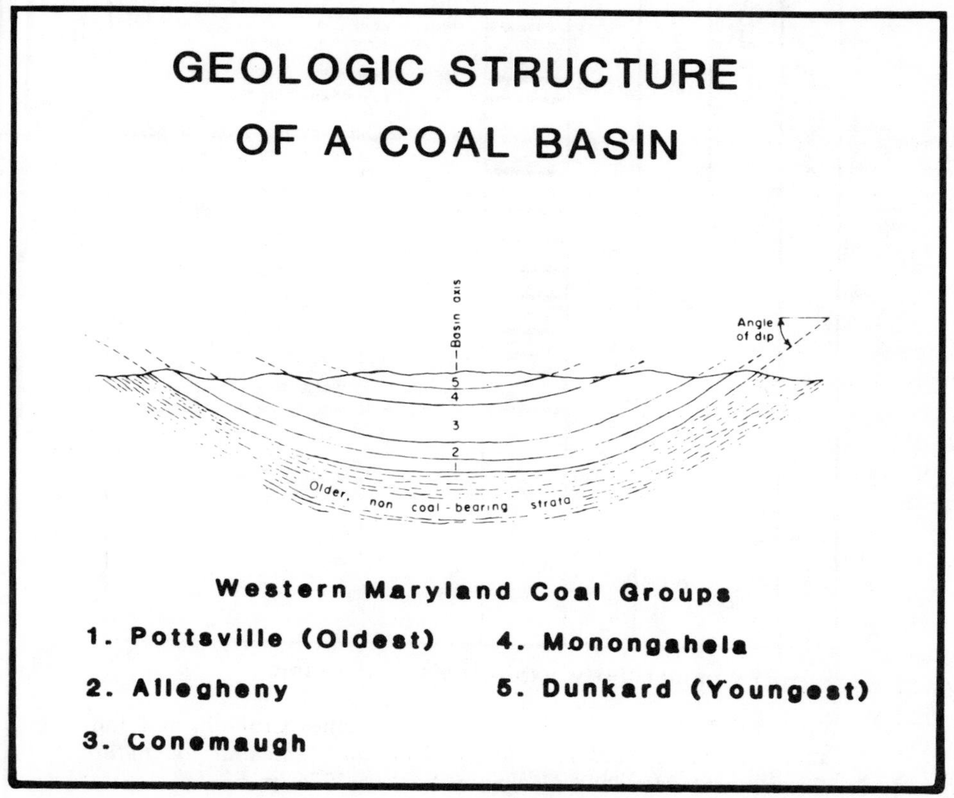

COAL BASIN GEOLOGY

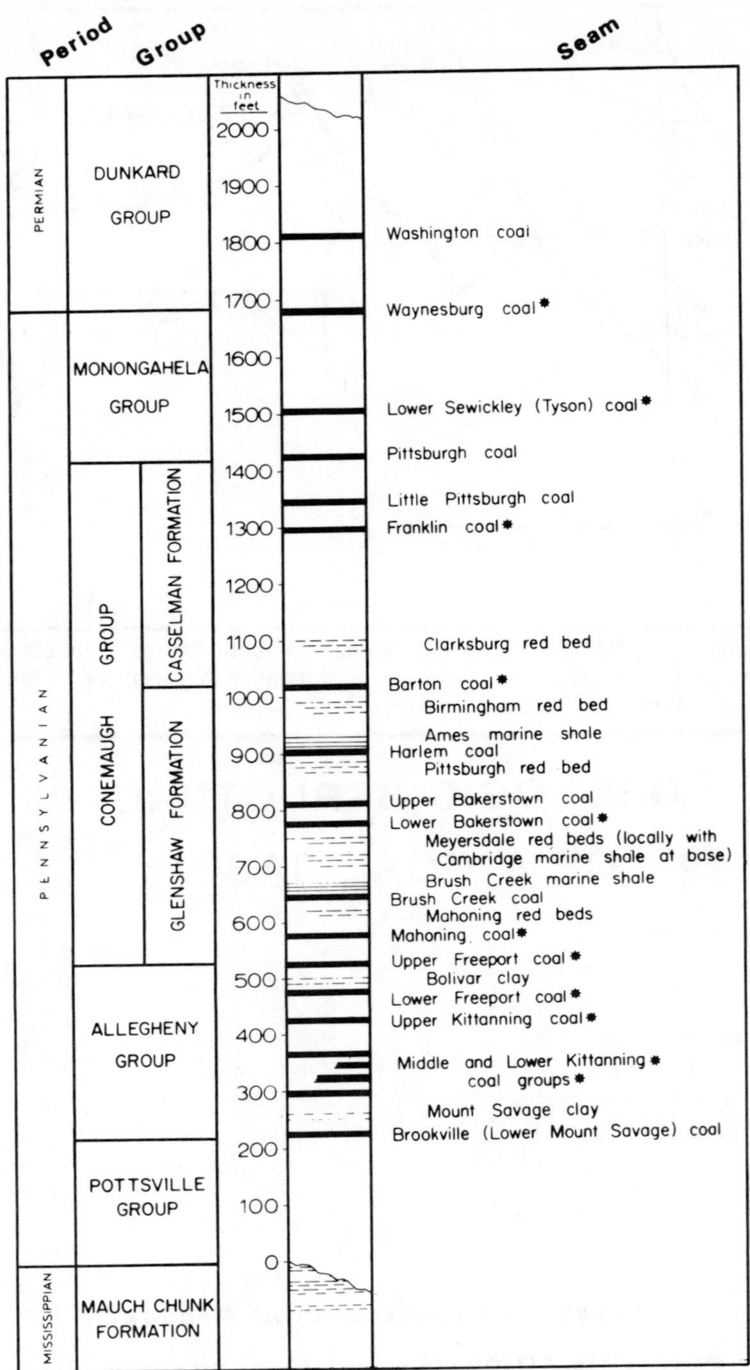

FIGURE 3.37. Source: Kenneth Weaver, James Croffoth, and Jonathan Edwards, *Coal Reserves in Maryland: Potential for Future Development,* Maryland Geological Survey, 1976, p. 6.

Garrett County (Table 3.12). The majority of the coal-bearing lands are in Garrett County; 400 sq mi (1,036 sq km) of its land are underlain by coal. Allegany County is underlain by 75 sq mi (194 sq km) of coal land in the Georges Creek basin.[52]

The Georges Creek basin is located between Big Savage Mountain on the west and Dans Mountain (Allegheny Front) on the east. The basin stretches twenty-one mi (33.8 km) from the Pennsylvania line (it continues in Pennsylvania as the Wellersbury basin) south to the Savage River. The most complete cross section of coal-bearing rock in Maryland is found in this basin. Most of the past mining activity in Maryland took place here, and numerous inactive deep mines dot this area. Over two-thirds of the coal mined in Maryland in the first half of this century came from the Georges Creek basin. The presence of the fourteen-foot-thick (4.27-meter), high quality Pittsburgh seam explains the high production. Although the Pittsburgh seam has been largely exhausted and production has subsided somewhat, the area is still responsible for almost half of the state's total production and much of its reserves (Tables 3.12, 3.13).[53]

The Upper Potomac basin is 30 mi (48.3 km) long and averages 3 mi (4.8 km) wide. The basin is transected between Maryland and West Virginia by the north branch of the Potomac River. This basin, which contains the largest contiguous reserve of coal in the state, is actually a continuation of the same synclinal structure as the Georges Creek basin. The basin lies between the Allegheny Front to the east and Backbone Mountain (a southern extension of Big Savage Mountain) to the west. The only significant settlements in the basin are four residential communities along the Potomac River: Bloomington, Kitzmiller, Shallmar, and Gorman. All other development is found along Maryland routes 135, 38, and 50; a few scattered farms are found in the hills above the Potomac. Considerable amounts of land suitable for mining still exist in the basin, although some land is in public ownership, for instance, the Potomac State Forest and federal land around the Bloomington Dam on the Potomac River.[54] Surface mining on public lands is prohibited by law.

The Casselman basin lies in central Garrett County; it is actually the southern end of the Somerset, or Berlin, basin of Pennsylvania. This basin is 18 mi (29 km) long and 5 mi (8 km) wide, running from Deep Creek Lake north to the state line; it ranks third in terms of total land area, reserves, and production of coal. In contrast to the Georges Creek and Upper Potomac basins, where coal mining dominates, the Casselman basin is diversified. Agriculture is more prevalent on the less-rugged terrain and richer soils. The coal seams here are not especially thick, and a good portion of the land is neither suitable nor available for coal surface mining. Residential areas around Grantsville and Jennings and those along Maryland routes 40, 48, and 495 limit the areas for surface mining, as do the state forest lands on the flanks of Negro and Meadow mountains.

In the extreme northwest corner of Garrett County lies the Lower Youghiogheny basin, which extends north into Pennsylvania and west into West Virginia. Winding Ridge is the eastern boundary, and Sang Run separates the basin from the Upper Youghiogheny basin. In Maryland, the basin is roughly triangular in shape, being 12 mi (19.3 km) long and a maximum of 6 mi (9.7 km) wide. Mining and development in this basin have lagged behind the three basins already described. The rugged Lower Youghiogheny area, with the Youghiogheny River flowing through it, is flanked by a deep gorge. Part of the gorge south of Friendsville is protected from surface mining by the state's Wild and Scenic Rivers program. Much potential for coal development exists in this basin. The National Freeway (U.S. Route 48) crosses the area providing easy access for coal trucks going to Cumberland and to Morgantown, West Virginia.

Located immediately south of the Lower Youghiogheny is the Upper Youghiogheny basin. Sang Run forms the northern

TABLE 3.12
COAL PRODUCTION 1978

Coal Seams in Allegany County	Production in Tons
Waynesburg	203,609.20
Sewickley	198,896.04
Redstone	70,100.00
Pittsburgh	444,902.23
Franklin	92,298.21
Wellersburg	1,032.00
Barton or Elklick	7,191.37
Bakerstown	50,391.34
Freeport	13,950.00
Total	1,082,370.39

Coal Seams in Garrett County	Production in Tons
Sewickley	25,437.97
Pittsburgh	113,963.27
Franklin	114,473.26
Barton or Elklick	58,149.51
Harlem	114,999.37
Bakerstown	411,238.29
Brush Creek	80,456.01
Mahoning	15,321.00
Freeport	431,165.75
Clarion	15,640.60
Kittanning	388,106.47
Total	1,768,951.50
Total Tonnage by Seam	2,851,321.89

Basins	Production in Tons
Lower Youghiogheny	273,754.05
Upper Youghiogheny	15,640.60
Casselman	202,688.85
Casselman (Cherry Creek)	185,132.58
Potomac	761,237.54
Georges Creek	1,412,868.27
Total	2,851,321.89

Source: Maryland Bureau of Mines, Fifty Sixth Annual Report 1978 (Annapolis: Dept. of Natural Resources, 1978).
Tonnes = .9 x tons

TABLE 3.13
RESERVES BY BASIN

Basin	Reserves in Tons
Georges Creek	354,100,000
Upper Potomac	223,500,000
Casselman	116,000,000
Lower Youghiogheny	107,000,000
Upper Youghiogheny	54,300,000
Total All Basin	854,900,000

Source: Kenneth Weaver, James Croffoth, and Jonathan Edwards, Coal Reserves In Maryland: Potential For Future Development (Annapolis: Maryland Geological Survey, 1976).

tonnes = .9 x tons

boundary, where a structural saddle separates the two synclinal basins. The basin extends west into West Virginia's Mt. Carmel Basin; on the east is found a series of knobs such as Roman Nose Mountain. The basin is 10 mi (16.1 km) long and 5 mi (8 km) wide. Little mining activity has occurred here recently. Large areas of state forests in the basin restrict surface mining, and future surface-mining activity in these thin coal-bearing strata is not expected to be significant. More potential exists for deep mining. Located nearby is the developed area in and around Oakland, the county seat of Garrett County, and the main rail line of the Chessie System (the Chesapeake and Ohio Railroad, which was combined with the Seaboard Coast Line in 1980 to form the CSX Corporation).

Deep and Surface Mining. Once again deep mining is beginning to play an important role in coal mining in western Maryland, as it did up to the time of World War II. The Mine Health and Safety Act of 1969 resulted in the closing of almost all deep mines in Maryland. With the increasing demand for coal, it is again becoming economically feasible to open deep mines; several are now in operation in the Upper Potomac basin. The newest deep mine, the Mettiki mine complex in western Garrett County financed by Japanese interests,[55] consists of three mine operations and a large coal preparation plant with storage and loading facilities employing several hundred people. In 1978 deep mining accounted for 13 percent of coal production in the state (Table 3.14). The resurgence of deep coal mining will benefit the region's economy: Deep mines have a life span of approximately fifteen years, while surface mine operations are often completed in one or two years; a deep mine requires six times more workers than a surface mine. Increased deep mining activity is expected in the future.

Surface mining has dominated the industry since 1960 (Figure 3.38). Surface mining is accomplished by successive parallel cuts in the earth. Maryland restricts the length of a cut and the amount of a site that may be exposed at one time. One completed cut is backfilled as another is dug, instead of removing the whole top of a mountain at once to expose the coal. A surface mine site resembles a gigantic but orderly construction site.[56]

Despite the increased deep-mining ac-

TABLE 3.14
SUMMARY OF 1978 STATISTICS -- COAL PRODUCTION IN MARYLAND

	Production in Net Tons			
Method of Mining	Allegany County	Garrett County	Total	Percentage of Total Production
Strip	1,080,250.24	1,373,438.29	2,453,688.53	86 %
Deep		379,872.61	379,872.61	13 %
Auger	2,120.15	15,640.60	17,760.65	1 %
TOTAL	1,082,370.39	1,768,951.50	2,851,321.89	100 %

Source: Maryland Bureau of Mines, Fifty Sixth Annual Report 1978 (Annapolis: Department of Natural Resources, 1978), p. 2.

tonnes = .9 x tons

FIGURE 3.38. A coal strip-mining operation located west of Frostburg, Allegany County.

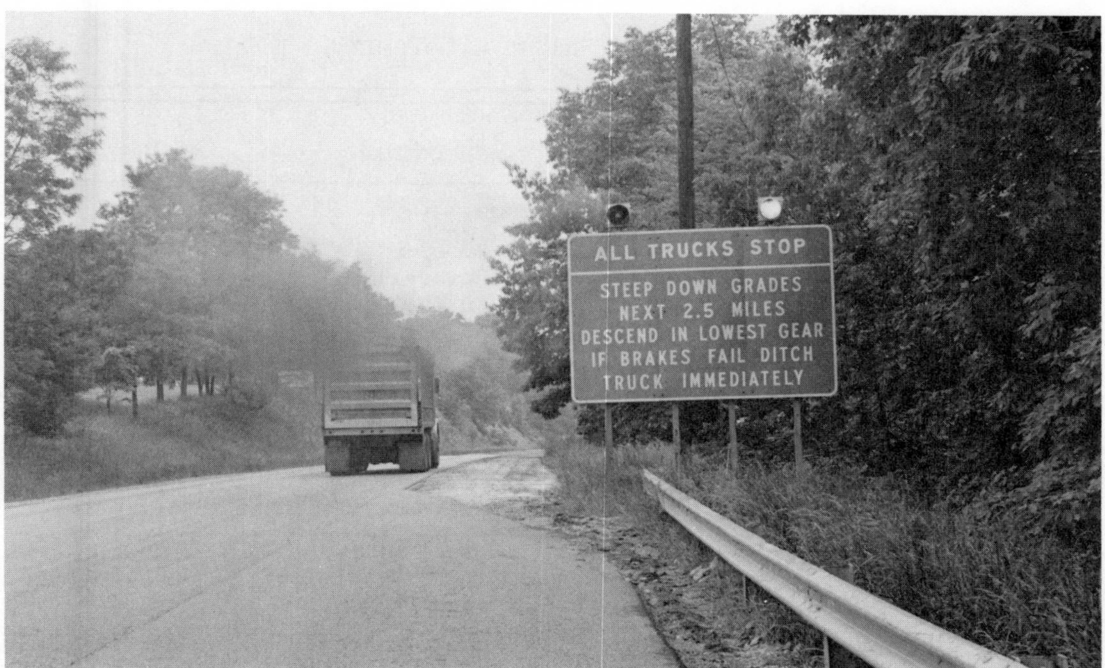

FIGURE 3.39. Coal trucks in western Maryland travel the steep, hazardous roads of the Appalachian highlands.

tivity, surface mining will maintain its present position for some time. There are still many tracts of land in each basin with seams not yet mined. With the extreme competitive market and the more stringent mining and reclamation regulations of the Federal Surface Mining Act of 1977, larger companies are coming to dominate the scene.

As surface mining increased after 1960, consolidation of production into the hands of large companies occurred. In 1977, 60 percent of total surface-mine production came from only five coal companies. Yet on a national scale, the companies in Maryland are small; there are no giant surface-mining firms such as Peabody Coal.

Coal Markets. Western Maryland coal is shipped in all directions for a number of uses. The two major markets are for *steam coal* used for the generation of electricity and *metallurgical coal* (met coal) used by steel companies to make coke. Before the coal is loaded and shipped to market, a number of critical factors must be considered. Coal companies must look at market size and location, coal output, location of the mine, quality of coal, and their ability to secure purchase orders.

Nearly 70 percent of Maryland's coal production is steam coal for the very competitive utility market. The largest consumer of local steam coal is the Virginia Electric Power Company (VEPCO) at Mt. Storm, West Virginia, which burns 300,000 tn (272,100 t) of coal per month. A smaller steam-coal customer is the Potomac Edison's R. Paul Smith generating station in Williamsport, Maryland.

Because terminal (loading and unloading) costs are so high for rail deliveries, most of the local short-distance coal shipments go by truck. Much of the Maryland coal going to VEPCO is shipped by truck over steep roads (Figure 3.39). Steam coal moves by rail to the Potomac Electric Power Company in Washington, D.C., and to other generating plants in central and

TABLE 3.15
METALLURGICAL COAL EXPORTED FROM THE CURTIS BAY TERMINAL 1977

Destination and Tonnage			
Argentina	331,948	Japan	3,406,424
Belgium	1,229,857	Korea	69,875
Brazil	92,680	Netherlands	86,065
China	43,053	Norway	34,571
Egypt	275,832	Rumania	124,117
England	168,658	Scotland	41,633
France	294,299	Sweden	219,570
Germany	135,231	Taiwan	49,226
Italy	76,197	Turkey	390,825
TOTAL			7,140,061

Source: Garrett County Development Corporation, "Feasibility Study for a Coal Preparation Facility," 1978.

tonnes = .9 x tons

eastern Maryland and in Delaware. Some Lower Youghiogheny basin coal is trucked to Masontown, Pennsylvania, or Morgantown, West Virginia, to be loaded on barges going to the Monongahela and Ohio rivers.

The demand for metallurgical coal is less than half that of steam coal, but the price is 50 percent greater, making the metallurgical coal market more competitive. Only premium-grade coals are sold as met coal, as the steel companies have stringent quality-control standards for coal they use to make coke. Large companies like U.S. Steel and Bethlehem Steel have so-called captive mines that almost entirely supply their needs. Much of the Maryland met coal is of marginal quality and must be blended with premium-grade coking coals. This means that only those coal brokers who can buy large quantities of various grades of coal and blend them can operate successfully in the domestic market. Maryland met coal eventually finds its way to companies such as National Steel, Youngstown Steel, and Wheeling–Pittsburgh Steel.

More and more Maryland met coal is sold overseas, where there are less-stringent quality requirements. The coal fields of western Maryland have a major locational advantage: it is easy to transport the coal over a relatively short distance to Baltimore's harbor. Other ports are a greater distance from the coal fields. Unit trains of 100 cars, weighing 70 tn (63.5 t) per car, connect western Maryland and south-central Pennsylvania with Baltimore. All of the Maryland met coal for export is sold to a broker and shipped out of Baltimore's Curtis Bay Terminal, operated by the Chessie System (Table 3.15). Japan has traditionally been the largest buyer of met coal for its steel industry; it is also now beginning to buy some steam coal. The major market for steam coal exports is Europe.

Domestic and industrial users of coal are very minor at this time as few homes or businesses burn coal. The largest consumer of this type is the West Virginia Company (Westvaco) paper mill at Luke, Maryland (Figure 3.40). Westvaco produces much of its own coal from a nearby surface mine. Another significant local consumer of coal is the Kelly-Springfield Tire and Rubber Company in Cumberland. Both of these plants are in Allegany County and receive their coal from the Georges Creek basin.

The Baltimore Connection. The port of Baltimore has a clear locational advantage for the export of coal, as it lies close to the interior coal fields and is the terminus for several railroads connecting it to the coal fields of western Maryland, West Virginia, and Pennsylvania. Because of its geographic location and connectivity, many coal companies are compelled to do business through the large port.

The surge in foreign demand has overloaded U.S. coal ports. There has been a great increase in European demand for U.S. steam coal to generate electricity. High oil and natural gas prices have caused many European utility plants to convert to coal. One ton of bituminous coal contains the energy of four barrels of oil. Estimates are that steam coal exports will increase fifteen times by the year 2000. The United States, often called the "Saudi Arabia of Coal," will be exporting much more coal in the future, and Baltimore promises to be a major export center.

FIGURE 3.40. The West Virginia Company's paper mill at Luke, Allegany County.

The increased demand for coal has caused considerable congestion in U.S. coal ports. Ships must wait at anchor in Chesapeake Bay for up to fifty days before they can go on to Baltimore to load coal. Thirty to forty ships are often stretched out between the Bay Bridge and Thomas Point Light near Annapolis (Figure 3.41). It costs approximately $15,000 per day to keep a ship and crew waiting. These vessels and sailors must also be serviced, and Annapolis is not equipped to do so. As foreign sailors have overrun this colonial town, a degree of social disorder and adjustment has occurred.

Between 1980 and 1985 investments of $700 million in coal-loading facilities are anticipated. A number of coal companies have already purchased property to build new coal facilities. Presently, the only coal-loading facility is that at Curtis Bay Terminal, operated by the Chessie System (recently changed to CSX). Curtis Bay currently handles 15 percent of U.S. coal exports. Approximately 12 million tn (10,884,000 t) were loaded at the terminal in 1980. Baltimore is the nation's second coal port in volume, exceeded only by Hampton Roads, Virginia (Table 3.16).

Maryland state and local planners hope that the expansion of coal export facilities in Baltimore will produce a number of regional economic spread and multiplier effects, such as higher property assessments and taxes, jobs, port services, equipment

FIGURE 3.41. Coal ships must wait in Chesapeake Bay near the Bay Bridge because of the limited loading facilities in Baltimore. Reprinted by permission of the *Baltimore Sun*.

TABLE 3.16
U. S. COAL EXPORTS 1979

Port	Tons (Millions)	Percent
Hampton Roads, Va.	33.70	52.0 %
Baltimore, Md.	9.07	14.0 %
Mobile, Ala.	1.94	3.0 %
New Orleans, La.	1.30	2.0 %
Philadelphia, Pa.	.32	.5 %
By Rail to Canada and Mexico	18.47	28.5 %
TOTAL	64.80	100.0 %

Source: Coal Exporters' Association, 1980.

tonnes = .9 x tons

sales, and construction work. This optimism is offset by a number of serious current and potential problems. For instance, coal firms could use up much of the valuable, scarce waterfront property that could yield better returns from other activities. Competition will be tough. Already Hampton Roads is improving its infrastructure; New York has indicated an interest in exporting coal; and there are other new coal exporters such as New Orleans, Mobile, and Los Angeles.

Another problem is that the main channel into Baltimore's harbor is only 42 ft (12.8 m) deep. A ship can be loaded in Baltimore with up to 85,000 tn (77,095 t) of coal but then must go to Hampton Roads to top off the cargo with another 20,000 tn (18,140 t). The deeper channel in Virginia allows ships to load up to 127,000 tn (115,189 t) of coal. Plans to deepen the Baltimore channel to 50 ft (15.24 m) have become entangled in a local environmental battle over where to dump the dredged material.

Coal and the image of a new, vibrant, clean, and upbeat Baltimore could collide.[57] A constant succession of dusty, noisy 100-car unit trains stretching 5,000 ft (1,523 m) in length will have a degrading effect on the environment. In the 1980s, eight or nine trains per day may come to the port. In urban areas, these slow moving unit trains can take from one to one and a half hours to pass a point; the possibility of congestion worries planners. Another problem with coal development is that this highly automated, capital-intensive activity will not employ large numbers of people. The many negative aspects of this kind of economic growth should be assessed before a full commitment is made to making Baltimore the nation's leading coal port.

NOTES

1. Ronald R. Boyce, *The Bases of Economic Geography,* 2nd ed. (New York: Holt, Rinehart, and Winston, 1978), p. 25.
2. Ibid., p. 29.
3. Because 1980 data were not available at the time of this writing, the most recent data available in each category were used throughout Chapter 3.
4. *Maryland Statistical Abstract, 1979* (Annapolis: Maryland Department of Economic and Community Development, 1980), p. 104.
5. Derek Thompson, ed., *Atlas of Maryland* (College Park: Department of Geography, University of Maryland, 1977), p. 49.
6. Based on item from "Eyewitness News," Channel 13 television, Baltimore, Maryland (July 28, 1980).
7. *Maryland Agricultural Statistics Summary for 1978* (College Park: Maryland Department of Agriculture, 1979), p. 23.
8. Ted Shelsby, "Shore Tomato Canneries Dwindle With Crop," *Baltimore Sun* (August 24, 1980), p. K-7.
9. Pearl Blood, *The Geography of Maryland* (Boston: Allyn and Bacon, 1961), p. 35.
10. Sara Azrael, "No-Till Bodes Farming Revolution," *Baltimore Sun* (September 7, 1980), p. K-7.
11. Blood, *Geography of Maryland,* p. 46.
12. Henry S. Baker, Jr., *Maryland Tobacco: Certain Aspects of a 300-Year-Old Enterprise* (New Brunswick, N.J.: Rutgers University Press, 1957), p. 12.
13. Thompson, ed., *Atlas of Maryland,* p. 72.
14. Ibid., p. 73.
15. James Coddington and David Derr, *An Economic Study of Land Utilization in the Tobacco Area of Southern Maryland* (College Park: University of Maryland, 1939), p. 168.
16. John Alexander and Lay Gibson, *Economic Geography,* 2nd ed. (Englewood Cliffs, N.J.: Prentice-Hall Pub., 1979), p. 144.
17. Baker, *Maryland Tobacco: Certain Aspects of a 300-Year-Old Enterprise,* p. 22.
18. Donald M. Dozer, *Portrait of a Free State: A History of Maryland* (Cambridge, Md.: Tidewater Publishers, 1976), p. 508.
19. *Maryland Agricultural Statistics Summary for 1978,* p. 26.
20. James Gutman, "Chicken Restaurant Marks New Departure for Perdue," *Baltimore Sun* (February 8, 1981), p. K-7.
21. *Maryland Agricultural Statistics Summary for 1978,* p. 31.
22. Ibid., p. 37.
23. *Maryland Statistical Abstract, 1979,* p. 100.
24. Allan C. Fisher, Jr., "My Chesapeake Queen of Bays," *National Geographic* 158 (Oc-

tober 1980), p. 447.

25. William W. Warner, *Beautiful Swimmers* (New York: Penguin Books, 1976), p. 175.

26. Ibid., p. 127.

27. Ibid., p. 63.

28. Edward Papenfuse et al., eds., *Maryland: A Guide To The Old Line State* (Baltimore: Johns Hopkins University Press, 1976), p. 274.

29. "Oyster Industry Is Alive and Well," *Maryland Business Journal* (August–September 1980), p. 20.

30. Warner, *Beautiful Swimmers,* p. 11.

31. John J. Alford, "The Chesapeake Oyster Fishery," *Annals of the Association of American Geographers* 65, (1975):231.

32. Ibid., p. 233.

33. Dozer, *Portrait of a Free State,* p. 498.

34. "Keep on Shucking," *Baltimore Sun* (December 7, 1980), p. K-4.

35. Warner, *Beautiful Swimmers,* p. 90.

36. Ibid., p. 60.

37. This somewhat isolated island can be reached by the ferry *Island Belle* out of Crisfield. There are three communities on Smith Island: Ewell, Tylerton, and Rhodes Point. People with the name of Evans constitute about half the population of Ewell; Bradshaws dominate Tylerton; and the Tylers reign in Rhodes Point. This quaint island from an age past has no local government. The children go daily by school boat to Crisfield.

38. Jonathan Edwards, "Maryland's Metallic Mineral Heritage," *Maryland Conservationist* (August 1967), p. 1.

39. Ibid., p. 2.

40. Ibid.

41. Ibid.

42. Thompson, ed., *Atlas of Maryland,* p. 41.

43. Ibid.

44. Kenneth Weaver, James Croffoth, and Jonathan Edwards, *Coal Reserves in Maryland: Potential for Future Development* (Annapolis: Maryland Geological Survey, 1976), p. 1.

45. Carl Bode, *Maryland: A History* (New York: W. W. Norton, 1978), p. 90.

46. Ibid., p. 92.

47. Ibid.

48. Ibid.

49. "Feasibility Study for a Coal Preparation Facility" (Oakland, Md.: Garrett County Development Corp., 1978), p. 3.

50. Weaver, Croffoth, and Edwards, *Coal Reserves in Maryland,* p. 2.

51. "Feasibility Study for a Coal Preparation Facility," p. 3.

52. Ibid., p. 5.

53. Marsha Clark, "Coal in Western Maryland: A Closer Look," *Metro News,* Johns Hopkins University Center for Metropolitan Planning and Research, 6, no. 10 (February 1, 1978), p. 4.

54. Ibid., p. 2.

55. C. Fraser Smith, "Coal: Boom or Hazard for Baltimore?" *Baltimore Sun* (January 4, 1981), p. K-7.

56. Clark, "Coal in Western Maryland: A Closer Look," p. 2.

57. Smith, "Coal: Boom or Hazard for Baltimore?" p. K-7.

CHAPTER 4

MANUFACTURING, RECREATION, AND TOURISM

MANUFACTURING

Maryland is set within the American Manufacturing Belt and the high demand markets of megalopolis. In addition to its excellent relative location, Maryland is endowed with other factors necessary for manufacturing such as capital, labor supply, and transportation connectivity.

Both heavy and light industries are important in Maryland's economy. Heavy industries are represented by steel mills, shipyards, petroleum refineries, chemical plants, and truck assembly lines. Some of the leading light industries include food processing, printing and publishing, and clothing.

The Baltimore area traditionally has had the largest concentration of manufacturing in the state, with a wide range of activities ranging from sugar refining to production of chemicals and steel (Figures 4.1, 4.2, 4.3, 4.4). This area has economic and locational linkages of basic iron and steel, fabricated metals, and metal-using industries, resulting in the predominance of many durable manufacturing activities.[1] In western Maryland, manufacturing is centered at Hagerstown in Washington County and Cumberland in Allegany County; both are transportation centers. The largest plant in Hagerstown is the Mack Truck Company, employing 4,400 people; in addition there is a wide variety of other activities including apparel, printing and publishing, food processing, and machinery. Cumberland is noted for its textiles and apparel, plate glass (Pittsburgh Plate Glass Company), and tires (Kelly-Springfield Tire Company, the largest plant in Cumberland, employs 2838 people).

Montgomery and Prince Georges counties in the Washington, D.C., area are emerging as industrial growth areas. Montgomery County is a center for scientific research and development; Prince Georges County's industry is less research oriented, being primarily machinery, chemicals, food products, and miscellaneous goods. The Baltimore and Washington, D.C., metropolitan areas have contrasting manufacturing patterns: Baltimore is dominated by metals, engineering, and food products industries; Washington, D.C., by printing and publishing, food products, and machinery. Southern Maryland and Garrett County have only minor roles in manufacturing, but the Eastern Shore contributes significantly, especially in food products related to the area's seafood and agricultural activities.

Although Maryland's industry has been

FIGURE 4.1. Raw sugar being unloaded at the Domino Sugar Company's refinery in Baltimore harbor.

FIGURE 4.2. The Lehigh Cement Company plant in the port of Baltimore.

FIGURE 4.3. Procter and Gamble produces home soap products at this plant in the port of Baltimore.

FIGURE 4.4. Ship repairs and refittings are done in this Baltimore dry-dock complex.

dominated by primary metals, food products, and machinery, these currently are not growth areas. Over the past twenty years the major manufacturing growth has occurred in printing and publishing, paper products, machinery and electrical goods, and stone, clay, and glass products.[2] On the other hand, employment decreases are taking place in the primary and fabricated metals and apparel industries.

The wide range of manufacturing in Maryland shows up in the Standard Industrial Classifications of the Bureau of the Census: of the 451 different kinds of manufacturing included, 363 (over 80 percent) are represented in Maryland. Another index of diversity in manufacturing is the fact that of the eighteen leading manufacturing industries, not one accounts for more than one-sixth of the total manufacturing employment in the state.[3]

Measures of Manufacturing Activity

A number of standard variables are used to indicate the level of manufacturing activity in a region: employment, value added, earnings, and number of firms. The geographical patterns of each of these are described.

Employment. In 1980 Maryland ranked twenty-fifth among the states in number of people employed in manufacturing. The Baltimore metropolitan area has approximately 70 percent of Maryland's total 242,000 manufacturing employees (Table 4.1). The overall number of employees in the Baltmore area increased between 1976 and 1978, although slight decreases occurred in fabricated metal products, food products, and chemicals. The leading industry by employment, primary metals, is led by the Bethlehem Steel Corporation's

TABLE 4.1
MANUFACTURING EMPLOYMENT IN THE BALTIMORE SMSA BY SELECTED STANDARD INDUSTRIAL CLASSIFICATION (SIC)
ANNUAL AVERAGES: 1978, 1977, and 1976
(RANKED BY NUMBER OF EMPLOYEES IN 1978)

		Number of Employees (In Thousands)			Percentage Change	
SIC	Industry	1978	1977	1976	1978/77	1978/76
All Manufacturing TOTAL		164.3	161.2	160.8	1.9	2.2
Durable Goods Total		99.2	95.9	95.4	3.4	4.0
33	Primary Metal Industries	29.1	28.8	28.7	1.0	1.4
36	Electrical Equipment	19.8	18.5	18.2	7.0	8.8
37	Transportation Equipment	15.2	14.0	14.4	8.6	5.6
35	Machinery, Exclud. Electrical	11.3	11.0	11.1	2.7	1.8
34	Fabricated Metal Products	8.7	9.2	8.8	-5.4	-1.1
32	Stone, Clay & Glass Products	6.7	6.5	6.5	3.1	3.1
25	Furniture & Fixtures	3.1	2.9	2.8	6.9	10.7
38	Instruments & Misc. Manufacture	2.7	2.7	2.7	0.0	0.0
24	Lumber & Wood Products	2.6	2.3	2.2	13.0	18.2
Non-Durable Goods Total[a]		65.1	65.3	65.5	-0.3	-0.6
20	Food & Kindred Products	14.8	16.2	15.9	-8.6	6.9
27	Printing & Publishing	12.0	12.0	11.8	0.0	1.7
28	Chemicals & Allied Products	11.3	11.4	11.1	-0.9	1.8
23	Apparel & Related Products	10.9	10.4	10.5	4.8	3.8
26	Paper & Allied Products	7.7	7.6	7.7	1.3	0.0
30	Rubber & Misc. Plastic Products	6.1	5.7	5.7	7.0	7.0
22	Textile Mill Products	0.8	0.8	1.0	0.0	-0.2
29	Petroleum & Coal Products	0.9	0.7	1.0	28.6	-0.1

Source: Maryland Department of Human Resources, Nonagricultural Wage and Salary Employment, 1978.

[a]Nonadditive.

FIGURE 4.5. The Bethlehem Steel Corporation's Sparrows Point steel plant, one of the largest in the nation, occupies 2,100 acres just southeast of Baltimore on the Patapsco River near Chesapeake Bay. The plant turns out a variety of steel products such as plates, pipe, reinforcing bars, wire rods, wire, nails and staples, wire strand, sheets, blackplate, and tinplate. Alongside the plant, at the left of the photo, is Bethlehem's Sparrows Point shipyard, one of the major builders of tankers and cargo vessels in the United States. Courtesy Bethlehem Steel Corporation.

large Sparrows Point mill in coastal Baltimore County, employing 19,000 people (Figure 4.5). Table 4.2 shows that total manufacturing employment in the Baltimore Standard Metropolitan Statistical Area (SMSA) peaked at 209,700 in 1967. State employment peaked at 289,400 in 1969. Manufacturing employment in the Baltimore SMSA is nearly three times that in the Washington, D.C., SMSA.

Maryland has experienced a decline in manufacturing employment similar to states to the north, while states to the south have been experiencing gains (Table 4.3). It is clear from the information in Tables 4.1, 4.2, and 4.3 that manufacturing is not an employment growth sector for the state as a whole. Of all the states, Maryland had the second-lowest manufacturing employment growth rate between 1958 and 1972.[4]

The primary metals industry is followed in number of employees by food and kindred products, electrical equipment, and printing and publishing. Of these leaders, electrical equipment and printing and publishing have had the strongest growth rates (Table 4.4). Long-term trends for the durable and nondurable industries of Maryland are shown in Figure 4.6.

The majority of recent growth in the Maryland economy has been in the nonmanufacturing sector, yet manufacturing remains a major element in the state's economy, accounting for approximately 12.5 percent of total employment.[5]

Value Added. Value added by manufac-

TABLE 4.2
NUMBER OF EMPLOYEES IN MANUFACTURING:
MARYLAND AND SELECTED OTHER AREAS: 1963-1977

In Thousands

Year[a]	USA	South Atlantic[b]	Maryland	Baltimore SMSA	Washington SMSA[c]
1977	19,727.2	2,823.7	241.9	166.5	59.3
1976	18,753.0	2,734.5	242.8	164.9	61.8
1975	18,302.2	2,616.6	244.0	167.5	64.0
1974	19,844.8	2,845.5	259.3	181.6	62.8
1973	19,871.0	2,861.5	263.4	184.9	58.9
1972	19,026.8	2,739.1	255.6	179.7	54.9
1971	18,363.1	2,580.2	254.4	178.5	52.8
1970	19,217.2	2,618.0	272.4	194.8	55.2
1969	20,035.5	2,673.3	289.4	208.0	57.3
1968	19,527.6	2,572.4	284.7	206.7	55.1
1967	19,323.2	2,501.5	287.6	209.7	55.5
1966	19,024.0	2,415.5	288.6	206.5	55.1
1965	18,010.2	2,285.2	270.7	193.7	53.1
1964	17,268.5	2,182.0	263.0	190.2	52.5
1963	16,958.4	2,124.8	263.7	190.5	50.1

Source: U. S. Department of Commerce, Bureau of the Census, *1977 Census of Manufactures*, Preliminary Report issued October, 1979, Geographic Area Series and *Annual Survey of Manufactures 1973*, Area Statistics, M73 (AS)-6.

[a] 1972, 1967, and 1963 are census years and are recorded in the *Census of Manufactures*. All other years represent estimates derived from a representative sample of manufacturing establishments canvassed in the *Annual Survey of Manufactures* and may therefore differ from results that would have been obtained from a complete canvass of all manufacturing establishments.

[b] Includes: Maryland, Delaware, West Virginia, District of Columbia, Virginia, North Carolina, South Carolina, Georgia, Florida

[c] The definition of this SMSA was revised for 1972. Historical data prior to 1972 are based on the old definition. Data tabulated under the new 1972 definition differ by 5 percent or less from 1972 data tabulated under the old definition.

TABLE 4.3
NUMBER OF EMPLOYEES ENGAGED IN MANUFACTURING, MARYLAND AND SELECTED EASTERN STATES, REGIONALLY RANKED BY RATE OF GROWTH IN TOTAL EMPLOYEES: 1977 and 1972

Region and State	Total Employees		Production Workers		Total Employees
	1977 (1,000)	1972 (1,000)	1977 (1,000)	1972 (1,000)	1977/72 Percent Growth
UNITED STATES	19,727	19,027	13,713	13,527	3.7
MIDEAST					
Delaware	69	69	33	38	NC
Pennsylvania	1,347	1,418	938	1,015	-5.0
MARYLAND	242	256	162	177	-5.5
New Jersey	784	836	491	547	-6.2
New York	1,551	1,679	985	1,076	-7.6
SOUTHEAST					
South Carolina	375	345	301	283	8.7
Kentucky	277	259	208	200	6.9
Virginia	395	375	302	293	5.3
Alabama	340	323	272	262	5.3
Tennessee	488	467	373	367	4.5
Georgia	484	468	376	369	3.4
North Carolina	764	744	610	604	2.7
West Virginia	119	121	91	93	-1.7

Source: U. S. Department of Commerce, Bureau of the Census, 1977 Census of Manufactures, Preliminary Report issued October, 1979, Geographic Area Series and Annual Survey of Manufactures 1973, Area Statistics, M73 (AS)-6.

TABLE 4.4
MANUFACTURING EMPLOYMENT IN MARYLAND BY SELECTED STANDARD INDUSTRIAL CLASSIFICATION (SIC)
ANNUAL AVERAGES: 1978, 1977, and 1976
(RANKED BY NUMBER OF EMPLOYEES IN 1978)

		Number of Employees (In Thousands)			Percentage Change	
SIC	Industry	1978	1977	1976	1978/77	1978/76
All Manufacturing TOTAL		242.0	235.1	232.4	2.9	4.1
Durable Goods TOTAL		133.9	127.6	125.5	4.9	6.7
33	Primary Metal Industries	30.7	30.0	30.1	2.3	2.0
36	Electrical Equipment	27.7	25.5	24.0	8.6	15.4
37	Transportation Equipment	19.5	18.0	21.4	8.3	-8.9
35	Machinery, excluding Electrical	19.5	17.9	14.5	8.9	34.5
34	Fabricated Metal Products	11.6	12.1	11.9	-4.1	-2.5
32	Stone, Clay & Glass Products	9.7	9.5	9.7	2.1	0.0
38	Instruments & Misc. Manufacture	6.3	6.1	5.9	3.3	6.8
24	Lumber and Wood Products	4.9	4.6	4.3	6.5	14.0
25	Furniture & Fixtures	4.0	3.9	3.7	2.6	8.1
Non-Durable Goods TOTAL		108.1	107.5	106.9	0.6	1.1
20	Food & Kindred Products	29.8	31.1	31.8	-4.2	-6.3
27	Printing and Publishing	21.9	21.6	19.9	1.4	10.1
23	Apparel & Related Products	17.6	16.6	16.9	6.0	4.1
28	Chemicals & Allied Products	14.2	14.3	14.0	-0.7	1.4
30	Rubber & Misc. Plastic Products	10.3	9.8	9.6	5.1	7.3
26	Paper and Allied Products	9.9	10.0	10.2	-1.0	-2.9
31	Leather & Leather Products	2.0	2.0	1.9	0.0	5.3
22	Textile Mill Products	1.3	1.3	1.5	0.0	-13.3
29	Petroleum & Coal Products	1.1	0.8	1.1	37.5	0.0

Source: Maryland Department of Human Resources, Nonagricultural Wage and Salary Employment, 1978.

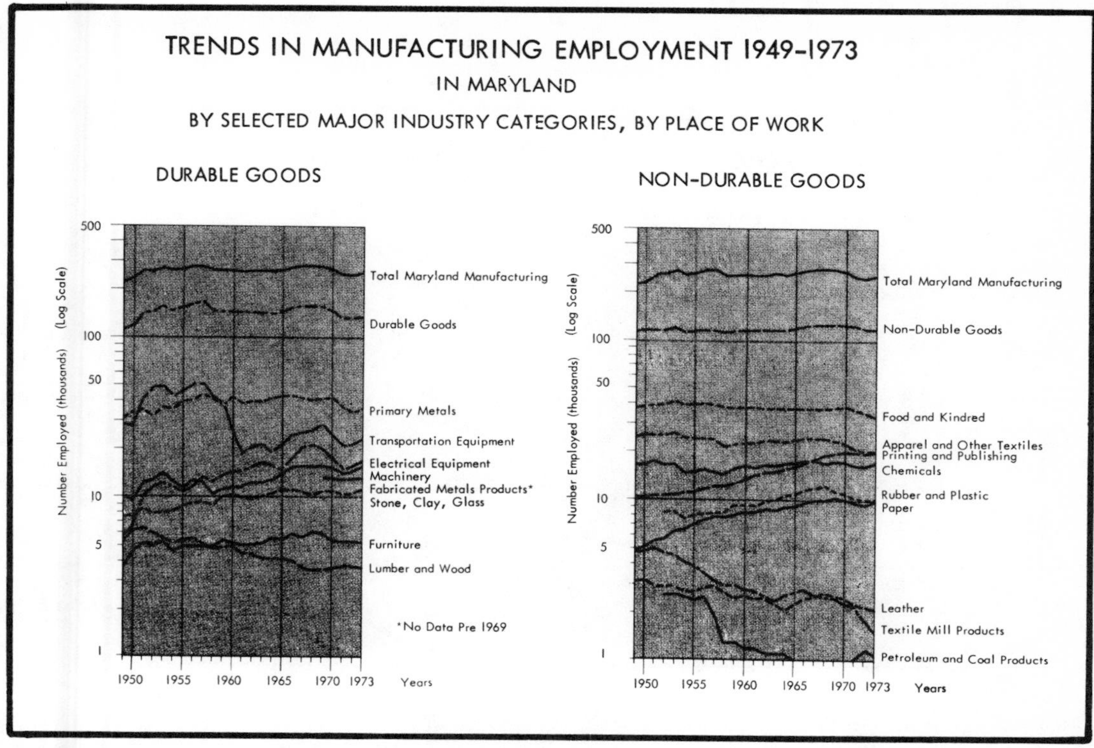

FIGURE 4.6. Source: Derek Thompson, ed., *Atlas of Maryland,* © 1977, p. 59 (College Park: Department of Geography, University of Maryland). Reprinted with permission.

turing is obtained by subtracting the cost of materials (raw materials, parts, supplies, fuel, goods purchased for resale, power, and purchased services) from the value of outgoing shipments.[6] Value added increased 51 percent in Maryland between 1972 and 1977 (Table 4.5). Food and kindred products led all industries in value added in 1977. The highest value-added growth rates have been in paper and allied products, electric and electronic equipment, and machinery. Compared with states to the north and south, the value added by manufacture in Maryland was lower than that in all except Delaware and West Virginia (Table 4.6).

The greatest increases in value added have occurred in the Baltimore–Washington, D.C., development corridor (Figure 4.7). Secondary areas of importance in Carroll, Frederick, Washington, and Allegany counties are centered on the cities of Westminister, Frederick, Hagerstown, and Cumberland respectively (see Figure 1.1 for locations).

Earnings. In 1978, Maryland workers in all jobs earned $19.42 billion; of this total, $4.114 billion (21 percent) was earned in manufacturing jobs. Weekly and hourly earnings are highest in the primary metals industry, followed by transportation equipment. The lowest wages are earned by workers producing textiles, apparel, and leather products (Table 4.7).

Number of Firms. In 1978 there were 2,344 manufacturing firms in Maryland. Baltimore, as the traditional dominant location for manufacturing firms in the state, had 841 (36 percent). However, from 1950 to 1978 the number of manufacturing firms in Baltimore City decreased from 1,738 to 841, while the number of firms in several surrounding suburban counties was increasing: in Baltimore County from 130 to

TABLE 4.5

VALUE ADDED BY PRINCIPAL MANUFACTURING INDUSTRIES IN MARYLAND
RANK BY DOLLAR VOLUME: 1977 and 1972

SIC	INDUSTRY	1977 ($1,000,000)	1972 ($1,000,000)	PERCENT CHANGE 1977/72
ALL	INDUSTRIES	$7,108.7	$4,706.9	51.0
20	Food and Kindred Products	1,021.9	687.9	48.6
36	Electric and Electronic Equipment	957.1	508.2	88.3
33	Primary Metals	843.4	626.5	34.6
35	Machinery, Excluding Electrical	714.6	396.2	80.4
28	Chemicals and Allied Products	683.9	415.0	64.8
37	Transportation Equipment	582.9	440.8	32.2
27	Printing and Publishing	480.8	345.2	39.3
26	Paper and Allied Products	326.0	159.5	104.4
34	Fabricated Metal Products	319.8	253.9	26.0
23	Apparel	294.9	216.5	36.2
32	Stone, Clay and Glass Products	260.3	228.7	13.8
24	Lumber and Wood Products	92.8	74.5	24.6
39	Miscellaneous	78.3	47.4	65.2
38	Instruments and Related Products	69.6	48.6	43.2
25	Furniture and Fixtures	49.2	40.4	21.8
29	Petroleum and Coal Products	40.0	33.5	19.4
31	Leather and Leather Products	33.5	25.0	34.0
22	Textile Products	18.1	19.2	-5.7
30	Rubber and Misc. Plastic Products	Not shown	140.0	

Source: U.S. Department of Commerce, Bureau of the Census, 1977 Census of Manufactures, Preliminary Report issued October, 1979, Geographic Area Series, MC77-A-21(P) and Annual Survey of Manufactures 1973, Area Statistics, M73 (AS)-6.

TABLE 4.6

VALUE ADDED BY MANUFACTURE, MARYLAND AND SELECTED EASTERN STATES,
REGIONALLY RANKED BY RATE OF GROWTH: 1977 and 1972

REGION AND STATE	VALUE ADDED ($1,000,000) 1977	1972	PERCENT CHANGE 1977/72
UNITED STATES	$585,798	$353,973	65.5
MIDEAST			
Pennsylvania	35,998	23,519	53.1
MARYLAND	7,109	4,707	51.0
New York	44,677	30,404	46.9
New Jersey	23,197	16,409	41.4
Delaware	1,618	1,292	25.2
SOUTHEAST			
Virginia	10,765	6,178	74.2
Georgia	12,500	7,386	69.2
Kentucky	9,440	5,682	66.1
Tennessee	12,635	7,662	64.9
North Carolina	18,105	11,015	64.4
South Carolina	8,095	4,966	63.0
Alabama	8,349	5,065	64.8
West Virginia	3,908	2,647	47.6

Source: U.S. Department of Commerce, Bureau of the Census, 1977 Census of Manufactures, Preliminary Report issued October, 1979, Geographic Area Series and Annual Survey of Manufactures 1973, Area Statistics, M73(AS)-6.

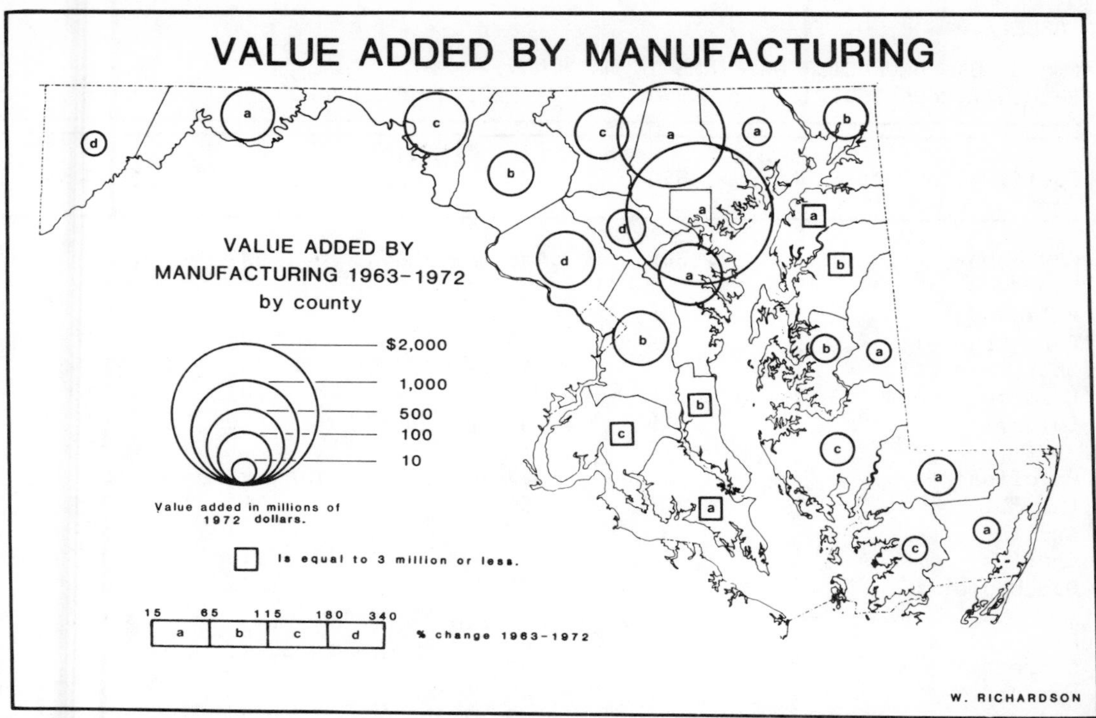

FIGURE 4.7. Source: U.S. Department of Commerce, Bureau of the Census, *Census of Manufacturers*, 1972 Area Series, Maryland, MC67(3), p. 21.

TABLE 4.7

AVERAGE WEEKLY AND AVERAGE HOURLY EARNINGS IN MANUFACTURING INDUSTRIES IN MARYLAND BY PLACE OF WORK: 1978 and 1976
(RANKED BY 1978 DOLLAR VALUE OF AVERAGE WEEKLY EARNING)

SIC	INDUSTRY	WEEKLY EARNINGS 1978	WEEKLY EARNINGS 1976	HOURLY EARNINGS 1978	HOURLY EARNINGS 1976
	All Manufacturing Average	$257.75	$218.59	$6.46	$5.52
	Durable Goods Average	293.35	246.83	7.19	6.14
	Non-durable Goods Average	216.06	186.03	5.54	4.77
33	Primary Metals Industries*	379.25	306.59	9.25	7.57
37	Transportation Equipment*	342.77	287.75	8.34	7.07
28	Chemicals & Allied Products	283.53	241.12	6.64	5.66
32	Stone, Clay & Glass Products*	282.46	234.99	6.94	5.86
35	Machinery, except Electrical*	273.88	221.91	6.68	5.69
27	Printing & Publishing	273.31	227.40	6.99	6.00
34	Fabricated Metal Products*	251.93	218.29	6.19	5.43
36	Electric & Electronic Equip.	226.59	194.25	5.54	4.82
26	Paper & Allied Products	212.27	182.74	5.19	4.49
20	Food & Kindred Products	208.83	185.02	5.41	4.72
38	Instruments & Miscellaneous Manufacturing*	203.60	N/A	5.09	N/A
24	Lumber & Wood Products*	182.28	N/A	4.65	N/A
25	Furniture & Fixtures*	175.64	N/A	4.38	N/A
22	Textile Mill Products	153.90	133.90	4.05	3.46
23	Apparel & Related Products	146.58	128.49	4.20	3.64
31	Leather & Leather Products	138.36	118.01	3.67	2.98

Source: Maryland Department of Human Resources, Research and Analysis Division.
*Durable Goods Industries

TABLE 4.8

NUMBER OF MANUFACTURING FIRMS IN MARYLAND, BY POLITICAL SUBDIVISION: 1978, 1977, 1970, 1960, 1950

POLITICAL SUBDIVISION	1978	1977	1970	1960	1950
MARYLAND	2,344	2,416	2,641	3,217	3,088
Allegany	55	57	56	81	67
Anne Arundel	111	115	99	104	59
Baltimore City	841	860	1,100	1,513	1,738
Baltimore	264	266	244	208	130
Calvert	9	10	17	20	7
Caroline	26	27	33	49	52
Carroll	56	56	67	89	83
Cecil	40	42	52	64	57
Charles	21	25	22	30	18
Dorchester	52	54	65	82	67
Frederick	65	66	67	83	78
Garrett	17	17	23	36	33
Harford	42	45	47	71	54
Howard	51	59	29	24	18
Kent	15	15	20	26	21
Montgomery	203	209	168	131	79
Prince George's	198	188	178	145	71
Queen Anne's	20	20	21	24	9
St. Mary's	9	12	23	39	20
Somerset	32	30	41	61	50
Talbot	37	41	51	58	44
Washington	78	77	103	114	124
Wicomico	72	74	77	102	112
Worcester	30	28	38	55	70
Nondistributable	0	23	0	8	27

Source: Maryland Department of Human Resources, Employment and Payrolls Covered by the Unemployment Insurance Law of Maryland, first quarter issue for the stated years.

264 and in Anne Arundel from 59 to 111. Much of this industrial decentralization has taken place in northern Anne Arundel County, in eastern Howard County close to Interstate 95 (I-95), and in eastern and central Baltimore County in the Hunt Valley industrial park. A similar pattern has emerged around Washington, D.C., in Prince Georges and Montgomery counties (Table 4.8). The geographical pattern of firms shown in Figure 4.8 reveals the primary dominance of Baltimore City and its surburban counties, the large number of firms near Washington, D.C., and outlying centers such as Salisbury in Wicomico County and Hagerstown in Washington

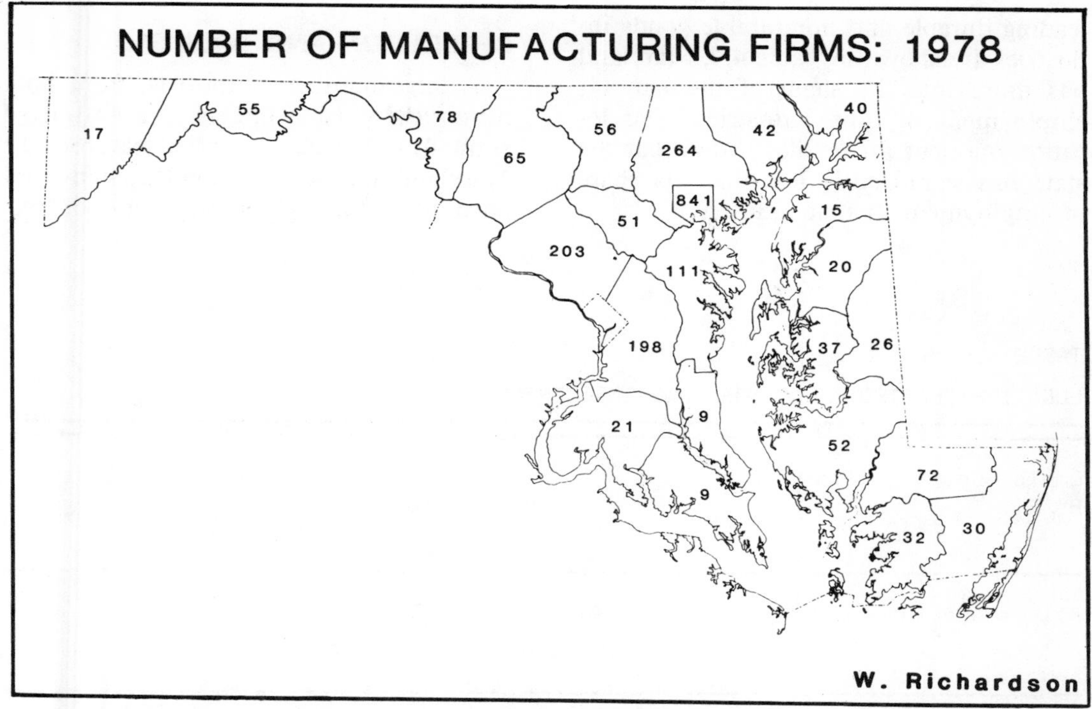

FIGURE 4.8. Source: Data from Maryland Department of Economic and Community Development, *Statistical Abstract of Maryland 1979.*

County (see Figure 1.1 for locations). This illustrates the geographical pattern of manufacturing, one of concentration at a few specific locations.

Measuring Industrial Location

Economic geographers have developed a number of indexes to measure industrial location. One of these is the location quotient, which measures the degree to which a specific region has more or less than its share of any particular industry.[7] The location quotient is a ratio of ratios. To illustrate: the ratio for the United States of the number of employees in primary metals industries to the total number of employees in manufacturing is

$$\frac{1{,}206{,}000}{19{,}727{,}000} = 6.1\%$$

The ratio of these two variables for Maryland is

$$\frac{30{,}700}{242{,}000} = 12.7\%$$

The location quotient for the primary metals industries of Maryland is found by dividing the state ratio by the national ratio. A location quotient of 1.0 means that Maryland has exactly its share of the nation's employment in primary metals manufacturing; a quotient greater than 1.0 means the state has more than its share, and, conversely, a quotient smaller than 1.0 indicates that the state has less than its share. For primary metal manufacturing, Maryland's location quotient is

$$\frac{.127}{.061} = 2.08$$

This shows that Maryland has considerably more than its share of the nation's employment in primary metals.

The location quotients for a number of

leading durable and nondurable goods industries are shown in Table 4.9; Maryland has more than its share of the nation's employment in nine industries. The location quotient for textiles shows that the state has significantly less than its share of employment in that industry.

RECREATION AND TOURISM

A large number of tourists, from both inside and outside the state, are attracted annually to Maryland's varied features. The Maryland landscape provides many opportunities for sight-seeing, outdoor rec-

TABLE 4.9

LOCATION QUOTIENTS FOR MARYLAND INDUSTRIES

Employment By SIC [a]	Maryland	U.S.	Location Quotient $\frac{C}{A} \div \frac{D}{B}$
All manufacturing	A	B	
	242,000	19,727,000	
Durable Goods	C	D	
33 Primary Metals	30,700	1,206,000	2.08
36 Electrical Equipment	27,700	1,967,000	1.14
37 Transportation Equipment	19,500	1,956,000	.82
35 Machinery--excluding Electrical	19,500	2,337,000	.67
34 Fabricated Metals	11,600	1,653,000	.57
32 Stone, Clay, Glass Products	9,700	696,000	1.14
38 Instruments & Miscellaneous	6,300	654,000	.79
24 Lumber & Wood Products	4,900	751,000	.53
25 Furniture & Fixtures	4,000	487,000	.68
Non-Durable Goods			
20 Food & Kindred Products	29,800	1,695,000	1.43
27 Printing & Publishing	21,900	1,181,000	1.50
23 Apparel & Related Products	17,600	1,315,000	1.09
28 Chemicals & Allied Prod.	14,200	1,088,000	1.04
30 Rubber & Misc. Rubber Products	10,300	749,000	1.08
26 Paper & Allied Products	9,900	702,000	1.14
31 Leather Products	2,000	251,000	.62
22 Textiles	1,300	911,000	.11
29 Petroleum & Coal Products	1,100	209,000	.45

Data Sources: Maryland Department of Economic & Community Development, Maryland Statistical Abstract 1979. U. S. Bureau of the Census, Statistical Abstract of the United States 1978.

[a] Standard Industrial Classification used by the U. S. Bureau of the Census.

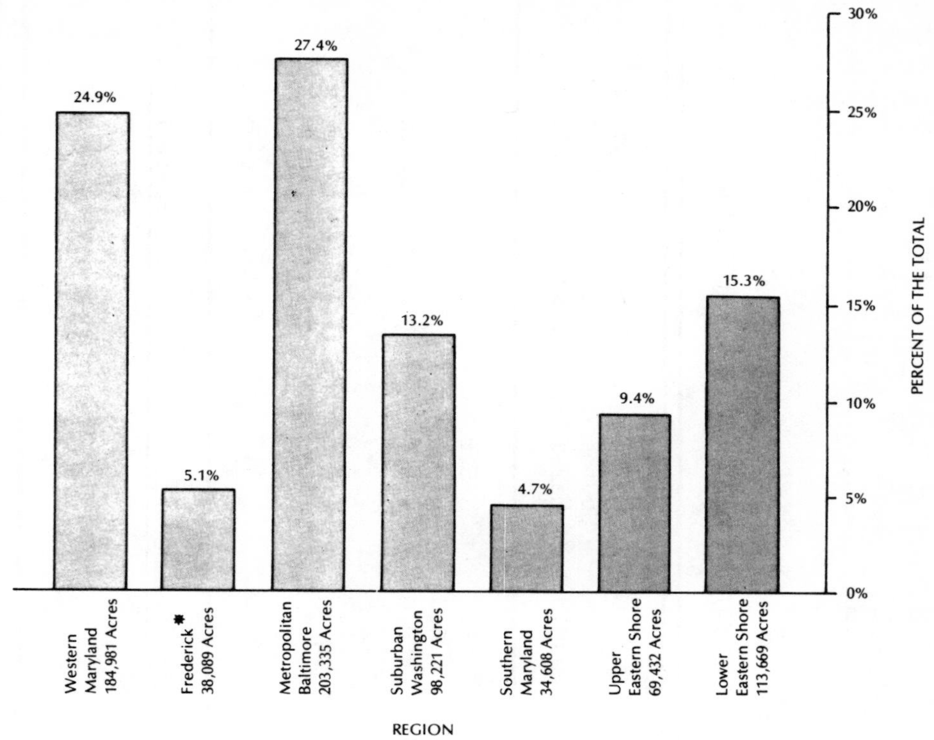

FIGURE 4.9. Source: Maryland Department of State Planning, *Maryland Outdoor Recreation and Open Space Plan,* 1978, p. 63.

reation, and visits to historic sites and special events. A Maryland Department of State Planning inventory of outdoor recreation areas and open spaces identifies over 5,000 such sites,[8] with a combined area of over 740,000 acres (299,700 ha) (Figure 4.9). The Baltimore metropolitan region contains nearly 28 percent of the total acreage, and western Maryland has nearly 25 percent; the smallest percentage (4.7) is in southern Maryland.

Much of the land used for outdoor recreation is open space that is publicly owned. The percentages of land in various ownership categories in the major regions of the state are shown in Table 4.10. The highest percentages of federal, county, municipal, and quasi-public ownership are found in metropolitan Baltimore; the largest ownership category in western Maryland is the state. Private ownership of open space and recreation areas is important on the upper and lower Eastern Shore.

A large part of the 900 sq mi (2,331 sq km) of publicly-owned outdoor recreation and open space land is in western Maryland. Considerably smaller areas are found in the Baltimore–Washington, D.C., urban corridor and the upper Eastern Shore (Figure 4.10).

TABLE 4.10
STATEWIDE OUTDOOR RECREATION AND OPEN SPACE AREAS: PERCENTAGE OF OWNERSHIP DISTRIBUTION BY REGION

Ownership	Western Maryland	Frederick County	Baltimore Metropolitan	Suburban Washington	Southern Maryland	Upper Eastern Shore	Lower Eastern Shore	State of Maryland
Federal	10.4	4.5	47.0	16.8	6.0	1.8	13.5	100 %
State	46.3	4.1	12.8	5.3	4.3	7.5	19.7	100 %
Regional	0.0	0.0	0.0	100.0	0.0	0.0	0.0	100 %
County	7.7	3.7	61.2	7.0	8.9	9.5	2.0	100 %
Municipal	6.2	25.2	62.4	2.2	0.0	1.4	2.6	100 %
Quasi-Public	5.3	2.9	34.3	24.9	2.5	29.3	1.8	100 %
Private	20.2	4.5	16.0	6.2	5.2	26.2	21.7	100 %
Total Acreage	24.9	5.1	27.4	13.2	4.7	9.4	15.3	100 %

Source: Maryland State Department of Planning, Maryland Outdoor Recreation and Open Space Plan, 1978, p.68.

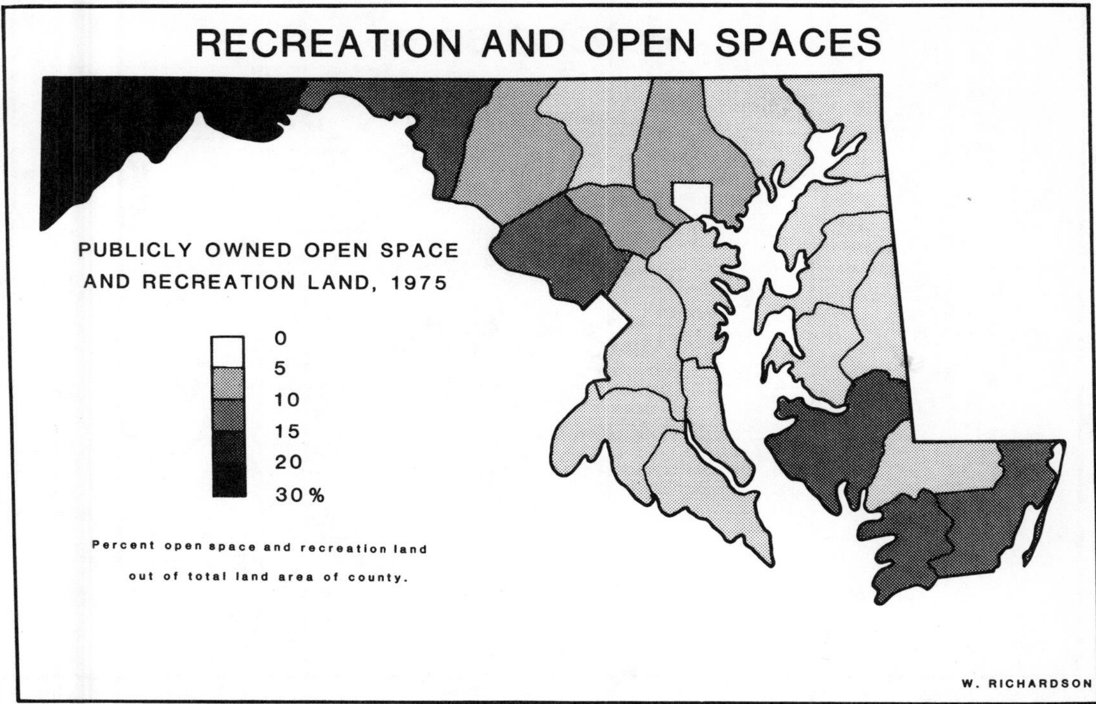

FIGURE 4.10. Source: Maryland Department of State Planning, *Maryland Outdoor Recreation and Open Space Plan,* 1978, p. 67.

Recreation and tourism are a significant part of the Maryland economy. General sight-seeing is especially important in areas with historic sites and special features, such as in and around Washington, D.C., Annapolis, and Baltimore. Other historic sites are widespread throughout the state (Figure 4.11). Boating is a major activity on Chesapeake Bay, especially in the lower Eastern Shore where there are many second homes. Summertime beach recreation is vitally important to Ocean City in Worcester County, a regional mecca for the fun-in-the-sun set. Also important in Ocean City is the business generated by conventions. The state's sales tax receipts from food, beverage, and lodging sales show the significance of recreation and tourism. In 1975, nearly 5.5 percent ($23 million) of all state sales tax receipts came from these three categories. Most of these sales tax revenues were generated in the urban corridor, but the tremendous importance of recreation and tourist-related revenues in Worcester County, centered on Ocean City, is shown in Figure 4.12.

Second homes play a small but growing part in the leisure economy of Maryland. Small portions of two major U.S. second-home areas are found in the state: the Atlantic-seaboard cottage belt and the Appalachian mountains recreation-home area.[9] About half of the second homes in the state are found in Worcester, Anne Arundel, Calvert, and Garrett counties (Figure 4.13).

Regional Features

The rugged mountains, high wooded ridges, and narrow stream valleys of western Maryland make this a prime outdoor recreation area. The considerable seasonal weather variations allow for winter sports as well as for summer boating, hiking, camping, and fishing. Historic sites include

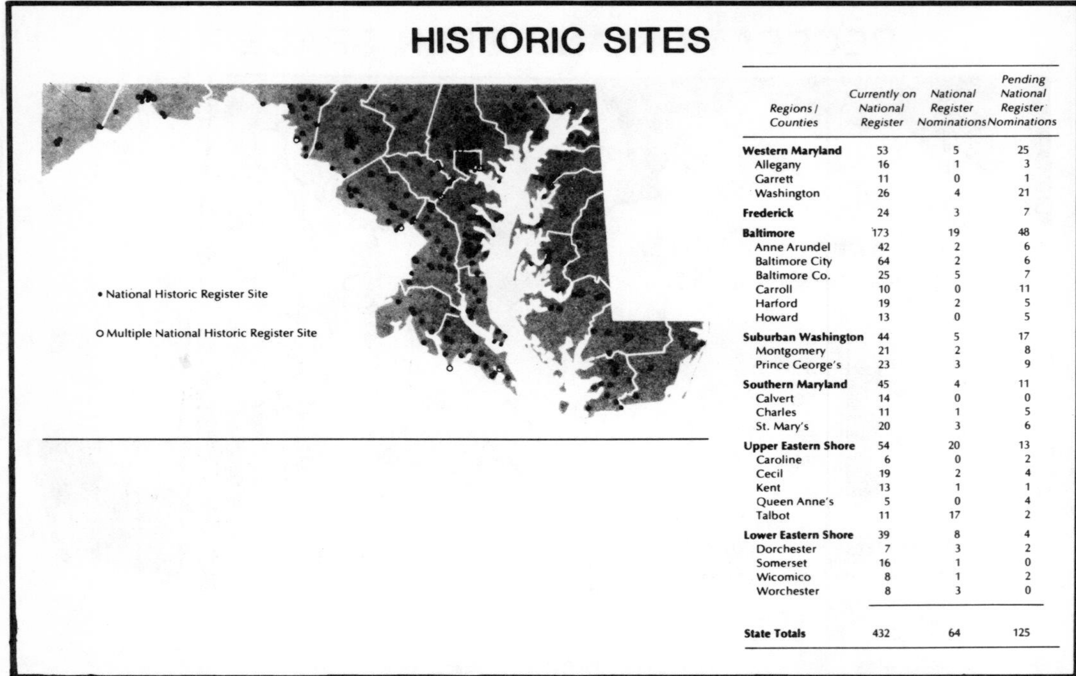

Regions / Counties	Currently on National Register	National Register Nominations	Pending National Register Nominations
Western Maryland	53	5	25
Allegany	16	1	3
Garrett	11	0	1
Washington	26	4	21
Frederick	24	3	7
Baltimore	173	19	48
Anne Arundel	42	2	6
Baltimore City	64	2	6
Baltimore Co.	25	5	7
Carroll	10	0	11
Harford	19	2	5
Howard	13	0	5
Suburban Washington	44	5	17
Montgomery	21	2	8
Prince George's	23	3	9
Southern Maryland	45	4	11
Calvert	14	0	0
Charles	11	1	5
St. Mary's	20	3	6
Upper Eastern Shore	54	20	13
Caroline	6	0	2
Cecil	19	2	4
Kent	13	1	1
Queen Anne's	5	0	4
Talbot	11	17	2
Lower Eastern Shore	39	8	4
Dorchester	7	3	2
Somerset	16	1	0
Wicomico	8	1	2
Worchester	8	3	0
State Totals	432	64	125

FIGURE 4.11. Source: Maryland Department of State Planning, *Maryland Outdoor Recreation and Open Space Plan,* 1978, p. 84.

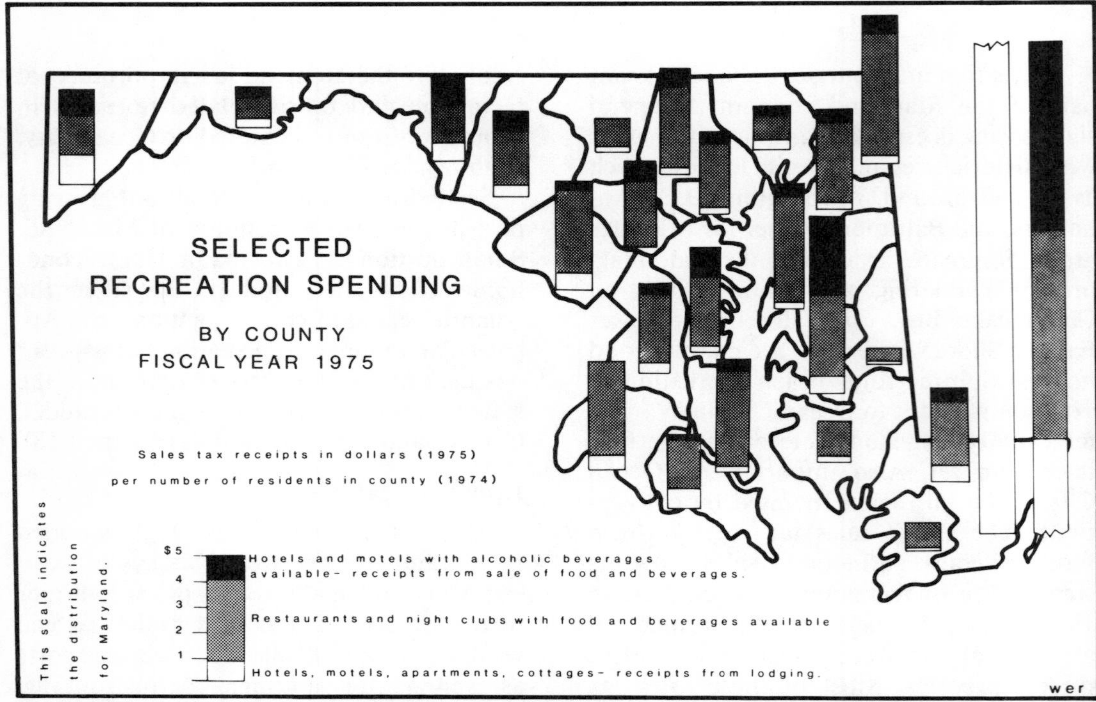

FIGURE 4.12. Source: Adapted from Derek Thompson, ed., *Atlas of Maryland,* © 1977 (College Park: Department of Geography, University of Maryland). Reprinted with permission.

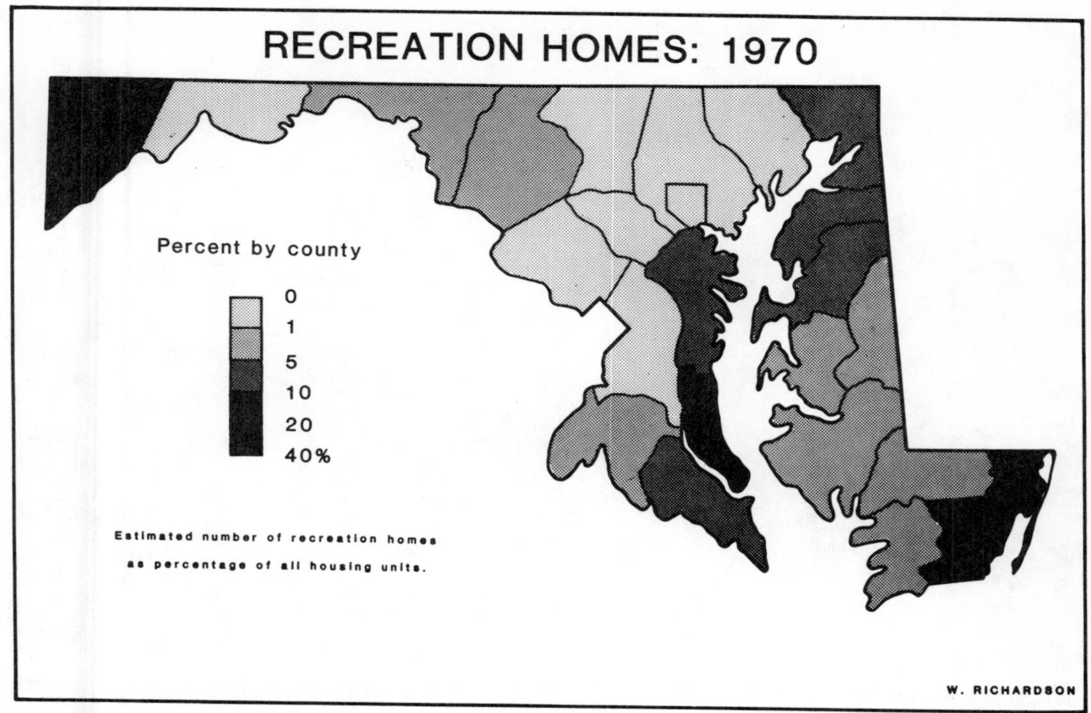

FIGURE 4.13. Source: Maryland Department of State Planning, *Maryland Outdoor Recreation and Open Space Plan,* 1978.

Fort Frederick, Antietam, and Smith Mountain battlefields, as well as the Chesapeake and Ohio (C&O) Canal National Park. There are many excellent state and local parks including Swallow Falls, Herrington Manor, New Germany, Rock Gap, Greenbrier, and Deep Creek Lake state parks (Figure 4.14). Also found in this area are two major trail systems, the Appalachian Trail and the Potomac Heritage Trail.

The Piedmont and Blue Ridge area centers on the broad lowland of the Frederick Valley. The region's economy is in transition, as it is affected by Baltimore-Washington metropolitan growth; it is changing from an agricultural base to one of manufacturing, trade, and services.[10] The area has a number of federal and state recreation areas including Catoctin Mountain National Park and Cunningham Falls State Park. The C&O Canal National Park traverses the area, and the newly designated Monocacy Battlefield National Park will be tied into a regional Civil War battlefield trail. Other outdoor recreation features include Gambrill State Park, Sugarloaf Mountain and its trail system, the Frederick Municipal Forest, Point of Rocks, and the Monocacy Scenic River.

Baltimore City and its surrounding metropolitan counties form a region dissected by more than six major river systems flowing through the Piedmont and Coastal Plain. Some 2.3 million people reside in this region, about 56 percent of the state's population. The region, centering on the city of Baltimore, has a highly diversified economy, a favorable location, and an interregional transportation network centered on the port and the Baltimore-Washington International Airport. The newly developed Harborplace on the Inner Harbor at Baltimore has been a heavily visited attraction since its opening in July 1980 (Figure 4.15). Another special feature of the area is the Preakness Festival in May, culminating in the Run for the Blackeyed Susans (Figure 4.16). Because the Baltimore region's pop-

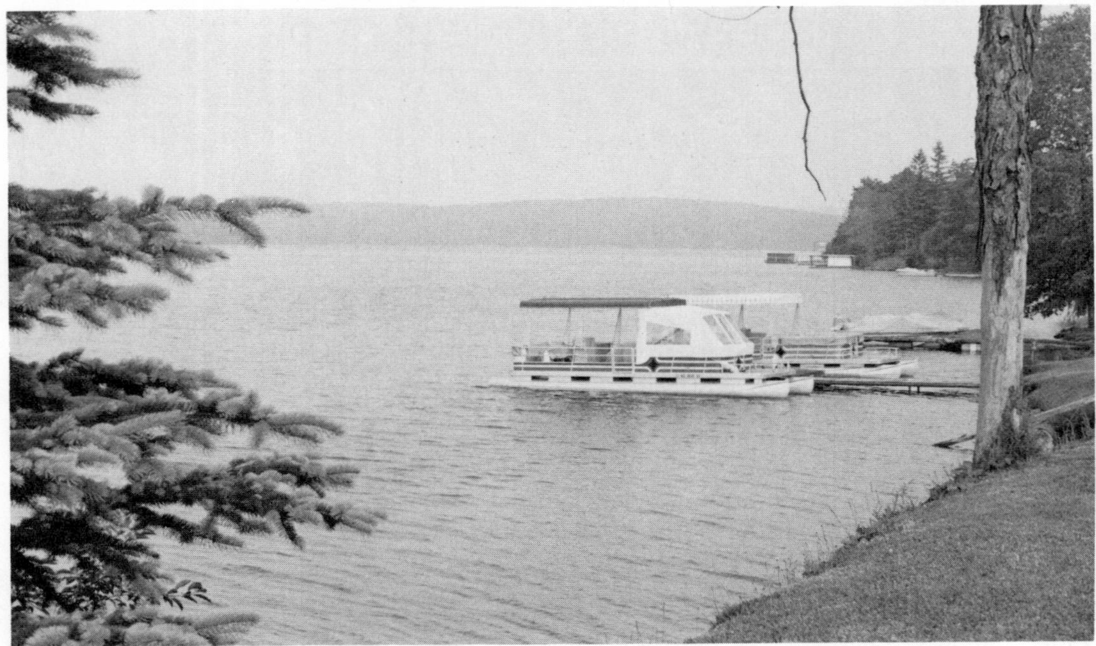

FIGURE 4.14. Deep Creek Lake in Garrett County is a favorite summer recreation spot in western Maryland.

FIGURE 4.15. Harborplace in Baltimore, built by the Rouse Company, has become a focus for the city. Courtesy, Baltimore Office of Promotion and Tourism.

FIGURE 4.16. The famous Preakness horse race is run in May at Pimlico Racetrack in Baltimore. Courtesy, Baltimore Office of Promotion and Tourism.

ulation is made up of so many different ethnic groups, on summer weekends the city sponsors a series of ethnic festivals that attract thousands of visitors (Figure 4.17). The concentrated urban population causes great competition for land, often rendering it difficult to satisfy the demand for recreation space. The majority of the inner-city population is restricted from use of many of the outlying parks, because they are not accessible to those without means of transportation. Some of the surrounding parks include Patapsco and Gunpowder state parks, as well as the Liberty, Loch Raven, and Prettyboy reservoirs. If the harbor channel is dredged and the spoil dumped behind a dike surrounding Hart and Miller islands, then a 1,000 acre (405 ha) state park on Chesapeake Bay will have been created to provide a 2-mile (3.22-kilometer) shoreline for boating, fishing, and picnicking.

From 1960 to 1970, 50 percent of Maryland's population growth occurred in Montgomery and Prince Georges counties in suburban Washington, D.C. The main stimulant to urbanization in the area has been growth and decentralization of government activities. This area has one of the finest stream valley and natural resource–oriented park systems in the country including Rock Creek, Cabin John, Sligo Branch, Cosca, Watkins, and Patuxent River parks. Other state and federal facilities include Seneca State Park, Rosaryville State Park, and the C&O Canal National Park; two wildlife-management areas in this region are the Merkle Wildlife and the McKee-Besher areas. The Maryland Department of State Planning has recommended that the Patuxent River zone be protected and preserved as a greenbelt between the Baltimore and Washington regions.

The largely agricultural southern Mary-

FIGURE 4.17. The Lithuanian festival is one of many ethnic festivals held annually in Baltimore. Courtesy, Baltimore Office of Promotion and Tourism.

FIGURE 4.18. The reconstructed colonial capitol on the original site in St. Mary's City.

FIGURE 4.19. Hunting ducks and geese has long been a favorite sport on the Eastern Shore. Courtesy, William Panageotou.

land region has 600 mi (965.4 km) of river and Chesapeake Bay shoreline and extensive areas of marsh and wetlands. The population of this area increased 33.4 percent between 1960 and 1970. While agricultural and seafood-industry employment has declined, urban employment and the recreation business have continually expanded. The region has five state parks, a state forest, two state environmental areas, and three natural resource–management areas. Boating, swimming, fishing, camping, picnicking, hiking, and sightseeing are popular in southern Maryland. The focus of visitor attention is on St. Mary's City, the original capital of Maryland (Figure 4.18). Travel to and within the region was greatly facilitated by the completion of the new Patuxent River Bridge connecting lower Calvert County with St. Marys County. The location of this area near the nation's capital is also an asset in attracting visitors.

The most significant recreation resource of the upper Eastern Shore is Chesapeake Bay and the major rivers, the Choptank, Chester, Sassafras, Elk, Northeast, and Susquehanna. Between 1960 and 1970 the population grew at a slow .8 percent per annum. Most of the growth occurred in the centers of Elkton, Chestertown, Denton, Federalsburg, and Easton. The four state parks in this relatively isolated region of the state are Elk Neck, Tuckahoe, Wye Oak, and Martinak.

The lower Eastern Shore is an area of extensive wetlands that provide unique habitats for wintering, migrating, and nesting waterfowl and other wildlife (Figure 4.19); recreation is restricted in the wildlife-management areas because of the delicate nature of much of these habitats. Wicomico and Worcester counties are the leading attractions, due primarily to Salisbury and Ocean City (Figure 4.20). Recreation is concentrated in Ocean City and Assateague, Milburn Landing, Shad Landing, and James Island state parks.

FIGURE 4.20. Ocean City is a regional vacation center for beach lovers and a meeting place for conventioneers. Courtesy, Maryland Department of Economic and Community Development.

NOTES

1. Derek Thompson, ed., *Atlas of Maryland* (College Park: Department of Geography, University of Maryland, 1977), p. 59.
2. Ibid.
3. *Maryland Manufacturers Directory 1979–1980* (Annapolis: Maryland Department of Economic and Community Development, 1979), p. xi.
4. Thompson, ed., *Atlas of Maryland,* p. 59.
5. *Maryland Statistical Abstract 1979* (Annapolis: Maryland Department of Economic and Community Development, 1980), p. 128.
6. Ibid.

7. John Alexander and Lay Gibson, *Economic Geography,* 2nd ed. (Englewood Cliffs, N.J.: Prentice-Hall Pub., 1979), p. 304.

8. *Maryland Outdoor Recreation and Open Space Plan* (Baltimore: Maryland Department of State Planning, 1978).

9. Thompson, ed., *Atlas of Maryland,* p. 45.

10. *Maryland Outdoor Recreation and Open Space Plan,* p. 229.

CHAPTER 5

MARYLAND'S PAST IN TODAY'S LANDSCAPE

The contemporary regions of Maryland, previously described in terms of their differentiating characteristics, can be best understood in a historical-geographical context. The present cultural landscape of Maryland has evolved over the last three centuries during four historical phases of development: colonization—seventeenth century, agrarian development—eighteenth century, early industrial period—nineteenth century, and mid-industrial period—nineteenth and twentieth centuries. Factors such as population, transportation, economy, culture, and environment will be reviewed for each historical period in order to understand the emergence of the isolated, rural, conservative Eastern Shore; the rural tobacco land of southern Maryland; the rugged mining area of western Maryland; the prosperous mixed-farming area of the Piedmont; and the metropolitan Baltimore-Washington corridor.

After finding Newfoundland too harsh an environment for settlement, Lord Baltimore secured the northern Chesapeake area for his proprietary colony. Human inadequacy and physical difficulties were profound, yet there were compensating factors that allowed the Maryland colony to take root. Primary among these factors were the overall similarities with the homeland's climate and vegetation. Cultural geographer Carl Sauer stated that, "It would be impossible, indeed, to cross an ocean anywhere else and find so little that is unfamiliar on the opposite side."[1] Little did Lord Baltimore realize that he had founded a future state in a new nation; a state that was to become a focus in the new country, a gateway to the west, a border state between north and south, and part of the great megalopolitan region.

COLONIZATION—SEVENTEENTH CENTURY

Cecilius Calvert, Lord Baltimore, had a vision of a feudal settlement system for the Maryland colony. He hoped to establish a manorial system with a stable social order; but this was not to be. Rapid economic development amid the primitive conditions of a newly settled frontier meant that poorer men were able to acquire land and wealth, thus disrupting the social order. Likewise, Lord Baltimore's vision of a dependent, proprietary colony based on nuclear families living in villages within a manorial system that was based on agriculture and some manufacturing proved unsuitable for the Chesapeake Bay region. Instead, what evolved was a Roman Catholic planter-gentry dominating Protestant tenants, all widely dispersed in small settlements along the many inlets of the Maryland shoreline.

By 1642, 83 percent of the settled land was located in sixteen manors concentrated in the hands of the Jesuit order and a half-dozen Catholic families.[2] Many of the immigrants were indentured servants who became freehold farmers after approximately five years of labor. The traditional European manorial system, which did not succeed on the primitive frontier, evolved into a New World variant, the plantation. Initially the plantations ranged from 250 to 500 acres (101.3 to 202.6 ha); in addition, many planters owned or rented scattered parcels of land. Eventually the term "plantation" identified a method of working and controlling the land, and it became a way of life.

In 1634, Governor Leonard Calvert and his fellow colonists made the initial settlement, landing at Blackiston's Island in what is now southern Maryland. An earlier minor settlement, a trading post on Kent Island, had been established in 1631 by a Virginian, William Claiborne. Calvert purchased land from the Yaocomico Indians and founded St. Mary's City.

The territorial expulsion, or physical elimination, of the Indians in Maryland seems to have followed the same general pattern as the removal of Indians in the other coastal colonies. Although the Maryland proprietors have a reputation in history books for a more enlightened treatment of the local Indians, the end result was the same as elsewhere.[3] By the end of the 17th century, Maryland's colonist population of 33,000 had replaced nearly all of the 11,000 Indians existing in 1630.[4]

The elaboration of the Maryland landscape was slow, owing to a lack of precise geographical information about the land and its resources. From St. Mary's, the population spread north and west along the shores of the Potomac River and the western shore (Figure 5.1). The fall line severely restricted early travel inland by water, so planters established themselves on the many tidewater peninsulas which form the shores of Chesapeake Bay, and there each planter's boat landing provided sufficient commercial access to the outside world. In such a natural and socioeconomic environment, commercial towns had no great functions and therefore never developed on the same scale as in New England, for example. This settlement pattern is reflected in the absence of large- and medium-sized commercial towns in southern Maryland even today. Maryland's transportation in the 1600s was locally oriented. The bay and its many tributaries were the main highways of Maryland; roads were few, consisting mainly of short, narrow, muddy paths leading from the plantations down to the river.

Seventeenth-century Maryland's landscape was one of isolated farms and plantations with a few small port towns specializing in the export of locally grown crops. Maryland farmers had readily accepted tobacco, along with its highly fluctuating market. New land was cleared and many new, small, independent farms were created to meet the growing demand for tobacco. Exports of tobacco rose dramatically from 50 tn (45.4 t) in 1640 to 8,000 tn (7,256 t) in 1690.[5]

Figure 5.1 shows that the population was clustered in southern Maryland in the 1630s and 1640s. Thereafter it shifted slowly northward along the western shore and onto the Eastern Shore. Between 1650 and 1700 the population of the Eastern Shore grew from only 11 percent of the colony's population to nearly half. During this period Eastern Shore farmers began to diversify from tobacco to include grains and livestock.[6] To better serve the needs of a more-dispersed population, in 1695 the capital was moved from somewhat isolated St. Mary's to Annapolis, which was more centrally located.

Another significant demographic change occurred in the late 1600s: tidewater Mary-

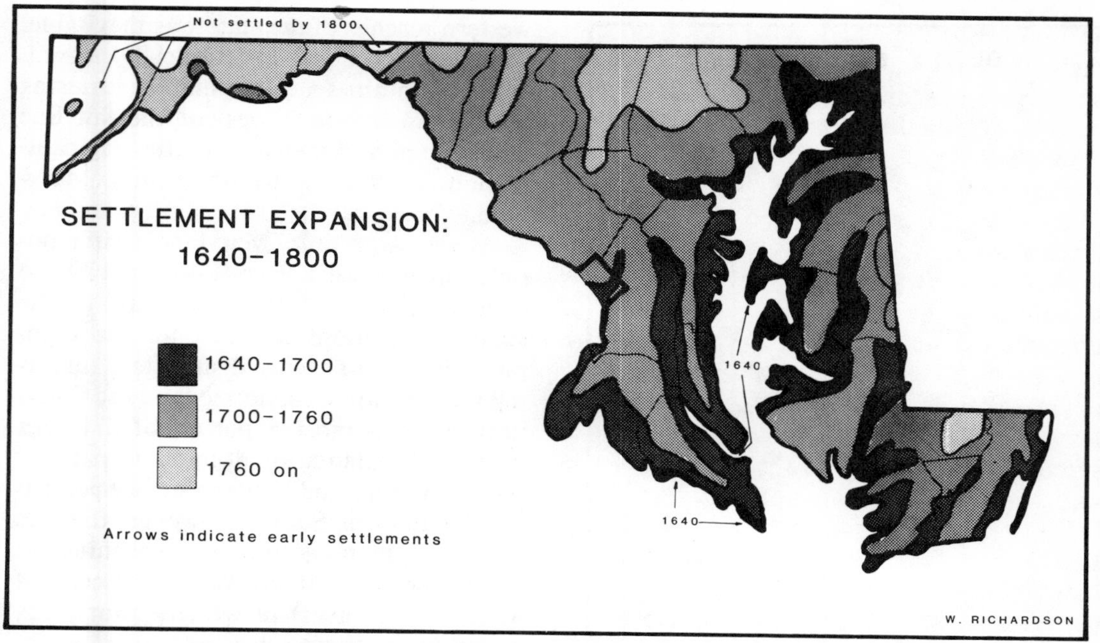

FIGURE 5.1. Source: Adapted from Robert D. Mitchell and Edward K. Muller, *Geographical Perspectives on Maryland's Past,* © 1979, p. 8 (College Park: Department of Geography, University of Maryland). Reprinted with permission.

land's economy was placed on a slavery basis. Most of the early laborers had been indentured servants, often teenage boys from the slums of London. By the late 1600s, as conditions in England improved, this source of labor proved too costly and eventually dried up. Soon Maryland planters, following the lead of the Dutch and Spanish in the New World, turned to slavery to supply the intensive labor needed to raise tobacco. An act was passed in 1671 encouraging the import of slaves from West Africa. In the 1670s indentured servants outnumbered slaves four to one in the labor supply, but by 1690 there were four times as many slaves as servants. In 1658 there were only 100 slaves in southern Maryland, accounting for 3 percent of that region's population; by 1710 there were over 3,500, comprising almost a fourth of the population.[7]

During the 1680s Maryland's nonslave population began to experience positive rates of natural increase. This was to lead to the creation of an American-born Maryland society.

AGRARIAN DEVELOPMENT—EIGHTEENTH CENTURY

Throughout the eighteenth century the basically rural-agricultural Maryland landscape developed into a more complex socioeconomic system. By the first federal census of 1790, the population had increased to 320,000. During the 1700s, Maryland's status went from that of a royal colony of England to a state in the new nation. As European market demand for tobacco and other products increased, the economy of Maryland grew; concurrently, settlements expanded westward as new crop and livestock areas were opened (Figure 5.1).[8]

During the 1730s the population increased steadily in the tidewater area and expanded westward into the Monocacy Valley. As the Piedmont was settled, increasing

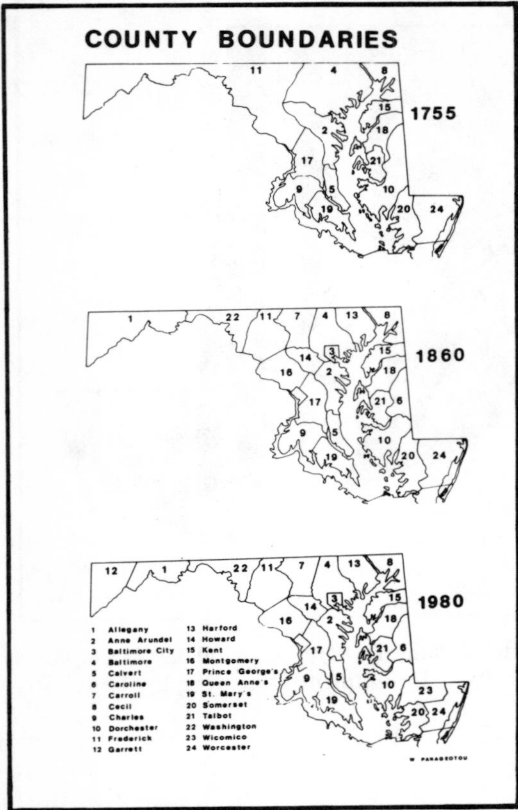

FIGURE 5.2.

numbers of non-English-speaking immigrants arrived. German-speaking immigrants settled along the fertile Monocacy Valley, while Scotch-Irish and English farmers pushed westward into the less desirable, but lovely, rolling hill country.

In 1748 Frederick County was formed (Figure 5.2); the population increased so rapidly that by 1755 it became the second most populous county, and Frederick Town soon replaced Annapolis as the second-largest town in the state. Inducements to settle the west were given settlers in the form of tax reductions. By 1756, Indian raids during the French and Indian wars had caused much of the area west of Frederick to be abandoned until hostilities ceased. The American Revolution once again slowed westward movement and development, but the settlement of the far western reaches of the state was inevitable. The emergence of an ethnically mixed, yeoman-dominated population raising wheat and livestock west of the fall line added a new dimension to the regionalization of late eighteenth-century Maryland.[9]

At the same time, Maryland's slave population increased from 4,400 in 1700 to over 111,000 in 1790—one third of the state's population! By 1790, the black population was unevenly distributed, reflecting the prevailing economic land use found in the state. Almost 42 percent of all blacks were in the plantation-dominated parts of southern Maryland and another 39 percent on the Eastern Shore. However, the ties of slavery to tobacco were weakening, as there were 13,000 blacks (90 percent of whom were slaves) in western Maryland, where little tobacco was grown.

The urban population was also growing. After the 1740s, significant changes in the low-order urban hierarchy began to occur. In 1750 Annapolis had only 800 residents, Baltimore merely 150, and Frederick 1,000. By 1776, Baltimore was an urban settlement of over 5,000; it was followed in size by two relatively new western towns, Frederick and Hagerstown, with 1,800 and 1,500 people respectively. Baltimore's growth, centered on its port, continued rapidly thereafter until by 1790 it was the fifth-largest city in the United States (Table 5.1). Enlightened and visionary Baltimore businessmen united to consolidate the position of their port city as the leading trade center of the Chesapeake region by 1785 (almost 200 years later the Baltimore business community was once again to muster its resources to help build the "new" Baltimore). It has been claimed that the rise of the western towns was tied to the tobacco and wheat trade with accompanying needs for transportation, storage, and processing.[10] The evolving economic-geographical pattern, however, began to focus more and more on the port city of Baltimore.

In preindustrial eighteenth-century Maryland, the principal source of wealth

TABLE 5.1
TWENTY LARGEST CITIES BY POPULATION, 1790-1970

	1790		1830		1870
Rank	City	Rank	City	Rank	City
1	New York, N.Y.	1	New York, N.Y.	1	New York, N.Y.
2	Philadelphia, Pa.	2	Baltimore, Md.	2	Philadelphia, Pa.
3	Boston, Mass.	3	Philadelphia, Pa.	3	Brooklyn, N.Y.
4	Charleston, S.C.	4	Boston, Mass.	4	St. Louis, Mo.
5	Baltimore, Md.	5	New Orleans, La.	5	Chicago, Ill.
6	Salem, Mass.	6	Charleston, S.C.	6	Baltimore, Md.
7	Newport, R.I.	7	Cincinnati, Ohio	7	Boston, Mass.
8	Providence, R.I.	8	Albany, N.Y.	8	Cincinnati, Ohio
9	Gloucester, Mass.	9	Brooklyn, N.Y.	9	New Orleans, La.
10	Newburyport, Mass.	10	Washington, D.C.	10	San Francisco, Cal.
11	Portsmouth, N.H.	11	Providence, R.I.	11	Pittsburgh, Pa.
12	Brooklyn, N.Y.	12	Richmond, Va.	12	Buffalo, N.Y.
13	New Haven, Conn.	13	Pittsburgh, Pa.	13	Washington, D.C.
14	Taunton, Mass.	14	Salem, Mass.	14	Newark, N.J.
15	Richmond, Va.	15	Portland, Maine	15	Louisville, Ky.
16	Albany, N.Y.	16	Troy, N.Y.	16	Cleveland, Ohio
17	New Bedford, Mass.	17	Newark, N.J.	17	Jersey City, N.J.
18	Beverly, Mass.	18	Louisville, Ky.	18	Detroit, Mich.
19	Norfolk, Va.	19	New Haven, Conn.	19	Milwaukee, Wis.
20	Petersburg, Va.	20	Norfolk, Va.	20	Albany, N.Y.

	1910		1950		1970
Rank	City	Rank	City	Rank	City
1	New York, N.Y.	1	New York, N.Y.	1	New York, N.Y.
2	Chicago, Ill.	2	Chicago, Ill.	2	Chicago, Ill.
3	Philadelphia, Pa.	3	Philadelphia, Pa.	3	Los Angeles, Cal.
4	St. Louis, Mo.	4	Los Angeles, Cal.	4	Philadelphia, Pa.
5	Boston, Mass.	5	Detroit, Mich.	5	Detroit, Mich.
6	Cleveland, Ohio	6	Baltimore, Md.	6	Houston, Tx.
7	Baltimore, Md.	7	Cleveland, Ohio	7	Baltimore, Md.
8	Pittsburgh, Pa.	8	St. Louis, Mo.	8	Dallas, Tx.
9	Detroit, Mich.	9	Washington, D.C.	9	Washington, D.C.
10	Buffalo, N.Y.	10	Boston, Mass.	10	Cleveland, Ohio
11	San Francisco, Cal.	11	San Francisco, Cal.	11	Indianapolis, Ind.
12	Milwaukee, Wis.	12	Pittsburgh, Pa.	12	Milwaukee, Wis.
13	Cincinnati, Ohio	13	Milwaukee, Wis.	13	San Francisco, Cal.
14	Newark, N.J.	14	Houston, Tx.	14	San Diego, Cal.
15	New Orleans, La.	15	Buffalo, N.Y.	15	San Antonio, Tx.
16	Washington, D.C.	16	New Orleans, La.	16	Boston, Mass.
17	Los Angeles, Cal.	17	Minneapolis, Minn.	17	Memphis, Tenn.
18	Minneapolis, Minn.	18	Cincinnati, Ohio	18	St. Louis, Mo.
19	Kansas City, Mo.	19	Seattle, Wash.	19	New Orleans, La.
20	Seattle, Wash.	20	Kansas City, Mo.	20	Phoenix, Ariz.

Source: James E. Vance, Jr., "Cities in the Shaping of the American Nation," *The Journal of Geography*, 75:1, (January 1976), 41-52. Reprinted by permission of the National Council for Geographic Education.

was land. The size of landholdings ranged from 255 acres (103.3 ha) in Worcester County and 282 acres (114.2 ha) in St. Marys County to 370 acres (149.9 ha) in Frederick County and 372 acres (150.7 ha) in Cecil County and even to 473 acres (191.6 ha) in Anne Arundel County.[11] Freeholding farmers were more numerous on the Piedmont and to the west than on the western shore.

Eighteenth-century Maryland had an economy dominated by tobacco, grains, and livestock, with some lumber and iron production. Unlike Virginia to the south, which remained heavily dependent on tobacco, Maryland diversified earlier as food processing and small manufacturing were added to its economy.

By 1755 there were four distinct regions on the Maryland landscape: the Eastern Shore, southern Maryland, the Baltimore area, and western Maryland. David Curtis Skaggs noted that, "While population and economic power moved northward and westward, the center of social and political influence remained in the tidewater homes of tobacco planters and the drawing rooms of Annapolis."[12] Of these four regions, the Eastern Shore had the most-diversified economy and the least-variable population size. Population there increased from 16,000 in 1750 to 108,000 in 1790 (50 percent of the state's population). The counties with the best soils (Talbot, Queen Annes, Kent, and southern Cecil) produced tobacco, wheat, and corn. Marginal soils in Worcester, Somerset, and parts of Caroline and Dorchester counties were used for lumbering, especially for export to England. During the Revolution the northern counties of the Eastern Shore sent wheat, flour, corn, cattle, and salted fish to Philadelphia; these commodities left Oxford and Chestertown by water for Elkton at the head of Chesapeake Bay, where they were loaded onto wagons.[13] By the end of the eighteenth century, the export trade of the Eastern Shore was dominated by wheat, shipped mainly to Baltimore.

Tobacco and corn dominated in southern Maryland. There, the population reached 89,000 by 1790 (25 percent of the state's population). Annapolis was unable to hold off competition from Baltimore and became a quiet market town serving a rural hinterland.

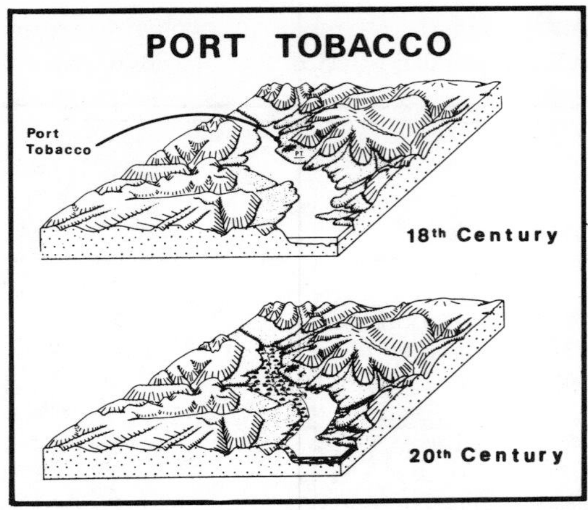

FIGURE 5.3. Source: L. C. Gottschalk, "Effects of Soil Erosion on Navigation in Upper Chesapeake Bay." Reprinted from the *Geographical Review,* vol. 35, 2 (April 1945) p. 232, with permission of the American Geographical Society.

Near the end of the century soil erosion in the coastal tobacco-corn areas was evident, and silting began to affect the navigability of small ports such as Port Tobacco in southern Maryland and Joppa north of Baltimore (Figure 5.3). Although Port Tobacco was still used at the time of the Civil War, today neither it nor Joppa are ports. In 1608 when Captain John Smith first saw the Patapsco River, whose main estuary forms Baltimore harbor, the limit of the open water was 7 mi (11.3 km) farther inland than it is today.

The rise of the Baltimore area was evident on the eighteenth-century Maryland landscape, and it was linked to the changing economic landscapes of the other regions of the state. In 1711 a flour mill was established at Jones Falls, and in 1723 iron furnaces were built at the mouth of Gwynns Falls. As roads were opened into western

Maryland and a public tobacco-inspection warehouse was sited in the city, Baltimore's centrality was strengthened. After reaching a population of 13,500 in 1790, a period of rapid growth followed; by 1800 the population had more than doubled to 31,500![14]

Throughout the eighteenth century, western Maryland was being opened up to settlement, and it developed at a phenomenal rate. In the 1740s, this region had only 8,000 people or less than 5 percent of the state's population; by 1790 it had 85,000 inhabitants, comprising over 25 percent of the state's population. Growth was clustered in several fertile lowlands, especially the Monocacy Valley in Frederick County and the Hagerstown Valley in Washington County. The agricultural emphasis was on livestock and grains, particularly wheat and rye; tobacco did not become very important in this area.

Despite the major culture hearth in the Chesapeake tidewater area, the settlers of western Maryland were mainly influenced by the cultural characteristics of the southeastern Pennsylvania, or Midland, culture hearth.[15] These were yeomen-freeholders carrying on mixed agriculture of wheat, rye, flax, and cattle on 200- to 400-acre (81- to 162-hectare) farms. Through Maryland, the Chesapeake and Midland cultural traditions penetrated to influence the Midwest and upper South during the nineteenth century.

EARLY URBAN INDUSTRIAL PERIOD—NINETEENTH CENTURY

During the nineteenth century a number of basic structural changes, part of a national process, occurred on the Maryland landscape. The last frontiers in Garrett County were finally settled (Figure 5.1). Maryland merchants began to encounter stronger domestic and foreign competition in commerce; the state's farmers faced new and increasing competition from the newly opened western lands. In response, some farmers took advantage of their relatively better geographic location and diversified to meet the needs of the growing urban areas. Some rural people moved to the cities to work in the new and growing industries; they were joined there by an influx of foreign-born immigrants. Baltimore was the center of this vortex of forces, and it grew into the stereotypic mid-century American commercial city—large, bustling, and heterogeneous.[16] By 1830 Baltimore had become the second population center of the country (Table 5.1). As the population grew, so did Baltimore's dominance of the state's manufacturing activities, especially shipbuilding, food processing, weaving, iron works, and printing. The chief items of Baltimore's export activities remained tobacco and grains for the European market.

The cultural, economic, and social regional contrasts of Maryland came to be more sharply defined during the nineteenth century. The initial thirty years of the century witnessed a stagnation in Maryland's still basically agricultural economy. This was the period of the Embargo of 1807, War of 1812, and depression of 1819–22. Outdated farming methods were accompanied by soil erosion and exhaustion and poor yields.[17] As people left Maryland for destinations west, the population increased by only 127,000 between 1790 and 1830. Baltimore City accounted for 53 percent of this increase; the northern Eastern Shore lost population; and southern Maryland remained stable.

After the 1830s, a number of agents of change began to flourish in Maryland: agricultural reform, transportation improvements, coal mining, immigration, and industrial development.[18] The rural-urban dualism had become clear by 1850. Differences in the character of farming and fishing on the rural Eastern Shore, tobacco plantations in southern Maryland, burgeoning Baltimore, and the western coal fields were sharpened.

Not until the middle of the 1800s, following the adaptation of steam power to water and rail, did important changes occur in the transportation system of Maryland. In the early 1800s turnpikes had been built from Baltimore to Frederick and north into Pennsylvania, but by the 1820s the emphasis on canals and railroads lessened the attention to roads. By 1830 turnpikes were no longer the predominant lines of transportation, but had become feeders to the railroads and canals. Responding to the beginning of coal production in western Maryland and the desire of mercantilists to break the isolating trade barrier of the mountains, the legislature in 1826 passed a bill to canalize the Potomac River to Cumberland. Fearing that the proposed Chesapeake and Ohio Canal (C&O) would enable Georgetown to rival their city, Baltimore merchants chartered the Baltimore and Ohio Railroad (B&O) west. Construction on both the C&O and B&O was started in 1828.

In 1842, the B&O Railroad reached Cumberland. By the 1850s, Baltimore had rail connections to the Ohio and Mississippi valleys. The 13-mile-long (20.9-kilometer) Chesapeake and Delaware Canal connecting Chesapeake Bay with the Delaware River, which opened in 1829, also contributed to the growing centrality of Baltimore.[19] When completed, the C&O Canal moved flour, agricultural produce, and coal to Georgetown, but Baltimore was secure as the leading commercial center of the region, thanks to the efforts of its businessmen and its geographical position. In the 1870s and 1880s the C&O Canal declined in use, after damage from a number of floods.

As transportation improved and the costs of movement decreased, more farmers had access to the large urban markets. Agricultural reforms in Maryland were noticeable, such as the use of lime and guano fertilizers and crop diversification. Dairying and orchards developed on the Piedmont and in western Maryland. Fruit and vegetable production on the Eastern Shore led to the establishment of canneries, while truck farming of perishable fruits and vegetables for the urban markets developed around Baltimore and Washington, D.C. Despite all of this change, there was a stubborn persistence of tobacco farms and slaves in southern Maryland; the results of this resistance are still evident on the landscape there today. Although there were many miles of roads in Maryland, it was still rough going for travelers. By 1900, about 90 percent of Maryland's 14,483 mi (23,303 km) of road were still dirt surfaced; the rest had been improved with stone, gravel, and shells.[20]

From 1830 to 1860, Maryland's population increased by more than a third, reaching 687,000; this was a gain of 240,000. Baltimore City accounted for over 50 percent of this growth. Population data show a considerable decline in the population of Baltimore County between 1850 and 1860, but this is due largely to the separation of Baltimore City, which became a separate political entity in 1851. During the 1870s every county increased in population, except Allegany, from which Garrett County had been carved. Baltimore City and Washington, D.C., were also growing rapidly during the late nineteenth century (Figure 5.4).

By 1860, the number of free blacks nearly

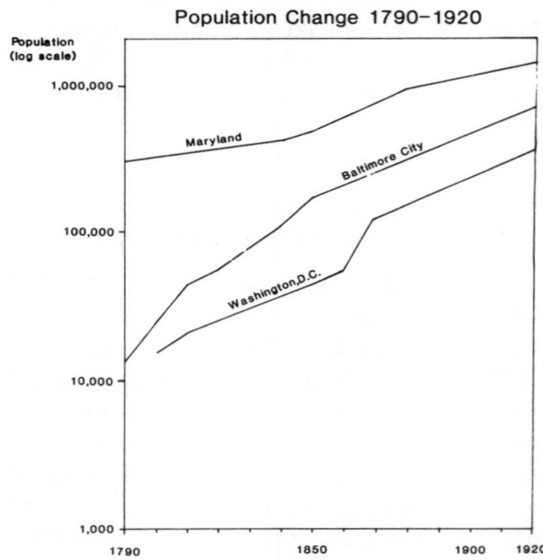

FIGURE 5.4. Source: U.S. Department of Commerce, Bureau of the Census.

equaled the number of slaves, who now accounted for only 25 percent of the population. Because of the population influx of immigrants, more and more Marylanders were unfamiliar with slavery and black people. However, in southern Maryland, slaves still were 45 percent of the population prior to the Civil War, partly because the number of foreign immigrants in southern Maryland and on the Eastern Shore was small, with most staying in Baltimore or moving west. After the Civil War, Baltimore attracted large numbers of free blacks from southern states, and between 1870 and 1900, Baltimore became one of the largest centers of urban blacks in the United States.

Between 1830 and 1860 rapid population growth occurred in Cecil County, in Baltimore City, on the Piedmont, and in western Maryland. In terms of growth rate, immigrants, and black population, western and north-central Maryland were drifting farther from the Eastern Shore and southern Maryland. Baltimore, with its influx of Irish Catholics and Germans, was becoming exotic to the whole state.[21]

One major scene of nineteenth-century industrialization was Allegany County. The coming of the railroad and canal to western Maryland opened up coal production, and more and more miners came to Maryland from the British Isles and Germany. By 1860, nearly 20 percent of Allegany County's population was foreign born. The coal company towns, mines, and foreign-born population contrasted with the dispersed rural-mountain folk culture of western Maryland.

Another area of major industrialization was Baltimore. By 1860 it had over 1,100 industrial establishments employing nearly 20,000 people. New industries developed, e.g., ready-made clothing, iron works, and railroad shops. Travelers were impressed with Baltimore's urbanity and modernity—its density, diversity, and dispersal.[22] The regularity and simplicity of the red-brick early row houses had become part of the city's personality.

MID-INDUSTRIAL PERIOD—LATE NINETEENTH CENTURY AND EARLY TWENTIETH CENTURY

The Civil War had a disrupting effect on the economic and social structure of this border state, but after the war industrialization continued, and farmers turned more to perishable crops to supply the growing Baltimore and Washington, D.C. urban markets. During the war, the federal government found it necessary to keep Maryland loyal to the Union so as not to isolate Washington, D.C., as an enclave in the south. Union troops occupied much of Maryland, especially the key rail links at Baltimore connecting Washington and the north. The war-depressed farm economy finally picked up as a result of the federal government's need for food, supplies, and transportation.

After the Civil War, Maryland agriculture changed. Tobacco production was more costly without slaves, and wheat farmers were faced with competition from the western plains. Farmers turned more to perishable fruits, vegetables, and dairy products that were carried to urban markets on the expanding railroads. Tobacco farming retreated to the better soils of southern Maryland. Fruits and vegetables became popular on the Eastern Shore and in Prince Georges and Anne Arundel counties; Piedmont farmers turned to forage crops and dairying; orchards were planted in the western mountain valleys and on the slopes. With new crops, fewer staple products, smaller farms, more machinery, and out-migration, the rural landscape of Maryland experienced significant changes.[23]

Even though agriculture was still the leading economic activity in the state until 1900, other sectors of the economy had developed a strong, basic infrastructure for future growth. After the disruption of the Civil War, agriculture slowly declined in importance, and by 1900, more Marylanders were employed in industry than in agriculture. The shift in employment emphasis from primary activities, especially agriculture, to secondary manufacturing activities is a part of the development process that has been well documented by economists. Today the development process has produced an employment structure with a greater emphasis on tertiary service and government jobs.

By 1910, Maryland had nearly doubled its 1860 population, and the majority of Marylanders lived in towns and cities of 2,500 or more. The state's cities and towns settled largely into the mold of a central-place system. By 1910 there were only fourteen settlements with a population over 2,500, and half of them had fewer than 5,000 people.[24] The ports of Cambridge and Crisfield developed oyster packing and fish processing; Salisbury developed flour milling, vegetable canning, and timber products. West of the Catoctin Mountains, only Hagerstown and Cumberland experienced industrial growth, chiefly iron foundries, railroad repair yards, and machine shops. Coal and its transportation were the basis of Cumberland's manufacturing and commercial activities. Most of the immigrants stayed in urban areas; the rural population was only 4 percent foreign born. The number of blacks in rural areas declined between 1860 and 1910, many going to Baltimore and Washington, D.C. Still, southern Maryland remained 40 to 50 percent black, the Eastern Shore 25 to 33 percent, while the Piedmont and western Maryland had only small black populations. By 1910, while 43 percent of all Marylanders lived in the culturally plural city of Baltimore with its growing ethnic neighborhoods, nearly 75 percent of all Maryland's foreign-born population lived in that city. The largest group was Germans; other groups that grew significantly in size were the Poles, Eastern European Jews, and Italians.

The waterpower sites in the state lost their importance with the coming of steam and electric power. Some canning of vegetables, timber processing, and seafood processing remained in rural areas, but by 1900 most of the industry was in the Baltimore area; the value-of-manufactures patterns shown on the maps in Figure 5.5 indicate that Baltimore had become the central focus of manufacturing by 1920.

By 1900, Baltimore City had become the center of the state in many ways: it had over 40 percent of the state's population, 33 percent of the black population, 75 percent of the foreign born, 66 percent of the industrial workers, and 60 percent of the total value of production.[25] Manufacturing became the leading activity in Baltimore by 1910, exceeding the value of foreign commerce. New, large industries such as steel and petroleum refining were established in Baltimore. Smaller industries requiring semiskilled hand labor, such as men's clothing, remained in the city, while newer heavy industry located in surrounding suburbs. Baltimore was largely a branch-plant town, not an industrial-headquarters town. The fire of 1904 destroyed most of its downtown, but Baltimore rebuilt and by 1910 this sprawling metropolis had over 500,000 people, making it the seventh largest city in the nation (Table 5.1).

A number of distinct ethnic neighborhoods grew in Baltimore: German, Jewish, Italian, Polish, and black. Industrialization brought with it congested housing, poor santitation, diseases, and poor working conditions, especially for women and children. These conditions were accompanied by political corruption. Although Baltimore entered the twentieth century with serious challenges to its economic and social structure, the quality of its neighborhood communities and the varied delights of its heterogeneity made it attractive; this industrial metropolis was to many a city of homes.[26]

Although the story of the Maryland landscape told here points to the growing differences among the regions of the state, in reality the regions have all become structurally interlinked and focused on Baltimore. The legacy of Maryland's past geography still is present today in the distinct and diverse, yet connected, regions of the state.

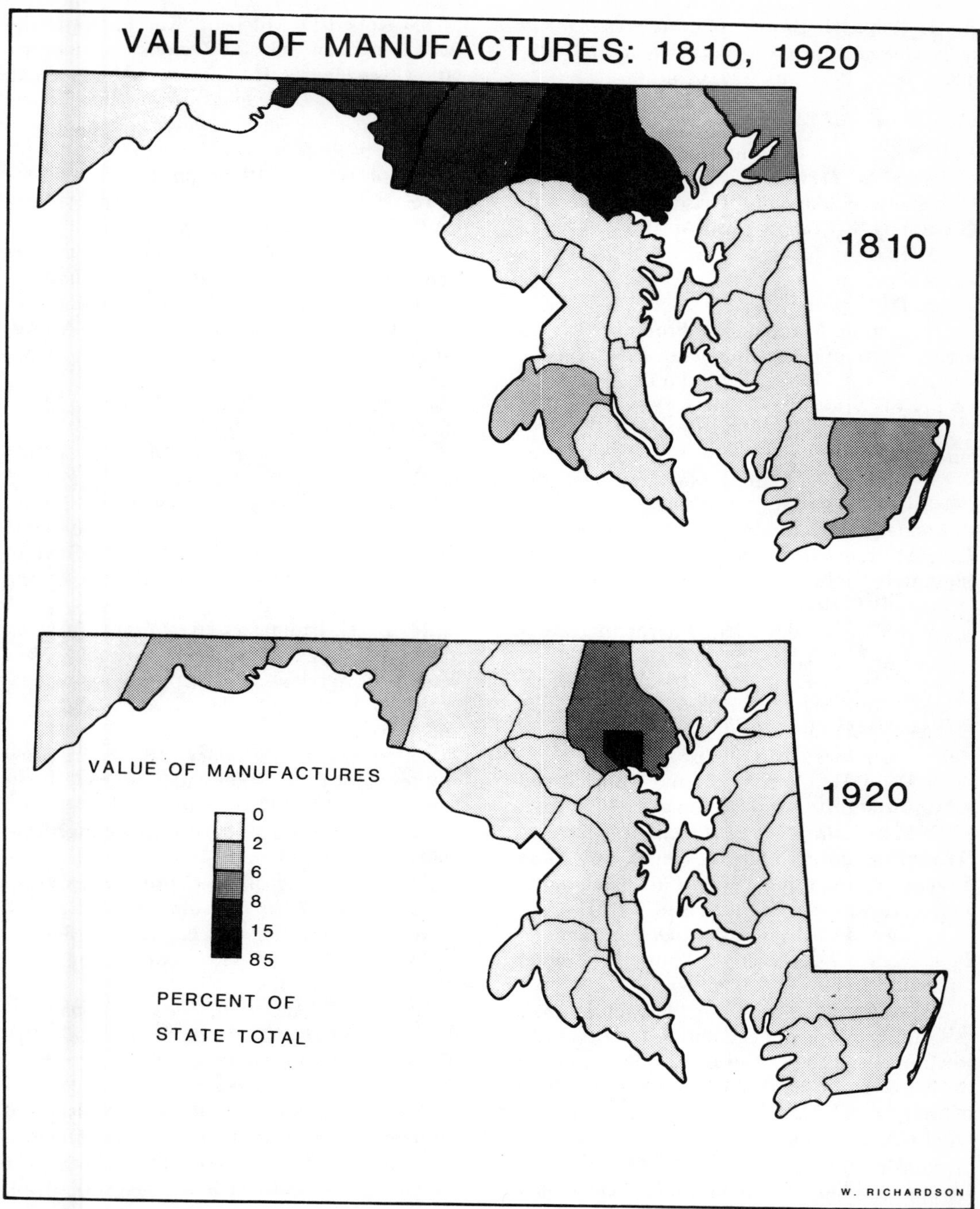
VALUE OF MANUFACTURES: 1810, 1920
1810
1920
VALUE OF MANUFACTURES
0
2
6
8
15
85
PERCENT OF
STATE TOTAL
W. RICHARDSON

FIGURE 5.5.

NOTES

1. Ralph H. Brown, *Historical Geography of the United States* (New York: Harcourt, Brace, and World, 1948), p. 7.

2. Robert D. Mitchell and Edward K. Muller, "Interpreting Maryland's Past: Praxis and Desiderata," in Mitchell and Muller, eds., *Geographical Perspectives on Maryland's Past* University of Maryland, Occasional Papers in Geography 4 (College Park: April 1979), p. 7.

3. Ibid., p. 6.

4. Ibid., p. 7.

5. Ibid., p. 9.

6. Paul G. E. Clemons, "From Tobacco to Grain: Economic Development on Maryland's Eastern Shore, 1660–1750" (Ph.D. diss., University of Wisconsin, 1974).

7. Mitchell and Muller, "Interpreting Maryland's Past," p. 10.

8. Gloria L. Main, "Maryland and the Chesapeake Economy, 1670–1720," in Aubrey C. Land, L. G. Carr, and E. C. Papenfuse, eds., *Law, Society, and Politics in Early Maryland* (Baltimore: Johns Hopkins University Press, 1977), pp. 134–152.

9. Mitchell and Muller, "Interpreting Maryland's Past," p. 12.

10. Carville Earle and Ronald Hoffman, "Staple Crops and Urban Development in the Eighteenth-Century South," *Perspectives in American History* 10 (1976):7–78.

11. Paul H. Giddens, "Land Policies and Administration in Colonial Maryland, 1753–1769," *Maryland Historical Magazine* 28 (1933):156; and Clarence P. Gould, *The Land System in Maryland, 1720–1765* (Baltimore: Johns Hopkins University Press, 1915), p. 10.

12. David Curtis Skaggs, *Roots of Maryland Democracy 1753–1776* (Westport, Conn.: Greenwood Press, 1973), p. 37.

13. Edward C. Papenfuse, "Economic Analysis and Loyalist Strategy during the American Revolution: Robert Alexander's Remarks on the Economy of the Peninsula or Eastern Shore of Maryland," *Maryland Historical Magazine* 68 (1973):173–195.

14. Richard M. Bernard, "A Portrait of Baltimore in 1800: Economic and Occupational Patterns in an Early American City," *Maryland Historical Magazine* 69 (1974):341–360.

15. Robert D. Mitchell, "The Formation of Early American Cultural Regions: An Interpretation," in James R. Gibson, ed., *European Settlement and Development in North America: Essays on Geographical Change in Honour and Memory of Andrew Hill Clark* (Toronto: University of Toronto, 1978), pp. 66–90.

16. Mitchell and Muller, "Interpreting Maryland's Past," p. 23.

17. James S. Van Ness, "Economoic Development, Social and Cultural Changes: 1800–1850," in Richard Walsh and William L. Fox, eds., *Maryland: A History 1632–1974* (Baltimore: Maryland Historical Society, 1974), pp. 188–190.

18. Mitchell and Muller, "Interpreting Maryland's Past," p. 29.

19. Edward Hungerford, *The Story of the Baltimore and Ohio Railroad, 1827–1927,* 2 vols. (New York: Arno Press, 1928); and Joseph C. G. Kennedy, *Preliminary Report on the Eighth Census, 1860* (Washington, D.C.: U.S. Government Printing Office, for the Bureau of the Census, 1862), pp. 231–234.

20. Derek Thompson, ed., *Atlas of Maryland* (College Park: Department of Geography, University of Maryland, 1977), p. 17.

21. Mitchell and Muller, "Interpreting Maryland's Past," p. 34.

22. Robert I. Alexander, "Baltimore Row Houses of the Early Nineteenth Century," *American Studies* 16 (1975):65–76.

23. Mitchell and Muller, "Interpreting Maryland's Past," p. 43.

24. U.S. Bureau of the Census, *U.S. Census of Population, 1910* (Washington, D.C.: U.S. Government Printing Office, 1910), p. 849.

25. Mitchell and Muller, "Interpreting Maryland's Past," p. 45.

26. Alan D. Anderson, *The Origin and Resolution of an Urban Crisis: Baltimore 1890–1930* (Baltimore: Johns Hopkins University Press, 1977), pp. 57–64; and James B. Crooke, "Maryland Progressivism," in Richard Walsh and William L. Fox, *Politics and Progress: The Rise of Urban Progressivism in Baltimore, 1895–1911* (Baton Rouge: Louisiana State University, 1966).

CHAPTER 6

THE PEOPLE: A STORY OF DIVERSITY

GENERAL ASPECTS OF THE POPULATION

The recent national demographic trends of slower population growth, reduced immigration rates, increased numbers of nonfamily households, an older age-profile, and the revival of nonmetropolitan growth all can be clearly seen in the changing demographic structure on the Maryland landscape. Although it is nearly 75 percent white, Maryland's population is surprisingly heterogeneous (Figure 6.1).

As might be expected in an area as diverse as Maryland, there is considerable variation in growth rates and population composition among the political subdivisions. From 1970 to 1980, Maryland's population grew from 3,923,897 to 4,216,446, an increase of 7.5 percent. During this period, the fastest-growing county was Howard County, which grew in population by an amazing 89.8 percent (most of this growth was due to the continued development of the planned city of Columbia, to be described in Chapter 8). Other counties that experienced considerable growth were Calvert, 65.9 percent, and Charles, 51.7 percent; both are in the state's urban corridor close to Washington, D.C. At the other extreme are Allegany County, which lost 4.3 percent of its population, and Baltimore City, which lost 13.5 percent.

Maryland's land area is larger than that of nine other states, but its population exceeds that of thirty-three other states. With 427 people per square mile (164 per sq km), Maryland has a population density exceeded only by the northeastern states of Massachusetts, Connecticut, Rhode Island, and New Jersey. But density figures are not meaningful without accompanying information as to how the population is geographically distributed. It can be seen in Figure 6.2 and Table 6.1 that the population is unevenly distributed; the largest cluster is in the Baltimore–Washington, D.C., metropolitan areas, which together hold 80 percent of Maryland's people. Population density runs as high as 9,959 people per sq mi (3,830 per sq km) in Baltimore, but is well under 100 (38) for much of the Eastern Shore and between 100 and 200 (38 and 77) for many nonmetropolitan counties across the state.

Although suburban growth continues, during recent years many of the more rural nonmetropolitan areas of Maryland also have grown at a rapid rate. Many counties on the Eastern Shore and in western Maryland are experiencing population increases. Maryland's population-growth pattern is symptomatic of its position as a *hinge* between the North and South; it is expe-

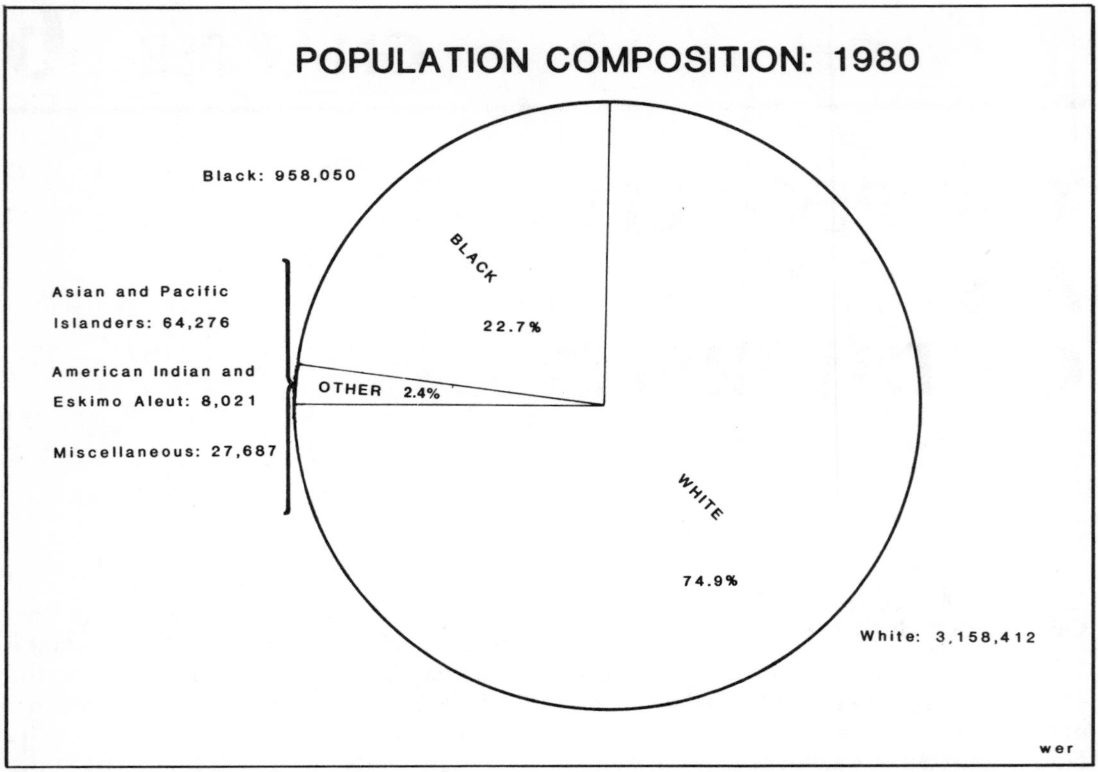

POPULATION COMPOSITION: 1980
Black: 958,050
BLACK
22.7%
Asian and Pacific
Islanders: 64,276
American Indian and
Eskimo Aleut: 8,021
Miscellaneous: 27,687
OTHER 2.4%
WHITE
74.9%
White: 3,158,412
wer

FIGURE 6.1 (*above*). FIGURE 6.2 (*below*). Source for both figures: Data from U.S. Census of Population, 1980.

MARYLAND POPULATION: 1980
Population by county
0–24,999
25,000–49,999
50,000–99,999
100,000–199,999
200,000–399,999
400,000–800,000
W. RICHARDSON

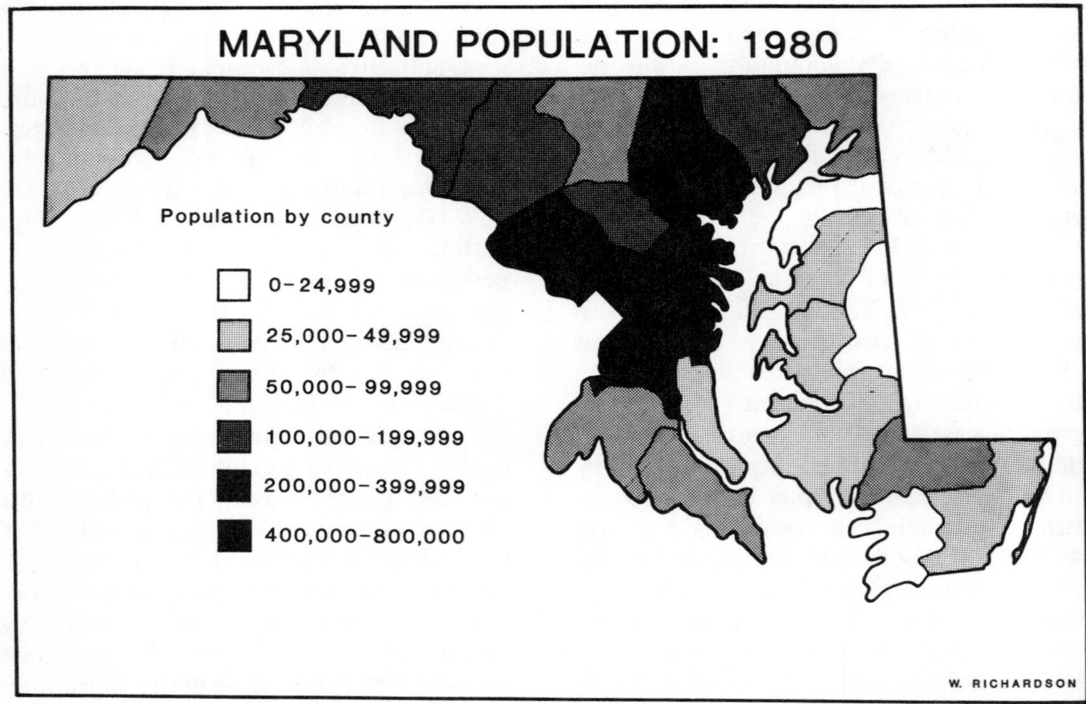

TABLE 6.1
POPULATION DENSITY: 1980

Subdivision	Land Area (Sq Mi)	Population 1980	Population Density (People/Sq Mi)
MARYLAND	9,874	4,216,446	427.0
Baltimore City	79	786,775	9,959.2
Prince George's [a]	485	665,071	1,371.3
Montgomery [a]	443	579,053	1,307.1
Baltimore [b]	608	655,615	1,978.3
Anne Arundel [b]	417	370,775	889.1
Howard [b]	250	118,572	474.3
Harford [b]	448	145,930	352.7
Washington	462	113,086	244.8
Carroll [b]	453	96,356	212.7
Allegany	426	80,548	189.1
Frederick	664	114,263	172.1
Cecil	352	60,430	171.7
Wicomico	380	64,540	169.8
St. Mary's	367	59,895	163.2
Charles	458	72,751	158.8
Calvert	219	34,638	158.2
Talbot	279	25,604	91.8
Caroline	320	23,143	72.3
Queen Anne's	373	25,508	68.4
Worcester	483	30,889	64.0
Kent	284	16,695	58.8
Somerset	332	19,188	57.8
Dorchester	580	30,623	52.8
Garrett	662	26,498	40.0

Source: Land area compiled by the Geography Division, Bureau of the Census, U. S. Department of Commerce, *Maryland Manual* 1977-1978. Population data are from the U. S. Bureau of the Census, *1980 Census of Population Housing*.

[a] Washington, D.C., metropolitan area

[b] Baltimore metropolitan area

sq km = 2.6 x sq mi

riencing population growth in its nonmetropolitan areas similar to that in the Sun Belt, while the population losses in the large cities and slowdown of growth in many of the suburban counties are similar to trends in the older industrialized areas of the Northeast and Midwest. (The position of Maryland as an interface between the Sun Belt and Frost Belt will be discussed in Chapter 9.)

The structure of the Maryland population reveals some important differences between its major components. Figures 6.3 and 6.4 are age-sex pyramids of Maryland's white and nonwhite populations respectively. For both groups, the increasing percentage of females relative to males in the older age-cohorts represents the generally longer life span of women. The nonwhite population is younger than the white pop-

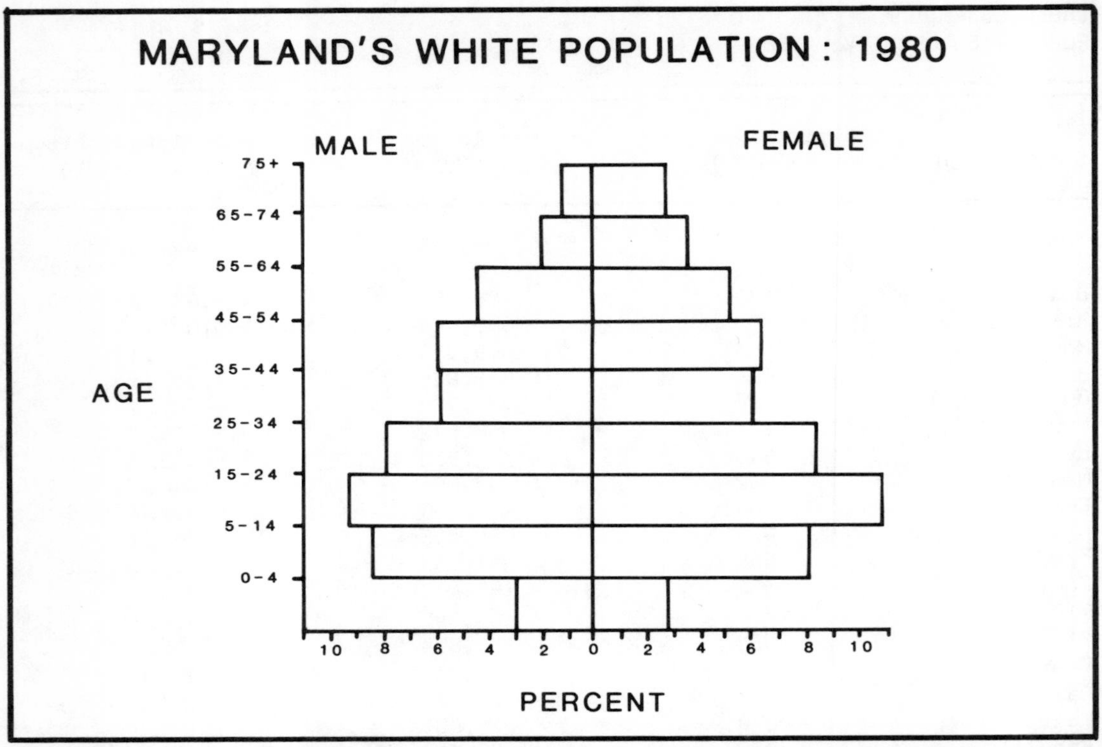

MARYLAND'S WHITE POPULATION: 1980

FIGURE 6.3 (*above*). FIGURE 6.4 (*below*). Source for both figures: Data from U.S. Census of Population, 1980.

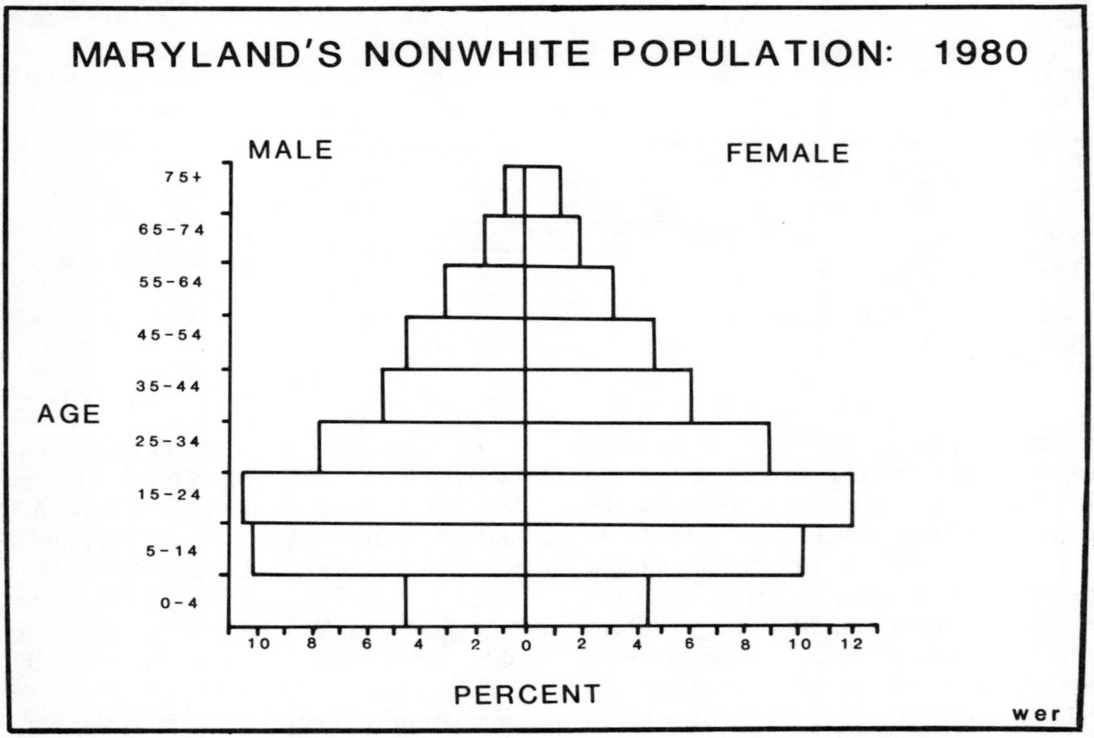

MARYLAND'S NONWHITE POPULATION: 1980

ulation. The infant mortality rate per 1,000 live births is 25.7 for nonwhites and 13.7 for whites, while the crude birthrate per 1,000 population is 17.1 for nonwhites and 11.5 for whites.[1] Crude death rates per 1,000 population are 7.3 for nonwhites and 8.1 for whites. Although nonwhites suffer from higher infant mortality rates, the excess of the birthrate over the death rate (9.8 percent) indicates that the nonwhite population will continue to grow at a faster rate than the white.

As with the population in general, the geographical distribution of the white and nonwhite populations is highly uneven. Of the 1,058,328 nonwhites in Maryland in 1980, nearly 42 percent (441,380) resided in Baltimore City. As a result of the growth of the black population, coupled with the loss of white population (which declined 28 percent from 1970 to 1980), the majority of Baltimore's population is now black.

There have been some strong suburbanization trends of the nonwhite population in Maryland, especially in those areas immediately adjacent to Baltimore and Washington, D.C. For example, in Prince Georges County, nonwhite increase was matched by white decrease in the 1970s. The result was that the total population remained about the same between 1970 and 1980, but in 1980 41.9 percent of the population was nonwhite, whereas in 1970 it was only 15 percent nonwhite. Similar suburban nonwhite growth occurred in Baltimore, Montgomery, and Howard counties, but the white populations did not decrease there. In 1970, 15 percent of the blacks who lived in the Baltimore metropolitan area lived in the suburban counties; by 1980 that figure had reached 24 percent. The white population, with the exception of that in Harford County, increased in those counties containing the outer suburbs of Baltimore and Washington, D.C.: Carroll, Harford, Frederick, Charles, and Calvert counties.

Most of the Eastern Shore, Piedmont, and western Maryland counties remained heavily white in 1980; for example, Allegany County was 98 percent white, Carroll 96 percent, Frederick 94 percent, Talbot 78 percent, and Wicomico 84 percent. Of these areas, the Eastern Shore has historically contained the largest nonwhite population.

Like most of the United States, Maryland has experienced significant demographic changes since 1970. Nonmetropolitan areas of the state are growing at a more rapid rate than metropolitan areas. The well-connected highway network of Maryland has facilitated the process of people moving from urban areas to residences in rural areas, while still maintaining their jobs in the metropolitan areas. In addition, the spread of jobs to the outer rings of the metropolitan areas has added to the attractiveness of rural exurbs as places of residence. The commuter field of the urban corridor has extended into southern Maryland and the Eastern Shore, to which the Chesapeake Bay Bridge has provided good access.

In terms of the national pattern, the states in the Northeast and Midwest are growing more slowly than Maryland, while those in the South and West are growing more rapidly. After 1930, Maryland's rate of population growth was faster than the national rate, especially during the 1960s. By the 1970s, the state's growth rate had settled down to about the national rate. Maryland's growth in this century has been tied to the assets of its varied economy and to the influence of federal government jobs and related employment in and around Washington, D.C.

SOCIOECONOMIC CHARACTERISTICS

In general, residents of Maryland are affluent, well educated, and well housed. Yet Maryland still has particular segments of the population that do not share in the society's generally high standard of living: poor, inner-city dwellers of Baltimore, sharecroppers in southern Maryland, and seasonally unemployed workers in western

Maryland and on the Eastern Shore. A number of key socioeconomic characteristics of the population, as well as their geographic patterns, must be identified in order to understand present needs and to plan for future requirements.

Housing

While the overall characteristics for housing in Maryland are those of good quality and high values, there are significant variations from place to place in the age, quality, and type of structures. The greatest differences are seen between housing in the urban corridor and other areas, although there is also significant variation in housing within the urban corridor. The two large cities located at the ends of the urban corridor differ in housing characteristics. Baltimore has a larger share of renter-occupied, single-family, prewar housing; in Washington, D.C., there are more large, black-occupied, multiple-family housing units, reflecting an emphasis on the construction of high-rise and garden-complex apartments in recent years.[2]

Age. The age of structures varies around the state. Over 30 percent of the houses on the Eastern Shore were built before 1940; in western Maryland this percentage reaches 45. Between 1970 and 1980, the number of housing units in Howard County increased an amazing 135 percent, due largely to the growth of the planned city of Columbia. The development in and around Ocean City caused Worcester County's housing units to increase 118 percent during the 1970s; many of these units are vacation homes and high-rise condominiums (Figure 6.5). Significant growth also occurred in southern Maryland as Washington, D.C., spread its influence into tobacco country: the rate of Calvert County was 61 percent, Charles County 68 percent, Anne Arundel 45 percent, and St. Marys 50 percent. Other areas of notable housing

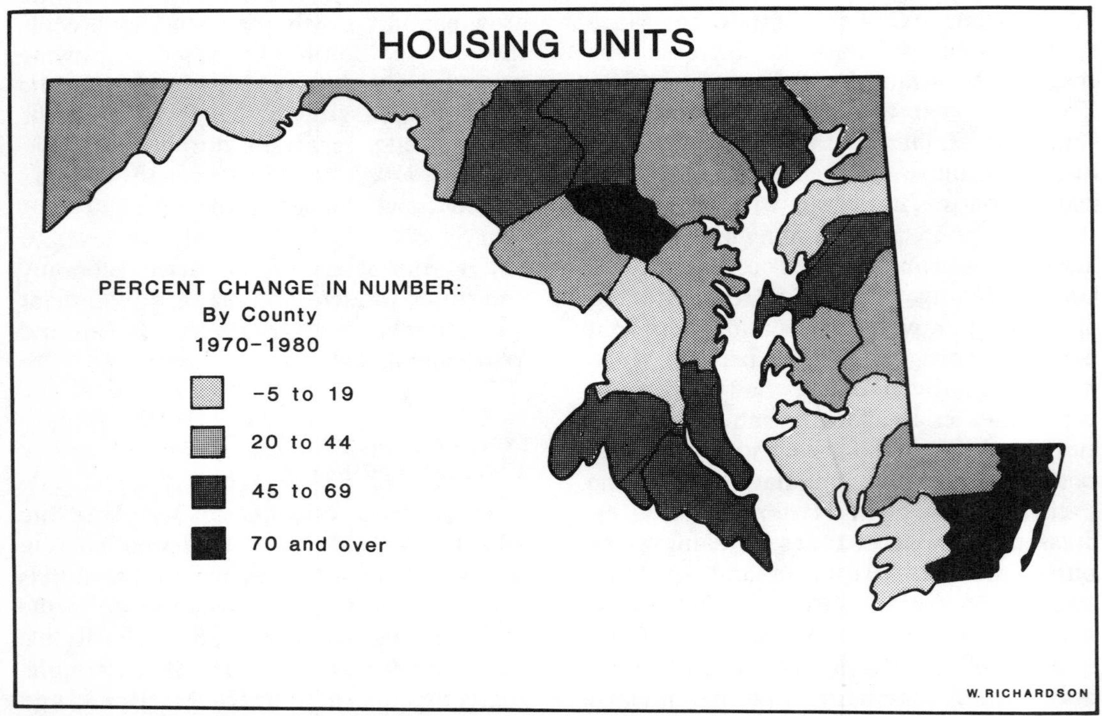

FIGURE 6.5. Source: Data from U.S. Census of Population, 1980.

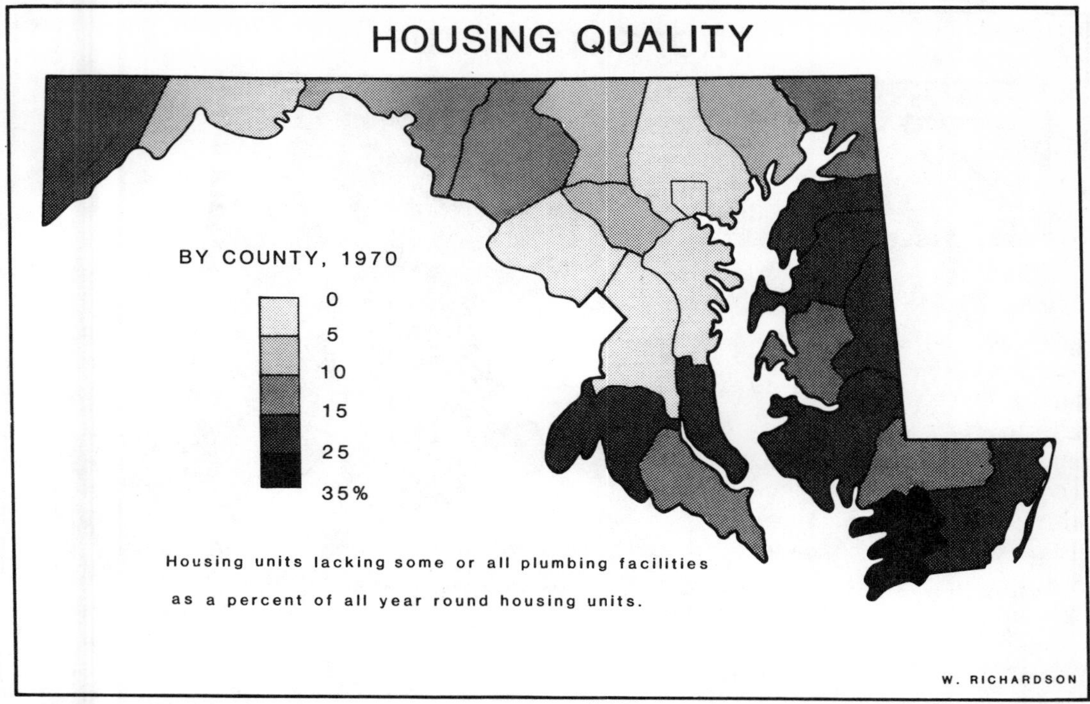

FIGURE 6.6. Source: U.S. Census Bureau, *Census of Housing, 1970.*

growth during the 1970s were Carroll, Frederick, Harford, and Queen Anne counties. On the other end of the scale, Baltimore City lost 1.2 percent of its housing units and Allegany County gained a mere 7.2 percent during the 1970s.

Quality. Quality of housing has been interpreted from the latest available U.S. Census data on the basis of the percentage of housing lacking some or all plumbing facilities (Figure 6.6) (plumbing facilities included in the census are piped hot and cold water inside a structure, a flush toilet, and tub or shower for use only by occupants of the housing unit).

In many of the counties of the Eastern Shore and in southern Maryland, over one-fifth of the houses lack some or all plumbing; the highest proportion is 34 percent in Somerset County. Again, it is the housing in the urban corridor which has the highest quality. As few as 1 percent of the housing units in Montgomery County lack some plumbing, followed by low figures in Baltimore City (2 percent) and Baltimore county (2 percent).

Ownership. Home ownership is a goal of many Marylanders. In 1980 nearly 58 percent of the state's housing units were owner occupied. Occupancy by owners ranged from a high of 74 percent in Howard County to a low of 40 percent in Baltimore City. The greatest valuation of property in Maryland occurs in Montgomery, Baltimore, and Prince Georges counties, and Baltimore City in that order (Figure 6.7).

Type. Housing is a basic fact of human geography reflecting culture, current fashion, functional needs, and the positive and negative aspects of the noncultural environment.[3] Building styles that evolved during the colonial period, before professionalism in architecture for homes was widespread, are referred to as *folk housing.* As a topic, folk housing has been largely ignored by architects and anthropologists

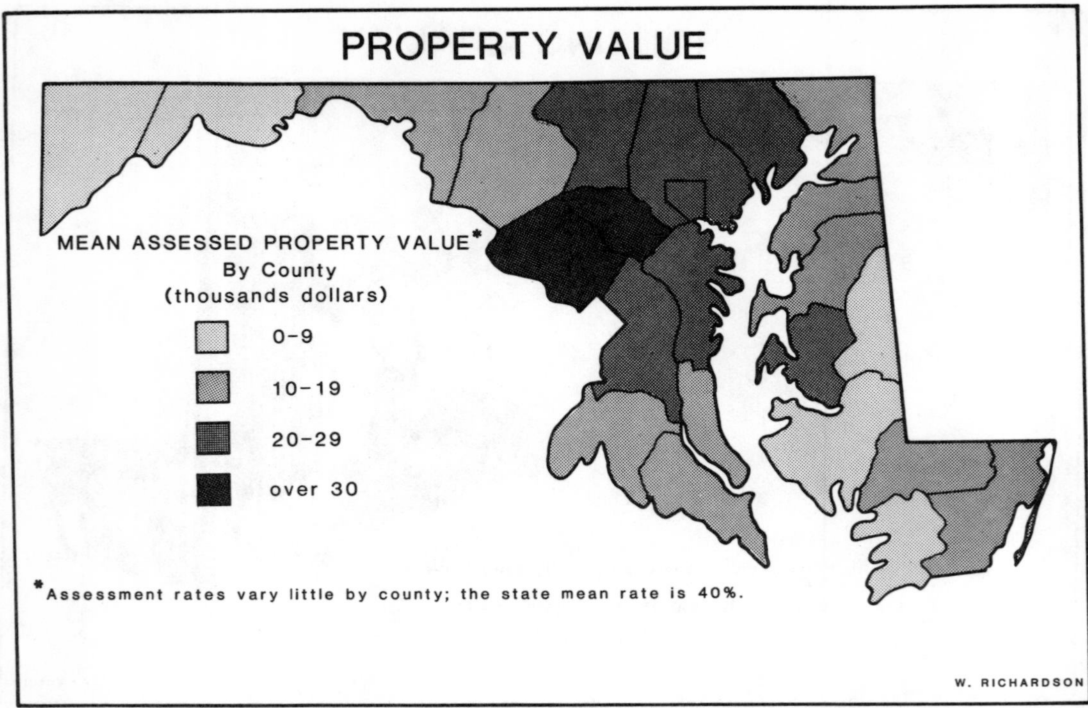

FIGURE 6.7. Source: Data from Maryland Department of Assessments and Taxation, *1979 Annual Survey Assessment Ratios.*

in the United States; only a few geographers have given the topic serious attention. Foremost among the cultural geographers interested in folk housing is Fred Kniffen, who disagrees with the notion that U.S. settlement patterns are so young and so marked by ferment, mixture, and makeshift that they are amorphous and their study can lead to no significant results.[4]

Another cultural geographer, Wilbur Zelinsky, describes the house as the product of a complex set of societal and psychological factors, all filtered through the sediments of history. House form tells us about physical locale, technology of the era, source and dates of the builder, and the class, occupation, and religion of the original occupant.[5] By 1790, three well-defined colonial culture source areas had developed in the eastern United States: southern New England, the Midland region centered on southeastern Pennsylvania, and the Chesapeake Bay area. Each of these culture source areas developed its own set of house types, which diffused into other parts of the country and were modified according to local materials and environments (Figure 6.8).

In Maryland, while some of the designs and materials for homes of the wealthy were imported intact from western Europe, the average house is a composite of European and native elements. The hearth of the Chesapeake Bay folk house was from tidewater Maryland and Virginia, much of northern and western Maryland was influenced by the Midland culture, and styles in the interior of the state represent a fusion of the other two styles.

The concern here is with structures built before about 1850, as the styles of those built after that time reflect date of construction rather than territorial location. By 1850 there had been enough mixing of the colonial house types to produce a set of national architectural forms. The role

FOLK HOUSING BY 1850

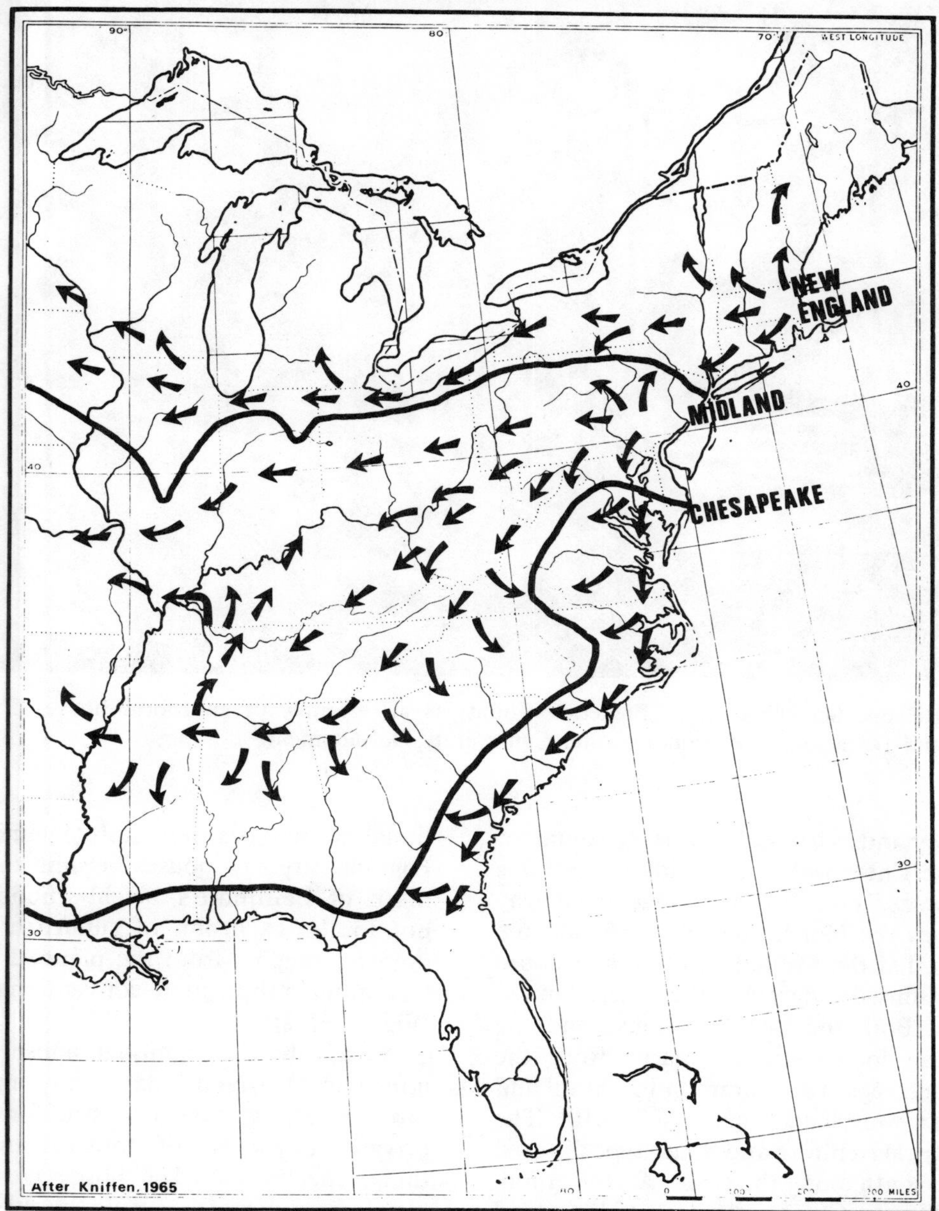

FIGURE 6.8. Source: Adapted from Fred Kniffen, "Folk Housing: Key to Diffusion," *Annals Association of American Geographers,* 55, December 1965, p. 560.

FIGURE 6.9. Schiefferstadt in Frederick County is an example of an I-form house. Courtesy, Maryland Department of Economic and Community Development.

of Maryland as a so-called mixing container for the Chesapeake and Midland cultures reinforces its position as a hinge or gateway between the North and South. Figure 6.8 shows that the Midland culture and house form diffused widely over the eastern United States. Both the English I-house and the German log-constructed barns from the Midland region are common in central and western Maryland (Figures 6.9, 6.10). The Chesapeake culture and house type diffused to the south along the coast. A typical folk house in the Chesapeake area of Maryland has end chimneys with a front gallery or porch where much of the social life of the family took place during the warmer seasons (Figure 6.11).

As Maryland developed and became more urbanized in the late nineteenth century and the twentieth century, newer national house types were built (Figure 6.12). High-density row houses became the hallmark of Baltimore's neighborhoods, but not to the exclusion of suburban development, ranging from the planned city of Columbia to some more conventional types (Figure 6.12).

As a subset of national house forms, homes in Maryland today incorporate features reflecting buyers' desire for space, privacy, quickness of construction, and things mechanical. The house is a completely appropriate capsule world incorporating the main principles, myths, and values of the larger culture.[6]

Income

Income data describe Maryland as one of the more affluent states. Constituting 2 percent of the nation's population, Mary-

FIGURE 6.10. Pennsylvania German barns with overhand forebays and ground-level access to the second floor are common in north-central Maryland. Courtesy, Carroll County Farm Museum in Westminster.

FIGURE 6.11. This lower Chesapeake tidewater-type house is located on Kent Island.

FIGURE 6.12. Home types vary greatly around Maryland. *Top left,* high-density old homes in Baltimore; *center left,* a new high-density area—Coldspring Village in Baltimore; *bottom left,* suburban single-family detached home; *top right,* suburban townhouses; *center right,* farm in Carroll County; *bottom right,* clam workers' shanties on Kent Island.

landers earned 2 percent of the nation's total personal income in 1978 and ranked sixteenth among the states.[7] The average household, consumer-spendable income (household income after all federal, state, and local taxes have been deducted) for Maryland was $20,407 in 1978, compared to $18,460 for the nation as a whole (Table 6.2). Of the states in the mideastern and southern parts of the country, only New Jersey had a higher average household, consumer-spendable income. The distribution of families by consumer-spendable income is interesting. Of the states listed in Table 6.2, only New Jersey had a smaller percentage of families with income under $8,000; Maryland had the highest percentage of families with income of $25,000 and over. Within Maryland, the metropolitan areas are the leaders. Montgomery County has the second-highest average disposable income ($28,658) of any county in the United States, and Baltimore, Prince Georges and Charles counties all have average disposable incomes of over $20,000 per household. On the lower end of the scale are Garrett, Caroline, Calvert, and Worcester counties, all under $13,000.

A more common measure of income is per capita income. Maryland ranked thirteenth among the states in per capita income in 1978.[8] Of the states listed in Table 6.2, only New Jersey and Delaware had higher per capita incomes. The pattern within Maryland is in agreement with, and related to, the previously described patterns of housing and disposable income (Figure 6.13). The highest per capita incomes were found in Montgomery and Howard counties with their large numbers of professional people. The next-highest category in Figure 6.13 included Baltimore County and Prince Georges County. Thus the four counties with the highest per capita incomes were in the urban corridor. The third-highest category included Harford County, Baltimore City, and Anne Arundel County in the urban corridor, as well as five other counties on the Eastern Shore and in central-western Maryland. In this category, most of the counties that are outside of the urban corridor have a sizable urban center in which incomes are higher than in the surrounding area: Worcester County has Ocean City; Wicomico County—Salisbury; Harford County—Bel Air; Frederick County—Frederick; and Washington County—Hagerstown. Talbot County's center, Easton, is smaller, but the county also is the residence of a number of high-income retired people, as well as some wealthy families who bought land and built estates here during the 1920s and the Great Depression.[9] The remainder of the state, including far-western Maryland, southern Maryland, and the remainder of the Eastern Shore, falls into the lowest income categories. Much of the employment in these low-income areas is in primary economic activities, e.g., farming, lumbering, mining, and fishing, all of which are seasonal and have fluctuating market prices.

The income information thus far presented tells the story of a generally affluent state, but data that are geographically aggregated at the state and county levels mask many pockets and locales of extreme poverty in Maryland. In 1970 (the latest year for which figures are available) there were nearly 75,000 Maryland families, 10 percent of the state's families, living below the poverty level, a designation used by the federal government as one means of identifying areas and persons with income levels so low that some economic hardship is present. Various levels have been determined depending on family size, sex of family head, number of children, and type of residence; the poverty-level threshold for 1970 averaged $3,750.[10]

Unlike Washington, D.C., which has an income profile similar to its surrounding suburban counties and a median income higher than most cities, Baltimore City has an income profile more like rural areas: many people living in economic hardship.[11] Baltimore City alone has 40 percent (30,000) of the state's families living below the poverty level. Low incomes are not only localized geographically, but are also con-

TABLE 6.2

AVERAGE HOUSEHOLD CONSUMER-SPENDABLE INCOME, MARYLAND AND SELECTED EASTERN STATES: 1978

State	Average Household Consumer-Spendable Income [a]	Percentage Distribution of Families, by Consumer-Spendable Income Group				
		Under $8,000	$8,000-9,999	$10,000-14,999	$15,000-24,999	$25,000 and over
United States	$18,460	6.1	11.1	18.7	30.3	33.8
Mideast						
MARYLAND	20,407	4.9	8.4	16.7	31.5	38.5
New York	18,981	5.9	9.2	17.7	29.9	37.3
New Jersey	21,211	4.4	7.9	17.2	32.1	38.4
Pennsylvania	18,392	7.1	12.3	20.8	30.1	29.7
Delaware	20,289	5.0	9.9	18.1	30.6	36.4
Southeast						
Virginia	18,969	6.7	11.4	17.6	28.9	35.4
West Virginia	15,652	9.3	17.3	22.4	27.8	23.2
North Carolina	16,302	8.8	15.6	21.1	27.7	26.8
South Carolina	16,071	8.6	15.6	21.2	28.5	26.1
Georgia	16,751	8.1	13.5	19.4	28.7	30.3
Florida	16,135	6.9	12.4	17.6	26.9	36.2
Mississippi	14,981	9.7	17.7	20.7	26.2	25.7
Kentucky	15,977	8.6	15.5	21.0	28.0	26.9
Tennessee	15,361	9.3	15.9	20.8	27.4	26.6
Alabama	15,700	9.3	16.3	21.0	27.4	26.0

Source: Standard Rate and Data Service, Inc., 1-1-79 SRDS Consumer Market Data Summary, issued Aug. 12, 1979.

[a] Household income after all federal, state, and local taxes have been deducted.

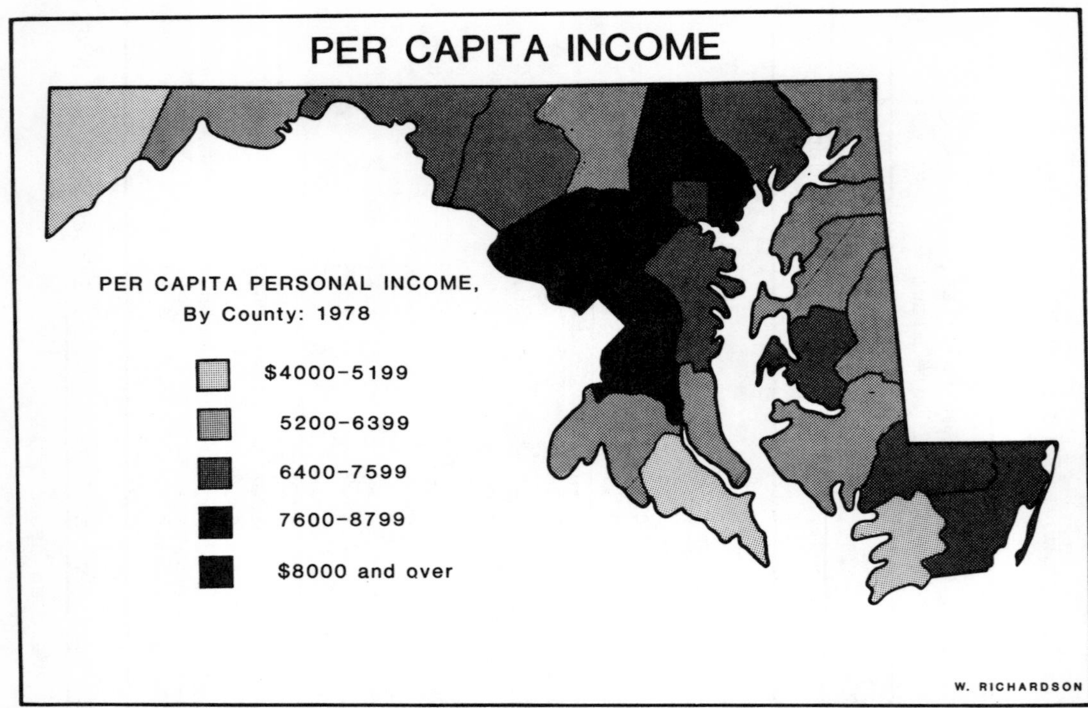

FIGURE 6.13. Source: U.S. Department of Commerce, Bureau of Economic Analysis, *Regional Economic Information System,* April 1978.

centrated in certain population segments, e.g., blacks, the elderly, and female heads of households. Income differences between some rural and urban places in Maryland are offset by the overall lower cost of living in areas outside the urban corridor where housing, food, insurance, and transportation are usually less expensive.

Education

In 1694 the Maryland General Assembly provided for a free school, the first in what is now the United States. The school opened as King William's School in Annapolis in 1696; today it is St. John's College. In 1864 the schools of Maryland were put under the supervision of the State Board of Education, and in 1900 a state superintendent of schools was appointed.[12]

Maryland high schools graduated approximately 56,000 students in 1978; of these, 42 percent continued into higher education. In the same year there were over 28,000 full-time students in the twenty two-year colleges of Maryland, and nearly 99,000 students in the twenty-eight four-year colleges and universities. If part-time students are included, over 215,000 students were enrolled in institutions of higher education in the state during 1978;[13] the largest by enrollment were the University of Maryland at College Park (37,000), Towson State University (15,000), and Johns Hopkins University (10,000).

Baltimore is the educational center of the state with its many colleges and universities; the major ones are the Johns Hopkins University, University of Maryland at Baltimore, St. Mary's Seminary and University, College of Notre Dame of Maryland, Loyola University, Morgan State University, Mt. St. Agnes College, Coppin State College, Maryland Institute of Art, Peabody Institute, and University of Baltimore. Nearby are the University of Maryland at Baltimore County in Catonsville

FIGURE 6.14. The U.S. Naval Academy in Annapolis. Courtesy, Baltimore Office of Promotion and Tourism.

and Towson State University and Goucher College in Towson. A number of other colleges are located around the state, including the United States Naval Academy in Annapolis (Figure 6.14).

The geographic pattern of socioeconomic contrasts between the urban corridor and the rest of the state is reinforced by the educational attainment levels of the population (Figure 6.15). Differences between the suburban counties and Baltimore City are also evident. The median number of school years completed for all of Maryland's population in 1970 was 12.1; the median for the United States was also 12.1 years. Figure 6.15 shows that the only areas of the state at or above the median were those in the urban corridor and extending into southern Maryland, along with Allegany County in the west. Great contrasts also existed within the urban corridor; Baltimore City's population aged twenty-five and older had a median educational level of 10.0 years, while that group in Montgomery County had the highest in the state, 13.0 years. The entire Eastern Shore fell below the median; Somerset County was the lowest in the state. The highest educational attainment levels found on the Eastern Shore were in Cecil County, Talbot County, and Wicomico County, which has a sizable state college at Salisbury.

The differences in education between white and nonwhite people are striking. The nonwhite population of Maryland had a median level of only 10.0 years of school completed, compared to more than 12 years for whites. The percentage of blacks with college degrees was only half that of whites; the percentage of blacks with high school work was only two-thirds that of whites. Contrasts also existed between the rural and urban areas; the percentage of urbanites in Maryland who were college educated

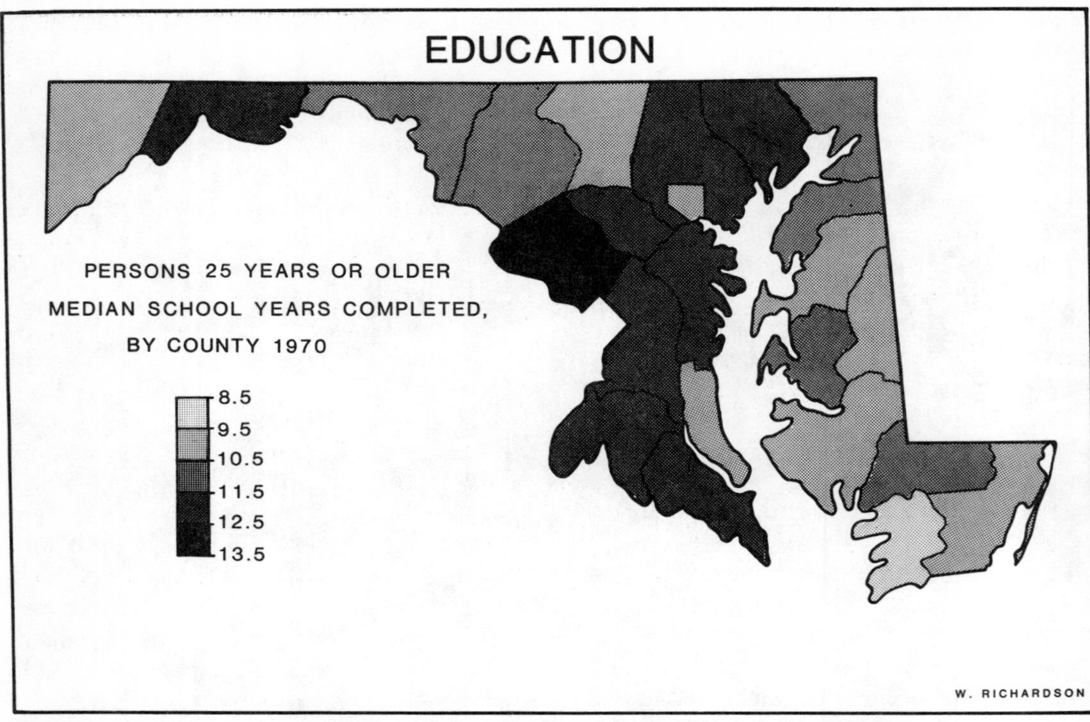

FIGURE 6.15. Source: U.S. Bureau of the Census, *Census of Population,* 1970.

was nearly twice that of the rural nonfarm and farm populations.

The geographic pattern of high school retention rates is interesting. Over 90 percent of the high school students in Montgomery and Howard counties graduated, as did over 80 percent in all of the other suburban counties except Prince Georges. Graduation in Allegany and Garrett counties also reached over 80 percent. On the other end of the spectrum were Baltimore City, southern Maryland, and Queen Annes and Somerset counties, where less than 70 percent of the students completed high school. These low retention rates corresponded to high percentages of blacks in the population.[14]

ETHNIC GROUPS

Various peoples have made significant contributions to the shaping of the Maryland landscape. The term *ethnic* has no definite meaning. This old word stems from the ancient Greeks, who used it to mean "heathen," in the sense of non-Greek and therefore barbarian. The English used the word to mean anyone not Christian or Jewish. In the United States today, "ethnic" has come to mean any person who is not Anglo Saxon.[15]

Ethnicity, therefore, is defined from one's particular perspective. American Indians viewed the newly arrived, strange European settlers as ethnics. The Europeans viewed the Indians as savage ethnics who had to be converted to Christianity.

Over the past 300 years numerous groups of people have come to Maryland for reasons ranging from religious oppression to economic opportunity. It is remarkable that over this period of time these various ethnic groups have not completely melted into a new American race. Instead, ethnic identities run strong in Maryland, even though the various groups have developed livable relationships, become friends, and intermarried. Throughout the state ethnic festivals are celebrated annually, especially in Baltimore City. Ethnic groups support their own churches, newspapers, radio and television stations, and various other civic organizations. The ethnic peoples of Maryland are indeed an important and contributing element of the culture of the state.

It is important to study ethnicity in order to know more about the society, its heritage, its social problems, and its possibilities. Ethnic awareness and feeling, very visible in Maryland today, are not new phenomena. Ethnicity has always been present in Maryland's society, but it was not always embraced with a tolerant attitude.

Prior to the 1890s, the largest numbers of immigrants to Maryland came from northern and western Europe and, via forced immigration, from Africa. As this "old" immigration declined, more immigrants from eastern and southern Europe and Russia began to arrive. The first waves of immigrants had settled the state and pushed west to the coal fields of Garrett County. Most of the "new" immigrants after 1890 settled in and around Baltimore City. The shift in source areas for Maryland's immigrants is shown in Table 6.3. By 1920, Baltimore City contained over 80 percent of the foreign born in Maryland. The large numbers of immigrants caused alarm among some native-born citizens. Indeed, there was a strong nativist sentiment against immigrants in Maryland.

Although Baltimore City attracted the bulk of the immigrants, every region of the state had immigrant residents. The Eastern Shore attracted the fewest, while central Maryland (Baltimore, Carroll, Frederick, Harford, and Howard counties) attracted the most. After Baltimore City, Baltimore County had the largest number of foreign born in the state for many years. By 1970, the pattern had shifted. The Maryland suburbs of Washington, D.C., were the leading regions for foreign born and foreign stock (which includes U.S.-born residents of foreign parentage and the foreign born) rather than Maryland's traditional magnet, the Baltimore region (Table 6.4).

In 1970, there were 410,680 ethnic people in Maryland, comprising 10.5 percent of the total population (Table 6.5). The largest ethnic groups in Maryland were German, Spanish speaking, Italian, Soviet, and Polish, in that order. Germans have been in Maryland since colonial times, when they migrated from Pennsylvania

TABLE 6.3

FOREIGN BORN POPULATION OF EUROPEAN BACKGROUND LIVING IN MARYLAND

	1890		1930	
	Number	%	Number	%
Northwestern Europe	29,119	30.9	15,853	16.6
Central Europe	57,382	60.9	38,424	40.4
Eastern Europe	4,258	4.5	23,391	24.8
Southern Europe	1,512	1.6	12,770	13.4
All Europe	92,271	97.9	90,438	95.2

Source: Ethnic Affairs Committee of Baltimore County, Ethnic Heritages and Horizons: An Expanding Awareness, 1980, p. 123.

TABLE 6.4

FOREIGN BORN AND FOREIGN STOCK IN SELECTED JURISDICTIONS: 1970

	Foreign Born		Foreign Stock	
	#	%	#	%
Montgomery	35,914	6.8	110,743	21.1
Baltimore City	28,710	3.1	100,235	11.0
Prince George's	24,639	3.7	81,989	12.4
Baltimore	18,157	2.9	87,323	14.0
Anne Arundel	5,915	1.9	27,492	9.2

Source: Ethnic Affairs Committee of Baltimore County, Ethnic Heritages and Horizons: An Expanding Awareness, 1980, p. 125.

TABLE 6.5

ETHNICITY IN MARYLAND 1970

Source Area	Number
Asian	
Chinese	6,520
Filipino	5,170
Japanese	3,733
Other	8,370
European	
Austrian	13,516
Czech	11,111
Danish	2,461
Dutch	3,312
French	6,519
German	59,680
Greek	12,508
Hungarian	7,817
Italian	49,619
Lithuanian	9,090
Norwegian	3,385
Polish	39,334
Swedish	4,546
Swiss	2,437
USSR	46,332
Yugoslavian	3,148
Other European	15,069
American	
American Indian	4,329
Canadian	25,300
Spanish speaking	52,974
Other	15,490
TOTAL	410,680

Source: U.S. Department of Commerce, Bureau of the Census, U.S. Census of Population, 1970.

into western Maryland. A sect of Germans, the Mennonites, have spread out of southeastern Pennsylvania into southern Maryland. In 1970, nearly 15,000 German ethnics resided in Baltimore. Of the nearly 53,000 Spanish-speaking persons, 32,000 resided in metropolitan Baltimore, 3,000 in and around Annapolis, and the remainder throughout the state with a cluster in the Washington suburbs. Most of the Spanish-speaking people were from Latin America and had arrived since 1960. Although Italians were spread throughout the state, there was a distinct cluster in the area of Baltimore called Little Italy. The large number of ethnics from the USSR included mainly Jews, Russians, Byelorussians, and Ukrainians. Polish people were found throughout the state, with a large concentration of over 14,000 in Baltimore.

Notable among the smaller ethnic groups found in Maryland are the American Indians. A few descendants of the Piscataways of southern Maryland, Nanticokes of the Eastern Shore, and Susquehannocks from the Maryland-Pennsylvania border area still lived in Maryland. The largest concentration of Indians was the Lumbees in Baltimore; numbering 2,500, these people are from a number of various eastern tribes, mainly from North Carolina.

NOTES

1. *Annual Vital Statistics Report, 1980* (Annapolis: Maryland Department of Health and Mental Hygiene, Maryland Center for Health Statistics, 1981).
2. Derek Thompson, ed., *Atlas of Maryland* (College Park: Department of Geography, University of Maryland, 1977), p. 97.
3. Fred Kniffen, "Folk Housing: Key to Diffusion," *Annals of the Association of American Geographers* 55 (1965):549.
4. Ibid.
5. Wilbur Zelinsky, *The Cultural Geography of the United States* (Englewood Cliffs, N.J.: Prentice Hall, 1973), p. 88.
6. Ibid., p. 94.
7. *Survey of Current Business, August 1979* (Washington, D.C.: U.S. Department of Commerce, Bureau of Economic Analysis, 1979).
8. Ibid.
9. Boyd Gibbons, *Wye Island: The True Story of an American Community's Struggle to Preserve Its Way of Life* (Baltimore: Johns Hopkins University Press, 1977), pp. 88–89.
10. *Census of Population 1970, General Social and Economic Characteristics,* Final Report PC (1) C22, Maryland (Washington, D.C.: U.S. Department of Commerce, Bureau of the Census, 1970).
11. Thompson, ed., *Atlas of Maryland,* p. 89.
12. Harold E. Vokes, *Geography and Geology of Maryland,* revised by Jonathan Edwards, Jr. (Baltimore: Maryland Geological Survey, 1968), p. 17.
13. *Profile of Higher Education in Maryland, 1979* (Annapolis: Maryland Board of Higher Education, 1980).
14. Thompson, ed., *Atlas of Maryland,* p. 93.
15. *Maryland, Our Maryland, An Ethnic and Cultural Directory* (Baltimore: Baltimore Council for International Visitors, 1975), p. 3.

CHAPTER 7

SERVICES TO PEOPLE

Maryland ranks high in the nation by most of the standards used to indicate provision of services to the people. Some form of higher education is available to almost everyone within a short distance of his or her residence. Transportation facilities for intrastate and external travel are readily accessible. Local and state government agencies provide a wide range of special welfare services, and health-care facilities range from among the best in the nation to at least adequate in some of the rural areas.

GOVERNMENT

Maryland is organized into twenty-four counties, including Baltimore City, which is legally a county. Four counties are in western Maryland, eight in the central part of the state, three in southern Maryland, and nine on the Eastern Shore. Most of the counties are between 250 and 500 sq mi (648 and 1296 sq km) in size, but Baltimore, Dorchester, Frederick, and Garrett are larger and Calvert and Baltimore City smaller.[1]

Counties are the most important form of government in Maryland. They gradually have taken over provision of basic services—such as schools, police and fire protection, and public works—which elsewhere are usually the responsibility of municipalities. There are only fifty incorporated places in Maryland; of these, only eight have a population exceeding 25,000: Baltimore City, Bowie, Rockville, College Park, Annapolis, Cumberland, Hagerstown and Salisbury. Places such as Towson, Catonsville, Dundalk, Wheaton, Silver Spring, and Bethesda have over 50,000 people, yet they are unincorporated and have no city government.

The key to the structure of Maryland's government is local responsibility for the implementation of area functions and services, under the broad policy guidance of the state. Economic and social change has been more easily accommodated because of the great amount of flexibility in the system. Over the past three centuries, Maryland has created and sustained a system of local government that is so uniform and responsive, it may well prove to be among those state systems most capable of responding appropriately and quickly to the severe challenges of urban development.[2]

Maryland is one of twenty-nine state systems with no township government, and one of four with no independent school districts. The total Maryland system of local government has only 351 units; forty-three states have more local governmental units than Maryland.[3] The counties and municipalities that form Maryland's basic units of government have a high degree of basic uniformity; the absence of the clutter and multiplication of local governments that so often compound and clog the local process is one of the main strengths of the system. It is also flexible enough to adjust for the great variety of physical, social, cultural, and economic environments that exist in different parts of the state. Each local government in Maryland reflects, in its operations and relations, both the prominent features of its own environment and the general requirements and limitations of constitutional and legislative provisions.[4] A good example of the flexibility in local government allowing for the expression of concerns of the local population in environmental issues is the case of Wye Island in Queen Annes County. In 1974, developer James Rouse (a native of Easton in Talbot County, Maryland) announced his plans to buy most of Wye Island and to develop it in a careful and planned manner. After a series of exhaustive socioeconomic and physical geographical studies, the Rouse Company presented its plan at a public session in Centerville; the reception by the public and the Queen Annes county commissioners was not supportive. The local government refused to rezone Wye Island below the minimum five-acre plot, and shortly afterward the Rouse Company withdrew its plan that had cost nearly $900,000 to prepare.[5]

The county originally started out as a broad geographic area within which judicial and record-keeping functions were performed locally. These activities were centered in the county seat, usually located near the geographic center of the county; the guiding principle was that the county seat should be no more than one day's ride by horseback from any point in the county.[6] (The series of maps in Figure 5.2 shows the development of the present pattern of counties in Maryland.)

In 1683, Maryland's legislature passed the "town act," which systematized the establishment of city and town municipalities. Municipal governments were given the responsibility of providing services such as public health, construction and maintenance of public thoroughfares, and some fire and police protection. A county and an incorporated municipality serve largely different, yet partially overlapping, populations. Municipal governments often serve densely settled populations in small areas, whereas the county governments serve populations that are spatially clustered as well as dispersed over larger geographic areas. Municipalities and counties traditionally have divided responsibilities in a functionally complementary manner.

Since 1950 the population patterns in the state have greatly changed, with counties in the urban corridor experiencing growth of urban population clusters. The suburban growth of Washington, D.C., and Baltimore City in particular, but also of the smaller cities, has demonstrated the need for greater cooperation between municipal and county governments. Two prime examples are Prince Georges County as it relates to Washington, D.C., and Baltimore County as it relates to Baltimore City. Maryland has responded to these demographic changes, but not by creating new local governments; not since 1953 has a new municipal government been incorporated in Maryland.[7] Instead, a number of counties have assumed responsibilities usually left to municipalities, for example, water, garbage removal, sewage disposal, planning and zoning, and police and fire protection. Baltimore and Howard counties, in fact, remain without any incorporated places. As a result of these responses, Maryland has a high ratio of population to local government (the third highest in the nation) and continues with its strong reliance on local government.

TRANSPORTATION

The people of Maryland are served by a superb network integrating all of the various modes of transportation. Historically, the state has developed its transportation network concomitant with its settlement and growth.

The Port of Baltimore

The port of Baltimore is in many ways the heart of the state's economy, and nearly everyone living in Maryland is affected in some way by its operations. Each year more than 4,000 ships call at the port, carrying diverse cargoes such as teak from Burma and India to be used in cabinet making, coral from the Pacific for button makers in Caroline County, hemp from the Philippines for the brush industries of Frederick County, and iron ore and manganese from Venezuela and Liberia for one of the world's largest steel mills at Sparrows Point. As the export of many local and national products is also part of the port's activities, it puts Maryland on the interface of the international exchange of goods. By most standards, the port and foreign trade are Maryland's largest single economic asset—an asset based on the geographic location of the port.

The port of Baltimore began operations in 1706, predating the establishment of the city by twenty-three years. Early competition from Annapolis, Oxford, and the tobacco ports of southern Maryland was keen, but Baltimore's latent geographical-location advantages soon won out over the other ports. Because of the configuration of the coast, Baltimore is located farther inland and hence closer to the Midwest than other East Coast ports. As the interior of the country developed and railroads were built connecting Baltimore to the Midwest, the port's geographical advantages led to growth.

In the 1700s the port's Inner Harbor was a mud flat that could accommodate only small sailing vessels, and the only settlement was on the waterfront at Fells Point. In 1758, Dr. John Stevenson gave a lift to the small port when he began to ship grain from the port to customers up north and overseas. In the following years a port infrastructure developed: piers and warehouses, shipbuilders, financiers, merchants and brokers, and so forth.

During the Revolutionary War the port was left open despite a British blockade; this has been attributed to the British taste for the colony's tobacco exported through the port.[8] During the War of 1812, Baltimore was not as fortunate. The British attack on the city culminated in the bombardment of Fort McHenry, which to this day sits protecting the entrance of the harbor (Figure 7.1). Another lasting outcome of the British attack was the "Star Spangled Banner" written by Francis Scott Key. After the War of 1812, the port rebounded and developed a lucrative trade with South America and China (one section of the port, Canton, is named for the port of Canton, China). By the 1830s the Baltimore shipyards at Fells Point were turning out the famous Baltimore clippers, the fastest sailing vessels afloat. Even today, Baltimore remains a major commercial shipbuilding port.

By the 1860s, Baltimore had become a railroad port, with its rail line connections to the Midwest. Baltimore soon benefited from the discovery of oil in western Pennsylvania; refineries were developed at the port and U.S. oil was shipped all over the world. During this period Baltimore became the world's largest refiner of copper, as well as the country's leading fertilizer and chemical producer, based on the importation of Peruvian guano.

Although trade slowed down during the Civil War, it was quickly reestablished afterwards. The port's main ship canal was enlarged, thanks mainly to the efforts of Major William P. Craighill. By the late 1880s, the railroads had built huge grain elevators in the port; Baltimore is still one of the world's leading grain-shipping ports. It was during this time that the port also became a major shipper of coal and a fueling depot for steam-powered ships. These factors combined to make Baltimore the world's sixth-largest port by 1876.[9]

When the Panama Canal was built in 1914, the port of Baltimore once again benefited; for many years it handled more

FIGURE 7.1. Fort McHenry stands at the entrance to Baltimore's Inner Harbor. Courtesy, Maryland Department of Economic and Community Development.

cargo westward bound through the canal than any other East Coast port. During World War I the port grew even more; and by the time of World War II, Baltimore was ready to support the war effort. Between 1941 and 1945 Baltimore shipyards turned out 608 ships! The first liberty ship, the S. S. *Patrick Henry,* was built in Baltimore. After the war, the state became more involved in the administration of the port, and in 1956 the Maryland Port Authority (now the Maryland Port Administration) was established.

Through the port of Baltimore pumps the lifeblood of contemporary Maryland's economy. The port has 45 mi (72 km) of shoreline with containerized cargo facilities at Dundalk Marine Terminal and North Locust Point Terminal, huge storage facilities equivalent to 53,700 railroad cars of cargo, bulk cargo facilities, passenger liner facilities, and automobile import areas (Figure 7.2).

Baltimore's geographical location still gives it advantages. The port can be approached from the south through Chesapeake Bay and from the north via the toll-free Chesapeake and Delaware Canal. Being

PORT OF BALTIMORE

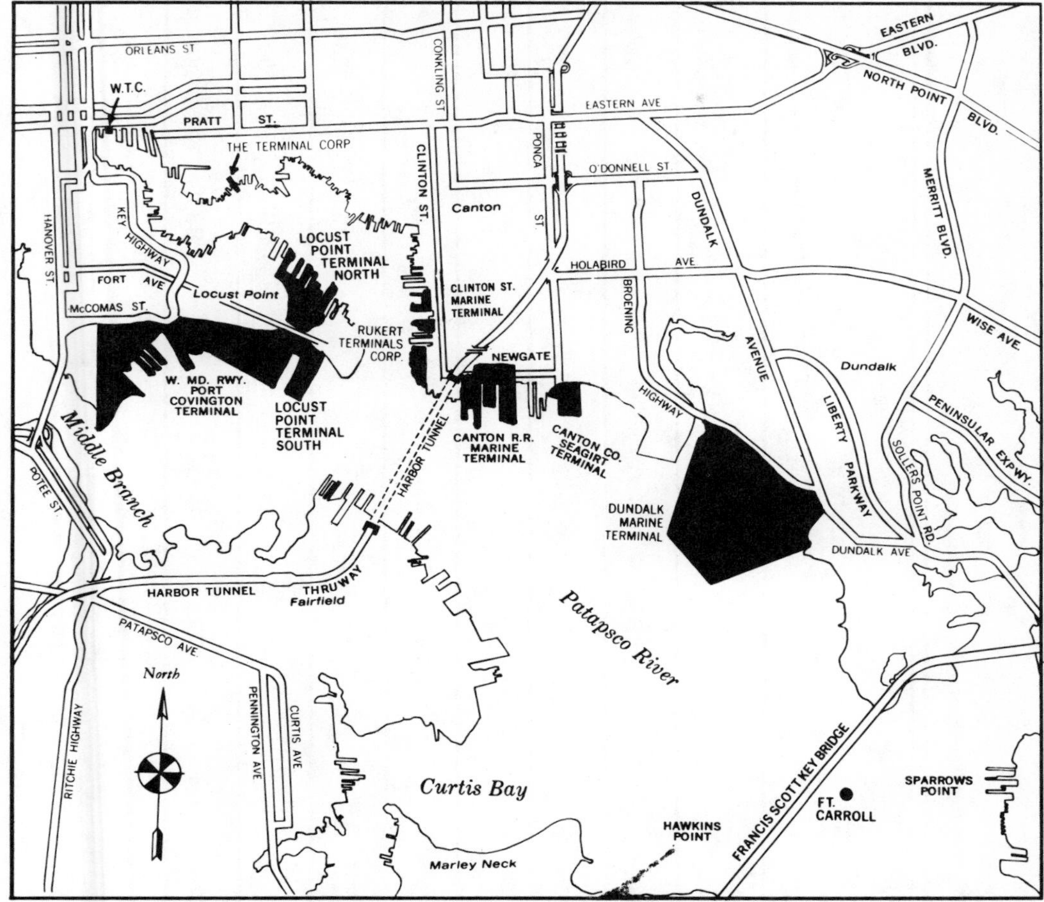

FIGURE 7.2. Courtesy, Maryland Department of Transportation, Maryland Port Administration.

located nearer the Midwest than other ports, Baltimore long has been known as the economy port of the East Coast (Table 7.1). Baltimore also is linked to Maryland's excellent transportation system, one of the most complete, sophisticated, and varied intermodal systems in the country. Three major trunk-line railroads, superb highways, and an international airport all serve the port.

Baltimore is a leading U.S. port by any standard. In foreign waterborne exports, the port ranks fifth in the nation by tonnage and third by value (Table 7.2). Export trade is carried on with many countries (Table 7.3). Japan is the leading export customer by tonnage; Saudi Arabia by value. Much of the export to Japan is coal, while many manufactured goods go to Saudi Arabia. Major exports through the port include coal, corn, wheat, soybeans, fertilizer, machinery and transport equipment, chemicals, and manufactured products. A specialty of the port is shipping disassembled industrial plants overseas to be reassembled.

In terms of imports, Baltimore's rank in the nation is seventh by tonnage and

TABLE 7.1

BALTIMORE'S PROXIMITY TO U.S. INTERIOR: COMPARATIVE RAIL DISTANCES

	To: Baltimore		Philadelphia		New York City	
From:	Miles	Kilometers	Miles	Kilometers	Miles	Kilometers
Pittsburgh	313	503	360	579	436	701
Cleveland	444	714	490	788	562	904
Columbus	479	770	545	877	621	999
Cincinnati	560	901	644	1036	724	1165
Detroit	604	972	637	1025	631	1015
Indianapolis	650	1046	723	1163	799	1286
Chicago	767	1234	814	1310	890	1432
Milwaukee	831	1337	878	1413	881	1417
St. Louis	891	1434	958	1541	1040	1673

Source: Baltimore Economic Development Commission, 1980.

TABLE 7.2
LEADING 15 U.S. SEAPORTS IN EXPORT OF FOREIGN WATERBORNE TRADE: 1978

	Exports by Tonnage		Exports by Value	
	Thous. Tons	Rank	$(Millions)	Rank
UNITED STATES	301,573		$ 79,055	
Baltimore	14,339	5	6,444	3
Baton Rouge	11,374	6	1,917	9
Charleston			1,685	10
Corpus Christi	5,863	10		
Galveston	3,776	15	1,125	14
Houston	20,050	1	7,222	2
Long Beach	6,983	8	2,173	8
Los Angeles			2,221	7
Mobile	4,852	13		
New Orleans	17,020	4	5,127	4
New York	6,220	9	11,877	1
Newport News	5,262	12		
Norfolk	17,310	2	4,540	5
Oakland			3,135	6
Philadelphia	4,378	14	1,595	11
Portland, Ore.	9,596	7	1,298	13
Savannah			1,011	15
Seattle			1,397	12
Tacoma	5,762	11		
Tampa	17,058	3		

Source: Maryland Department of Transportation, Maryland Port Administration, Foreign Commerce Statistical Report, 1978.
Tonnes = .9 x Tons

sixth by value (Table 7.4). The major source countries for imports are shown in Table 7.5. Canada is the leading source of imports by tonnage, while Japan is the leading source by value. Much of the Canadian imports consists of primary industry products such as lumber, paper, and iron ore; the high-value Japanese imports are largely automobiles and electronic appliances. Major bulk imports include iron ore, manganese ore, petroleum, sugar, molasses, bauxite, gypsum, and fertilizer.

Port-dependent industries can be found in every part of Maryland; examples are the aluminum and tire factories in western Maryland and tool makers in northern Maryland. Nearly 169,000 jobs throughout the state (1 out of every 10) are directly or indirectly related to the port.[10] The port's annual economic impact is $2.5 billion, or 10 percent of the Gross State Product.[11]

Air Transportation.

Maryland is served by three major, international airports and thirty-nine smaller airports and heliports. The leading commercial air facility in the state is Baltimore-Washington International Airport (BWI) in Anne Arundel County, just off the Balti-

TABLE 7.3

EXPORT TRADE OF THE PORT OF BALTIMORE
ARRANGED BY PRINCIPAL COUNTRIES AND BY TRADE AREAS: 1978

COUNTRY OF UNLADING IN ORDER OF TONNAGE	SHORT TONS [a]	COUNTRY OF UNLADING IN ORDER OF VALUE	VALUE
Japan	2,812,804	Saudi Arabia	$539,344,686
Russia	1,276,453	West Germany	493,330,691
Spain	985,911	France	409,652,422
Belgium & Luxembourg	780,850	Belgium & Luxembourg	393,778,038
Rumania	696,772	United Kingdom	333,495,965
United Kingdom	625,855	Japan	319,651,438
Italy	598,944	Iran	272,802,683
France	588,606	Venezuela	209,385,394
Republic of Korea	565,614	Brazil	209,102,536
Poland	471,764	Russia	197,658,900
Taiwan	417,864	Spain	188,780,888
Portugal	399,566	Netherlands	188,456,175
West Germany	373,266	Italy	187,437,771
Egypt	339,700	Republic of Korea	145,598,069
Netherlands	320,834	Republic of So. Africa	139,142,703
Greece	319,334	Taiwan	134,976,902
Sweden	275,545	Nigeria	134,126,281
Iran	193,950	Sweden	126,514,405
Saudi Arabia	175,561	Colombia	119,328,801
Pakistan	155,795	Kuwait	98,316,201
Turkey	149,709	Switzerland	95,283,732
Argentina	140,181	Argentina	82,064,642
Norway	125,798	Hong Kong	82,017,291
Venezuela	121,219	Egypt	81,228,639
Brazil	116,732	Israel	75,069,057
China	93,440	Portugal	67,948,348
Israel	90,847	Poland	66,094,999
Canary Islands	76.551	Australia	66,079,398
Yugoslavia	63,832	United Arab Emirates	48,922,780
Finland	59,775	Greece	47,855,853

Source: Maryland Department of Transportation, Maryland Port Administration, Foreign Commerce Statistical Report, 1978.

[a] Short Ton = 2000 lb.

TABLE 7.4
LEADING 15 U.S. SEAPORTS IN IMPORT OF FOREIGN WATERBORNE TRADE: 1978

	Imports by Tonnage		Imports by Value	
	Thous. Tons	Rank	$(Millions)	Rank
UNITED STATES	601,653		$118,865	
Baltimore	19,185	7	4,898	6
Baton Rouge	20,838	6	1,743	13
Boston	7,504	14	1,607	14
Corpus Christi	26,067	4	2,180	11
Houston	42,440	2	6,863	3
Jacksonville, Fla.			2,078	12
Long Beach	9,286	12	6,294	4
Los Angeles	12,671	10	7,747	2
Marcus Hook, Pa.	15,348	9		
Mobile	18,260	8		
New Orleans	21,100	5	4,881	7
New York	60,818	1	24,087	1
Norfolk	6,106	15	3,011	9
Oakland			2,842	10
Paulsboro, N.J.	12,270	11		
Philadelphia	31,329	3	4,458	8
Portland, Me.	8,905	13		
Savannah			1,462	15
Seattle			5,640	5

Source: Maryland Department of Transportation, Maryland Port Administration, *Foreign Commerce Statistical Report, 1978.*
Tonnes = .9 x Tons

more-Washington Parkway (Figure 7.3). The other two major airports in the region are Washington National and Dulles International in nearby Virginia. Since the early sixties, all three airports have competed for the region's market, which stretches north into Pennsylvania to include York and Harrisburg. BWI has emerged as the leader.

After World War II, when aviation technology had proved that flying boats were no longer necessary for crossing the ocean by air, an inland location for a new airport was selected at the site of Friendship Church in Anne Arundel County. In June 1950, President Harry S Truman dedicated the new Friendship International Airport, owned by the city of Baltimore. This modern airport was the first in the country with the new pier concept of design, and until 1962, it was the only airport in the region capable of handling large, passenger jet aircraft. During the 1960s Friendship's air service eroded under the pressure of competition from Washington National and Dulles International airports. In 1972, the State of Maryland purchased the airport from Baltimore for $36 million; it changed the name to Baltimore-Washington International Airport in 1973. Improvements

TABLE 7.5

IMPORT TRADE OF THE PORT OF BALTIMORE
ARRANGED BY PRINCIPAL COUNTRIES AND BY TRADE AREAS: 1978

Country of Origin in Order of Tonnage	Short Tons	Country of Origin in Order of Value	Value
Canada	4,925,760	Japan	$1,143,533,900
Venezuela	4,084,191	West Germany	750,980,167
Brazil	979,532	United Kingdom	334,163,258
Algeria	778,262	Venezuela	243,852,984
Liberia	746,520	France	224,933,214
West Germany	742,625	Italy	205,614,749
Japan	579,145	Canada	153,284,917
Netherlands Antilles	564,756	Brazil	149,221,048
Trinidad and Tobago	454,329	Sweden	149,027,901
Australia	393,478	Norway	141,071,925
Norway	385,389	Taiwan	108,328,752
Italy	273,378	Spain	79,344,233
Spain	266,351	Belgium & Luxembourg	71,168,478
Philippines	259,897	Philippines	64,812,318
Republic of S. Africa	244,227	Republic of Korea	63,815,670
Sweden	233,974	Hong Kong	60,942,428
Mexico	228,738	Republic of S. Africa	55,997,952
United Kingdom	221,645	Australia	55,895,811
France	207,815	Finland	53,251,438
Bahamas	200,209	Netherlands	50,087,811
Netherlands	194,895	Dominican Republic	44,274,185
Rumania	161,626	Netherlands Antilles	43,375,208
Dominican Republic	143,769	Iceland	43,152,694
Colombia	114,256	Trinidad and Tobago	34,671,705
Costa Rica	111,476	French Pacific Islands	32,316,035
Chile	110,457	Switzerland	27,768,473
Finland	102,354	Chile	26,424,317
Guiana	101,197	Liberia	23,796,860
Taiwan	100,764	Rumania	23,741,456
Libya	94,989	Russia	22,309,797

Source: Maryland Department of Transportation, Maryland Port Administration, Foreign Commerce Statistical Report, 1978.

Tonnes = .9 x tons

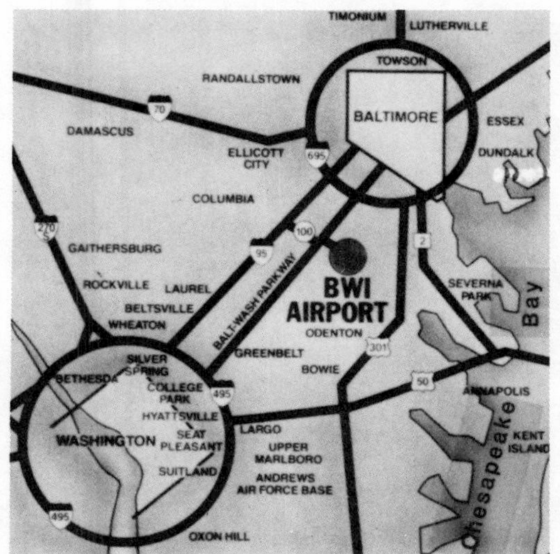

FIGURE 7.3. Courtesy, Maryland Department of Transportation, State Aviation Administration.

were made, and passenger and cargo traffic have increased dramatically since 1973 (Figure 7.4). BWI offers 500 direct flights to 77 U.S. cities and many international cities in addition to handling over 50 percent of the region's air cargo traffic. In 1980, the country's first intercity air-rail passenger station was opened at BWI, just six minutes away from the terminal along Amtrak's Washington–New York–Boston line.

The thirty-nine other air facilities in Maryland are spread among twenty-two of the state's twenty-four counties. Some of these airports are served by air commuter lines, a rapidly growing segment of the airline passenger industry.[12] The largest of these airports are in Easton, Frederick, and Hagerstown, and in Montgomery County (Figure 7.5).

Highway and Rail Transportation

Maryland is crisscrossed with an extensive network of over 25,000 mi (40,225 km) of highways and 1,000 mi (1,609 km) of rail routes. The highways consist of 3,862 mi (6,214 km) of municipal roads, 16,703 mi (26,875 km) of county roads, and 5,258 mi (8,460 km) of state roads.[13] Most parts of the state are easily accessible via multilaned, limited-access highways (Figure 7.6). Some 350 common- and contract-carrier trucking firms operate in Maryland. The state's highways are well connected into the U.S. interstate system: many cities in the eastern half of the United States can be reached by truck in one to two days; Boston, Buffalo, Pittsburgh, and New York overnight; Chicago and St. Louis in two days. Thirty-seven percent of the U.S. industrial market and 31 percent of the nation's population is within overnight delivery distance by truck.[14] Over 150 communities in Maryland are served by two major, public, intercity bus systems centered on Baltimore and Washington, D.C., as well as by several smaller operators.

The rail freight system in Maryland focuses primarily on Baltimore (Figure 7.7) with over 100 inbound and outbound trains serving the city daily. Specialized facilities in Baltimore include piggyback, container, rail-to-truck transfer, and coal, grain, and ore loading and storage. Hagerstown and Cumberland are secondary rail centers. Rail traffic is heaviest on the lines into western Maryland and along the urban corridor both north and south of Baltimore. Rail commuter service exists from Washington, D.C., to Baltimore, with service continuing north. Nearly one-fifth of the passenger traffic between New York City and Baltimore or Washington is by rail.[15] A number of the short-line, light-density rail routes throughout the state are currently operated with state and federal subsidies, for instance, the Midland Railroad in Frederick and Carroll counties. Many of these lines, especially those on the Eastern Shore and in southern Maryland, are being considered for abandonment.

COMMUNICATIONS

Maryland is near the top of the national mass-media communications hierarchy

FIGURE 7.4. Baltimore-Washington International Airport is the major air facility serving Maryland. Courtesy, Maryland Department of Transportation, State Aviation Administration.

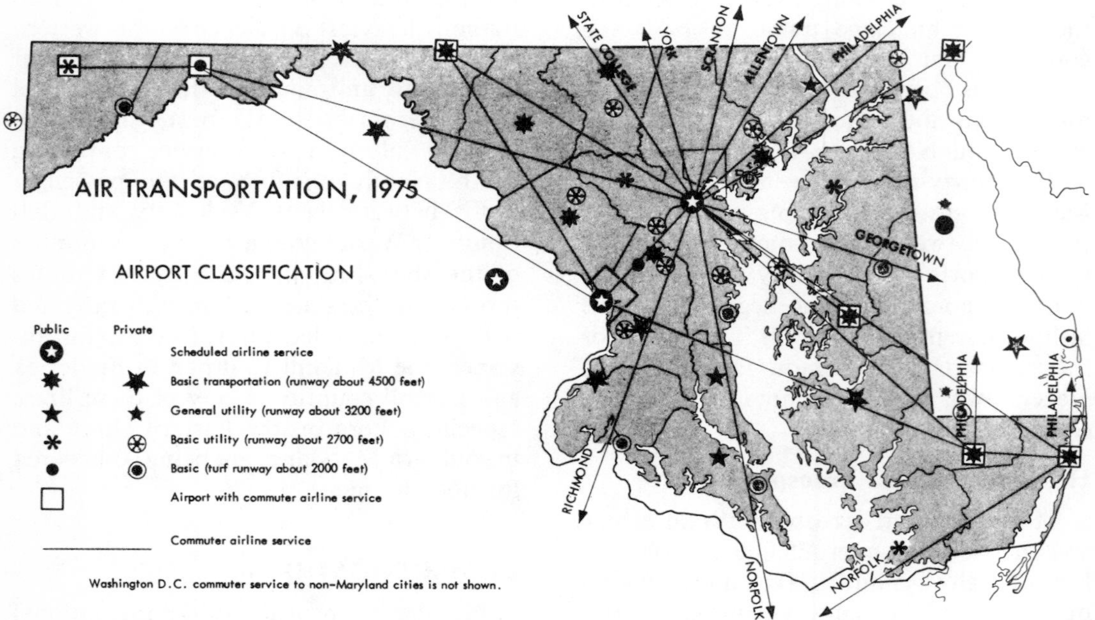

FIGURE 7.5. Source: Derek Thompson, ed., *Atlas of Maryland,* © 1977, p. 103 (College Park: Department of Geography, University of Maryland). Reprinted with permission.

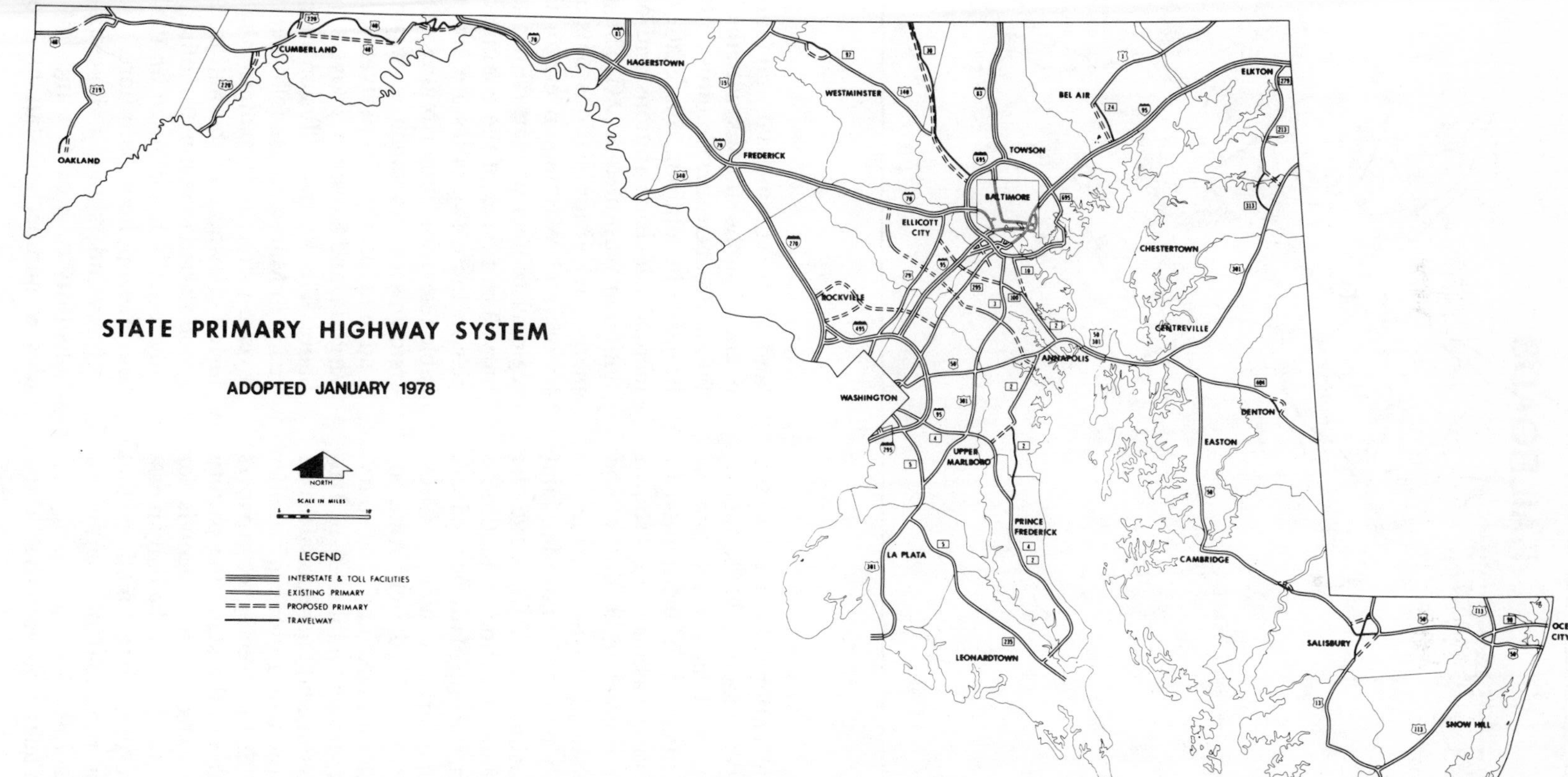

FIGURE 7.6. Courtesy, Maryland Department of Transportation, State Highway Administration.

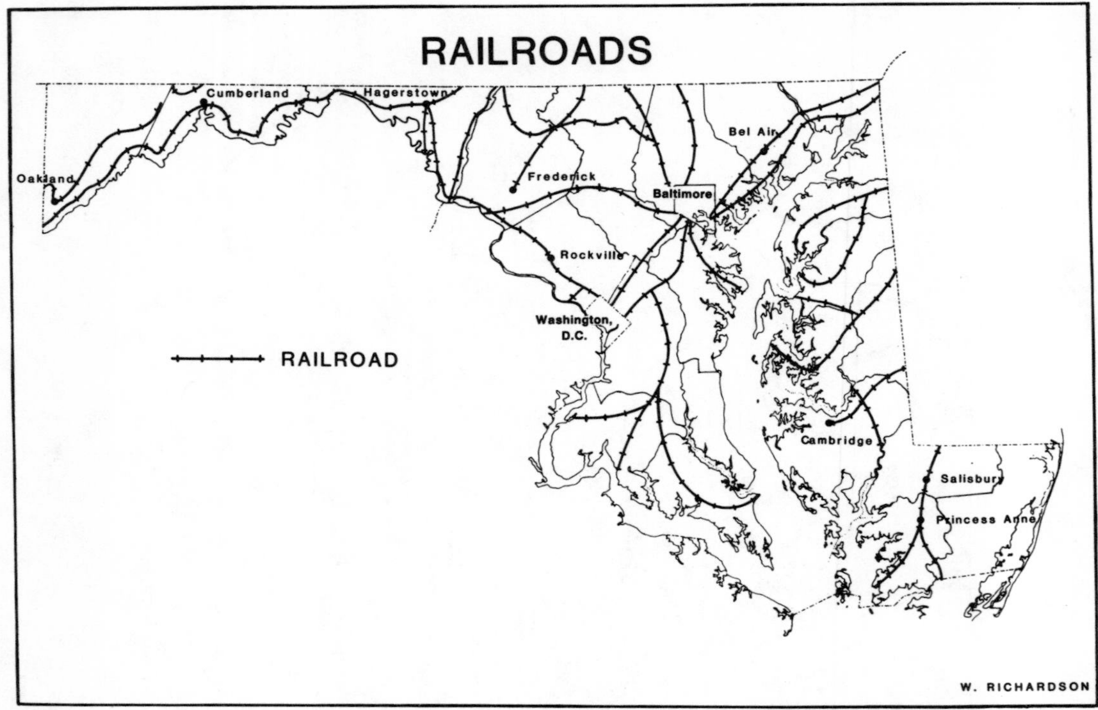

FIGURE 7.7.

with two major national centers in the Baltimore and Washington, D.C., metropolitan areas, as well as several smaller, local regional centers. The distribution of newspapers and broadcasting centers shown in Figure 7.8 is a good indication of the hierarchy of urban places in the state.

Fourteen daily newspapers in Maryland and two in Washington, D.C., serve the people of Maryland. Outside of Baltimore and Washington, the only daily newspapers are in the regional urban centers of Cumberland, Hagerstown, Frederick, Annapolis, Easton, Cambridge, and Salisbury. Weekly newspapers are published in Baltimore, Washington, and the regional urban centers, in addition to a group of smaller urban centers. Eighty weekly newspapers are published across the state; the pattern of lower-order weekly newspapers is far more dispersed than that of the daily newspapers, higher-order urban functions that require a larger threshold population for support (Figure 7.8).

There are ten television stations in Maryland; six are commercial, and four are state-operated public stations, with the Maryland Public Broadcasting Commission being the licensee. In addition, there are five commercial television stations and one public station in Washington, D.C. The only commercial television stations outside of Baltimore and Washington are in the major regional centers of Hagerstown and Salisbury. The ranges of the commercial channels in those two cities are augmented by cable television subscription systems; Hagerstown's covers much of western Maryland and nearby Pennsylvania and West Virginia, and Salisbury's covers the Eastern Shore. The spatial diffusion of cable television in Maryland has followed the typical reverse-hierarchical pattern that has occurred elsewhere in the nation: cable television started in nonmetropolitan areas and only recently has diffused up the hierarchy into metropolitan Baltimore.

Marylanders have a choice of radio stations (fifty each of AM and FM stations), plus a number of stations broadcasting

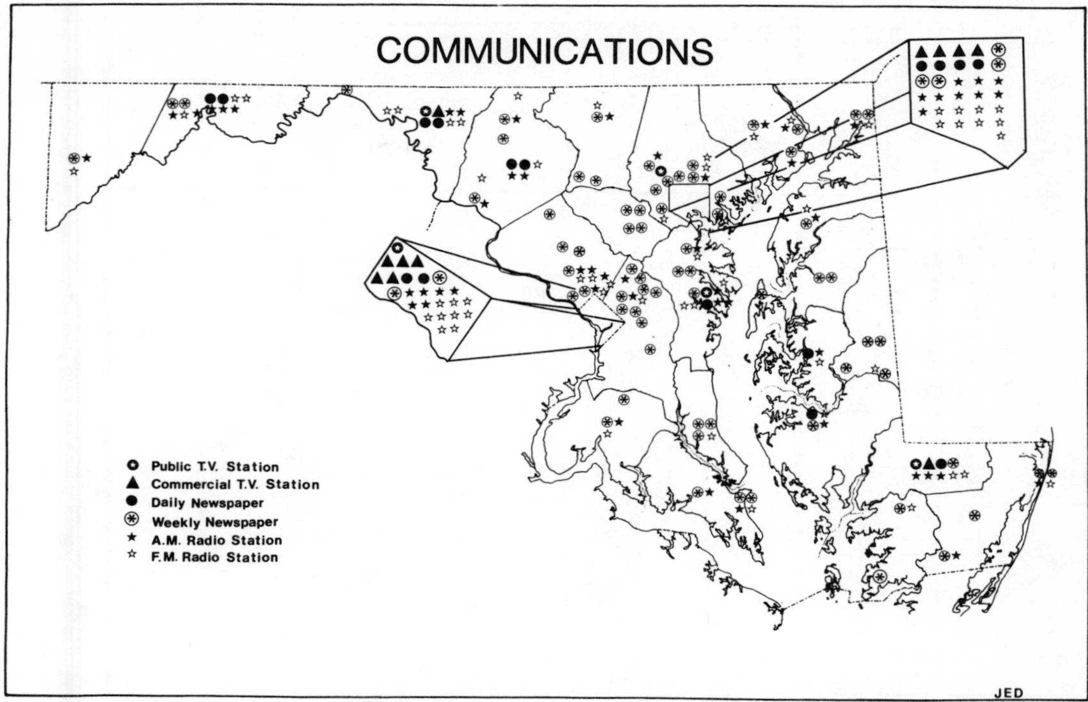

FIGURE 7.8. Source: Data from Department of Economic and Community Development, *Maryland Statistical Abstract, 1979.*

from Washington, D.C. It is apparent that people in Maryland have a broad latitude in the availability of mass communications media.

HEALTH CARE

In the aggregate, Maryland has an impressive array of health-care facilities and personnel. The geographical patterns of health care reveal a strong hierarchical system ranging from few alternatives in several parts of the state to highly sophisticated, specialized facilities at the top of the hierarchy in Baltimore. Most of the state's general and specialized hospitals are located in the Baltimore and Washington, D.C., metropolitan areas, with a limited number of hospital beds in western and southern Maryland and on the Eastern Shore. The urban corridor contains 84 percent of the 22,139 hospital beds in the state (Table 7.6),[16] while the outlying areas lack specialized medical centers.

The distribution of nursing homes is much the same as that of hospitals; however, the pattern shows more dispersal into rural areas where the population density is insufficient to support local hospitals.[17]

The distribution of physicians providing direct care again shows the attraction of the higher-order medical centers of Washington and Baltimore (Figure 7.9). Baltimore City has 1 physician for every 219 people, while in many rural counties the ratio is 1 primary-care physician for every 1,000. At the extreme are Caroline and Queen Annes counties on the Eastern Shore with in excess of 3,000 people for every physician. The suburban counties fall in between the extremes (with the exception of Montgomery County, a popular residential area for physicians who have offices there and in Washington, D.C.). The densities of population per physician shown in Figure 7.9 reflect the concentration of physicians in urban centers, e.g., Cumberland, Hagerstown, Cambridge, and Salis-

TABLE 7.6
DISTRIBUTION OF PHYSICIANS, AND NUMBER OF BEDS IN HOSPITALS IN MARYLAND

Counties by Region	Number of Beds in Hospitals [a]	Number of Beds in Licensed Institutions [b]	Persons per Physician Providing Direct Patient Care [c]
Metropolitan Baltimore	15,651	14,252	799
Anne Arundel	1,390	838	1,085
Baltimore	3,466	6,353	960
Baltimore City	7,952	5,694	219
Carroll	1,874	892	1,019
Harford	434	395	1,063
Howard	535	80	449
Metropolitan Washington, D.C. [d]	2,934	5,443	599
Montgomery	1,404	3,031	290
Prince George's	1,530	2,412	908
Western Maryland	1,566	2,439	1,233
Allegany	659	288	682
Frederick	226	598	1,207
Garrett	72	199	2,132
Washington	609	1,354	910
Southern Maryland	305	304	1,590
Calvert	111	133	1,500
Charles	108	105	1,909
St. Mary's	86	66	1,362
Eastern Shore	1,683	1,941	1,702
Caroline		52	3,688
Cecil	174	255	1,797
Dorchester	586	168	654
Kent	86	41	867
Queen Anne's		12	3,229
Somerset	36	64	2,213
Talbot	226	419	350
Wicomico	575	853	545
Worcester		77	1,977

Sources: Maryland State Department of Health and Mental Hygiene, Div. of Licensing & Certification, Directory of Acute General Hospitals & Special Hospitals, May 1978. Also, the Directory of Licensed Institutions, May 1978. The Medical & Chirurgical Faculty of the State of Maryland, Characteristics of Physicians in Maryland: December 31, 1977 (based on data obtained from the American Medical Association, July 1979).

[a] Includes General Hospitals, Chronic Disease Hospitals, Mental Institutions, Tuberculosis Institutions, hospitals in Penal Institutions and Special Hospitals, May 1978.

[b] Includes Nursing Homes, Intermediate Care Facilities, Domiciliary Care, and Residential Treatment Centers for Emotionally Disturbed Children and/or Adolescents, May 1978.

[c] Data concerning the number of physicians are as of December 31, 1977 - the reader is cautioned that physicians may register by county of residence rather than by county of practice. Population estimates are for July 1, 1977 issued by the Department of Health and Mental Hygiene.

[d] This includes the Maryland portion only.

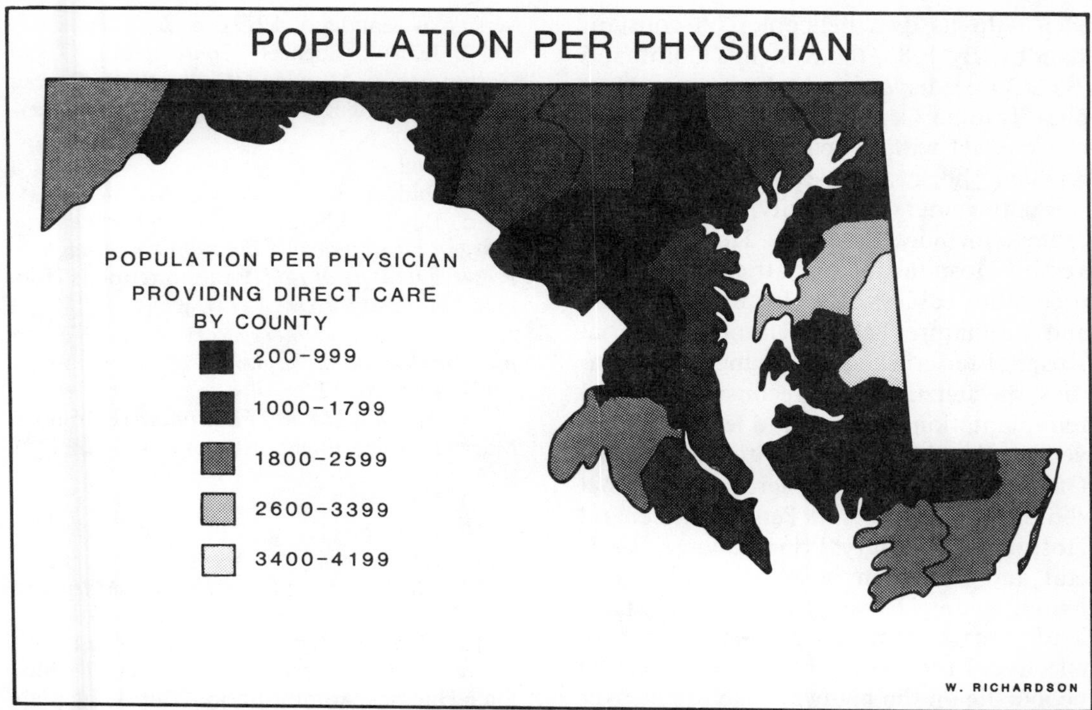

FIGURE 7.9. Source: Data from Maryland Department of Health and Mental Hygiene.

bury, as well as in the more affluent counties such as Talbot. As a region, southern Maryland has the largest number of people to be cared for per physician (Table 7.6).

At the top of this hierarchical health-care ladder is Baltimore, a recognized worldwide leader in health care. Two large teaching hospitals, the Johns Hopkins and the University of Maryland, in addition to over twenty-five general and nine specialty hospitals, provide extraordinarily high-quality care.[18]

> Baltimore is a medical town that has produced surgeons like Holstead and Blalock, internists like Osler, opthamologists like Wilmer and pediatricians like Taussig. Biologists from Baltimore figured heavily in the conquest of polio. Bufferin comes from Baltimore and the increasingly popular "belly button" sterilization procedure for women was developed there as well. Medicine, like steel, is one of Baltimore's principal exports and its practice is viewed locally with a reverence approaching awe.[19]

The nation's first major shocktrauma center was opened in Baltimore at the University of Maryland Hospital in 1969. For a number of years, the Maryland state police had tried to get the federal Department of Transportation (DOT) to fund the purchase of helicopters to monitor traffic and chase criminals, but DOT judged the helicopters not to be cost effective. Then the police joined the trauma unit in requesting the helicopters for combined police and medical evacuation use, with a priority given to medical emergencies; in 1968 Maryland got its aircraft. Each helicopter has a medic in addition to the pilot. (A state police helicopter carrying the governor of Maryland once landed and left him on the side of the highway, so that a medical emergency could be answered.[20])

In 1973 the Maryland Institute for Emergency Medical Services was formally created by executive order of the governor. The state is divided up into a number of regions, each with its own helicopter on constant standby. By 1980, the System's Command (SYSCOM) dispatcher at University Hospital Trauma Center in Baltimore had direct contact with helicopters, a number of regional shocktrauma centers, and major specialty centers in the city. The specialty centers include the Johns Hopkins University Hospital for pediatric trauma and premature babies; City Hospital for burns and premature babies; Union Memorial Hospital for crushed and mangled extremities, specializing in the reconstruction and reimplantation of hands and feet; and University Hospital for the critically injured. Outside of Baltimore there are regional shocktrauma centers at Peninsula General Hospital in Salisbury, Prince George's General and Suburban hospitals, and Washington County Hospital for western Maryland. This system has proven to be very effective. In the United States over 50,000 people die on the highways each year, over 800 in Maryland alone. Many accidents occur at night when labs are closed and hospitals are not fully staffed, but in Maryland, a team leader in a Baltimore trauma unit is ready for emergencies at all times with superior equipment, supplies, and specialists. Arrangements have even been made to fly the president of the United States, if seriously injured in Washington, to the shocktrauma unit at Baltimore's University Hospital.

NOTES

1. Derek Thompson, ed., *Atlas of Maryland* (College Park: Department of Geography, University of Maryland, 1977), p. 2.
2. Jean E. Spencer, *Contemporary Local Government in Maryland* (College Park: Bureau of Government Research, University of Maryland, 1965), p. 1.
3. Ibid.
4. Ibid., p. 4.
5. Boyd Gibbons, *Wye Island—The True Story of an American Community's Struggle to Preserve Its Way of Life* (Baltimore: Johns Hopkins University Press, 1977), p. 91.
6. Spencer, *Contemporary Local Government in Maryland,* p. 4.
7. Ibid., p. 12.
8. *The World Port of Baltimore* (Baltimore: Maryland Department of Transportation, 1978), p. 6.
9. Ibid., p. 7.
10. Ibid., p. 11.
11. Ibid.
12. Thompson, ed., *Atlas of Maryland,* p. 103.
13. *Highway Mileage on State, State Toll, County, and Municipal Systems* (Annapolis, Md.: State Highway Administration, Bureau of Highway Statistics, 1979).
14. *Baltimore Metro Business Facts* (Baltimore: Economic Development Council of Greater Baltimore, 1980), p. 20.
15. Thompson, ed., *Atlas of Maryland,* p. 103.
16. *Maryland Statistical Abstract, 1979* (Annapolis: Maryland Department of Economic and Community Development, 1980), p. 62.
17. Thompson, ed., *Atlas of Maryland,* p. 111.
18. *Baltimore Metro Business Facts,* "Health Care."
19. Jon Franklin and Alan Doelp, *Shocktrauma* (New York: St. Martin's Press, 1980), p. 108.
20. Ibid., p. 142.

CHAPTER 8

THE URBAN SYSTEM

CHARACTERISTICS OF URBAN CENTERS

Maryland presents an interesting urban network with its national, regional, and local centers; the story of this system has been woven into the previous chapters of this book. The elements of the system, ranging from Baltimore down to the smallest rural settlement, have been described in terms of their economic employment, population, transportation, communications, historical development, and natural and regional setting. In this chapter the major functions of settlements will be summarized in an integrative manner to demonstrate how they form a functioning and interacting system. Some of the urban settlements with special characteristics of plan, function, and size will be described in more detail, for example, Greenbelt, Columbia, Baltimore, and nearby Washington, D.C.

The Importance of Cities

The size, number, and spacing of settlements over the earth is an important basis for comprehension of many other activities. For example, the location of poultry-processing plants on the Eastern Shore and the steel mill at Sparrows Point are partially explained by proximity to urban markets. The location of cities can be understood by considering five major items: (1) the distribution of rural population; (2) the location of space-using activities such as agriculture, forestry, and mining; (3) the location of transportation routes; (4) the industrial structure and government needs; and (5) the functions that cities perform.[1]

Cities are directly important to the surrounding territory that they serve and influence, the tributary area or hinterland. It is in the cities that decisions concerning the use and development of the earth are made. From the cities radiate laws, economic decisions, and cultural trends such as music and language. In the cities are found banks, institutions of higher learning, industries, arts, libraries, and all of the other elements that, added together, control the development of the landscape. The rural areas of Maryland are associated with their local urban centers in a complementary manner, and the whole system focuses up the ladder on the port city of Baltimore. It is in the cities of Maryland that the geographies of production and consumption interlink.

Interurban Relationships

Scholars who have studied the structure of regions in terms of sizes of service centers have found that as the size category (usually measured by population or number of urban functions) increases, the number of settlements per category decreases. This pattern has been called the rank-size relationship. The number, size, and distribution of settlements on the landscape form a hierarchy of cities; developed regions, such as Maryland, have a rather well-balanced hierarchy with the number of centers decreasing in a regular manner as the settlement-size hierarchy is ascended. Lesser-developed regions often do not display a balanced hierarchical pattern; in these areas there may be many smaller-size settlements, with few intermediate-size settlements between these and the large city, often called a primate city, at the top of the hierarchy.

It is common among urbanologists to speak of the *order* of a settlement. In the United States, New York City is the first-order center, while Chicago, Los Angeles, and Philadelphia are examples of second-order cities. Although Baltimore and Washington, D.C., are usually ranked as third-order centers,[2] they are important components of the national urban hierarchy; in 1976 they ranked fifteenth and eighth respectively in population among the metropolitan areas of the nation.[3]

The settlements in a hierarchy are interrelated in a functional manner. Large centers like Baltimore and Washington are attached to other large centers in the nation and the world by communications and transportation. Strong information flows radiate from these high-order centers; new trends in fashion, music, and technology usually appear first in the high-order centers and then diffuse down the hierarchy to towns and rural areas.

Maryland's Settlement Hierarchy. The settlement hierarchy in Maryland shows in Table 8.1. The only city over 250,000 population is Baltimore. As the hierarchy is descended, there are more settlements in each successive category; at the bottom of the hierarchy are 271 rural settlements. The U.S. Bureau of the Census uses a population size of 2,500 to differentiate between the urban and rural places.

The smallest settlements in Maryland are *roadsides:* isolated establishments such as a gasoline station, small general store, or motel located along a highway. The next larger rural settlement is the *hamlet,* which

TABLE 8.1

UNINCORPORATED AND INCORPORATED PLACES IN MARYLAND: 1980

Population	Number of Places
Urban	
Over 250,000	1
100,000 - 250,000	3
50,000 - 99,999	13
25,000 - 49,999	28
10,000 - 24,999	33
5,000 - 9,999	70
2,500 - 4,999	91
Rural	
Under 2,500	271

Source: Tabulated from 1980 U.S. Census of Population and Housing, PHC80-V-22, Advanced Report, Maryland.

has about 150 people. Glenn Trewartha has described the hamlet, "The unincorporated hamlet represents the first hint of thickening in the settlement plasma. It is neither purely rural nor purely urban, but neuter in gender, a sexless creation midway between the more determinate town and country."[4] A large number of hamlets are found across Maryland, the common functional factor often being the presence of a rural post office. The *village* has more functions and a population of approximately 150 to 1,000. In addition to the functions found in the hamlet, the village has others such as an automobile dealer, hardware store, drug store, churches, and a grade school. In Maryland there are 121 settlements in the roadside, hamlet, and village categories. The largest rural settlement is the *town,* with 1,000 to 2,500 people and additional functions such as a high school, bank, professional services (doctor, lawyer, dentist), and sometimes a weekly newspaper. (It should be noted that in New England and Wisconsin, towns are subdivisions of counties and can be much larger than those described for Maryland.)

The urban settlements indicated in Table 8.1 range from small centers to intermediate and large *cities.* On the lower end of the spectrum of cities are urban places that service a small, local, rural hinterland. A number of intermediate-sized cities are regional business centers, with an urban base that reaches beyond the immediate rural area. Others are transportation centers, special function centers (e.g., for government administration or next to military installations), or suburbs of Maryland's highest order center—the *metropolis.* Maryland's large metropolitan milieu is a complex, throbbing system with industrial parks, traffic jams, shopping centers, pollution problems, cultural amenities, vitality and decay.

Classification by Type. During the 1950s, a number of urban geographers devised systems for classifying cities by type. One of these systems, developed by Howard Nelson, was based on the number of people employed in various occupations and the degree to which the city's number deviated from the national mean. Some of the larger cities of Maryland are classified according to the Nelson system in Table 8.2. Annapolis is classified as strongly professional service and public administration; this is expected because it is the state's capital. Baltimore, Cambridge, Hagerstown, and Salisbury are diversified; they are near the national mean. Cumberland is classified as strongly transportation, while Frederick is strongest in public administration employment.

Maryland's Overall Pattern of Urban Centers

The urban system in Maryland has a distinctive pattern: a dominating concentration stretching from Baltimore to Washington, D.C., a number of smaller cities around the state serving as regional centers, and many smaller towns and villages serving very local areas.

The large metropolitan areas of Baltimore and Washington are a complex tangle of industrial plants, transportation routes, townhouses, office buildings, pollution, education systems, and other facets of urbanism. The sprawl of these large cities has been rapid, especially since the 1960s. Interstate 695 (I-695), the circumferential highway around Baltimore, has had a remarkable amount of development along it. Known locally as the "Golden Horseshoe," this corridor is capturing much of the productive activity of the metropolitan area.[5] A number of large facilities are located near I-695, including Bethlehem Steel's plant at Sparrows Point, employing over 30,000 people, and the U.S. Social Security Administration's new Woodlawn site, employing over 13,000. Towson, the county seat of Baltimore County, is located along I-695. It has grown into a complex minicity with hospitals (Greater Baltimore Medical Center, St. Joseph's, and Sheppard-Pratt), a college and a university (Goucher College and Towson State University), and numerous government offices.

TABLE 8.2

SELECTED MARYLAND CITIES CLASSIFIED BY THE NELSON SYSTEM

City	Functional Specialization	
Annapolis	Pf_3	Pb_2
Baltimore	D_1	
Cambridge	D_1	
Cumberland	T_3	
Frederick	Pb_1	
Hagerstown	D_1	
Salisbury	D_1	

D - Diversified
Pb - Public administration
Pf - Professional Service
T - Transportation and Communication
Numbers represent plus standard deviations above the national employment mean for that category.

Source: Adapted from Howard Nelson, "A Service Classification of American Cities," Economic Geography, 31 (1955), pp. 185-210.

To the south, the Capitol Beltway (I-495) around Washington has become the main street for the District of Columbia's metropolitan area.[6] Located near the beltway are many federal agencies and private corporate business offices, such as those of Time-Life, Marriott, VISA, and Mobil Oil.

In the remainder of Maryland, most of the urban places are surrounded by well-defined rural hinterlands. This is true of Oakland, Frostburg, Westernport, Hancock, Brunswick, Westminster, Bel Air, Elkton, Lowel, Annapolis, Centerville, Easton, and Crisfield. A few of these cities do have economic ties reaching beyond the locality, for instance, Frederick, Hagerstown, Cumberland (a major transportation center), Salisbury (center for processed foods that are marketed nationwide), and Ocean City (an east coast resort and convention center). Elsewhere in the state, towns and villages are tied to local farming, fishing, or mining.

Figure 8.1 shows the immediate trade areas of the major cities of Maryland. The entire area within the major trade boundary is served by Baltimore and Washington, D.C. Within this major trade area are nested a number of more local regional trade areas, centered on smaller cities. Parts of West Virginia and Virginia are included on Figure 8.1, as Washington's trade area and that of Cumberland extend into those states. Cecil County is included as part of the Wilmington, Delaware, trade area, while Caroline County is within the Dover, Delaware, trade area.

PLANNED TOWNS, THEN AND NOW

The building of *new towns* is an old concept that came to the United States from England. Columbia, the most recent new town in Maryland, is predated by

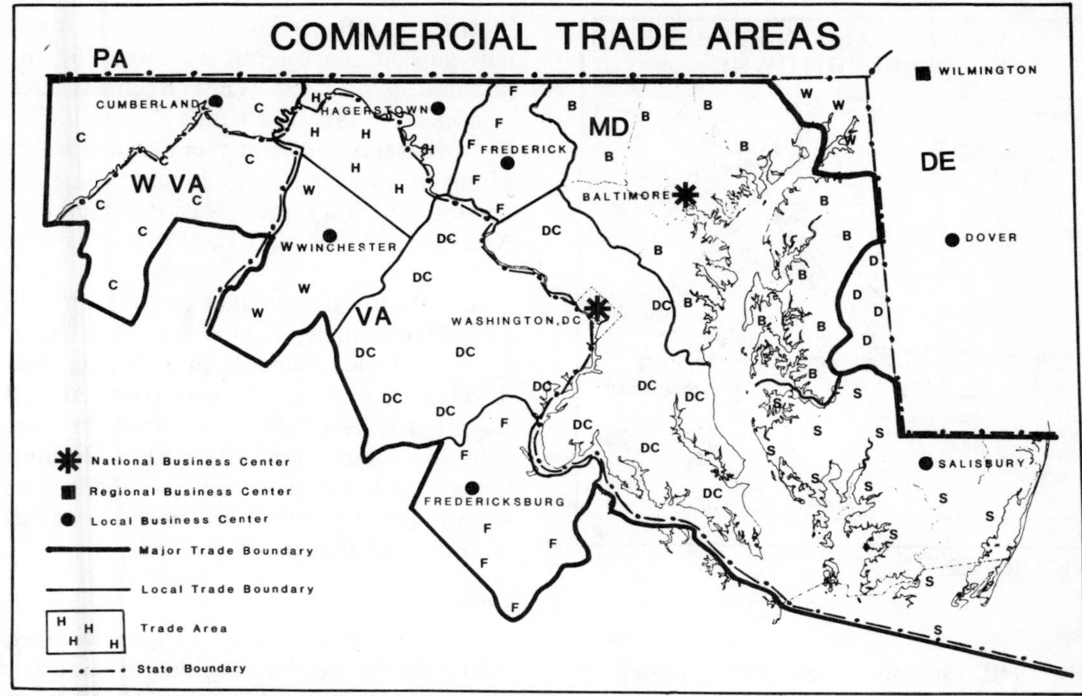

FIGURE 8.1.

another Maryland new town, Greenbelt. Before Greenbelt, there was Radburn in New Jersey. The Radburn idea included several elements: (1) superblocks to replace the usual narrow, rectangular blocks; (2) roads planned and built for one specialized use such as express highways, service roads, and parking areas; (3) overpasses and underpasses to separate automobile and pedestrian traffic; (4) houses turned around with the main door and the living and sleeping rooms facing the gardens and the back door and service rooms toward the road; and (5) large, open-area parks in the center of the superblocks. The depression starting in 1929 hurt the Radburn developers, and only two superblocks were built.

Greenbelt

In 1935, President Franklin D. Roosevelt created the Resettlement Administration. Its Suburban Resettlement Division was responsible for the planning and development of three new towns: Greenbelt, Maryland; Greenhills, Ohio (5 mi or 8 km north of Cincinnati); and Greendale, Wisconsin (7 mi or 11.3 km from Milwaukee). The planners laid out Greenbelt on a 3,370-acre (1,365-hectare) tract in Prince Georges County, just 13 mi (21 km) from downtown Washington, D.C., (Figure 8.2). The land was second-growth woodland and worn-out tobacco farmland.

Intended as low-cost housing for low-income families, Greenbelt incorporated elements of Ebenezer Howard's English "garden city" as well as of Radburn. In 1937 Greenbelt was incorporated as a town, and the first hand-picked residents moved in. The two requirements placed on the selection process were that families had to have low income (earnings between $1,000 and $1,200 per year) and that the community must reflect the nation's current religious mix (63 percent Protestant, 30 percent Catholic, and 7 percent Jewish).[7]

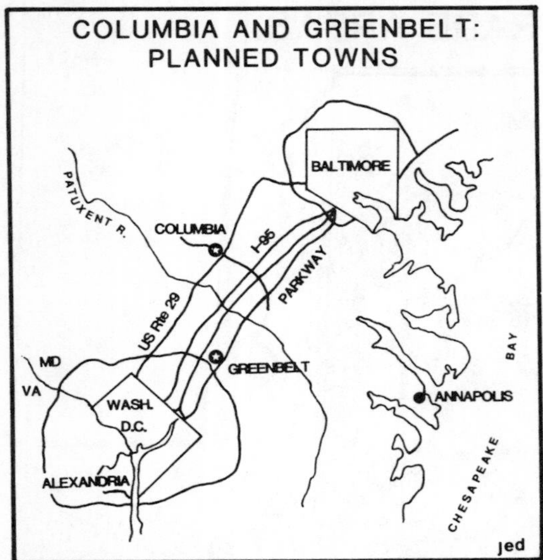

FIGURE 8.2.

By 1940, Greenbelt had slowly grown to 2,831 people, but World War II was to bring changes.

With heavy employment needs in the capital's defense agencies during the war, a housing shortage developed. In 1941, 1,000 frame row houses were constructed in Greenbelt. These houses were not well planned; they faced the streets, had narrow setbacks, and lacked interior parks and playgrounds. After this, little residential construction took place until after 1960. Between 1952 and 1954, the federal government sold Greenbelt to a housing cooperative and to developers; a tract of 1,362 acres (552 ha) was deeded to the U.S. National Park Service and has been developed as Greenbelt Regional Park.

In 1954, the Baltimore-Washington Parkway was completed with a four-way exit at Greenbelt that generated heavy traffic on Greenbelt Road, which connected into U.S. Route 1 at College Park. Strip commercial establishments and a regional shopping center were built along the road. In 1964 the circumferential beltway I-495 was completed with two accesses into Greenbelt. With this new accessibility, Greenbelt became a prime area for development.[8] Starting in 1962, developers built many new garden apartments, and by 1967 the population doubled. The Greenbelt idea disappeared; Greenbelt today is no longer the low-income town it was planned to be. Major employers nearby include the University of Maryland, National Security Agency, and the Goddard Space Flight Center.

The Radburn principles can be seen only in old Greenbelt (Figure 8.3). The green space sold to developers in 1954 has been developed, and the town is trisected and fragmented by major roads. As acres were split into minimum lots with minimum houses built on them and wooded acres were bulldozed into submission, it was as if Greenbelt had never existed.

Columbia

The second new town to be developed in the Baltimore-Washington corridor was Columbia in Howard County. After having observed with dismay the unplanned development in Prince Georges County, developer James Rouse decided to provide a better alternative. Born and raised in Easton, Talbot County, Rouse wanted to create a community with the neighborly life he knew there.

In the early 1960s, Rouse built the Village of Cross Keys in northwest Baltimore. Cross Keys is a mixture of high-rise and garden apartments, town houses, office buildings, and a village square with stores around it. This was a step toward the development of Rouse's goal for Columbia: a planned community designed to enhance the lives of the people in it and to earn a profit at the same time.[9]

The Rouse Company planners found that on the eastern seaboard, there were just two areas bracketed by the dual pressures of two major metropolitan centers less than 50 mi (80.5 km) apart: the Providence-Boston corridor and the Baltimore-Washington corridor. Since a sizable tract of land was not available between Providence and Boston, Rouse turned to the open land of Howard County in Maryland.

FIGURE 8.3. *Above,* these original Greenbelt homes have the main living rooms facing an interior garden behind the houses; *below,* this underpass leads from a residential area to the town commercial center; notice the blighted appearance of the structure.

By quietly buying piece by piece, Rouse acquired 15,200 acres (6,156 ha) by 1964;[10] the land had to be purchased in secrecy in order not to alert the local landowners and drive the price of land sky-high. Eventually Rouse's company owned 10 percent of Howard County (Rouse borrowed much of the needed money from Connecticut General Life Insurance Company).

In October 1963, Rouse confronted the Howard County commissioners with the fact that he owned a good part of the county and wished to build a new town on it. He argued that it would be impossible for Howard County to remain rural forever and that his was a good alternative to the uncoordinated growth being experienced in other parts of the state. Throughout 1964 Rouse traveled around the county presenting his plans to the people.[11] Finally, in August 1965, the commissioners voted to pass the New Town District Zoning Ordinance. One year later, construction on the new town of Columbia began.

Community Research Development, Inc. (CRD), the developers of Columbia, held a series of weekend seminars to develop their community concept; experts in transportation and the behavioral and social sciences were invited. The group felt that the nucleus of the residential community would be the *neighborhood,* consisting of 500 to 600 families grouped around a lower school, a convenience store, nursery, tot lots, and other neighborhood facilities. Five or six neighborhoods would comprise a *village* of 2,500 to 3,500 families. The village center would feature a library, higher-order shopping establishments, and a junior high school and senior high school. A cluster of villages would comprise the *town.* The town center would be the focal point of the area with a concentration of urban functions including office buildings, department stores, theaters, hospital, shopping center, and other units (Figure 8.4).

By the mid 1970s, some 20,000 people had jobs in Columbia and 700 businesses had located there. Today office buildings in the town center have tenants such as A & P, Shell Oil, Hershey Foods, and Connecticut General Life Insurance Company. With 53,100 residents in 1980, Columbia has nearly half the population of Howard County. By the early 1980s, some 100 businesses per year were moving into Columbia, contributing to a rate of growth in the city's employment base of 12 percent per year. Unemployment in Howard County at the end of 1979 was only 3.2 percent.[12] At the edges of Columbia are industrial parks. The most spectacular location decision was that made by General Electric to invest $250 million in the General Electric Appliance Park East, the largest investment of the sort in Maryland's history. Several other parks were established, and Howard County is seeking more land to locate more industries. The demand for industrial and commercial land in the Baltimore-Washington corridor is so great that it cannot be satisfied.[13]

Columbia has become a city of families; there are few older couples and singles. By 1975, the median household income was $26,000; nearly 90 percent of household heads had gone to college, and 42 percent had done graduate work.[14] Columbia has an innovative school system, with higher education available at Howard Community College in addition to classes offered by Antioch College, Johns Hopkins University, and Loyola College of Baltimore.

But not all is rosy in Columbia. In 1971, a team of psychologists visiting Columbia decided that they wouldn't want to live there. They called Columbia "plastic" and predicted that it too eventually would face common urban problems such as decay.[15] Residents of Columbia have high expectations, but Columbia is not utopia: there are problems of crime, integration, and self-government. By and large, however, residents of Columbia recommend it as a good place to live.

THE "NEW" BALTIMORE

Baltimore has most of the elements of other North American cities its size, but

FIGURE 8.4. The center of the planned town of Columbia is shown here. Courtesy, the Howard Research and Development Corporation.

also has its own rhythm and its own pace that, along with its unique site and climate, give the city its character.[16] Baltimore is a dynamic organism whose morphology has greatly changed in recent years. Geographer Sherry Olson has described the city at the individual human scale,

> . . . the Baltimore economy not only produces steel for the North Atlantic community, and electric drills for the nation, distributes cars and groceries to six states, and fries chicken for Baltimoreans, but as a byproduct it produces Baltimore society—the class structures of consumption and the geographical structures of distribution. It produces in some measure a "Baltimore person," with a sense of competition and vulnerability, and an awareness of the limits on his ability to control his own personal life.[17]

Traditional Baltimore

A most persistent image of Baltimore is that of brick row houses with marble steps (Figure 8.5). Half of the people in the Baltimore metropolitan area live in row houses of many styles, each style reflecting a building-cycle period. Baltimore had a rather low, subdued skyline until recent years. A study of urban skylines in 1976 described Baltimore as having a low skyline index (based on number of buildings over 300 ft or 93 m), similar to other manufacturing-dominated towns such as Cleveland and Detroit.[18] Baltimore was ranked twenty-third among U.S. cities by skyline index. In recent years, as Baltimore has become more of a white-collar city, its skyline has grown.

FIGURE 8.5. Baltimore is widely known as "row house city." Courtesy, Baltimore Department of Housing and Community Development.

Another study in the early 1970s, by David Smith, addressed the questions of quality of life and social well-being in a place.[19] Smith developed an index of social well-being based on territorial social indicators; his main categories were income, wealth, employment, living environment, health, education, social order-disorder, social belonging, and recreation. A quantitative classification system was developed for the metropolitan areas of the nation: outstanding, excellent, good, adequate, and substandard. On his scale, Smith classified Baltimore as good and Washington, D.C. as excellent.

This city with a "good" quality of life (in 1970) is one of distinct neighborhood units, each with a sense of identity and cohesion. Topography reinforces the neighborhood units. In the Coastal Plain on the south and east are many points, or necks, along the irregular coastline of tidewater inlets; these govern the way roads and utilities are laid out. The railroads and industrial areas form additional barriers that separate neighborhoods, thus creating internal cohesion. On the Piedmont to the north and west, the stream valleys are often narrow and the land rolling. The chief factor in the layout of neighborhoods and roads here is slope.[20]

As areas were developed in Baltimore, it was often the case that planned elite neighborhoods (e.g., Roland Park, Guilford, and Homeland) excluded certain groups, particularly blacks, Jews, and Catholic Europeans. The excluded groups, therefore, formed their own building and loan societies to develop their own neighborhoods, thus reinforcing the pattern of differentiated social areas in the city. In a sense, Baltimore is a city of many different ghettos.[21]

Another general urban process that has

TABLE 8.3

SUBURBAN PERCENTAGE OF BALTIMORE AND WASHINGTON METROPOLITAN AREA EMPLOYMENT: 1970 - 1977.

	Baltimore			Washington		
	1970	1973	1977	1970	1973	1977
Total Employment	39.3	41.6	53.2	54.1	60.0	65.6
Manufacturing	47.4	48.8	55.4	57.6	65.5	68.0
Wholesale Trade	24.6	36.7	48.9	53.6	60.4	74.3
Retail Trade	46.9	50.9	65.0	65.7	72.3	77.4
F.I.R.E.*	21.3	24.2	39.5	47.7	53.5	57.7
Services	29.2	32.2	46.2	43.4	47.4	54.7
Business Services	20.2	23.4	54.5	51.9	57.6	67.9
Health Services	21.3	24.7	39.3	54.6	59.3	60.5

Source: U. S. Bureau of the Census, *County Business Patterns*.

*Finance, insurance, and real estate.

had its effect on Baltimore is suburbanization, resulting from such technological changes and social aspirations as the automobile, new roads, and the desire for a one-family detached dwelling. Suburbanization inevitably leaves some people behind: the geographical pattern of expansion in the suburbs is linked to the process of "underdevelopment" in the central city. The suburbanization of employment actually originated after World War I, but it greatly accelerated after 1960. Tables 8.3 and 8.4 show that the percentage of the Baltimore metropolitan area's employment in the suburbs has increased in all categories; the trend is even stronger for Washington, D.C. In the Baltimore suburbs, employment in wholesale trade, finance–insurance–real estate, services, business services, and health services all increased over 100 percent from 1970 to 1977. As the jobs have been moved to the suburbs, many people have been left jobless in the central city. Those who are unable to afford a home in suburbia or the daily transportation costs to commute to a job there are left behind to face the realities of a deteriorating environment.

Baltimore on the Move

Baltimore's first urban renewal began in 1904 with the great fire. After the fire, the city was immediately rebuilt, but it was much of the same style and layout. By 1960, the downtown was physically obsolete, financially stagnant, and psychologically demoralized.[22] In 1966, when Baltimore played in a World Series against the Dodgers, the media spotlighted a sleepy port town. Baltimore was called "mobtown," "Washington's Brooklyn," "a loser's town," "the last frontier," and "yesterday's town."[23] Baltimore's business leaders saw a do-or-die situation, and they pulled together to form the Greater Baltimore Committee (GBC). The GBC hired planners, and in 1968 unveiled the Charles Center Plan. After 33 acres (13.4 ha) were cleared, Charles Center was built downtown as an office building complex. The pleasant, public outdoor spaces of the center have a home-place atmosphere consistent with the Baltimore character (Figure 8.6). The strategy of Charles Center was to stimulate a multiplier effect to attract other businesses; in that sense, it has been a success. Part

TABLE 8.4
PERCENTAGE CHANGES IN EMPLOYMENT, CENTRAL CITY AND SUBURBS: 1970 - 1977

	Baltimore		Washington	
	Central City	Suburbs	Central City	Suburbs
Total Employment	-20	+ 41	- 9	+48
Manufacturing	-29	- 2	-23	-21
Wholesale Trade	-27	+115	-44	+38
Retail Trade	-26	+ 57	-19	+44
F.I.R.E.*	- 5	+128	- 4	+44
Services	+ 1	+109	+11	+75
Business Services	+17	+295	+ 1	+98
Health Services	+19	+181	+42	+80

Source: U. S. Bureau of the Census, County Business Patterns.

*Finance, insurance, and real estate.

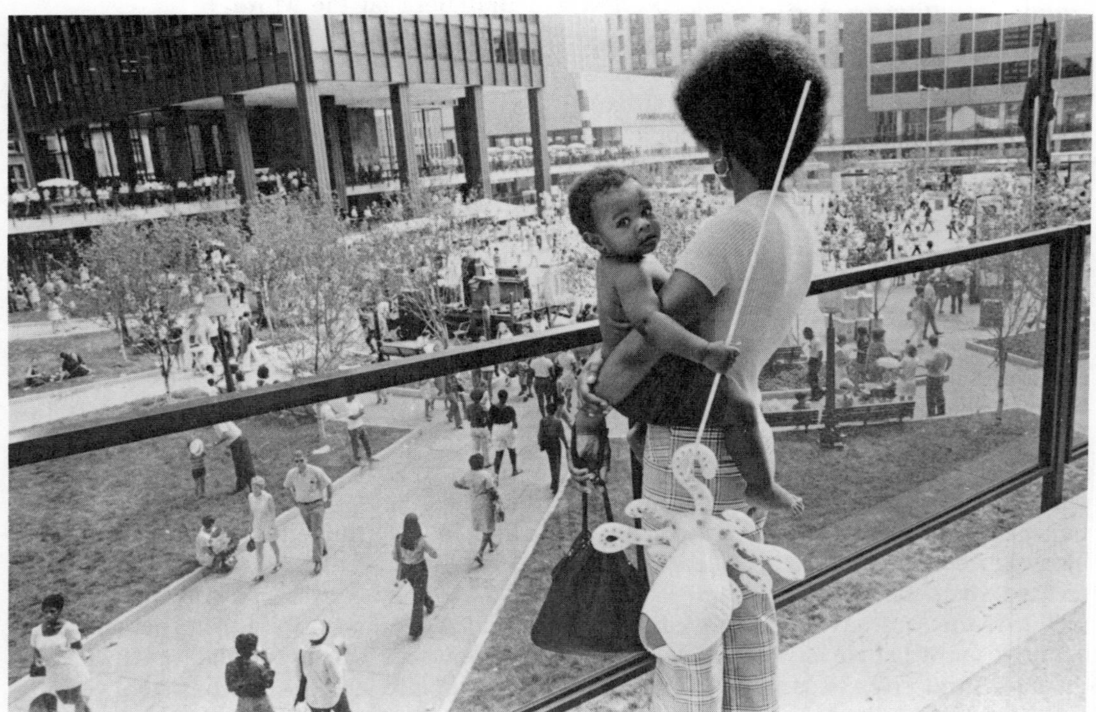

FIGURE 8.6. The plaza of the new Charles Center has become a focal point for city festivals, celebrations, and recreation. Courtesy, Baltimore Department of Housing and Community Development.

two of the commercial revitalization of downtown is the Inner Harbor project, where a U-shaped brick "boardwalk" has replaced the rotting wharves. A science museum and the National Aquarium sit opposite each other across the harbor; between them are the new pentagon-shaped World Trade Center skyscraper and Harborplace, a glittering pair of glass pavilions housing 130 shops and restaurants (Figure 8.7). Harborplace is the creation of James Rouse and architect Benjamin Thompson, who refurbished Boston's Quincy Market near Faneuil Hall. These days, Baltimore is often called "the renaissance city," "the best," "charm city," or "the city that works." *Life* magazine referred to Baltimore as the "most downright livable major city in the U.S."[24]

The overall grand design for downtown is called Metro Center (M.C.). M.C. has grown to include a new campus of the Community College of Baltimore, a new federal court house, a new Hyatt-Regency hotel, and buildings owned by IBM and U.S. Fidelity and Guarantee Company.

On the residential side, things are happening too, but they happen slowly in conservative, provincial Baltimore. (H. L. Mencken once said of his fellow Baltimoreans, "they change their shirts but once a day and their prejudices but once a generation.") During the "enlightened" urban renewal period of the 1960s and 1970s, Baltimore turned away from many of the federal programs that drove other northeastern cities near bankruptcy. Because massive clearance did not occur in the city, Baltimore entered the 1980s with a supply of good housing stock from the late 1800s.

The urban homesteading program has been used extensively in Baltimore, where it was launched in 1973, as well as in New York, Boston, and Philadelphia. The program involves returning previously abandoned housing to the marketplace (Figure 8.8). For one dollar each, the city sells an abandoned house to a buyer who agrees to renovate the house, bring it up to city codes within six months and then to live in it for at least another year and a half. By 1980, this "sweat equity" program had reclaimed 500 houses and attracted middle-class people back in from the suburbs.

Renewal for Whom?

Much controversy has surrounded the revitalization of Baltimore. One of the problems centers around the process called "urban gentrification," the movement of middle-class people back into the city. These people buy and renovate old structures, which the previous low-income tenants cannot then afford to rent. The net result is displacement of the poor from their homes. Baltimore still has many poor people; 21 percent of its residents live below the poverty level (annual income of $7,450 for a family of four). The majority of poor are black, jobless, and ill housed. The gleam of the Inner Harbor quickly recedes into the dying retail corridor to the west, the decayed neighborhoods of east and west Baltimore and the nearby "Block" with its nude or topless shows, massage parlors, and sex book shops.[25] Often cited by proponents of renewal is the *trickle-down* theory that describes the money being spent to attract new business and the urban gentry as filtering down in the form of more jobs and more city revenues. Those living at the bottom often see nothing trickling down but welfare payments, and during the 1980s government austerity is expected to reduce even these funds.

WASHINGTON, D.C.—AN IMPORTANT NEIGHBOR

Although not part of Maryland, Washington, D.C., directly influences much of the state, especially the surrounding counties of Montgomery, Prince Georges, and Charles. No geography of Maryland would be complete without a few comments on this city situated on land that was once part of Maryland.

Despite the importance of the United States in world affairs, its capital is only of modest size when compared to capital

FIGURE 8.7. The redeveloped Inner Harbor of Baltimore is shown here. From right to left are the World Trade Center, the U.S.F. *Constellation,* and one of the two Harborplace pavilions built by the Rouse Company. Courtesy, Maryland Department of Economic and Community Development.

FIGURE 8.8. Urban homesteading is popular and successful in Baltimore. Shown here are homes, *top,* before renewal; *center,* during renewal; and *bottom,* after renewal. Courtesy, Baltimore Department of Housing and Community Development.

FIGURE 8.9. Central core of Washington, D.C., with the Capitol in the foreground, the Mall at center left, the federal triangle at right center, and the central business district at right. Photograph by James P. Blair, © National Geographic Society.

cities such as London, Paris, and Tokyo. But the area and population sizes are not good indicators of the importance of Washington, D.C. While other, larger capitals are often multi-purpose urban places, Washington was built as, and largely remains, a single purpose city (Figure 8.9).

The city functions principally as the seat of the federal government. Even though employment in a wide variety of other activities (research firms, national headquarters of corporations and nonprofit organizations, interest groups, the tourism industry) has exceeded government employment, these activities support the national administrative decision-making role of Washington, D.C. The complexity of organization and administration of Washington can be understood only in the context of the entire metropolitan area that extends into Virginia (Arlington, Loudon, Prince William counties and the cities of Alexandria, Fairfax, and Falls Church) and Maryland (Montgomery and Prince Georges counties).

Between 1774 and 1789, the Continental Congress met in eight different towns and cities. The location for a new city to be the national capital was to be based on centrality and accessibility. It was decided to locate the capital on an estuary that was navigable for seagoing vessels; the northern states favored the Delaware estuary, the southern states the Potomac. The southerners eventually won out, and in 1790 George Washington was empowered to fix the location.[26] The site he selected along the Potomac lay close to the center of the thirteen states in terms of geographical area and population. George Washington expected the new capital to become the commercial center and leading seaport of the country, but the growth of nearby Baltimore outdistanced that of Washington and the capital became part of the former's hinterland.

The 10 by 10 mi sq (16 by 16 km sq) area for the capital was transferred to the federal government in 1791 by Virginia and Maryland and designated as the District of Columbia. Within the area were the ports of Alexandria on the Virginia side and Georgetown on the Maryland side. George Washington commissioned Pierre Charles L'Enfant, a French military engineer, to design the city plan. The L'Enfant plan was a rectangular grid superimposed with broad, diagonal-running avenues, many of which converged on the Capitol and the White House.

In 1800 the government was transferred from Philadelphia to its new seat, which in 1794 had acquired the name Washington City.[27] Most of the development took place on the Maryland side of the Potomac, and in 1846 the Virginia side of the District of Columbia (the District) returned by plebiscite to the state of Virginia.

Up until 1920, most of the population growth took place within the District of Columbia. Since then, the growth rate of the suburbs has been higher than that of the central city, and in 1953, the suburban population surpassed that of the District. Very little land remains for housing within the District, which has over 60 percent of its land in nontaxable public and semipublic ownership (including streets and parks), compared with an average of 34 percent in other U.S. cities.[28]

The bulk of civilian employment in the federal government is in the executive branch, with the legislative and judicial branches employing less than 10 percent of the total. In addition to the administrative functions of the many departments and agencies, the federal government also carries on extensive research in the area. Over fifty major research facilities are found in the metropolitan area; the major ones are the Smithsonian Institution, U.S. Geological Survey, Naval Observatory, Naval Research Laboratory, Walter Reed Army Medical Center, National Bureau of Standards, National Institutes of Health, Naval Medical Center, Navy's David Taylor Model Testing Basin, Goddard Space Flight Center, Beltsville Agricultural Research Center, National Weather Bureau, Naval Oceanographic Office, Central Intelligence Agency, and Defense Intelligence Agency.

Many private nonprofit research organizations and businesses specializing in research find it advantageous to be located in or near Washington, D.C., due to the contact with government personnel and the vast information resources of government libraries, archives, and files. Six major universities enhance the research environment: American University, Catholic University, Georgetown University, George Washington University, Howard University, and the University of Maryland. Nearly all of the nation's 500 largest corporations have some presence in the Washington area. As a result of the concentration of public and private research activities, Washington is second only to New York among U.S. metropolitan areas in the total number of scientists.

Another big industry in Washington is conventions and tourism. About 9 million visitors come to Washington each year. These visitors include tourists, conventioneers, politicians, diplomats, government officials, military persons, scientists, educators, businessmen, petitioners, and protecters.[29]

The Washington metropolitan area is the seat of an increasingly powerful federal government, as well as the location of a growing number of nongovernment activities. The merging of the fringes of the Washington and Baltimore areas has already occurred.

NOTES

1. Ronald R. Boyce, *The Bases of Economic Geography,* 2nd ed. (New York: Holt, Rinehart, and Winston, 1978), p. 277.

2. John Borchert, "America's Changing Metropolitan Regions," *Annals of the Association of American Geographers* 62 (1972):355.

3. Truman A. Hartshorn, *Interpreting The City: An Urban Geography* (New York: John Wiley and Sons, 1980), p. 87.

4. Glenn T. Trewartha, "The Unincorporated Hamlet," *Annals of the Association of American Geographers* 33 (1943):32.

5. Peter O. Muller, *Contemporary Suburban America* (Englewood Cliffs, N.J.: Prentice Hall, 1981), p. 172.

6. Ibid.

7. Donald M. Dozer, *Portrait of the Free State: A History of Maryland* (Cambridge, Md.: Tidewater Press, 1976), p. 188.

8. Virginia H. Moryadas, "Greenbelt and Columbia, Maryland," in *Nine Geographical Field Trips in the Washington, D.C. Area* (Washington, D.C.: Association of American Geographers, 1968), p. 38.

9. Dozer, *Portrait of the Free State,* p. 189.

10. Moryadas, "Greenbelt and Columbia," p. 39.

11. Edward G. Pickett, "Rouse Describes New City's Plans," *Baltimore Sun* (November 12, 1964), p. 56.

12. "Columbia The Gem of Howard County," *Maryland Business Journal* (August–September 1980), p. 7.

13. Jeff Kosnett, "Howard Hunts for More Land To Put Industry on," *Baltmore Sun* (February 22, 1981), p. K-7.

14. Dozer, *Portrait of the Free State,* p. 192.

15. Joann Rodgers, "Columbia Community Disenchants Visitors," *Baltimore News American* (December 2, 1971), p. C-1.

16. Sherry Olson, *Baltimore* (Cambridge, Mass.: Ballinger Pub. Co., 1976), p. 1.

17. Ibid., p. 45.

18. Larry R. Ford, "The Urban Skyline as a City Classification System," *The Journal of Geography* 75 (1976):154–164.

19. David A. Smith, *Geography of Social Well-Being in the United States* (New York: McGraw Hill Book Co., 1973).

20. Olson, *Baltimore,* p. 11.

21. Ibid., p. 13.

22. Ibid., p. 50.

23. Eric Garland, "The End of Baltimore as a Blue Collar Town," *Baltimore Magazine* (December 1980), p. 53.

24. "Look What's Happened to Baltimore," *Life Magazine* (September 1980), pp. 91–94.

25. Garland, "The End of Baltimore as a Blue Collar Town," p. 56.

26. Robert Harper and Frank Ahnert, *Introduction To Metropolitan Washington* (Washington, D.C.: Association of American Geographers, 1968), p. 3.

27. Ibid., p. 6.

28. Ibid., p. 8.

29. Ibid., p. 14.

CHAPTER 9

FUTURE PROSPECTS

The major binding element in Maryland is the urban system that focuses on the Baltimore-Washington urban corridor. As much as people on the Eastern Shore or in western Maryland would like to protect their life-styles from the strong and spreading development of the urban corridor, they ultimately depend upon that conurbation for their livelihoods. The symbiotic relationships between Baltimore's large market and port facilities and the coal miners of western Maryland, dairy farmers of the Piedmont, and watermen of the Eastern Shore have been described throughout this book.

By most national socioeconomic standards, for instance, those of housing, income, health, and education, Maryland measures up as a prosperous and stable state. Yet these data at the aggregate state level do not reveal the poverty conditions and social pathologies experienced by those living in Appalachia, the inner area of Baltimore, and some rural areas. Although it has an overall well-organized and developed landscape, Maryland still contains significant distess areas. Disparities in standards of living among the people of the state should not be overlooked.

Several urbanologists have suggested a reorganization of state political boundaries in the United States to more clearly reflect economic, cultural, and political functional units. Stanley Brunn suggested sixteen new states with Baltimore as the capital of "Mid Atlantica."[1] Etzel Pearcy proposed thirty-eight states, with Maryland included as the core of "Chesapeake";[2] while Joel Garreau placed Maryland within one of his nine nations of North America, "The Foundry."[3] All of these proposals recognize Maryland as a place that has developed indigenous modes of thought, a personality, and a form of human ecology specific to the locality; in short, Marylanders have a strong sense of place.

What about future prospects for Maryland? In 1975 only 7.7 percent of the state's population was below the poverty level, as compared to a national average of 11.4 percent. By this measure of economic performance, Maryland outpaced every industrial state in the nation except Massachusetts and Connecticut. It outshone California, Texas, North Carolina, and Florida—states competing with Maryland for new economic activity—by a substantial margin.[4]

Maryland is a state with a mature industrial economy having many jobs in steel, metal fabrication, transportation and heavy equipment, along with growing employment in service and information processing. Diversification is still an important element of the Maryland economy. However, the substantial portion of the state's employment base comprised of jobs in mature industries is facing strong competition from other places. To remain productive, many Maryland industries must spend large amounts of money to modernize, but this will mean fewer jobs. Competition has caused many of Maryland's backbone industries—e.g., steel, chemicals, apparel, transportation equipment, and fabricated metals—to decline in recent years; this has been in line with national trends.

The economic future of Maryland depends on its ability to expand in the sectors where it has shown competitive strength: electronics, electrical equipment, instruments, machinery, and specialized services. Both the state government and local governments have made strong efforts in recent years to attract new firms and to devise a well-thought-out economic strategy. The Maryland Port Administration maintains offices in Baltimore, New York, Chicago, Pittsburgh, Brussels, Hong Kong, London, and Tokyo. Largely through the efforts of the Maryland Department of Economic and Community Development, some large firms have remained in Maryland, investing millions of dollars to improve their competitive positions in the future.

A major problem for Maryland in the future will be a mismatch between skills of the labor force and skills needed in the growth sectors. Even today there are more unskilled and semiskilled workers than there are jobs, while there are more jobs for skilled workers, craftsmen, and technical and managerial personnel than there are persons to fill them. As the Maryland economy becomes even more complex, qualified and reliable labor will become more important. Even blue-collar workers will need to understand diagrams, systems analysis, and mathematics in the near future. The burden of training and educating the people of the state falls heavily on the state's education system.

In 1980, Maryland's spending per student was only slightly above the national average, but it was significantly below that of other industrial states that are improving their competitive positions by providing the trained and skilled labor needed in the growth sectors. In higher education there is a symbiotic relationship between colleges and universities on the one hand and commercial institutions of science and technology on the other. Maryland is not exploiting these links, especially in public higher education, where the state ranks in the lowest spending-per-student quartile in the nation. The value of strong, long-term commitments to education can be seen in Massachusetts, a state with a depressed economy that blossomed in the early 1980s. The economic revival in Massachusetts reversed a trend of losing business to the Sun Belt; the revival has been based on the state's tremendous attraction as a center of higher education.[5] To be prepared for the necessary structural economic changes in the future, Maryland must also make a strong commitment to education.

An interesting development has been the attempt to expand the market for Maryland by combining the resources of Baltimore and Washington, D.C. The Washington/Baltimore Regional Association was formed by an alliance of the business communities of the Baltimore SMSA and Washington SMSA in addition to Calvert, St. Marys, and Frederick counties. By presenting the region as one market, the organization (popularly known as the Baltimore/Washington Common Market) seeks to stimulate economic growth in the future by means of attracting domestic and international investment. By the mid 1970s, economic and population growth in Baltimore and Washington, D.C., had slowed or declined. The region faced an identity crisis: was the Baltimore-Washington area the southernmost part of the economically distressed Northeast or was it the gateway to the economically growing Sun Belt? Maryland is truly a border state between the Frost Belt and the Sun Belt—sometimes more accurately called the Tax Belt and Growth Belt.[6] Maryland has research and high technology industries, yet it still has many low-wage jobs characteristic of the South.

With characteristics of both the northern Tax Belt and southern Growth Belt, Maryland has the opportunity to create a prosperous future. The geographical location of the state within a large market, with excellent transportation linkages and a major port, can enhance the future of the economy. Whether or not Maryland continues to prosper in the future depends on its ability to develop its human resources, for human beings are the active agents who produce capital, exploit natural resources, build social, economic, and political organizations, and carry forward development.

NOTES

1. Stanley D. Brunn, *Geography and Politics In America* (New York: Harper and Row, 1974), p. 424.
2. John F. Rooney, Jr., *A Social and Cultural Atlas of the United States* (Chicago: Denoyer Geppert Co., 1979), p. 59.
3. Ibid., p. 62.
4. Gail Garfield Schwartz, "Growth Potential In Maryland," *Metro News,* Johns Hopkins University Center for Metropolitan Planning and Research, 9, no. 10 (June 15, 1981), p. 4.
5. Clayton Jones, "A Surprise Called High Tech—Bay State Enjoys Economic Revival," *Christian Science Monitor* (March 11, 1981), special section.
6. Niles Hansen, "The New International Division of Labor and Manufacturing Decentralization in The United States," Department of Economics, University of Texas, 1980.

APPENDIX

MARYLAND POPULATION DATA SHEET

Subdivision or County	Population, April 1, 1980	Population, April 1, 1970	Percent Change 1970-1980	Rank Order of Population Size, 1980/1970	Projected Population, Year 2000[1]	Land Area, Square Miles/Rank Order	Persons per Sq. Mile of Land Area, 1980/Rank Order	Births per 1,000 Population, 1978[2]	Deaths per 1,000 Population, 1978[2]	Infant Mortality Rate, 1976-1978[2]	Marriages per 1,000 Population, 1978	Divorces per 1,000 Population, 1978	Net Migration as a Percent of 1970 Population, 1970-1978	Per Capita Income, 1977	Black Population, % of Total, 1980	Percent of Population Aged 65 and Over, 1978	Death Rate, Heart Disease, 1978[3]	Death Rate, Cancer, 1978[3]	Motor Vehicle Death Rate, 1980[3]	Population per Physician, 1978-1979	Unemployment Rate, 1980	Crime Rate, 1979/Percent Change, 1978-1979[4]	School Expenditures per Pupil, 1979-1980[5]	Percent of Land in Farms, 1978	
THE STATE	**4,216,446**	**3,923,897**	**7.5**	**—**	**4,764,000**	**9,891**	**426**	**13.4**	**8.8**	**15.4**	**10.9**	**4.0**	**0.4**	**$6,561**	**22.7**	**8.7**	**308.9**	**182.5**	**18.5**	**520**	**6.4**	**6,297/ 8.3**	**$2,271**	**43**	
BALTIMORE CITY	**786,775**	**905,787**	**-13.1**	**1/1**	**719,000**	**78/24**	**10,087/1**	**14.7**	**12.2**	**23.1**	**9.9**	**4.9**	**-14.9**	**5,242**	**54.8**	**12.6**	**479.3**	**266.1**	**9.0**	**250**	**9.1**	**9,471/ 5.0**	**2,857**	**—**	
BALTIMORE SUBURBAN	**1,387,248**	**1,165,229**	**19.1**	**—**	**1,705,000**	**2,181**	**636**	**12.3**	**6.9**	**11.7**	**9.2**	**3.7**	**10.8**	**6,844**	**9.1**	**7.8**	**278.6**	**165.8**	**21.0**	**870**	**6.3**	**5,552/ 8.5**	**—**	**37**	
Anne Arundel	370,775	298,042	24.4	5/5	479,000	423/13	877/5	13.6	6.1	12.1	9.2	3.9	13.4	6,367	11.6	6.4	209.0	160.6	20.0	1,090	5.0	4,825/ 2.4	2,089	18	Anne Arundel
Baltimore	655,615	620,409	5.7	3/3	705,000	598/3	1,096/4	11.2	8.2	11.7	9.1	4.0	-0.3	7,366	8.2	9.5	349.7	190.6	19.4	760	7.7	6,761/11.2	2,467	26	Baltimore
Carroll	96,356	69,006	39.6	10/10	127,000	456/10	211/9	12.3	6.9	11.6	9.6	2.4	29.0	5,484	2.9	9.7	265.9	160.0	15.6	860	6.1	2,839/28.5	1,782	61	Carroll
Harford	145,930	115,378	26.5	6/6	176,000	453/11	322/7	13.2	5.6	12.4	9.3	3.8	17.6	6,024	8.3	5.4	231.9	126.5	38.3	1,000	5.8	3,956/ 1.6	1,979	40	Harford
Howard	118,572	62,394	90.0	7/11	218,000	251/22	472/6	13.3	4.2	8.9	9.4	2.2	76.3	7,522	11.7	3.8	167.2	99.5	16.0	950	3.0	5,326/10.1	2,299	36	Howard
WASHINGTON SUBURBAN	**1,244,124**	**1,184,528**	**5.0**	**—**	**1,359,000**	**980**	**1,270**	**13.4**	**5.8**	**14.9**	**9.6**	**3.8**	**-3.1**	**8,058**	**24.0**	**6.0**	**203.9**	**138.6**	**14.9**	**510**	**3.8**	**6,398/14.6**	**—**	**31**	
Montgomery	579,053	522,809	10.8	4/4	628,000	495/5	1,170/3	11.6	6.1	12.7	10.1	3.1	4.5	9,470	8.8	7.7	225.0	149.0	13.4	340	3.2	5,243/17.3	2,906	36	Montgomery
Prince George's	665,071	661,719	0.5	2/2	731,000	485/6	1,371/2	14.9	5.4	16.4	9.2	4.3	-9.2	6,850	37.3	4.5	185.6	129.6	16.3	940	4.4	7,402/ 5.0	2,345	25	Prince George's
SOUTHERN MARYLAND	**167,284**	**115,748**	**44.5**	**—**	**255,000**	**1,049**	**159**	**16.1**	**6.2**	**14.9**	**8.7**	**3.1**	**20.8**	**5,211**	**19.1**	**6.1**	**197.8**	**135.6**	**37.1**	**1,390**	**6.0**	**4,145/17.5**	**—**	**37**	
Calvert	34,638	20,682	67.5	16/20	62,000	217/23	160/15	15.2	7.5	12.3	7.5	3.2	43.4	5,131	22.2	8.0	174.6	190.5	46.2	940	10.3	3,076/19.4	2,276	37	Calvert
Charles	72,751	47,678	52.6	12/14	109,000	459/8	158/16	14.8	5.4	16.2	8.8	3.2	30.0	5,447	20.3	4.9	205.7	117.7	38.5	1,690	3.9	4,842/22.8	2,037	31	Charles
St. Mary's	59,895	47,388	26.4	15/15	84,000	373/16	161/14	18.1	6.5	14.9	9.2	3.0	1.6	4,967	15.9	6.4	201.5	125.7	30.1	1,490	7.8	3,902/ 9.8	2,002	44	St. Mary's
FREDERICK COUNTY	**114,263**	**84,927**	**34.5**	**8/8**	**157,000**	**665/1**	**172/11**	**14.4**	**7.5**	**12.5**	**9.3**	**3.6**	**21.5**	**5,430**	**5.5**	**8.5**	**294.7**	**159.4**	**29.8**	**1,070**	**7.1**	**3,797/14.2**	**1,961**	**59**	

	Population, 1980	Population, 1970	% Change, 1970-1980	Population Rank	Proj. Pop., 2000	Area/Rank	Pop. Density/Rank	Birth Rate	Death Rate	Infant Mortality	Marriage Rate	Divorce Rate	Net Migration	p.c. Income	% Black	% 65+	Heart Disease	Cancer	Motor Veh.	Pop. per M.D.	Unemployment	Crime Rate	School Exp.	Farmland	
WESTERN MARYLAND	**220,132**	**209,349**	**5.2**	—	**227,000**	**1,546**	**142**	**12.3**	**10.1**	**12.6**	**19.1**	**4.1**	**0.2**	**4,806**	**2.8**	**12.6**	**428.6**	**229.7**	**22.3**	**780**	**10.0**	**3,004/ 5.8**	—	**33**	
Allegany	80,548	84,044	-4.2	11/9	76,000	428/12	188/10	11.6	12.4	10.8	15.1	3.8	-5.9	4,705	1.6	15.4	570.4	273.9	21.1	610	9.6	2,913/ 9.4	2,102	18	Allegany
Garrett	26,498	21,476	23.4	19/19	33,000	659/2	40/24	15.1	9.1	17.7	37.3	3.2	15.4	3,512	0.2	10.2	332.0	204.6	34.0	1,730	13.0	2,310/15.5	1,894	30	Garrett
Washington	113,086	103,829	8.9	9/7	119,000	459/8	246/8	12.2	8.6	12.3	17.6	4.5	2.1	5,185	4.2	11.2	348.5	203.5	20.3	840	9.6	3,235/ 2.2	2,064	51	Washington
UPPER EASTERN SHORE	**151,380**	**131,322**	**15.3**	—	**178,000**	**1,600**	**95**	**13.2**	**9.5**	**12.0**	**35.6**	**3.7**	**7.8**	**4,990**	**13.4**	**11.9**	**404.3**	**189.4**	**35.0**	**820**	**8.2**	**3,659/15.0**	—	**64**	
Caroline	23,143	19,781	17.0	22/21	28,000	321/19	72/18	14.3	11.7	7.4	17.8	3.6	11.9	4,165	16.9	14.9	502.2	257.8	13.0	2,810	11.0	3,036/42.6	1,906	65	Caroline
Cecil	60,430	53,291	13.4	14/13	70,000	362/17	167/13	13.7	7.2	14.7	73.1	3.6	-1.2	5,012	5.3	8.1	297.9	134.8	34.8	980	9.0	4,253/17.0	1,847	39	Cecil
Kent	16,695	16,146	3.4	24/24	16,000	281/20	59/21	13.1	12.2	16.1	11.7	4.1	0.5	4,810	22.1	16.2	611.1	240.7	65.9	610	9.5	3,161/17.6	2,411	77	Kent
Queen Anne's	25,508	18,422	38.5	21/23	38,000	375/15	68/19	13.0	9.0	9.4	7.2	3.2	28.1	5,036	16.0	10.3	369.7	193.3	35.3	2,640	7.5	2,853/ 2.3	2,058	72	Queen Anne's
Talbot	25,604	23,682	8.1	20/18	26,000	261/21	98/17	11.3	11.1	9.4	10.9	3.9	13.9	5,719	21.3	16.5	451.5	212.7	35.2	350	4.9	3,952/ 4.3	2,216	70	Talbot
LOWER EASTERN SHORE	**145,240**	**127,007**	**14.4**	—	**164,000**	**1,793**	**81**	**13.7**	**11.5**	**14.6**	**13.1**	**4.8**	**7.1**	**4,697**	**26.1**	**13.2**	**424.3**	**251.3**	**24.8**	**730**	**11.3**	**6,253/17.4**	—	**38**	
Dorchester	30,623	29,405	4.1	18/16	31,000	594/4	52/23	12.4	12.7	16.6	8.3	4.1	4.1	4,684	29.7	14.2	549.0	271.2	29.4	650	10.6	4,265/13.3	2,388	36	Dorchester
Somerset	19,188	18,924	1.4	23/22	19,000	339/18	57/22	14.4	14.0	11.0	11.1	4.1	0.9	3,459	34.6	15.4	513.1	329.8	31.4	1,510	17.6	3,173/13.3	2,049	31	Somerset
Wicomico	64,540	54,236	19.0	13/12	76,000	381/14	169/12	14.1	10.1	16.6	14.2	5.9	8.5	5,167	21.8	11.5	335.0	226.1	15.5	540	9.2	5,529/10.9	1,992	44	Wicomico
Worcester	30,889	24,442	26.4	17/17	39,000	479/7	64/20	12.9	11.4	10.7	17.4	3.6	12.1	4,572	26.2	14.3	420.9	230.2	35.6	1,760	12.6	12,137/26.9	2,441	40	Worcester
WASHINGTON, D.C.	**637,651**	**756,668**	**-15.7**	—	**630,000**	**61**	**10,453**	**14.0**	**10.5**	**26.6**	**6.9**	**5.1**	**-14.6**	**7,074**	**70.3**	**10.8**	**325.8**	**282.3**	**7.2**	—	**7.2**	**8,602/11.1**	—	—	
UNITED STATES	**226,504,825**	**203,302,031**	**11.4**	—	**266,497,000**	**3,540,023**	**64**	**15.3**	**8.8**	**14.4**	**10.5**	**5.2**	**1.7**	**5,751**	**11.7**	**11.0**	**334.3**	**181.9**	**23.5**	—	**7.1**	**5,522/ 8.1**	—	**46**	

Source: The Maryland Population Data Sheet of the Population Reference Bureau, Inc., © 1981. Reprinted by permission of the Population Reference Bureau, Inc., Washington, D.C.

SELECTED BIBLIOGRAPHY

CHAPTER 1. INTRODUCTION: THE MOSAIC OF MARYLAND

Alexander, John, and Gibson, Lay. *Economic Geography.* 2nd ed. Englewood Cliffs, N.J.: Prentice-Hall, 1979.

Alexander, Lewis. *The Northeastern United States.* Princeton, N.J.: D. Van Nostrand Co., 1967.

Birdsall, Stephen, and Florin, John. *Regional Landscapes of the United States and Canada.* New York: John Wiley and Sons, 1978.

Caudill, Henry M. *Night Comes to the Cumberlands.* Boston: Little, Brown and Co., 1962.

Directory of Maryland Manufactures, 1979–80. Annapolis: Maryland Department of Economic and Community Development, 1980.

Gottmann, Jean. *Megalopolis: The Urbanized Northeastern Seaboard of the U.S.* New York: 20th Century Fund, 1961.

"Maryland, Come for the Biggest Incentive of All." *Business Week,* no. 2629, March 24, 1980, pp. 21–38.

Munro, J. M. "Planning the Appalachian Development Highway System: Some Critical Questions." *Land Economics* 45 (1969): 160–161.

Paterson, J. H. *North America.* 6th ed. New York: Oxford University Press, 1979.

Thompson, Derek, ed. *Atlas of Maryland.* College Park: Department of Geography, University of Maryland, 1977.

CHAPTER 2. THE LAND

Baumann, Duane, and Sims, John. "Flood Insurance: Some Determinants of Adoption." *Economic Geography* 54 (July 1978):189–196.

Besley, F. W. *Thirty Important Forest Trees of Maryland.* Annapolis: Maryland State Board of Forestry, 1922.

Blood, Pearl. *The Geography of Maryland.* Boston: Allyn and Bacon, 1961.

Clark, Wm. Bullock, and Mathews, Edward. *The Physical Features of Maryland.* Baltimore: The Johns Hopkins University Press, for the Maryland Geological Survey, 1906.

Compendium of Natural Features Information. Vol. I. Baltimore: Maryland Department of State Planning, 1975.

Dando, W. A., and Rabenhorst, Thomas. *Introduction to Maryland.* Fenton, Mich.: American Geographic, 1970.

Davis, Penny, and Fahle, Vernon. *Economic Rationale for the Preservation of the Ocean City Beaches.* Annapolis: Maryland Department of Economic and Community Development, 1980.

Dolan, Robert; Lins, Harry; and Stewart, John. *Geographical Analysis of Fenwick Island, Maryland, A Middle Atlantic Coast Barrier Island.* Washington, D.C.: Government Printing Office, for the U.S. Geological Survey, 1980.

Environmental Effects Report for Interim Beach Maintenance at Ocean City, Maryland. Annapolis: Maryland Department of Natural Resources, Tidewater Administration, 1980.

Ferguson, Roland. *The Timber Resources of Maryland.* Bulletin NE-7. Washington, D.C.: Government Printing Office, for the U.S. Forest Service, 1967.

Fisher, Allan C., Jr. "My Chesapeake Queen of Bays." *National Geographic* 158 (October 1980):428–467.

Forest Vegetation in Maryland. Baltimore: Maryland Department of State Planning, 1974.

Franklin, Ben. "Chesapeake Bay Pollution Fight Pits Oyster Against Automobile." *New York Times,* April 27, 1980, pp. 1, 60.

Franklin, Jon. "350 Million Years of Geology Link Baltimore with Frostburg." *Baltimore Sun,* October 2, 1972, p. C-1.

______. "Volcanoes Rumbled Here Millions of Years Before the Dinosaur." *Baltimore Sun,* October 3, 1972, p. C-1.

______. "Blue Ridge Story: Mountains Too Are Transient." *Baltimore Sun,* October 4, 1972, p. D-1.

______. "Opposite Geological Actions Formed Two Great Valleys: Great Valley Province." *Baltimore Sun,* October 5, 1972a, p. C-1.

______. "Coastal Plain Young in Geological History." *Baltimore Sun,* October 5, 1972b, p. C-1.

______. "Fairview Mountain Marks Edge of Beautiful Rugged County: Valley and Ridge Province." *Baltimore Sun,* October 6, 1972, p. C-1.

Horton, Tom. "Official Efforts to Save the Bay Have Pointed the Wrong Way: Look at the Land for Solutions." *Baltimore Sunday Sun,* June 15, 1980, pp. A-1, A-8.

Hurley, George, and Hurley, Suzanne. *A Pictorial History of Ocean City.* Virginia Beach, Va.: Donning Publishers, 1979.

Integrity of the Chesapeake Bay. Publication 184. Baltimore: Maryland Department of State Planning, 1972.

McDermott, John S. "America's Abused Coastline." *Time,* September 15, 1980, pp. 28–29.

Maryland Outdoor Recreation and Open Space Plan. Baltimore: Maryland State Department of Planning, 1978.

Maryland Statistical Abstract, 1979. Annapolis: Maryland Department of Economic and Community Development, 1980.

Michener, James A. *Chesapeake.* New York: Fawcett Crest Books, 1978.

Miller, Fred P. *Maryland Soils.* Cooperative Extension Service Bulletin no. 212. College Park: University of Maryland, 1967.

Natural Soil Groups of Maryland. Baltimore: Maryland Department of State Planning, 1973.

Rouse, Parke. "Chesapeake: The Noblest Bay." *Vista,* Spring 1979, pp. 19–22.

Simon, Anne W. *The Thin Edge: The Coast and Man in Crisis.* New York: Harper and Row Pub., 1978.

Vokes, Harold. *Geography and Geology of Maryland.* Revised by Jonathan Edwards. Geological Survey Bulletin 19. Baltimore: Maryland Geological Survey, 1968.

Weeks, John R. *Our Climate: Maryland and Delaware.* Baltimore: Maryland State Weather Service, 1941.

"What Will the Bay Be Like in Twenty Years?" *Chesapeake Citizen Report,* no. 14 (July–August 1980).

CHAPTER 3. HOW THE LAND IS USED: PRIMARY ACTIVITIES

Alford, John. "The Chesapeake Oyster Fishery." *Annals of the Association of American Geographers* 65 (1975):229–239.

Annual Reports. Annapolis: Maryland Bureau of Mines.

Azrael, Sara. "No-Till Bodes Farming Revolution." *Baltimore Sun,* September 7, 1980, p. K-1.

Baker, Henry S., Jr. *Maryland Tobacco: Certain Aspects of a 300-Year-Old Enterprise.* New Brunswick, N.J.: Rutgers University Press, 1957.

"Baltimore's King Coal." *Baltimore Sun,* June 15, 1980, p. K-4.

Bode, Carl. *Maryland: A History.* New York: W. W. Norton, 1978.

Clark, Marsha. "Coal in Western Maryland: A Closer Look." *Metro News,* Johns Hopkins University Center for Metropolitan Planning, 6, no. 10 (February 1, 1978):1–4.

Coddington, James, and Derr, David. *An Economic Study of Land Utilization in the Tobacco Area of Southern Maryland.* College Park: University of Maryland, 1939.

Dozer, Donald M. *Portrait of a Free State: A History of Maryland.* Cambridge, Md.: Tidewater Publishers, 1976.

Edwards, Jonathan. "Maryland's Metallic Mineral Heritage." *Maryland Conservationist,* August 1967, pp. 1–4.

Fisher, Allan C., Jr. "My Chesapeake Queen of Bays." *National Geographic* 158 (October 1980):428–467.

Horton, Tom. "Shad: Decimation of a Bay Fishery Shows Peril of Managing by Crisis." *Baltimore Sun,* June 29, 1980, p. A-1.

———. "Border Dispute Dates Back Centuries." *Baltimore Sun,* March 8, 1981, pp. B-1, B-6.

Maryland Agricultural Statistics Summary. College Park: Maryland Department of Agriculture (annual).

Maryland Economic Atlas. Annapolis: Maryland Department of Economic Development, 1967.

Mindus, Paul. "Coal Fever: Exports Raise Hopes, Question for Port." *Baltimore Sun,* March 9, 1981, p. A-1.

———. "Coal Fever: Technology May Limit New Jobs." *Baltimore Sun,* March 10, 1981, p. A-1.

———. "Demands of Exporting Raise Questions About the Railroads." *Baltimore Sun,* March 11, 1981, p. A-1.

———. "Exports Hopes Stir Environmentalists' Concern for Communities' Welfare." *Baltimore Sun,* March 12, 1981, p. A-1.

———. "Dredging Harbor Seen as Key to City's Export Capacity." *Baltimore Sun,* March 13, 1981, p. A-1.

———. "Baltimore Faces Competition, Foreign Skepticism Over Coal." *Baltimore Sun,* March 14, 1981, p. A-1.

"Oyster Industry Is Alive and Well." *Maryland Business Journal,* August–September 1980, p. 20.

Shelsby, Ted. "Shore Tomato Canneries Dwindle With Crop." *Baltimore Sun,* August 24, 1980, p. K-7.

Warner, William W. *Beautiful Swimmers.* New York: Penguin Books, 1976.

Weaver, Kenneth; Croffoth, James; and Edwards, Jonathan. *Coal Reserves in Maryland: Potential for Future Development.* Annapolis: Maryland Geological Survey, 1976.

CHAPTER 4. MANUFACTURING, RECREATION, AND TOURISM

Directory of Maryland Exporters-Importers. Annapolis: Maryland Department of Economic and Community Development, 1976.

Employment Report for Maryland and Metropolitan Baltimore. Baltimore: Maryland Department of State Planning, (monthly).

A Guide to Maryland: Sharing the Heritage of America. Annapolis: Maryland Department of Economic and Community Development, 1978.

Maryland Manufacturers Directory. Annapolis: Maryland Department of Economic and Community Development (annual).

Maryland: The Mountains, The Bay, The Oceans—Recreation In Maryland's Parks and Forests. Annapolis: Maryland Park Service, 1973.

Maryland 1980 Guidebook. Annapolis: Maryland Office of Tourist Development, Department of Economic and Community Development, 1980.

Maryland Outdoor Recreation and Open Space Plan. Baltimore: Maryland Department of State Planning, 1978.

Maryland Statistical Abstract. Annapolis: Maryland Department of Economic and Community Development, 1980.

The National Register of Historic Places. Washington, D.C.: U.S. Department of the Interior, 1970.

State and Federal Land Inventory. Baltimore: Maryland Department of State Planning, 1974.

CHAPTER 5. MARYLAND'S PAST IN TODAY'S LANDSCAPE

Bernard, Richard M. "A Portrait of Baltimore in 1800: Economic and Occupational Patterns in an Early American City." *Maryland Historical Magazine* 69 (1974):341–360.

Brown, Ralph H. *Historical Geography of the United States.* New York: Harcourt, Brace and World, 1948.

Buford, Carol B. "The Distribution of Negroes in Maryland 1850–1950." Master's thesis, Catholic University of America, 1955.

The Chesapeake and Delaware Canal. Philadelphia: U.S. Army Corps of Engineers, 1979.

Clark, Wm. Bullock. *The Geography of Maryland.* Baltimore: The Johns Hopkins Press, 1906.

Clemons, Paul G. E. "From Tobacco to Grain: Economic Development on Maryland's Eastern Shore, 1660–1750." Ph.D. diss., University of Wisconsin, 1974.

Dozer, Donald M. *Portrait of the Free State: A History of Maryland.* Cambridge, Md.: Tidewater Publishers, 1976.

Giddens, Paul H. "Land Policies and Administration in Colonial Maryland, 1753–1769." *Maryland Historical Magazine* 28 (1933): 150–165.

Hungerford, Edward. *The Story of the Baltimore*

and Ohio Railroad, 1827–1927, 2 vols. New York and London: G. P. Putnam's Sons, 1928.

Land, Aubrey C. "Tobacco Staple and the Plantor's Problems: Technology, Labor, and Crops." *Agricultural History* 43 (January 1969):69–81.

Main, Gloria L. "Maryland and the Chesapeake Economy, 1670–1720." In Aubrey C. Land, L. G. Carr, and E. C. Papenfuse, eds. *Law, Society, and Politics in Early Maryland.* Baltimore: Johns Hopkins University Press, 1977.

Mathews, Edward. "The Counties of Maryland, Their Origins, Boundaries, and Election Districts." *Maryland Geological Survey* 6 (1907): 419–572.

———. "History of the Boundary Dispute Between the Baltimores and Penns Resulting in the Original Mason and Dixon Line." *Maryland Geological Survey* 7 (1908):105–203.

Mitchell, Robert D., and Muller, Edward K., eds. *Geographical Perspectives on Maryland's Past.* Occasional Papers in Geography, no. 4. College Park: University of Maryland, 1979.

Porter, Frank W. "Expanding the Domain: William Gooch and the Northern Boundary Dispute." *Maryland Historian* 5 (Spring 1974):1–13.

———. "From Backcountry to County: The Delayed Settlement of Western Maryland." *Maryland Historical Magazine* 70 (Winter 1975):329–349.

Sanderlin, Walter S. "The Great National Project: A History of the Chesapeake and Ohio Canal." *Johns Hopkins University Studies in History and Political Science* 64 (1946).

Skaggs, David Curtis. *Roots of Maryland Democracy 1753–1776.* Westport, Conn.: Greenwood Press, 1973.

CHAPTER 6. THE PEOPLE: A STORY OF DIVERSITY

Annual Survey Assessment Ratios, 1979. Annapolis: Maryland State Department of Assessments and Taxation, 1980.

Annual Vital Statistics Report. Annapolis: Maryland Department of Health and Mental Hygiene.

Facts About Maryland Public Education 1978–1979. Annapolis: Maryland State Department of Education, 1979.

Gibbons, Boyd. *Wye Island: The True Story of an American Community's Struggle to Preserve Its Way of Life.* Baltimore: Johns Hopkins University Press, 1977.

Kniffen, Fred. "Folk Housing: Key to Diffusion." *Annals of the Association of American Geographers* 55 (December 1965):549–577.

Maryland Our Maryland, An Ethnic and Cultural Directory. Baltimore: Baltimore Council for International Visitors, 1975.

Maryland Population, 1930–1970. Baltimore: Maryland Department of State Planning, 1971.

Profile of Higher Education in Maryland, 1979. Annapolis: Maryland Board of Higher Education, 1980.

Salganik, M. William. "Nonwhite Gains Noted in City, D. C. Suburbs." *Baltimore Sunday Sun,* March 29, 1981, pp. B-1, B-4.

Zelinsky, Wilbur. *The Cultural Geography of the United States.* Englewood Cliffs, N.J.: Prentice Hall, 1973.

CHAPTER 7. SERVICES TO PEOPLE

Baltimore Metro Business Facts. Baltimore: Economic Development Council of Greater Baltimore, 1980.

Baltimore-Washington International Airport Master Plan Summary 1950–1995. Annapolis: Maryland Department of Transportation, Maryland State Aviation Administration, 1980.

BWI: 30 Years of Service. Annapolis, Md.: Baltimore-Washington International Airport Administration, 1980.

The Chesapeake and Delaware Canal. Philadelphia: U.S. Army Corps of Engineers, 1979.

Comparative Summary of Activity for Calendar Year 1978. Annapolis: Maryland Department of Transportation, Maryland State Aviation Administration, 1979.

Directory of Maryland Exporters-Importers (annual). Annapolis: Maryland Department of Economic and Community Development.

Foreign Commerce Statistical Report (annual). Annapolis: Maryland Department of Transportation, Maryland Port Administration.

Franklin, Jon, and Doelp, Alan. *Shocktrauma.* New York: St. Martin's Press, 1980.

Gibbons, Boyd. *Wye Island: The True Story of an American Community's Struggle to Preserve Its Way of Life.* Baltimore: Johns Hopkins University Press, 1977.

Highway Mileage on State, State Toll, County, and Municipal Systems. Annapolis, Md.: State Highway Administration, Bureau of Highway Statistics, 1979.

1978 Maryland Transportation Plan. Baltimore: Baltimore-Washington International Airport, Maryland Department of Transportation, 1978.

Port of Baltimore (monthly). Annapolis: Maryland Department of Transportation, Maryland Port Administration.

"Port of Baltimore," *Baltimore Sunday Sun,* September 25, 1977, special pullout section.

Port of Baltimore Directory (annual). Annapolis: Maryland Department of Transportation, Maryland Port Administration.

"The Port of Baltimore: A Private User's Perspective." *Metro News,* Johns Hopkins University Center for Metropolitan Planning and Research, 8, no. 9 (May 15, 1980):2–3.

Spencer, Jean E. *Contemporary Local Government in Maryland.* College Park: Bureau of Government Research, University of Maryland, 1965.

"U.S. Ports." *Christian Science Monitor,* June 16, 1980, pp. B-1, B-12.

The World Port of Baltimore. Annapolis: Maryland Department of Transportation, Maryland Port Administration, 1975.

CHAPTER 8. THE URBAN SYSTEM

Abler, Ron, ed. *A Comparative Atlas of America's Great Cities.* Minneapolis: University of Minnesota Press, 1976.

"Baltimore Awakens to a Municipal Renaissance." *Christian Science Monitor,* January 8, 1981, p. 10.

Baltimore's Housing and Community Development Programs. Baltimore: Department of Housing and Community Development, 1981.

"Columbia The Gem of Howard County." *Maryland Business Journal,* August–September 1980, pp. 7–8.

Commercial Atlas and Marketing Guide, 1981. Chicago: Rand McNally Inc., 1981.

Garland, Eric. "The End of Baltimore as a Blue Collar Town." *Baltimore Magazine,* December 1980, pp. 50–58.

Harper, Robert, and Ahnert, Frank. *Introduction to Metropolitan Washington.* Washington, D.C.: Association of American Geographers, 1968.

Hoppenfeld, Morton. "Sketch of the Planning-Building Process for Columbia, Maryland." *Journal of the American Institute of Planners* 33 (November 1967):170–182.

"Look What's Happened to Baltimore." *Life Magazine,* September 1980, pp. 91–94.

Mayer, Albert. "Greenbelt Towns Revisited." *Journal of Housing* 24 (1967):57–62.

Moryadas, Virginia H. "Greenbelt and Columbia, Maryland." in *Nine Geographical Field Trips in the Washington, D.C. Area.* Washington, D.C.: Association of American Geographers, 1968.

Olson, Sherry. *Baltimore.* Cambridge, Mass.: Ballinger Pub. Co., 1976.

______. "Baltimore Imitates the Spider." *Annals of the Association of American Geographers* 69 (1979):557–574.

Tannenbaum, Robert. "Planning Determinants for Columbia." *Urban Land* 24 (April 1965): 72–85.

Urban Atlas: Baltimore, Maryland. Washington, D.C.: Government Printing Office, for the U.S. Bureau of the Census and Manpower Administration, 1974.

Urban Atlas: Washington, D.C. Washington, D.C.: Government Printing Office, for the U.S. Bureau of the Census and Manpower Administration, 1974.

"Where Things Are Going Right in America: Vacancy Slums Spell Opportunity in Baltimore." *U.S. News and World Report,* December 28, 1978, p. 75.

CHAPTER 9. FUTURE PROSPECTS

The Baltimore-Washington Common Market Economic Fact Sheet. Washington, D.C.: Washington/Baltimore Regional Association, 1979.

"The Baltimore-Washington Common Market: The Economic Future of a Region." *Metro News,* Johns Hopkins University Center for Metropolitan Planning and Research (June 15, 1979):1–3.

Cohen, Saul B. "Misguided Federal Focus on the Sun Belt." *New York Times,* January 4, 1981, p. 45.

Economic Analysis of the Baltimore/Washington Common Market. Washington, D.C.: Washington/Baltimore Regional Association, 1980.

"Economic Forecast for Maryland." *Maryland,* Winter 1975, pp. 44–47.

An Economic Profile. Washington, D.C.: Washington/Baltimore Regional Association, 1980.

Hansen, Niles. "The New International Division of Labor and Manufacturing Decentralization in the United States." Department of Economics, University of Texas, 1980.

Lyall, Katharine C. "Baltimore in the 80s: What the Experts Say." *Metro News,* Johns Hopkins University Center for Metropolitan Planning and Research (March 1, 1980):1–7.

"Maryland: Come for the Biggest Incentive of All." *Business Week,* no. 2629, March 24, 1980, pp. 23–38.

Schwartz, Gail Garfield. "Growth Potential in Maryland." *Newsletter* of the Johns Hopkins University Center for Metropolitan Planning and Research (June 15, 1981):4–7.

Zorthian, Barry. "Baltimore-Washington Common Market: A Dynamic, Exciting Reality." *Maryland Business Journal,* August–September 1980, p. 14.

INDEX